ENTANGLED FAR RIGHTS

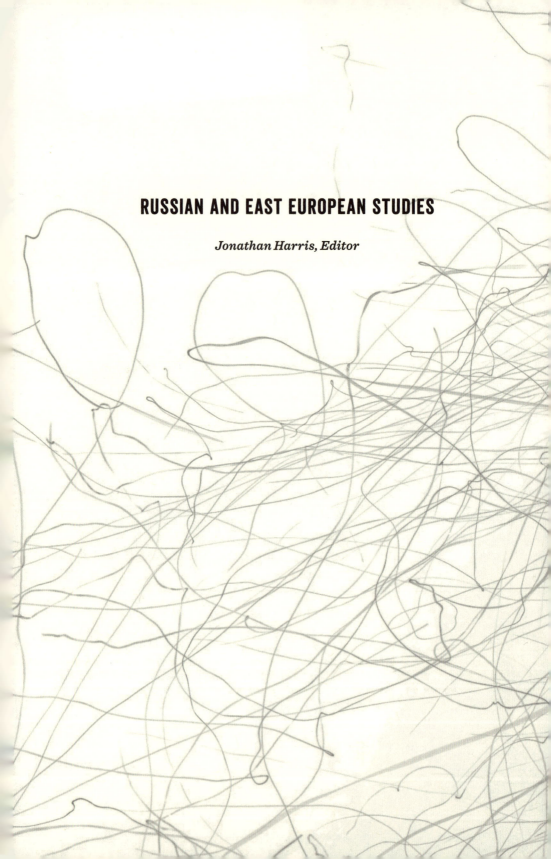

RUSSIAN AND EAST EUROPEAN STUDIES

Jonathan Harris, Editor

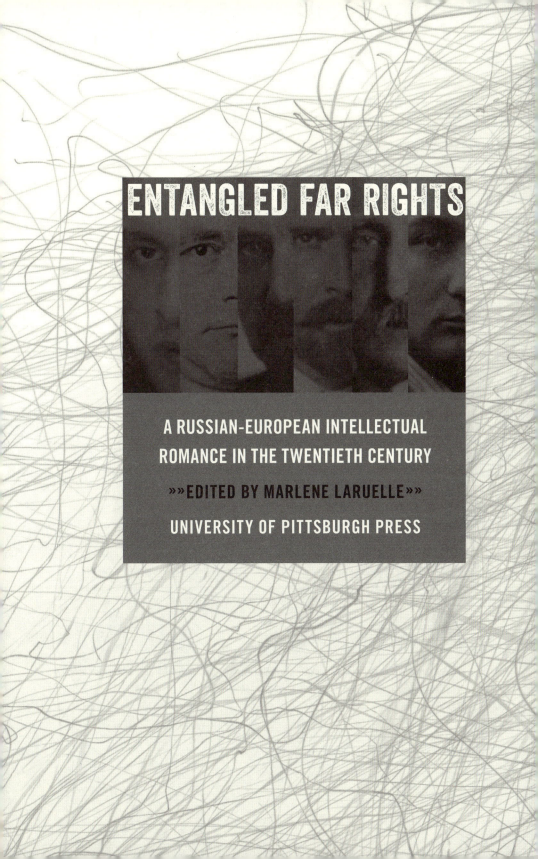

ENTANGLED FAR RIGHTS

A RUSSIAN-EUROPEAN INTELLECTUAL
ROMANCE IN THE TWENTIETH CENTURY

»»EDITED BY MARLENE LARUELLE»»

UNIVERSITY OF PITTSBURGH PRESS

Published by the University of Pittsburgh Press, Pittsburgh, Pa., 15260
Manufactured in the United States of America
Printed on acid-free paper
10 9 8 7 6 5 4 3 2 1

Cataloging-in-Publication data is available from the Library of Congress

ISBN 13: 978-0-8229-6565-7

Cover art: Collage of Julius Evola, Carl Schmitt, P. N. Savitskii, P. N. Trubetskoy, Karl Haushofer, and Lev Gumilev (*left to right*).
Cover design: Alex Wolfe

CONTENTS

INTRODUCTION

ENTANGLED FAR RIGHTS

A Russian-European Intellectual Romance in the Twentieth Century

Marlene Laruelle

Since the early 2010s and more visibly since the Ukrainian crisis in 2014, Russia's support for the European Far Right—and for conservative and populist leaders more globally—has become a cornerstone of the West's perception of Moscow as a "spoiler" on the international scene. Russia is now perceived as a danger to "established democracies": its support for far-right politics is interpreted as part of a broader strategy that also includes supposed meddling in elections and referendums—the 2016 U.S. presidential elections, Brexit, and the Catalonia referendum, among others.

Many observers expected that Russia, if it chose to intervene on the European political scene, would reactivate Soviet soft power toward the European Left. The fact that Russia's most fervent supporters are now to be found on the right of the ideological spectrum therefore came as a surprise.

Two key points explain the present reality. The first is that the European Left has undergone dramatic changes since the fall of the Berlin Wall and the collapse of the Soviet Union. Although the European Left's stance on international affairs may share some ideological features with Russia's position—such as being anti-NATO, cautious toward transatlantic institutions, and reluctant to see a too neoliberal European Union gain more power over nation-states—both are deeply divided on societal issues. Both the "old" Left, which maintains a certain proximity to communism, and the "new" Left, as it has emerged in Greece, Spain, and among many an-

1

tiglobalization movements, are very liberal in terms of gender values and militant on environmental issues—two elements that either do not speak to Russia's current regime or even directly clash with its ideological positioning. If there are indeed some sections of the European Left that (for geopolitical reasons) support Russia's policy today, a far larger segment sees Russia as a country with which it is difficult—or even impossible—to partner.

The second point, which is at the center of this volume, is that the European Right and Far Right have always had Russophile tendencies, but these were obscured during the Cold War, when rightist forces were decidedly anti-Communist. However, being anti-Communist did not mean being anti-Soviet, let alone anti-Russian. Being anti-Soviet without being anti-Russian is quite easy to reconcile, and was indeed a posture shared by many on the Cold War-era European Far Right who admired prerevolutionary Russia, whether for its autocratic regime or for the prominent role given to Orthodoxy. The fall of the Soviet Union, they believed, would result in the rebirth of an "eternal" Russia whose ideology would ally with far-right worldviews.

Being anti-Communist and not anti-Soviet is a more complex relationship to decipher. It requires understanding that for a segment of the European Far Right, the transatlantic world that emerged after 1945 was seen as more destructive to "authentic" European identity than the risk posed by communism. For all those who were vividly anti-American and who hoped for the rebirth of an independent, unified, and "white" European continent, the Soviet Union was far from the worst danger and could even be seen as a potential ally. As early as the late 1970s, figures such as Jean Parvulesco, a Romanian-born émigré who was close to the New Right, claimed that the Soviet Union's destiny was to save the white race.[1] Moreover, some far-right groups were impressed by the colossal forces unleashed by the Bolshevik revolution and could not help seeing similarities with interwar fascist regimes, including Nazi Germany. On the Russian/Soviet side, meanwhile, there was a complex magnetism toward the European Far Right.

This edited volume traces the "intellectual romance" that existed between European Far Right groups and their Russian/Soviet counterparts during the long twentieth century, their mutual borrowings, distorted interpretations, and phantasmagorical readings of each other.[2] It complements an earlier volume, *Eurasianism and the European Far Right: Reshaping the Russia–Europe Relationship* (2015), that investigated the role of the notorious neo-Eurasianist and neofascist geopolitician Aleksandr Dugin in cultivating contacts with the European New Right and, directly or indirectly, opening the way for the Russian authorities to find new fellow travelers among European Far Right groups.[3]

The Second World War continues to shape our perception of the relationship between the European Far Right, especially its fascist and national-socialist components, and the Soviet Union: the conflict was a fight to the finish between the two so-called totalitarian regimes. This memory is cultivated in Europe, and even more so in Russia, where the 27 million Soviet citizens who died fighting the German enemy are revered as national heroes and saviors of humanity. Alternative memories exist, but they remain marginal. In the Baltic states, Poland, and now Ukraine, the authorities, along with a large part of the historian community, have come to criticize this conventional reading of the war. They prefer to emphasize what they see as the shameful collaboration between the Soviet and Nazi regimes associated with the Molotov-Ribbentrop Pact of 1939–1941 and the mutually influenced patterns of violence in the occupied territories. These memory controversies have gained visibility in recent years, especially with the 2014 Ukrainian conflict, and have become an integral part of countries' foreign policy toolkits. The Putin regime warns against the threat of a "fascist junta" in power in Kyiv, while the Poroshenko government, following a trend that has grown in Ukraine since the Orange Revolution in 2004, puts the Nazi and Soviet pasts on an equal footing.

This volume investigates how diverse elements of the far-right repertoire have traveled between the European and Soviet/Russian spaces. This approach can sometimes be perilous due to the semantic confusion around the term "fascism." If the scholarly community has reached partial agreement on how to define it,[4] the use and abuse of the term in the public space, the lack of terminological consistency, its name-calling value, and countries' varying sensitivities based on their own memories of the Second World War make it difficult to study the term's transnational aspect, as well as its persistence throughout the twentieth century. In the United States, Europe, and Russia, "fascist" is used in the political and intellectual arenas as an epithet to identify and denounce enemies. The derogatory implication is so strong that the notion of fascism has become an insulting label that sometimes bears no connection to the actual ideological positions. In Soviet and post-Soviet culture, the semantic space of fascism is even more complex. The consensus around the Soviet Union's defeat of fascism remains the critical driver of Russia's social cohesion even today, and the mere suggestion that some Soviet citizens or contemporary political groups might refer to fascism positively is offensive to majority public opinion.

This volume has to face another significant methodological problem, namely its location at the intersection of diverse disciplinary approaches. It finds its inspiration in the trend of building a European transnational history that keeps the focus on pan-European phenomena, cultural transfers, and mutual borrowings beyond the borders of the nation-state. It also hopes to rehabilitate Russian intellectual history as an integral part of the European history of ideas and to affirm how much Russia has contributed to Europe's modern history, both as an object of debates and as an actor itself.

Beyond this broad framework, this book combines multiple ways of looking at the Far Right. Some chapters belong to intellectual history: they investigate how concepts critical to far-right ideology circulated in the wider Euro-Russian space. Others explore political history: they follow groups of activists, not concepts, people who had to decide in extreme political circumstances whether to ally with or fight against fascist regimes. A third set looks at individual trajectories and personal networks—it must therefore take into consideration the complexity of human life, the occasional contradiction between friendship and ideological commitments, and the evolution of political stances over time and space. Indeed, context matters: referring to fascism as a doctrine in a nonfascist state is not comparable to supporting the state ideology of Mussolini's Italy between 1922 and 1943 or Hitler's Germany between 1933 and 1945.

In the study of the transnational circulation of the far-right ideological repertoire, it is striking to note our knowledge gap regarding the Soviet space. Research may have been limited due to the heavy weight borne by the notion of *fashizm* in the post-Soviet space: many local scholars may, until recently, have engaged in self-censorship, intentionally avoiding this sensitive and potentially offensive topic. In the "Western" world, academic production likewise remains fragmented. The Soviet-German case remains the best known: a developed body of literature exists about the *Sonderverhältnis* (special relationship) between Germany and Russia in the nineteenth and twentieth centuries. It covers the comparative approach to the two so-called totalitarianisms that emerged after the end of the Second World War, conducted under the influence of Hannah Arendt until Ernst Nolte touched off the *Historikerstreit* of the late 1980s, as well as more recent studies of the "image of the other" and "entangled histories." Walter Laqueur carried out pioneering research for his book *Russia and Germany: A Century of Conflict* (1965), which goes beyond diplomatic history in an attempt to capture the feeling, on both the German and the Soviet sides, of a profound interaction and competition of cultures.[5] Leonid Luks recently added to this literature with an edited volume, *Zwei Sonderwege? Russisch-deutsche Parallelen und Kontraste (1917–2014)* (2016), that compares the Russian and German traditions of *Sonderweg*.[6]

Since the collapse of the socialist bloc and the Soviet Union, historical research has progressed enormously. The opening of Soviet archives allowed for the filling in of many previously blank pages, among them the "Holocaust by bullets," the Soviet occupation of Polish and Baltic territories, the Nazi occupation of Soviet territories, and collaborationism on all sides. Recent works include, among others, *Fascination and Enmity: Russia and Germany as Entangled Histories, 1914–1945* (2012), edited by Michael David-Fox, Peter Holquist, and Alexander M. Martin.[7] If German Russophobia has been well studied, German Russophilia has also become an object of research in recent years, with convincing demonstrations that a strong attraction to Russia was present across the political spectrum during the Weimar Republic.[8]

These entangled Russo–German histories contribute to a better understanding of the context in which intellectual and political interactions took place. Yet they cannot tell us the full story of this unknown page of European history. The case of France, for example, remains largely unstudied, a situation that is paradoxical, given the importance of the Russian émigré community in Paris, but also explicable, as that group remains reticent to expose its critical role in connecting the Russian and French Far Rights, and the alliance of some of its members with Nazi Germany against the Soviet Union. With the exception of John J. Stephan's book *The Russian Fascists: Tragedy and Farce in Exile, 1925–1945* (1978),[9] which focused on the history of Russian fascists in Manchuria and the United States, we are still missing a detailed history—based on archival works, memoirs, and diaries—of the mutual attraction between the European and Russian Far Rights throughout the twentieth century.

This work identifies different phases of dialogue and cultural transfer between what can loosely be called the far-right ideological repertoire and Russia/the Soviet Union. Both terms must be understood in a broad and fuzzy sense. In "far-right ideological repertoire" we include the movements that preceded the regime-fascism that was instituted in Italy in 1922 and in Germany in 1933; the German Conservative Revolution, which provided, wittingly or not, the intellectual framework of national socialism; the Nazi ideology of the war years; and the so-called postfascist movements of the Cold War, which attempted to revive the fight for the unity of white Europe. This work takes "Russia/the Soviet Union" to mean prerevolutionary Russia; the emigration of the interwar period; the territories that were occupied by the Soviet and Nazi armies between 1939 and 1945; and the post-Stalinist Soviet Union, as well as its dissident cultures. We leave aside post-Soviet Russia, which was the focus of the earlier volume and of a forthcoming monograph.

Four chronological phases shape the structure of the book. However, this volume does not seek to advance a linear analysis of these interactions across time—the whole twentieth century—and space—the whole of Europe and the Soviet Union. Instead, and more modestly, it sketches some critical historical moments, intellectual interactions, and personal trajectories.

Schematically, interactions around the far-right ideological repertoire can be divided into three concentric circles. The innermost circle is comprised of a small group that was openly collaborationist with Nazi Germany. This attitude could be found among European volunteers on the Eastern Front and was also a minority position among Russian émigrés and Soviet citizens living under Nazi occupation during the war.

The middle circle is structured around the notion of the Third Way, imbued with several ideological nuances and undertones. The Third Way doctrine allowed certain Russian political and intellectual groups to engage in discussion with their European counterparts during the interwar decades. During the Cold War, some Western European Far Right groups used it to display a paradoxical philo-communism or philo-Sovietism largely devoid of ideological content but aimed at promoting a conservative European continental unity against the transatlantic liberal "West." The term Third Way has seen a genuine revival with the collapse of the Soviet Union and offers a fascinating unifying metanarrative for Russia's ideological experiments around the notion of National Bolshevism. The latter concept has been repeatedly reinvested and remastered at different historical times—interwar, Cold War, and early twenty-first century—and in different national contexts. National Bolshevism is the term used to label Ernst Niekisch's theories of a Third Way for Germany, but it also describes Nikolai Ustrialov's vision for the future of Soviet Russia, and since the 1980s a section of the European New Right has claimed the label, too. In the 1990s, the term enjoyed a second renaissance in Russia with the birth of the National-Bolshevik Party of Eduard Limonov (and, initially, Aleksandr Dugin). National Bolshevism thus encapsulates the complex relationship between Russia/Bolshevism/the Soviet Union and ideologies that share some elements of "fascism," but is still waiting for a historian to study it in its *longue durée* and its multiple iterations.[10]

The outermost circle brings together an array of prerevolutionary and

Soviet ideological movements and figures with some beliefs that, in one way or another, may be considered to belong to the "ideological DNA" of the Far Right. This third circle displays high semantic confusion and encompasses the largest, most heterogeneous coalition of doctrines in time and space.

This volume focuses on two critical historical moments of this third circle. The first is that of prerevolutionary Russia, fertile soil for neo-Slavo-phile doctrines cultivating a reactionary utopia that closely resembled European protofascist ideologies, and for a strong far-right popular move-ment, the Black Hundreds (*Chernaia sotnia*), considered in many respects Russia's first fascist movement. The second is the three decades follow-ing Stalin's death (1953–1985). While several authors—including Walter Laqueur, Alexander Yanov, and Stephen Shenfield, among others—have traced the evolution, on the Soviet side of the Iron Curtain, of doctrinal elements that can be associated with the Far Right, it is difficult to as-sess the degree of their interaction with their European counterparts. In many respects, direct borrowings and entanglements were limited and/or clandestine, such that they are often discoverable only through memoirs, diaries, or interviews.

In this volume, we address two fertile zones and cultural niches in the Soviet Union where some doctrinal elements of the far-right repertoire were cultivated. The first was the specific case of ethnologist and histori-an Lev Gumilev (1912–1992), a semi-official, semi-dissident figure whose theories of ethnicity and territory share many tenets with the European New Right, though without any personal connections or interactions. The second belongs to Moscow's underground Bohemia, which in the 1960s–1980s rediscovered the esoteric aspects of fascism and national socialism, in particular Julius Evola's "spiritual racism" and neo-pagan Aryan theories. The dissident Yuzhinskii Circle, analyzed here, became the main conduit for introducing Far Right theoreticians to late Soviet Russian culture.

As with any edited volume, this book explores the complexities of the topic but does not pretend to exhaust it. The assembled chapters do not attempt to provide a full and comprehensive picture; instead, they dis-cuss some pieces of a very large puzzle and open new fields for research. Although this volume offers only sketches of a history still to be written, with multiple intellectual ramifications to be explored, we hope to con-tribute not only to a reassessment of the transnational aspect of Euro-pean history and Russia's legitimate place in it, but also to an expanded perspective on the state of contemporary affairs. The cross-fertilization between the Russian and European Far Rights goes deeper than shared posturing and lexicon; it is founded on more fundamental perceptions of what nations, nation-states, and the world order should be. The current honeymoon between Russia and European Far Right has its roots in the "intellectual romance" this volume discusses.

PART I

THE PREREVOLUTIONARY RUSSIAN RIGHT: A FASCISM AVANT LA LETTRE?

CHAPTER 1

LATE IMPERIAL SLAVOPHILISM IN THE CONTEXT OF FASCISTOGENIC IDEAS

A Case Study of Sergei Sharapov

Mikhail Suslov

Looking at late imperial Slavophilism from a bird's eye view, one sees its multiple synchronic and diachronic correspondences with the family of fascist ideas. This obviously does not imply a normative judgment of Slavophile thought, which cannot be held accountable for the atrocities of fascist regimes in the twentieth century. Still, one needs to be aware of the protean character of fascism, which can have many sources, topologies, and chronologies, not necessarily compartmentalized in interwar Western Europe.[1] By observing fascism beyond that term, and beyond the boundaries of the First World War, one can achieve a better understanding of the ideological foundations and heritage on which fascism has resurfaced in post-Soviet Russia. In spite of—or perhaps because of—Russia's status as a peripheral or even "subaltern" empire,[2] its intellectual life in the late imperial period was bustling and teeming with all sorts of hybrid and experimental "cultural software" products[3] designed to make sense of the traumatic processes of reinventing identity. Grounding its analysis in the writings of Slavophile journalist and theorist Sergei Sharapov (1855–1911), this chapter argues that late imperial Russia was not immune to fascism.

While not claiming that these Russian intellectuals were Hitler's teachers,[4] or, generally speaking, that European fascism could be presented as a unidirectional and linear story of birth, rise, and decline, the chapter offers an interpretation of late imperial Slavophilism (henceforth also referred to as "neo-Slavophilism") as one version of European early or protofascisms *avant la lettre*. This ideological stream was tightly embedded in the transnational networks of its Western European siblings, nurtured in the mélange of fascistogenic ideas and movements (the most obvious example being the Black Hundreds milieu), and persisted after the Revolution among the émigré intellectuals. Some of them were outright fascists who proclaimed their allegiance to Mussolini and Hitler, while others, such as Ivan Ilyin, dwelled in refined philosophical salons where they carefully preserved much of the spirit and the letter of prerevolutionary Slavophilism to be passed along to the present-day seekers of the Russian "Third Way." The chapter upholds and refines the idea of the proximity between late imperial Slavophilism and fascism offered in the much-criticized works of Aleksandr Yanov and Walter Laqueur, who situated the Russian fascist tradition within the late imperial radical Right and radical nationalism, mentioning Sharapov as one of the precursors of interwar fascism.[5] The academic orthodoxy, however, connects Russian forerunners of fascism mostly with the Union of the Russian People and the Black Hundreds in general.[6]

The extreme political flanks are not the only and perhaps not the most common habitat of fascist ideas; instead, they may find their strongest expression and universal presence in respectable and moderate niches.[7] In other words, fascism is not an issue of the quantitatively most radical "something," whether nationalism, conservatism, or religious fundamentalism; it is the issue of a qualitatively new conceptualization. It might seem counter-intuitive to believe that neo-Slavophilism—notwithstanding its history of fighting in the same camp with Constitutional Democrats, the aristocratic pedigrees of its supporters, and the traditions of liberal thinking—was an ideological testing ground on which components of the fascist ideology were produced and adapted to one another. An important reservation for this study is that neo-Slavophilism was never an ideological monolith or a single political party. There were at least three strands. First was the right-wing line, which closed ranks with the United Nobility and espoused pronounced monarchist, anti-revolutionary, and aristocratic attitudes. This faction was represented by such intellectuals as General Aleksandr Kireev (1933–1910), Prince Aleksandr Shcherbatov (1850–1915), Fedor Samarin (1858–1916), and Baron Mikhail Taube (1855–1924). The left-wing group, which bordered on Russian populism and non-Marxist socialism, encompassed Nil Durnovo, Konstantin Odarchenko, and Afanasii Vasil'ev. Finally, moderate Slavophilism did not fully sever ties with aristocratic conservatism, but steadily embraced elements of the radical ideology (Sergei Sharapov, Klavdii Stepanov, and Dmitrii Khomiakov are examples of this ideological mixture).[8] Although right-wing Slavophilism contributed to the fascistogenic atmosphere along with messianism, the heroic mythology of a golden age, geopolitical expansionism, and anti-Semitic sentiments, most of the ingredients of fascism were also present in the intellectual kitchens of the leftists and moderates.

INTERNATIONAL CONTEXT

In what sense can one speak of affinities between neo-Slavophilism and fascism? This chapter will pursue two lines of argumentation. First, it will briefly outline the international context of neo-Slavophilism, showing that it was firmly embedded in the fascistogenic milieu of its Western European peers, and second, it will draw ideological parallels, showing the proximity of neo-Slavophilism to the established fascist standard.

Neo-Slavophilism did not evolve in an ideological vacuum; it had multifarious international connections, especially with the French intellectuals close to Boulangist circles and later to the French anti-Semitic milieu, specifically Action Française.[9] As a typical Russian nobleman of that epoch, Sharapov was brought up in French linguistic and intellectual circles. The intellectual influences that he mentioned in his works include, among others, Léon Gambetta, Victor Hugo, Émile de Girardin, Louis Blanc, Charles Fourier, and Pierre-Joseph Proudhon.[10] In 1878–1880 he lived in Paris as a correspondent for *Novoe vremia* and met such intellectuals as Blanc[11] and Hugo. His conversation with Hugo, reported in *Novoe vremia*, discloses that early in his career, when he was still a democrat and a populist, he embraced pan-Slavic nationalism and messianic ideals.[12] Later in his life Sharapov developed ideas reminiscent of the Boulangist synthesis between nationalism and non-Marxist syndicalist Socialism, bequeathed from Louis Blanc.[13] Neo-Slavophilism blossomed when nationalism was grafted onto the trunk of Russian populism. Neo-Slavophilism and Boulangism identified the same demons: parliamentary democracy, the Jews, the urban lifestyle, and oligarchic capitalism. Importantly, the Russian sympathizers with the French revolutionary Right positioned themselves as equal and in some instances even as superior to their Western partners. Thus, Sharapov condescendingly commended General George Boulanger for his monarchist sympathies, expressing hope that a reborn France would emulate Russia in this regard.[14]

Sharapov corresponded with some leaders of the French radical Right, especially from the militarist and populist Ligue des patriotes, founded in 1882.[15] Its leader, Paul Déroulède (1846–1914), insisted on the necessity of military education and concocted revanchist projects against Germany.[16] Like his Russian friends, Déroulède spoke against the bourgeoisie, materialism, and parliamentarism. By 1886, Déroulède had adopted a revolutionary, radically oppositional rhetoric because he believed that the government was unable to put the idea of *revanche* into reality. This placed him side by side with Boulanger.[17]

Sharapov's periodicals succeeded in reaching a rapprochement with France and antagonizing Germany. He offered a publishing outlet for Lucien Millevoye (1850–1918), a Boulangist politician and editor of the nationalist *La Patrie,* with whom Sharapov started a correspondence in 1887. In 1888 Millevoye visited Russia on behalf of General Boulanger in order to promote the idea of a Russian–French alliance among the Russian Germanophobes.[18] One of Sharapov's articles asserted that the alliance would not only contain Germany, but also do away with the British influence. Millevoye generously proposed to divide up the world between Russia and France, so that the "civilizing mission" of France would be a boon for Africa just as that of Russia would benefit Asia.[19]

In 1901 Sharapov coordinated an attack on Sergei Witte's monetary reforms in concert with Édouard Drumont,[20] the notorious author of *La France juive* (1886; translated into Russian in 1895[21]) and the founder of the Ligue antisémite de France (1889). He also published Drumont's pieces in his journal *Russkoe delo.*[22] André Chéradame and Pierre Rocheverre,[23] two French journalists who wrote on the German threat, also entered into correspondence with Sharapov. Two of Chéradame's books were translated into Russian; one of them, *L'Europe et la question d'Autriche au seuil du XXe siècle* (1901), was published by the pan-Slavic activist and Sharapov's "brother-in-arms" Vissarion Komarov (1838–1907) in 1903.

In the last years of his life, Sharapov wrote on anti-German themes for a few French journals, most notably for *Le Radical*—which sometimes was accused of following the line of Action Française—and for *L'Opinion,* widely covering the theme of the German military threat.[24] Around the same time he started a correspondence with Roman Dmowski (1864–1939),[25] with whom he found a common language on the basis of anti-Semitism, Germanophobia, and some shared pan-Slavic ideas. Importantly, in the 1920s Dmowski developed a worldview close to that of the German Conservative Revolution, and mimicked some aspects of Mussolini's ideology.[26] Marian Zdziechowski was another Polish intellectual who corresponded with Sharapov. He started from the same Romantic pessimism regarding contemporary civilization and pan-Slavic sentiments, but belonged to the antifascist camp between the wars. Sharapov also mingled with Serbian intellectuals such as Nikola Pašić,[27] who was part of Ivan

Aksakov's circle in the 1880s and later developed a Serbian-style populist Slavophilism with a strong emphasis on communitarian aspects.[28]

An important caveat is that neo-Slavophilism, due to its heterogeneity and syncretism, attracted interest abroad not only among nationalists and protofascists, but also among religious activists, ecumenists, and scholars sympathetic to Russia and its intellectual developments. Two parallel international networks included Slavophile leaders: the Old Catholic movement, whose key supporter in Russia was Aleksandr Kireev (Sharapov supported the movement, too),[29] and the French "Slavophiles" grouped around Dmitrii Khomiakov (1841–1919).[30] This division again shows that there was no single intellectual route running through classic Slavophilism all the way to Hitler and Mussolini, but some of the busiest exits definitely led in this direction.

IDEOLOGICAL CORE: REDUCTIONISM AND SYNCRETISM

At the turn of the twentieth century, neo-Slavophile thinkers produced a pronouncedly protofascist worldview based on the intention to break away from West-centric modernity. They called for an alternative world order in which the most troubling contradictions—alienating social relations along with developing participatory political mechanisms; a pressing need to modernize the country while retaining its (imaginary) authentic core; Russia's desired role in international affairs and its perceived semi-colonial relations with the advanced Western countries—would recede and become irrelevant.[31]

Examining the idea of reductionism as the ultimate rationale of proto-fascist ideas, we can further follow the academic consensus on the "fascist minimum": the alternative world is more often than not envisaged in terms of "palingenetic" mythology, as a project of rejuvenation or rebirth based on the primordial fundamentals of a nation. Palingenetic mythology is con-structed from several elements: scathing criticism of the present, viewed as a period of degeneration and decline; the revolutionary thrust to create a new order; and the fundamentalist belief in the transformative powers of going "back-to-the-roots."[32] If we take the palingenetic mythology as the litmus test of fascism, neo-Slavophilism, given its anti-Westernism and its obsession with authentic national roots in the times of pre-Petrine Mus-covy, would probably hit the mark more than any of the other coterminous protofascisms. One can push this line of argumentation even further and support Hans Rogger's thesis of Russian fascism as the first European fas-cism. Indeed, if classic Slavophilism actually was the first anticolonial theoretical reflection,[33] informed by an emotional anti-Western *ressentiment*, it would inevitably ripen into an ideology of national renaissance.

Proceeding from two interrelated concepts, the reduction of social complexity and the idea of national rebirth, one can reasonably argue that fascism is a distinctive but "thin-centered" ideology;[34] that is, it has to outsource most of the biggest political questions to a contingent assortment of other ideologies. Hence, fascism represents a syncretic ideology, with the most common combinations including socialism, populism, nationalism, and conservatism, although it is not altogether hostile to the ideological peripheries of liberalism.[35] Neo-Slavophilism is a perfect exemplar of this kind of ideological syncretism. It is notoriously hard to pin down as either conservatism or liberalism; much depends on the prism through which it is observed by scholars. For students of Russian constitutionalism it represents a sort of liberalism,[36] whereas for specialists on the Russian Right it belongs in the domain of conservatism.[37] In this chapter I will show that the ideological fuzziness of Slavophilism may be explained in part by the inadequacy of the analytical apparatus applied to Russian ideologies, but also by the fact that neo-Slavophilism represented a new type of syncretic ideology that can better be understood within the context of European protofascisms.

Neo-Slavophiles shunned the idea that they represented a particular party or espoused a particular ideology; instead, they preferred to see Slavophilism not as an ideology, but as the natural Russian "worldview."[38] Sharapov struck this note when he emphasized that Slavophilism was complete in and of itself (*tsel'no*) because it attempted to translate people's "instincts" into political terms. Together with Nil Durnovo and Mikhail Taube, he interpreted Slavophilism as a philosophy that had already been established and needed only to be fully "cleared up."[39]

From this standpoint, Slavophiles avoided identifying themselves with either the Left or the Right. Explicating his ideological credo to the censor Evgenii Feoktistov, Sharapov specified that it was "neither liberal, i.e., *destructive* . . . nor conservative, i.e., *preservationist* (*okhranitel'noe*). . . . my foundation is *creative* (*zizhditel'nyi*)."[40] Elsewhere he explained that his "ardent love for freedom and hatred for any arbitrariness and violence" drew him near to the progressivists (i.e., the Octobrists and Constitutional Democrats), while on other important issues, such as local self-government, he sided with the United Nobility.[41] His understanding of freedom and violence should be contextualized within the broader Slavophile understanding of natural (organic) development. From this viewpoint, freedom is a synonym for unimpeded natural growth and, by extension, violence is a synonym for inorganic, unnatural intrusion into the processes of people's development.

Sharapov's interpretation of the concept of freedom was essentially different from the liberal vision of a person as an architect of his own fortune. This difference boils down to the central controversy between liberal and communitarian political philosophy: whether a human can and should step aside from his/her cultural background and critically assess it.[42] Claiming to be a "true liberal,"[43] Sharapov in fact was on the opposite side in this debate, because the ideological bedrock of his theorization was exactly the idea of harmony between rational planning and following the traditional ways. Little wonder that his understanding of "liberalism" was fairly unconventional. He was at pains to prove that democracy and especially parliamentarism—a "political syphilis," as he dubbed it[44]—contradicted "our historical instincts, people's beliefs, the order of things, and, simply, common reason,"[45] prioritized the Jews and the intelligentsia, and replaced the principles of solidarity and sympathy with the principles of partisan struggle and political animosity.[46]

At the same time, Sharapov carefully distanced himself from the rightists. His private correspondence is dotted with unappealing characterizations of them, such as "conservative rascals" (*konservativnaia svoloch*[47]), "hypocrites and cheats."[48] He tried to position Slavophilism as the "Third Way," equally intellectually alien to socialism and liberalism on the one hand and to conservatism on the other. Both extremes, in his view, represented the idea of an anti-national Westernization of Russia.[49] In return, conservatives did not recognize Sharapov as their ideological peer. Fedor Samarin, on the right flank of Slavophilism, refrained from joining the Ivan Aksakov Society, organized by Sharapov in 1906, on the grounds that he did not want to enlist in the ranks of Sharapov's associates.[50]

Sharapov's Romantic and religiously communitarian political philosophy rendered his take on socialism rather ambiguous. He criticized socialism as a doctrine of hatred and destruction,[51] even if he was by no means averse to socialist ideas. His intellectual trajectory—from radical populism to right-wing Slavophilism—was typical within the fascistogenic Russian intellectual landscape of the late imperial period, and was paralleled by the analogous developments made by Lev Tikhomirov (1852–1923), Petr Struve (1870–1944), and many others. Moreover, it reiterated the broader European model, epitomized by such intellectuals as Paul Déroulède.[52]

A *VÖLKISCH* THEORY OF SOCIETY

Sharapov's formative years coincided with the famous "going-to-the-people" movement and with the international vogue for socialist ideas of all types, developed and disseminated by Louis Blanc, Léon Gambetta, Nikolai Dobroliubov, Mikhail Bakunin, Aleksandr Herzen, and Dmitrii Pisarev. Echoing Herzen's idiosyncratic socialism, Sharapov confessed that during his youth, "a peasant (*muzhik*) was everything for me: a creature of the highest spirituality, a reservoir of historical wisdom, and a pillar of the Orthodox Church."[53] Likewise, at that time he entertained constitutional ideas and attacked the autocratic regime for its crackdown on civic freedoms. Later on, when he converted to Slavophilism and wrote extensively in opposition to socialism, he nevertheless promulgated many ideas from his youthful reading list and mingled with some visionaries of the utopian Christian-socialist persuasion, like Konstantin Odarchenko (+1905) and Afanasii Vasil'ev (1851–1929).

Sharapov worked with them on two interrelated themes: non-exploitative economy and direct democracy. In economics Odarchenko went as far as to suggest a currency system based on "labor money," which in the future would be replaced by non-monetary exchange. Adducing a typically Christian-socialist argument, he made his proposal contingent upon the spiritual improvement of humankind, and—in line with Russian populism and Slavophilism—upon active participation of local self-government in big business.[54] Elsewhere, Odarchenko drew on the populist gurus Sergei Iuzhakov (1849–1910) and Sergei Krivenko (1847–1906) to develop a vision of the economy grounded in professional cooperation between workers.[55] Sharapov approved of these ideas in general ("this is a fantastic study!") but advanced more practical—as he saw it—measures toward his own ideal of a just economic order based on a paper currency and the power of the autocratic tsar to spur economic growth by massive investment.[56] He also sided with Christian Socialists and Russian populists on the question of industrial and agricultural cooperation, whose primary unit would forever remain the peasants' commune.[57]

Not daring to lift a hand against private property, Sharapov elaborated an agricultural project that brought together *völkisch* visions of peasant communes as sources of the authentic Russian spirit and ideas of agricultural cooperation in the spirit of class harmony and reconciliation between small land proprietors and landlords. In so arguing, he did not move much beyond the position of Herzen, who infused Proudhon's utopia with messianic nationalism.[58] Still, considered in the context of the early twentieth century, when even the staunchest rightists supported the disintegration of peasant communes, these traditional ideas regained a sense of freshness, iconoclasm, and novelty.

Two aspects made Sharapov's agricultural project especially relevant to his contemporaries. One of them was his interpretation of property. He embraced the capitalist concept of property as an individual right, but at the same time he stipulated that "the property right is better secured outside of capitalism" because it cannot be alienated through the mechanisms of a market economy.[59] In this sense, the peasants' commune does not represent a seed of the would-be collective property, as Russian socialists averred, but a reasonable system for the collective exploitation of private property that privileges social justice and hard work and discourages speculation in land. The landed nobility, according to this line of thought, justly earned their estates by serving the state. This semi-feudal understanding of property as a privilege, rather than as capital, allowed Sharapov to make the right of possession contingent upon a person's productive labor and political loyalty.

Another aspect of Sharapov's vision was the emphasis on the reduction of social conflict. Sharapov was himself a middling landed nobleman, whose inherited estate in the Viaz'ma district became a testing ground for his—more often than not ill-conceived and ruinous—economic ideas. Sharapov tried to emulate his neighbor Aleksandr Engel'gardt (1832–1893), a famous scholar close to Russian populism. Importantly for our context, both of them shared a belief in the transformative powers of science (namely, agricultural chemistry) and positivist thought in general, which sharply separated them from the Romantic strain of Slavophilism. They both wanted to break away from the stereotypical role of a Russian landowner who would bleed his estate dry while squandering his money in the capital cities, and to offer a different model, in which a landowner would act as the manager of the rural economy of his peasants. As he described his experience, "Throughout the summer, I manage all the agricultural activities. I determine where to sow and where to fertilize."[60] Sharapov believed that, in the future, this model would morph into cooperation on shares, based on joint economic interest. He maintained that the peasants were glad to work with him and that they trusted him because it was their common cause; elsewhere he mentions that peasants were, "broadly speaking, my family."[61] Sharapov's vision of social solidarism in agriculture became his response to the challenge of capitalism. Like his understanding of property, this rustic idyll was a hybrid form of feudal land ownership, designed to survive in the troubled waters of capitalism.

Sharapov saw a panacea in the "back-to-the-land" movement, which proposed to enhance the "organic unity" of the society in such a way that there would appear a priest-farmer, a doctor-farmer, and a teacher-farmer.[62] Thus, the cardinal discrepancy between the "people and the public" (i.e., the intelligentsia), theorized by Ivan Aksakov, would wither. To recapitulate, Sharapov wanted to fight capitalism but not by means of socialism: "We Russians have to look for another way."[63] Sharapov moved in intellectual circles in which grassroots democracy, based on the Church's parochial self-government and peasant communes, was seen as a key to solving the dilemma between modernization and authenticity. This democratic tendency represented a strand of thought that aimed to make sense of the perceived lack of social cohesion and to offer an operational cure for this malaise. If nothing else, this concept of democracy alone would situate neo-Slavophilism within the broader context of the Europe-wide dissatisfaction with the alienating industrial *Gesellschaft* and vague longing for *Gemeinschaft*.[64] In a letter to Empress-Dowager Maria Fedorovna, Sharapov wrote: "[The government] mechanically managed the herd of the population. When the ruling mechanism had broken down, one part of this herd rebelled and the other part appeared to be utterly helpless. It is useless to call on this herd, to ask it to consolidate, until it is turned into an organized community of people."[65] He argued that the only way to do so was on the basis of the last remaining social bond—the bond of locality, reinforced by religiosity. Hence, in line with a large consensus among the reformist Orthodox thinkers Dmitrii Samarin (1827–1901), Aleksandr Papkov (1855–1920), Georgii Shechkov (1856–1920), and others, Sharapov intended to reinvigorate Russia's medieval parochial self-government as the heart of the country's religious, social, economic, and political life. In his view, the parochial organization was based on the "organic" neighborly and kindred relations of fraternal love, solidarity, and Christianity.

Locating the center of gravity of the political system at its most basic level, Sharapov proposed yet another hybrid: a participatory mechanism with a pronounced ethno-confessional coloration. Parishes, in his scheme, would exclude the non-Orthodox (and by extension, non-Russian) population of the Empire from political life, base it on the Orthodox clerics, peasantry, and nobility, and disadvantage urban dwellers. When in spring and summer 1905 the electoral law was being debated, Sharapov advanced the idea of organizing elections in parishes, where the influence of the intelligentsia would be minimal and the voices of the Church, noble landlords, and well-off peasants would be the loudest. During the revolution of 1905–1907 he persistently advocated the establishment of well-armed parochial fighting squads to confront revolutionaries. Importantly, he even suggested a "dictatorship of parochial self-government" as a way out of the revolutionary unrest.[66]

FÜHRERPRINZIP

The principle of the leader (*Führerprinzip*) requires an enduring Romantic tradition of perceiving the people in elevated terms, as the bearers of authentic national character and ideals. In this sense, fascism often appears to be a "surprisingly democratic" ideology.[67] A leader in this context is construed as an embodiment of the nation, who, energized by the collective will, carries out people's innermost desires and ideas. By the same token, a fascist tradition devoid of these *völkisch* associations is unlikely to develop a strong *Führerprinzip*.[68] The Slavophile theory of people's monarchy can be interpreted in this light.

Sharapov's elaborately depicted political model makes the syncretism of his thoughts especially salient. He described two sources of power and legitimacy: God's anointment of the tsar, who would control the most important imperial branches of government, such as foreign policy and security, finances, and railroads; and the will of the people, empowering local representatives who would manage education, sanitation, local police, business, and so on. Although Sharapov repeats the monarchist mantra of the divine provenance of the leadership, he does not draw on any theological substantiation of monarchist power, nor does he ever cite the biblical story about the first kings of Israel. His monarchist language is rational and managerial. In his model, the tsar has to stand completely outside of the bureaucratic system because he is not the highest functionary of the state apparatus, but the leader of the country, "a living Personality, standing at the top of the Russian state by God's Providence and by the people's will, [which] is the living embodiment of the collective historical organism."[69] In 1881, when Sharapov had just returned to Russia and joined Ivan Aksakov's circle, struck by the assassination of the tsar, he suggested in the draft of an unpublished article that the new monarch should altogether sever ties with "society" (i.e., with the intelligentsia and the bureaucracy) and that, "having leant upon the people, he would turn all existing order upside down and thereby would become a people's tsar in the strictest sense of the word."[70] The Slavophile theory of monarchy was a hybrid product of two processes: secularization of the theological concept of the tsar as a saint and democratization of politics. Whatever sophisticated theoretical substantiation of autocratic rule they embraced, the Slavophiles' vision of the tsar recalled the transitory period when his powers were seen as having a divine provenance and, at the same time, as being the "self-consciousness of the people, concentrated in one person."[71]

Sharapov refined this leadership principle in a series of utopian essays, *Diktator*, published in 1907–1908. Written in the classic model of a dialogue between the main character, the Dictator, and his collaborators, these stories offer a way out from what was perceived as revolutionary chaos and the degradation of the country. The salient feature of this narrative is how the figure of the Dictator is described. His name is Ivanov the 16th—the ordinal number refers to the Russian bureaucratic tradition of distinguishing functionaries with the same surname. (Here it is intended to highlight Ivanov's insignificant pedigree—and the very name "Ivanov" is deliberately ordinary, the most common Russian family name). He is a "simple colonel, who has never stood out and whose record of accomplishments is completely undistinguished. . . . We have thousands of such officers in Russia."[72] Likewise, Ivanov's right hand, the minister of finance, is Sokolov the 18th, who has similarly skyrocketed to Empire-wide prominence in spite of his complete obscurity.[73] All of the other members of Ivanov's team are depicted in similar terms: one came from the "modest ranks of our judicial circles," another is a retired professor who has peacefully passed his time in the countryside, yet another is a "modest priest from a remote village."[74] Elsewhere, Ivanov observes that if the revolutionaries were to kill him, his place would immediately be taken by "another unknown Ivanov, then a third one would come, and so on."[75] In addition, Sharapov emphasizes the intellectual ignorance of Ivanov, who had not read more than "five or six books" in his life.

This persistent debasement of the dictator is intended to highlight his separation from the intelligentsia and his unbreakable links with the grassroots. His ignorance allows him to express the people's interests and ideals, uncontaminated by foreign scholasticism and the treadmill of ideological polemics. Ivanov the 16th is, thus, an actual people's tribune, whose ultimate task is not to impose yet another invented socio-political constitution, but to excavate the primordial and half-forgotten Russian "constitution" from the layers of the people's common sense, everyday life, and ancient sagas.

In their practical decisions, Ivanov and his team show themselves to be advocates of decisive, often violent actions in line with "common sense" and in contradiction to the political conventions of the liberal West. For example, one liberal journalist who spreads lies about the tsar and the government is sentenced to flagellation; a workers' demonstration is broken up by the serious threat to use machine guns if the participants do not go back to work; elderly high-ranking bureaucrats are stripped of their lavish pensions in spite of energetic protests from the whole of the bureaucracy, and so on. Although the image of the dictator was deliberately debased, at the end of the day the dictator emerges as the real leader of the nation, the epitome of Sharapov's vision of an autocratic monarch, with elements of a cult of personality. In Sharapov's earlier utopia, *Cherez polveka* [Fifty years later] (1902), another dictator, "our genial Fedor Panteleev," is likewise an insignificant non-aristocratic landlord from the provinces, who in spite of this background (or rather because of it), emerges as the demiurge of a new Russia, reorganized on Slavophile bases.

NATIONALISM AND GEOPOLITICS

Grounding the system of political participation on ethno-cultural *Gemeinschaft,* Sharapov approached one of the central problems for neo-Slavophilism—that of nationalism. Roger Griffin's definition of fascism situates it within the more general phenomenon of ultranationalism.[76] This raises the question of the extent to which this could be applicable to neo-Slavophile imperial thinkers, who outspokenly opposed the nationalism of the Black Hundreds. Sharapov reproached their position: "For Russians, *Russland* is by no means *über Alles,*" he argued, because only God was "above everything."[77] Nationalism, as he defined it, was unacceptable for two reasons. First, in his view it contradicted Russia's divine mission: "Holy Russia," he explained, "is not for Russians, it is for God."[78] The second reason was a practical political one: as a multinational empire, Russia would fall apart if its Great Russian core professed nationalism. He admonished Vladimir Purishkevich (1870–1920) to stop the nationalist propaganda, because it would "pave the road along which the Roman Empire had once stumbled to collapse."[79] For the Slavophiles in general, "nationality" meant not so much an ethno-national or a civic political community, but rather a cultural one,[80] sounding Romantic and communitarian notes but also echoing some aspects of the concept of popular sovereignty. Afanasii Vasil'ev, for example, insisted that Russian history had been made "not by generals and privy councilors, but by the people."[81] The Slavophile newspaper *Moskovskii golos,* launched in 1906 by Klavdii Stepanov, proclaimed that the state could be based only on the principles and traditions worked out by the people.[82]

The Slavophile concept of the people's sovereignty, borrowing much from religiously colored communitarianism and cultural nationalism, reinforces *völkisch* and palingenetic visions as well as geopolitical reductionism. Sharapov's line of division between "us" and "them" reduced the national question to the "eternal" antagonism between the Slavs and the Germans. The Slavs, more often than not representatives of the patriarchal agrarian world, were increasingly seen not as Russia's younger brothers but as Russia's saviors. The united Slavs, he professed, were endowed with a messianic task: to create a "new civilization" that would "synthesize the East and the West, harmonize morality and law . . . and reunite the Christian churches."[83] The revolution of 1905 and the advent of parliamentarism were like a cold shower. Sharapov reflected on this: "I think that here is the end of Russia as such. We have to reach out to the Poles and yell at the top of our voices "Long live the Slavs!" Everything is rotten in Russia. . . . Russia has fizzled out and became corrupt as a state and as a nation. We cannot revive it by our own efforts. Our rebirth lies in Slavdom." From the standpoint of the Slavophile eschatology, the revolution of 1905–1907 and the advent of parliamentarism marked the end of "Russian Russia," which had to become "Slavic Russia," lest the Empire perish as Poland had in the eighteenth century.[84] After 1905 Sharapov repeatedly stressed that the decrepit Russian Empire needed the fresh forces of the Slavs, battle-hardened by their struggle to preserve their faith and independence. He emphasized that Russia was only a part of Slavdom, not Slavdom per se.[85]

Following the logic of this worldview, the referent "outside" group is "Germandom." Sharapov saw no possibility of avoiding war with Germany. His opinion was that Germans and Slavs could not live together—that the relationship was a zero-sum game, where Russia either assumed her mission as a Slavic leader, strengthened "the Latin world," contained Germany, and consolidated the predominant power of the Slavs in Europe; or renounced her historical mission, ceded the Slavic lands to Germany and Austria, and descended to the position of a second-rate state.[86] The idea that Europe was too small for two world-shaping forces—the Slavs and the Germans—was shared by virtually all neo-Slavophiles and propagated in the platform of the Slavonic Benevolent Society, where it was argued that Germanic tribes represented a wedge driven into the territory of the Slavic peoples; as long as Prussia and Austria existed in their present form, Slavdom would never feel safe. It could be said that neo-Slavophiles developed one of the first geopolitical programs, connecting the question of national security with some kind of an eternal "truth" about the territorial organization of states. The protagonist of Sharapov's utopia *Cherez polveka*, who has just woken up from a fifty-year slumber, marvels in front of a geographical map of the Empire: "Here you are, Mother-Russia! For a minute I was taken aback. . . . Now the western border starts near Danzig

... embraces the whole of East Prussia and Poznań ... then it steps into former Austria, embraces the Czech lands and Moravia, and descends to the Adriatic Sea past Salzburg and Bavaria and including Trieste."[87]

APPROACHING RACISM

On a greater scale, Sharapov envisaged a bloc of states, defined as "Aryan races," including the Slavic union, France, and the Anglo-Saxons, which would be strong enough to choke off the "Yellow race" and to secure the dominance of "White mankind" for centuries to come. Germany was deliberately excluded from this crusade on the grounds that it could "betray the White cause" and end up in the "yellow camp."[88] The most likely inspiration for this racial discourse is the journalist Mikhail Men'shikov (1859–1918) from *Novoe vremia*, who quoted from Houston Stewart Chamberlain and Otto Weininger, arguing that the Jews were the basest and most parasitic human species, who had contaminated the German host society and were killing it gradually.[89]

To do them justice, most of the Slavophiles did not embrace purely racist anti-Semitism, adducing mostly cultural and religious arguments against the Jews. The anti-Semitism of the Slavophiles was a tradition rooted in Ivan Aksakov's journalism, and represented the gloomiest elements of his "reactionary utopia." As has been shown by H. D. Löwe, Slavophile reactionary anti-Semitism stems from an aversion to modernity; the words "Jew," "capitalist," "liberal," and "revolutionary" are perceived as essentially synonymous.[90] For example, Kireev adhered to a culturally colored anti-Semitism, developing the argument that the Jews, due to their stateless status, were alien to the dearest Russian ideals, such as patriotism and monarchism. He suggested that the Jews' fate should be decided in a nationwide plebiscite.[91] Nevertheless, the speed with which some of the Slavophiles embraced the idea of marking and isolating the Jews was troubling. In particular, they demanded that the Jews should be punished for using Christian names and denied their rights to vote or hold office.[92] At the same time, the "old-fashioned" idea of the assimilation of the Jews—contingent upon their willingness to be baptized—still had some currency among the Slavophiles.[93]

Sharapov's exploration of the Jewish question in his writings shows us how the idea of segregation was taking hold in the minds of his contemporaries. In his previously mentioned utopia *Cherez polveka*, he depicts an imaginary neighborhood meeting dedicated to the Jewish question. The problem was that in Sharapov's renewed and regenerated Russia, the vibrant neighborhood organizations have undermined Jewish financial supremacy. Jews are boycotted and compelled to "subsist on their own, not by exploiting others." Masses of Jews are getting baptized and converting to Orthodoxy. This particular meeting discusses a bill of the Local Council of Russian Bishops, according to which parishes can accept the Jews only after testing the sincerity of their conversion and only after a five-year trial period. But the "true Russian patriots" consider these limitations insufficient, and the general opinion of the meeting is that the Jewish "essence" resides not in religion but in blood, and that to admit them to the parishes would mean to admit a hostile element into the fortress of Russian nationality. But at the same time, to leave the Jews starving on the streets would be contrary to the spirit of Christianity, so the meeting decides: let them first work on the land and become "spiritually regenerated," and then, when they have acquired habits of productive toil, they could be cautiously admitted to the parishes.[94] With some sympathy, Sharapov paints the image of an old converted Jew who had for years worked for the parish and who leaves this meeting in tears, but *dura lex, sed lex* ...

This episode shows an uneasy cohabitation of two anti-Semitisms in one mind, with the racial one gradually taking the upper hand. Later on, especially during and after the revolution of 1905–1907, Sharapov continued his ruminations on the corruptive essence of the Jews and on the Jewish–Masonic conspiracy and global hegemony. "Typical representatives of the Jews are the Jew-profiteers, the Jew-spongers, the Jew-exploiters," asserted Sharapov in 1906. He blamed the Jewish conspiracy for forcing Witte to introduce the gold standard and for promoting the October Manifesto in 1905, and constantly grumbled over the "Jewish dominance" in the press and in the Russian economy.[95] The gold standard, in his opinion, "fettered all peoples and states of the world with a single huge chain and threw them, like slaves, at the feet of the almighty Israel."[96] In a letter to Pavel Miliukov, Sharapov confessed that he was firmly convinced that the Jews and the Slavs were naturally different, "more different than sheep and wolves, grapes and phylloxera, hens and hawks."[97] The year 1905 was a period of ferment in anti-Semitic ideas. In August Sharapov claimed that the Jews would remain enemies of the Russian state in times to come, although as we can judge from the context, the reason he had in mind was their religion, not race.[98] When he resumed publication of his journal after a break in October, an editorial called the Jews "misanthropic in their religion and parasitic in their racial essence," suggesting that their legal status in the Empire should be reduced to the status of foreigners.[99] After the revolution, Sharapov's anti-Semitism sounded unambiguously segregationist and racist. In another of his utopias, *Kabinet diktatora* (1908), even baptized Jews are excluded from the public sphere, including the press, where the editors-in-chief have to sign a statement that they will never hire a Jew.[100]

In spite of Sharapov's dissatisfaction with the Great Russian nationalism of the Black Hundreds, his own program implied a more radical version of nationalism, based on palingenetic revivalism, racism, anti-Semitism, and the expansive geopolitics of *Lebensraum*. A Slavic Russia, as envisaged in his pan- and supra-nationalist program, was seen as the hegemony of racially defined Slavs, with Jews expelled from the public sphere.[101]

PALINGENETIC MYTHOLOGY

The *völkisch* legacy of the classic Slavophiles became the foundation on which late imperial neo-Slavophiles built their anticolonial ideas and conceptualized the supposed lack of recognition of Russia as the embodiment of a geopolitical anti-Westernism. Their contemporaries, too, were vulnerable to disillusionment, resentment, and eschatological fears.[102] All this produced a specific intellectual atmosphere in which Russian messianism, severely wounded by the collision with reality, began a fundamental transformation from an expansive messianism that saw Russia as the savior of the world to an introverted messianism aimed at the restoration of some mythical primordial "covenant" whose clauses had been abandoned at some point in history, a covenant that had to be reinstated in order for Russia to regain its lost sense of historical importance and mission.[103] This reinterpretation of messianism inspired critical attacks against the present social order, the creation of palingenetic mythology, and Promethean revolutionary musings in the writings of neo-Slavophiles.

Thus, Sharapov gained fame as an intransigent critic of post-Petrine Russia with its bureaucracy, inert and impoverished population, and predatory capitalism, and its lack of civilized habits of work, leisure, and polemics. Mounting his criticism, he followed the analysis of the classic Slavophiles who had developed the concept of an inauthentic, borrowed culture. As Ivan Kireevskii argued in the 1840s, repeating Johann Gottfried Herder's premises, a transplanted flower would wither away on foreign soil; furthermore, it would block the natural development of the "native flora." Hence, borrowed cultural forms could never raise the cultural level of the locals, but could only multiply their barbarity and passive lack of creativity.[104] Sharapov continued thinking along these lines, arguing that the borrowed political forms of Prussian bureaucracy had morphed into the "St.

Petersburg regime," a "horrendous tumor on the body of humankind."[105] The affective universe of Sharapov's published works is evident in terms such as "rotting away," "dirt," "contamination," and "decomposition." For example, in a New Year's editorial of his journal he penned: "Russia has started to rot away slowly,"[106] so that Russian life is compared to a "cesspit," and to "suffocating, rotting and stinking slush" (*udushaiushchaia, gniiushchaia i zlovonnaia zhizha*).[107] He called the post-Petrine epoch "one hundred fifty years of systematic debasement (*opodlenie*), suffocation of the spirit, contamination of the most holy [ideals] of the Russian soul and heart, and turning the whole of Mother Russia into a gigantic prison camp."[108] Elsewhere he pointed at Russia's "deadly slumber, flabbiness, degeneration (*izmel'chalost'*), cowardice, meanness, and low spirits."[109]

Against this background, the war and the revolution were perceived as a salutary and beneficial way out.[110] Striking the same note, Aleksandr Kireev averred that the Russians were "heroes, not workers," and pessimistically observed that today's world required crafts and trade, not heroic feats.[111] Stringing together populist, messianic, anti-Semitic, and antiliberal ideas, Sharapov proclaimed that Russia's universal mission would be accomplished only if Russia could become "heroic and national (*narodnaia*), not Jewish, liberal, bureaucratic, and parliamentary."[112] He employed two interrelated metaphors connected to revolutionary transformation: the yoke and liberation from it; and destruction followed by regeneration. He envisaged the imminent catastrophe as a revolutionary uprising, civil war, military debacle, and financial bankruptcy,[113] but his depiction of it manifests a kind of thanatological attraction to it. He repeatedly says that the forthcoming downfall of Russia would become the first salutary step toward its rebirth. In his private correspondence, Sharapov wrote: "There is no hope whatsoever. We are useless militarily, and [the enemy] could take us with their bare hands. . . . I have already gone over much suffering in my heart, [imagining] our shameful conditions in the future: how we surrender armies and fortresses, how [the enemy] enters Moscow, how the bureaucratic Russian state is destroyed. . . . But in any case, [we will see in Russia's future] *liberation and rebirth*. As for the impending catastrophes, [I must admit that] they have to come precisely in order to allow for our *regeneration*."[114]

He believed that this "regeneration" would mean, first and foremost, the moral rebirth of the people, with a subsequent thorough bottom-up transformation of the political system, and social and economic reforms. As a result, a "spiritual unity" would emerge where now there was merely a "herd of people," and there would arise talented political figures and military leaders.[115] Kireev mused similarly, hoping that losing the war with Germany would "reunite the tsar and the people."[116] In a more general sense, the Slavophiles' craving for catastrophe mirrored their Romantic attraction to the sublime nature of the terrors of war and violence. Sharapov, for example, wished to wash away the dirt of contemporary civilization by means of "great wars with their terrors, calamities, and conquests, [which would] regenerate and morally elevate humankind."[117]

The scale and the method of the transformation suggested in Sharapov's model are truly radical; hence his attitude to the revolution of 1905 is ambivalent. As might be expected for a nobleman of the Slavophile persuasion, the revolution posited the greatest challenge to his populist and messianic worldview, destroying the ideal images of the "peaceful Russian people" and of Russia's unique path between the Scylla of industrial backwardness and the Charybdis of mass proletarianization. Unlike the majority of the Russian rightists, however, Sharapov and Dmitrii Khomiakov, armed with Slavophile theory and palingenetic mythology, related the revolutionary events to the sweeping process of degeneration, which in their view had started long before the propaganda of the social democrats—namely, with Peter the Great's revolution of the early eighteenth century. Today, they maintained, two revolutions met to produce an outburst of violence on an unprecedented scale. There were "revolutionaries in work shirts" from below and the "revolutionaries in uniforms" (meaning bureaucrats) from above.[118] Echoing these views, another neo-Slavophile, Iurii Bartenev (1866–1908), expressed the Conservative-Revolutionary spirit of the doctrine in the following words: "We are looking for transformations (*preobrazovaniia*), but these [transformations should bring about] new forms that would remind us of our beloved past."[119]

Stressing the radical and comprehensive character of the proposed reforms, Bartenev's paper recognizes that the Slavophiles' radicalism differs essentially from the revolutionary tradition motivated by certain universal rational principles.[120] Instead, philosophically, it resonates with the representatives of the "Conservative Revolution,"[121] when it emphasizes the importance of the particular, the traditional, and calls for the liberation of the people from abstract ideals and a return to the old paths of "natural" development—the exact opposite of what socialist revolutionaries wanted. Still, the very idea of a revolutionary transformation was not alien to Sharapov and his circle, so time and again right-wingers accused him of inspiring the revolution.[122]

CONCLUSION

Sharapov was not one of the Slavophile luminaries, although at times he managed to rally a quite visible group of supporters and subscribers for his papers. In today's Russia his writings have been unearthed and popularized by anti-Semites and religious fundamentalists. For example, ultra-nationalist Oleg Platonov claims that Sharapov explicated some of the most important elements of the "Russian civilization," namely, its concept of the state, local self-government, and the economy.[123] Slavophilism in general is again in vogue among such figures as Aleksandr Dugin, Egor Kholmogorov, Mikhail Leontiev, and Natalia Narochnitskaia, who are trying to represent it as Russia's ideology of the Third Way. Thus, there is something in Slavophilism that continues to resonate with the radical nationalists and provide satisfactory answers to their most burning questions. What made late imperial Slavophilism relevant to its contemporaries was its reductionist program, based on an ideational framework that combined non-Marxist communitarian socialism with *völkisch* nationalism. This framework supported a counter-revolutionary utopia, featuring radical denial of Englightenment universalism and embodying an imagined primordial and racially pure pan-Slavic unity, whose internal cohesion was based on religious and political ties with the tsar as a people's tribune, and externally tempered by anti-German and anti-Semitic antagonisms. The *völkisch,* racial, and palingenetic elements of this utopia were not contingent and marginal, but were central to this syncretic and hybrid ideology, which attempted both to make sense of and to mediate the country's transition to capitalist modernity. As an ideological "interface" designed to tackle internationally universal and important issues, neo-Slavophilism echoed elements of French Boulangism and populist radicalism in general, and undoubtedly contributed to the creation of the prewar European fascistogenic milieu.

CHAPTER 2

A REACTIONARY UTOPIA

Russian Black Hundreds
from Autocracy to Fascism

Giovanni Savino

L ate imperial Russia had fault lines, but the main ones were almost certainly those related to the "nationalities question." The nationalizing policy pursued by the tsarist authorities caused tensions not only in the newly colonized spaces of Central Asia, but even more so in the western borderlands of today's Belarus, Ukraine, Moldova, and Poland. Continuous resistance by local constituencies, and competing ideologies such as the Polish national revival movement, prevented the accomplishment of Russification. However, the critical issue, as stressed by historian Alexei Miller, was that "the Romanov Empire did use the nationalist resources, but at the same time actively opposed 'nationalization' for the large part of the nineteenth century."[1] It thus inadvertently contributed to the emergence in the western borderlands and in central Russia of another social movement, composed of local intellectuals, Orthodox priests, nobles, and officials who perceived themselves as bearers of Russianness.[2] They had to face the contradiction of being the "state nationality" indirectly celebrated in the "Autocracy, Nationality, Orthodoxy" triad elaborated under Nicholas I, and at the same time being in opposition to the Romanovs. This Russian nationalist movement focused on deciding who was to be included in and who excluded from the nation. Two concepts were in competition: the religious—Russia is everywhere there is an Orthodox or an Old Believer church—and the linguistic—Russia is everywhere where people speak

Russian. Both Orthodox Karelians and Catholic Belarusians, respectively, could then be included in the "Russian" nation.[3]

However, the main feature of this Russian nationalist movement was its politicization in the early twentieth century, at a time when the Russian Empire was experiencing mass social and economic transformations and the need for political reforms. In such a context, the 1905 Revolution gave birth not only to a strong worker and trade-unionist movement, but also to a vivid reactionary one, embodied by the Black Hundreds (Chernaia sotnia). The Black Hundreds are often considered to be the precursor of fascism not only in Russia but also in Europe more generally. While fascism as a political movement was officially founded in postwar Italy in 1919 by Benito Mussolini,[4] many far-right groups, parties, and associations had developed all over Europe even earlier, characterized by organized violence, conspiracy theories, and populist claims that combined nationalist and socialist characteristics. In a seminal article published in 1964, "Was There a Russian Fascism? The Union of the Russian People," the historian Hans Rogger convincingly analyzed the differences between the Black Hundreds, a movement structured on loyalty to the tsar and the autocracy, and Fascism and National Socialism, which aimed at the creation of a "new order." If this is indeed a major difference, the Black Hundreds movement can still be considered as the starting point of a genuinely Russian fascist tradition in the broad sense.

THE RISE AND DECLINE OF THE RUSSIAN ASSEMBLY, THE CRADLE OF RIGHT-WING POLITICS IN RUSSIA

The emergence of a more or less organized right-wing politics, autonomous but linked to the upper echelon of the imperial authorities, had its roots in various informal networks and places. At the end of 1870s, rightist salons (*pravye salony*)[5] rose to prominence among aristocratic and intelligentsia circles as liberal tendencies and "cosmopolitanism" came to be considered a threat to the future of the Empire and its culture. In the late years of Aleksandr II's rule, important figures in the tsar's court and bureaucracy met at the palace of Prince Vladimir P. Meshcherskii (1839–1914) to listen to music, read poetry, and discuss political matters. Another famous salon of the 1880s was at the home of General Evgenii V. Bogdanovich (1829–1914), where the future president of the Russian Assembly, Prince Dmitrii P. Golitsyn-Muravlin (1860–1928), was a frequent guest. In the late autumn of 1900, Aleksei S. Suvorin (1834–1912), editor of the newspaper *Novoe vremia*, actively promoted the establishment of a national-conservative force, the Russian Assembly (Russkoe sobranie), loyal to the tsar and to Russia's interests, and capable of defending a "love for the fatherland" that was seen to be in decline. The poet Vasilii L. Velichko (1860–1903) described the Russian Assembly as "working for the elevation of national consciousness. . . . [T]he specific and peculiar position of the Russian Assembly is evident in the goodwill and mutual trust of its members."[6]

At its beginning, the Russian Assembly stayed focused on intellectual and cultural matters, and its political aims emerged only later. Among the founders were professor and academic Konstantin Ya. Grot (1853–1934); director of the Saint Petersburg Imperial Public Library Nikolai P. Likhachev (1862–1936); writer Sergei N. Syromiatnikov (1860–1933); and poet Nikolai A. Engel'gardt (1867–1942).[7] On January 26, 1901, the society began its official activities, devoted to "affirm[ing] in everyday life the traditions of Russian people."[8] Its tasks were listed in a charter with a preamble that emphasized three points: (1) study of Russian popular and national life in both past and present; (2) discussion of questions related to philology, arts, ethnography, law, and national economy, and the study of various manifestations of spiritual and everyday Russian and Slav peculiarities; and (3) maintenance of the purity and correctness of the Russian language.[9] Contrary to many similar societies shaped by Slavophilism, the Russian Assembly was more focused on promoting all things "Russian." To carry out these aims, the society was authorized to organize public and members' rallies, lectures, musical evenings, and exhibitions, and to promote literary and artistic contests. Notably, one paragraph stated the importance of lobbying activity within the government and the bureaucracy for the achievement of the society's goals. An anonymous member of a competing institution, the Saint Petersburg Slav Benevolent Society, publishing under the name of "Old Slavophile," mentioned a split inside the society between a "young party" and the old regime, with the former more interested in becoming a political force.[10]

A key founding father of the Russian Assembly was Prince Dmitrii Golitsyn-Muravlin, a future State Council member but at that time an eccentric bureaucrat with modest literary talent and a career as a minor novelist.[11] In his works Prince Golitsyn opposed the new currents coming from the West that were influencing Russian prose and poetry, standing in defense of traditional values and in favor of raising the public consciousness and revitalizing the supposedly corrupted spirit of people.[12] In February 1901 Golitsyn's efforts were blessed by his election as first president of the Russian Assembly by a council composed of army officers, including the generals Mikhail M. Borodkin (1852–1919) and Nikolai F. Geiden (1856–after 1918),[13] high-ranking bureaucrats, and conservative intellectuals such as Suvorin and Velichko.[14] Around 40 percent of the members of the Russian

Assembly were from the upper echelons of the state administration, and around a third were army and naval officers; there was an annual fee of ten rubles in Saint Petersburg and five in Kharkov and Kiev.[15] Ethno-confessional homogeneity was the mark of the Russian Assembly, with few members of Polish or German origin, and a majority consisting of Russians as well as Little Russians and Belorussians who self-identified as Russians.[16]

Elitism, defense of Orthodoxy, service to the autocracy, and a commitment to strengthening Russianness within the Empire's borders were the main stated goals of the Russian Assembly. Some of its founders would be called to play an important role in governmental policies on the nationalities question, among them General Mikhail Borodkin (1852–1919), an expert on Finnish affairs; the statistician Akim M. Zolotarev (1853–1912); the former rector of Dorpat Iurev University, Anton S. Budilovich (1846–1908); and Professor Platon A. Kulakovskii (1848–1913). This group formed the Russian Assembly's "borderlands section" (*okrainnyi otdel*) and started a cycle of lectures about the Russian cause in the borderlands, promoting a hard-line Russification policy and attacking other nationalist movements as part of a plot to "destroy Russia." This special section expanded further, and by 1908 formed the bulk of the Russian Borderlands Society (*Russkoe okrainnoe obshchestvo*).[17]

The Russian Assembly attracted members from provincial cities, usually mid-level civil servants or intellectuals who wanted to be better connected to the political and cultural life of the capital, Saint Petersburg. Within just a few months the society had attracted members in Moscow, Warsaw, Kiev, Odessa, Tula, Pskov, Riazan, Novgorod, Kazan, Smolensk, Kursk, Irkutsk, and Vilno. A group of professors, intellectuals, and officials, headed by future deputy Andrei S. Viazigin (1867–1919), asked permission to open a branch in Kharkov in 1902.[18] The Assembly's central council was initially reluctant, afraid of losing the centralized character that the society was promoting, but after a long exchange of letters with Viazigin, Golitsyn supported the idea.[19] Opened in March 1903, the Kharkov branch actively worked with the support of two newspapers, *Mirnyi trud* and *Iuzhnii krai*, and became the bulwark of Viazigin's political career and the birth of the Union of the Russian People in Kharkov governorate.[20] After Kharkov, other branches rapidly formed: in 1904 in Warsaw, Vilno, Ekaterinoslav, Orenburg, and Odessa, followed by Saratov, Kazan, Ufa, and Perm in European Russia; Kielce and Radom in Privislinskii Krai (then part of the so-called Congress Poland); Irkutsk and Verkhneudinsk in Siberia; and Kiev, Simferopol, Poltava, and Kherson in the Ukrainian governorates. Historian Igor Omelianchuk rightly observes that the presence of the Russian Assembly in the Empire's main borderland cities reflected the growing forces of local Russian nationalism.[21]

Despite its extended geographical presence in the main cities of the country, the Russian Assembly was never able to advance a robust nationwide political agenda. Its membership never exceeded a few thousand, with a progression from less than a thousand members in 1901 to almost four thousand in 1907.[22] The Assembly's shift toward politics came on the eve of the year 1905, with growing discontent in public opinion, the disastrous war against Japan, and mounting calls for more freedom. On December 31, 1904, the Assembly, worried about the creation of a national representative or advisory chamber, met with Nicholas II to try to prevent a move toward parliamentarianism. The promulgation of the October 1905 Manifesto—giving Russia its first constitution and first legislative body, the Duma—was interpreted by the Assembly not as abolishing the autocracy, but as restoring the lost unity between the tsar and the people.[23] The Assembly's new program, adopted in 1906, called for the defense of Russian religious values,[24] invoked the "Autocracy–Orthodoxy–Nationality" triad, and denied the right of Jews to become equal citizens because of their supposed plans to dominate the world.[25]

The indecisiveness and apathy of the Assembly's central council during the 1905 turmoil caused the departure of some of the future leaders of the Black Hundreds. Breaking with the Assembly's elitist approach, they tried to organize meetings with butchers, shopkeepers, and doormen (*dvorniki*) in defense of autocracy.[26] The Assembly also lost about 200 of its officers after the Ministry of War prohibited army and navy officers from taking part in politics. After the 1905 Revolution, the Assembly attempted, with little success, to unify all rightist movements in defense of autocracy. For example, it organized a first "Russian Congress" of representatives of all the monarchist associations in Saint Petersburg on February 8–12, 1906. With an attendance of some 350 delegates, the congress represented more than thirty organizations, including the Russian Monarchist Party, the Union of the Russian People, the Union of Russian Men, and others,[27] but it failed to reach its goal of creating a central body to coordinate campaigns for Duma elections. Despite this failure, the Russian Assembly organized more congresses—in Moscow in April, in Kiev in October 1906, and in Moscow again in April 1907—but was progressively overshadowed by the Union of the Russian People. With Prince Mikhail L. Shakhovskoi (1855–1915) elected as its new chairman in 1906,[28] the Russian Assembly participated, in a joint slate with the Union of the Russian People and other monarchist organizations, in the Duma campaigns of 1906 and 1907, but none of its candidates were elected.[29]

From 1907 until the February Revolution a decade later, the Russian Assembly focused on educational activities, which it saw as the best way to invest in the future of rightist ideas in a rapidly changing Russia. It opened its own gymnasium in the Assembly's quarters at Bazhenov Palace in Saint Petersburg,[30] and another one in Irkutsk,[31] and focused on school issues aimed at promoting a "Russian education." But it declined as a political organization in 1911 following internal quarrels related to the rivalry between Nikolai Markov and Aleksandr Dubrovin (see below) over control of the Union of the Russian People. Only with the advent of the First World War did the Assembly experience a brief revival, with the formation of a Committee for War Invalids and the opening of a field hospital at Tsarskoe Selo, but these efforts did not revitalize the society and it was disbanded after February 1917.[32] Even if unsuccessful, the Russian Assembly played a critical role as an "incubator" of rightist ideas in Russia and inspired other institutions and political parties that would move toward more radical political concepts.

THE BLACK HUNDREDS, A MASS REACTIONARY MOVEMENT

It was the 1905 Revolution that enabled a significant rightist movement to emerge and gain mass support. The engagement of citizens in politics, the popular mobilization in urban centers and in the regions of the Empire, the birth and growth of political militancy, and last but not least, the joining of national and social elements in the insurgency against the autocracy contributed to the birth of a reactionary movement. Aristocratic organizations such as the Union of Russian Men and the United Nobility could not respond to the challenges posed by the revolutionaries; only a party with at least some level of popular legitimacy in the two capital cities and in the governorates could respond and strive to save the autocracy. This would be the task of the Union of the Russian People (URP), whose core was made up of the Black Hundreds. The term "Black Hundred" originally applied to guilds of small tradesmen in medieval Muscovy.[33] At the end of the nineteenth century it came to include all movements that aimed to unite the various local anti-Semitic, chauvinist organizations loyal to the tsar.

Aleksandr I. Dubrovin (1855–1918), a Saint Petersburg pediatrician and a member of the Russian Assembly, emerged as the driver of a more militant and popular mood for the monarchist movement. He founded a circle "In Defense of Autocracy," met with semi-religious societies from various part of the Empire such as the Society of Banner Carriers (Obshchestvo khorugvesnotsev) in Moscow, and with the help of friends such as Vladimir M. Purishkevich (1870–1920)[34] launched the Union of the Russian People in November 1905, less than three weeks after the proclamation of the October

Manifesto.[35] The party's first public event was a meeting on November 8 at the Mikhailovskii Riding Hall, the Saint Petersburg Manege, where more than 2,000 people cheered the speakers defending autocracy and the tsar and warning against the risk of political chaos. Even more than in Saint Petersburg or Moscow, the URP rapidly gained support in the provinces, where it attracted local monarchist groups. One of the reasons for the URP's success was the attention it devoted to the press: the URP's first newspaper, *Russkoe znamia*, launched on November 27, soon began to circulate in provincial cities, and some local branches started their own publications. It is possible that, as it was claimed, more than thirteen million pamphlets were distributed by the URP between May and November 1906.[36] As historian Don C. Rawson noted, "In an era of rising literacy in Russia, when the printed word was becoming a significant instrument of persuasion, the Union of the Russian People, more than any other rightist organization, excelled in this form of propaganda."[37]

On December 23, 1905, in Tsarskoe Selo, the tsar received a delegation of URP representatives led by Dubrovin. They expressed their support for autocracy and the need to defend the country against any attempts at reform, and they gave the tsar a URP badge.[38] Was Nicholas II himself supportive of the URP? That is not clear. What we know for sure is that the tsarist central and local administration welcomed the Black Hundreds' actions and rewarded them for their loyalty to the autocracy. In the provinces, governors received URP delegations and supported, sometimes financially, the activities of the Black Hundreds, as in Kishinev, where the city council gave 5,000 rubles to the party.[39] In his memoirs, Sergei E. Kryzhanovskii (1862–1935), deputy minister of internal affairs in several Stolypin cabinets, revealed that he could spend at his discretion three million rubles a year from a government reserve fund to support "friendly" forces and newspapers, one of which was the Black Hundreds.[40] Money was given not to the organization itself but to its main representatives, for example, Dubrovin, Purishkevich,[41] and Father Ivan Vostorgov (1864–1918). Secret funds were also used to publish pamphlets such as the anti-Semitic and anti-Kadets essays of the famous polemicist Ilia Ya. Gurland (1868–1921).[42] Nikolai Markov, one of the most influential Black Hundreds leaders in the Duma, received 12,000 rubles a month from 1909 to 1916, as he confessed to a commission of inquiry in 1917.[43]

This intimate connection between the Black Hundreds and the tsarist authorities became even more evident during the pogroms that spread all over western Russia in the early twentieth century (see below). Proclaiming that they were simply protecting the Empire against Jews and revolutionaries, the Black Hundreds gained the support of the local authorities, and especially of the police, despite the violence. In some cities, like Odessa, they were very well organized in paramilitary brigades called the "yellow shirts."[44] In Saint Petersburg, URP activists organized meetings in several police stations.[45] The police even provided logistical support, as in the case of Captain Mikhail Kommissarov in Saint Petersburg, who used presses confiscated from revolutionary movements to print pogromist flyers in the police station basement.[46] The Russian Orthodox Church also supported URP activities, a merger exemplified by the popular monk (later canonized) Yoann Kronshtadtskii (1829–1909), who was a URP member and blessed the movement's flag.[47] The presence of clerics was invaluable in bringing new members into the movement and strengthening the URP's legitimacy. In Kazan, the URP newspaper *Rus' pravoslavnaia i samoderzhavnaia* was directly published by the local eparchial printers.

The Black Hundreds believed in Russian national purity and the need to secure it through mass Russification and the relocation of some non-Russian groups. Jews, for example, were to be expelled to Palestine.[48] Black Hundreds local newspapers, especially those in the western borderlands, advanced a very bellicose narrative against all ethnic minorities. A good example is one of the most influential local branches of the URP, centered around the Pochaev monastery in Volhynia, a very diverse region straddling today's Poland, Ukraine, and Belarus. In 1897 the first all-Russian census recorded a rural population of 69 percent Little Russians (mainly Ukrainians), 10 percent Jews, 4 percent Poles, 4 percent Germans, and other, smaller communities such as Czechs. In contrast, the regional nobility was majority Polish, with 52 percent, compared to 36 percent Little Russian and 12 percent Russian.[49] The Pochaev monks used the influence of the monastery to disseminate a pro-"Russian" position and to fund the local newspaper, *Pochaevskie izvestiia*, with the aim of mobilizing the peasantry against the so-called Jewish threat. Volhynia became one of the centers of URP activism, with more than 600 village branches opened in 1907, and 1,155 before the First World War, under the leadership of Bishop Antonii (Khrapovitskii), honorary president of the Volhynian URP.[50] Because there was no official registered membership, it is impossible to have an accurate estimate of the URP's real numbers. Markov affirmed that there were millions of party activists,[51] a clear exaggeration, but after surveying newspapers and archival evidence, Rawson gives a plausible number of more than a thousand branches, each with several tens or hundreds of members.[52]

Unlike other elite-centered monarchist movements, the Union of the Russian People actively sought popular support. A mixture of conspiracy theories, prejudices, and populist arguments were at the core of its outreach. Some

URP members called for expropriating the property of major land owners, linking the national and social questions by arguing that "foreigners"—read, Polish and German nobility—possessed the lands while the Russian peasants were dispossessed. Count Vladimir A. Bobrinskii (1867–1927), one of the organizers and leaders of the Russian National Union,[53] in a speech to the National Club in Saint Petersburg on March 19, 1910, denounced the condition of the peasants in Kholm region: "Russians are day laborers in Kholmshchina, dispossessed peasants without land, and they can do nothing more than sell their labor to the Polish landlords. . . . Peasants are so fearful of losing work that at night they go to Orthodox clergy to receive the sacraments."[54] On another occasion, he emphasized that the Polish *szlachta* was the enemy of the Russian peasantry.[55] Some other URP members, warning of a Jewish plot to obtain land, called for a total "Russification" of property in Russia.

"BEAT THE JEWS": THE BLACK HUNDREDS AND THE URP'S ROLE IN POGROMS

Anti-Semitism was widespread in late imperial Russia. Pogroms devastated Russian Jewry in 1881–1884, after the assassination of Aleksandr II, destroying houses, shops, and the lives of Jewish communities in the Pale of Settlement (the Empire's western borderlands, including much of present-day Ukraine).[56] Aleksandr III imposed new restrictions on Jews in 1882 with the May Laws, which forbade settlement in the countryside, and these opened the way to other discriminatory laws. In 1887 quotas were introduced in high schools and universities, with no more than 10 percent of Jewish students to be enrolled within the Pale, 5 percent outside, and 3 percent in Saint Petersburg and Moscow. In 1891, the Jewish community was expelled from Moscow.[57] Authorities tended to see in every Jewish student a potential revolutionary, and anti-Semitic prejudices were widely distributed from the lower to the upper levels of society. The Orthodox clergy was not immune. Iliodor, a fanatical monk active in the Volhynian branch of the URP, recalled in his memoir, "All I had been taught about the Jews was this: the Jew drinks human blood, the Jew regards it as a pious deed to kill a Christian, the anti-Christ will spring from Jewish stock, the Jew is accursed by God, the Jew is the source of all evil in the world. My hatred of Jews was thus based wholly on religious fanaticism. I did not know any Jew in private."[58]

Pavel A. Krushevan (1860–1909),[59] editor of the Kishinev newspaper *Bessarabets* and later a URP leader, played a critical role in creating the hysterical atmosphere that led to the 1903 Kishinev Easter Pogrom. Krushevan saw the Jews as an evil force in the world, and it seems that for him no tactic against the local Jewish community was too vile. *Bessarabets* played a major role in inciting the lower classes toward the pogrom by publishing a false story about the ritual murder of a Christian boy.[60] Over two days, April 6–7, 1903, more than fifty people were killed and 495 wounded.[61] At the beginning of 1905, threats of pogroms hung in the air, with nationalist feelings heightened by war with Japan: Jews were the "enemies" behind defeats and revolutionary events, together with Poles, Ukrainians, Finns, and other national minorities. Several Black Hundreds organizations distributed flyers that called for smashing all enemies. The following was written by the Russian Monarchist Society, a local Black Hundreds organization:

> Beat the damned traitors everywhere and all over, wherever you find them and with whatever [you can], beat the Yids, destroyers of Russian tsardom ... beat the instigators of the sedition and strikes, beat ... the student, even if he is your son, brother, or relative, all the same, he's a traitor ... beat him, he's a complete wretch and is the destroyer of the people and the Russian land, and the more of them we destroy, the better for Russia and [for] the people, the more of them we kill, the less sedition there will be in Russia and Russia will be on the path to redemption.[62]

The slogan "Death to the Revolutionaries," spread by Black Hundreds organizations beginning in summer 1905,[63] often took the meaning of "Death to the Jews." The interpretation that the revolutionary actions were being orchestrated by Jews was not only a Black Hundreds reading of the 1905 events. It was shared even by Nicholas II, who wrote in his correspondence: "[T]he people became enraged by the insolence and audacity of the revolutionaries and socialists, and because nine-tenths of them are Yids, the people's whole wrath has turned against them."[64] After the promulgation of the October Manifesto, a new wave of pogroms started in the Pale of Settlement, with about 600 cities and towns experiencing anti-Semitic violence. In Kiev, on October 19, 1905, a loyalist demonstration quickly degenerated into a massive pogrom, with 5,000 people attacking the Jewish quarter.[65] Soldiers sent to suppress the pogrom joined the crowd, according to a Kiev vice-governor's report.[66] After the June unrest and the Battleship Potemkin mutiny, the city of Odessa, too, became a place of virulent anti-Semitic propaganda: a four-page broadside that appeared after the repression of the June strike, called *Odesskie dni*, accused the Jews of being revolutionary agents.[67] On October 18, clashes erupted between loyalists and anti-government demonstrators, and pogromists began attacking the Jewish quarter of Moldavanka. Over four days, the pogromists acted virtually without interference by the police, and only at the end of the pogrom did officials intervene, after at least 400 Jews had been killed (some estimates place the number even higher, between 600 and 2,500), and over 1,600 Jewish houses, apartments, and shops had been destroyed.[68]

At this time, the Union of the Russian People had not yet been officially launched, but local Black Hundreds organizations were actively calling for violence against the Jews. During the second major upsurge of anti-Semitic violence, in 1906, with pogroms in Gomel, Yalta, and Bialystok, URP branches played an active and identifiable role in organizing attacks against the Jews; URP activists also shot a Kadet representative of Jewish origin, Mikhail Ya. Herzenstein (1859–1906).[69] URP leaders were never prosecuted by tsarist authorities for organizing pogroms or assassinations. The Herzenstein case confirmed that they had protection from the upper echelons of the bureaucracy: because Herzenstein was shot in Terijoki, at that time part of Grand Duchy of Finland, a Finnish jury declared URP members Sergei Aleksandrov (one of Dubrovin's bodyguards) and Nikolai M. Yuskevich-Kraskovskii to be guilty, but they were amnestied by Nicholas II on December 30, 1909.[70]

NOSTALGIA FOR MUSCOVY? THE BLACK HUNDREDS IDEOLOGY

The URP ideology was founded on several inherent contradictions. The first was political. Although Nicholas II signed the October Manifesto, the introduction of parliamentarism was interpreted by URP as a plot against autocracy.[71] To attack the Manifesto would be to go against the tsar's will, so how could one fight for the tsar against the tsar himself? The URP thus focused on confronting the tsar's advisers, such as Sergei Witte, on the grounds that they were influencing him in an anti-autocratic way.[72] Yet even as the URP violently criticized parliamentarism, URP leaders such as Nikolai Markov, Vladimir Purishkevich, and Vasilii V. Shul'gin (1878–1976), participated in the Duma system and campaigned for election. At the opening of the Third Duma, in November 1907, they even thanked the emperor for having re-established the union between the people and the sovereign through the Duma.[73]

URP ideology can be defined as a reactionary utopia. It called for a return to pre-Petrine Russia, before the advent of the Romanov dynasty in 1613. It hoped to replace the State Duma with the older *zemskii sobor*, an assembly of the feudal estates, to which the URP proposed to add peasant representatives of every district. Moreover, the holiness of the tsar as a symbol was now contradicted by the URP members' low esteem for Nicholas II. Boris V. Nikol'skii (1870–1919), one of the URP ideologues, referred to the tsar as an "idiot" in private correspondence.[74] Lev A. Tikhomirov (1852–1923), a former populist who joined the monarchist camp and became a kind of guru for rightist intellectuals, remarked in February 1906 that autocracy was finished in October 1905 and that the tsar would not be able to go back.[75]

The second inherent contradiction was economic. For the URP ideologists, capitalism and the market economy were the fruit of a Jewish plot to take complete control over Russia's natural resources. Industrial modernity was a Jewish myth imposed by force over a Russia that was a country of artisans, peasants, and small traders. At the same time, it was impossible to imagine a powerful Russian Empire without factories and industrial production. The Black Hundreds thus advocated for a "nationalization" of capital, with incentives to support "Russian" business and to expropriate non-Russians. The same ambivalence is noticeable in the URP's perception of the agrarian question. It called for respecting traditional hierarchy and at the same time sponsored the expropriation of non-Russian landlords. A fierce anti-Semitism fueled the URP worldview: linking the ruble to gold was considered a threat to the Russian national economy because the Jews supposedly controlled gold.[76]

Between 1907 and the First World War, the Black Hundreds movement faced several schisms and quarrels, related in part to personal competition between its leaders but also to the difficulties in solving the inherent contradictions of the movement. In 1907, after a conflict with Dubrovin, Purishkevich founded his own organization, the Russian Popular Union of St. Michael Archangel (Russkii narodnyi soiuz im. Mikhaila Arkhangela), whose program was identical to the URP's, except that it did not recognize the State Duma as a link between the tsar and the people.[77] In 1911, Dubrovin, who was never elected to the Duma and vehemently opposed every kind of participation in the government, rejected Markov's decision to support some of Stolypin's decisions that were favorable to the destruction of peasants' communes and the creation of a class of small landowners. Dubrovin then left the URP and formed the All-Russian Dubrovinian Union of the Russian People (Vserossiiskii dubrovinskii soiuz russkogo naroda).[78] Markov remained the main URP spokesman until the February Revolution.

CONCLUSION: THE BLACK HUNDREDS AND FASCISM AFTER THE OCTOBER REVOLUTION

In many respects, the Black Hundreds shared the main ideological patterns of fascist movements in Europe. In their calls for a metaphysical unity of the nation, a return to the past, and anti-capitalist and anti-Semitic rhetoric combined with the promotion of a mythical rural authenticity and Orthodoxy, the Black Hundreds were very similar to Corneliu Codreanu's Romanian Iron Guard, for example. However, the Black Hundreds' determination to defend the status quo of autocracy and to restore an idyllic and ideal Muscovite past, without accepting any aspects of the modern world, distinguished them from the Italian Fascists and German Nazis, who saw themselves as revolutionary forces against the old order. Although intellectual figures of the Russian Right such as Sergei Sharapov were well integrated into the West European debates of their time, as Mikhail Suslov showed in the previous chapter, the Black Hundreds had few contacts with or influences from any similar West European trends. Not until the interwar period was there any direct mutual emulation between émigré groups and German *völkisch* themes.

The only contact we can document between nationalist movements in Europe and Russian Black Hundreds is that of the journal *Okrainy Rossii*.[79] After brief participation in URP in the first months of its existence, the group eventually joined the All-Russian National Union, a nationalist party that officially emerged in 1908 from the fusion of the moderate right and some nationalist factions in the Third Duma.[80] Russian nationalists were generally oriented against the so-called German threat,[81] and were active in supporting the Slavic cause during the Balkan Wars.[82] Many of them were positioned as pro-Entente before the First World War, although URP leader Markov had a more pro-German stance. After the war began, support for the Entente was unanimous, from the Kadets to the Black Hundreds.[83]

However, despite the lack of direct personal interaction between the Black Hundreds and their European counterparts, the Black Hundreds' legacy shaped many fascist movements that emerged in the interwar Russian emigration, in particular the Russian Fascist Organization based in Harbin, Manchuria, and disbanded by the Chinese government, and later the Russian Fascist Party, which was supported by Japanese occupation authorities during the 1930s and the Second World War.[84]

The Black Hundreds also influenced the birth of National Socialism in Germany itself. In his book *The Russian Roots of Nazism*, Michael Kellogg explores the links between the *völkisch* White émigré association headquartered in Munich, Aufbau (Wirtschafts-politische Vereinigung fur den Osten), and Adolf Hitler's National Socialist Party, concluding that "Aufbau left a powerful anti-Bolshevik and anti-Semitic legacy to National Socialism after 1923."[85] The chairman of Aufbau was General Vasilii V. Biskupskii (1878–1945), a former commander of the Russian Army during the First World War.[86] He claimed to be close to Dubrovin, although his name appears nowhere in the URP documents and archival materials, and membership in a party was officially prohibited for officers. Member or not, Biskupskii was without any doubt a Black Hundreds supporter. During the civil war he fought in the ranks of Pavel Skoropadskii's army in Ukraine before going into exile in Germany in 1919. There, he contributed to the spread of the Black Hundreds' legacy and especially the infamous *Protocols of the Elders of Zion*, published for the first time in Germany in 1919 by Ludwig Müller von Hausen, leader of the Association against the Presumption of Jewry. That same year, the group of White officers around Lieuteunant Petr Shabelskii-Bork, son of URP members Aleksandr Bork and Elsa Shabelskii-Bork,[87] began publication of a Russian-language journal, *Prizyv*, full of anti-Semitic and anti-Bolshevik materials.[88] In September 1920 the official newspaper of the German National Socialist Party, *Völkischer Beobachter*, claimed that a White investigation of the Romanovs' execution in Yekaterinburg found that Jews had murdered the tsar and his family.[89]

The most important Black Hundreds figure, Nikolai E. Markov (1866–1945), former leader of the Union of the Russian People and of the rightists' faction at the Third and Fourth Dumas, played a critical role in linking the Black Hundreds legacy to Nazism. Based in Germany, he became the chairman of the Supreme Monarchical Council, in open conflict with Aufbau for the leadership of White Movement and for the succession to the Romanov throne—Markov supported Nikolai Nikolaevich, Aufbau supported Grand Prince Kirill. Markov appealed to France to support a White Army attack on the Soviet Union in 1922.[90] He left Germany for France in 1926, then returned to Nazi Germany in 1935 to take leadership of the Russian Section of *Welt-Dienst: Internationale Korrespondenz zur Aufklärung über die Judenfrage,* the anti-Semitic International Media Network launched by Hitler. He died on April 22, 1945, in Wiesbaden, during the last days of the Nazi regime. During the Third Duma, Markov was already famous for his violent anti-Semitism, seeing Jews as enemies of mankind: "From the creation of the world, Jews were always antihuman, they always hated all peoples with which history put them in contact, they were always hated by all peoples, they're hated even now by all people without exception, including, of course, by the Russian people."[91]

The Black Hundreds' main legacy thus remains its ferocious anti-Semitism and its critical role in spreading conspiracy theories around the *Protocols of the Elders of Zion*. Its ambiguous status as both a "puppet" of the tsarist authorities and a genuine popular movement could inspire many modern forms of totalitarianism. It is not by chance that the dystopian authoritarian state described by Jack London in his masterpiece *The Iron Heel*, published in 1908, had a militia called the Black Hundreds.[92]

PART II

INTERWAR MUTUAL DISCOVERIES: EURASIANISM AND THE GERMAN CONSERVATIVE REVOLUTION

CHAPTER 3

THE "THIRD CONTINENT" MEETS THE "THIRD WAY"

Eurasianism's Reading of Fascism

Marlene Laruelle

Scholarship on classical Eurasianism has mostly focused on the study of the movement's ideological arguments and its main figures, as well as its Russian roots—the Slavophile and pan-Slavist school, Silver Age philosophers and poets—in order to trace its intellectual genealogy.[1] The academic community has focused less on placing Eurasianism in its European time and context, probably because of the conventional dividing lines between "Russianists" or "Sovietologists," on the one hand, and historians of Western Europe, on the other. Nevertheless, Eurasianism significantly appropriated cultural and political ideas from contemporary Europe. As part of the vital and vocal Russian émigré communities scattered across various European capitals, Eurasianists engaged passionately with their host communities and were influenced by the European zeitgeist.

The most important interactions were those between Eurasianism and the various strands of "fascism." In one of his major texts criticizing Eurasianism, philosopher Nikolai Berdiaev (1874–1948) proposes that the "maximalism" of Eurasianism be interpreted as a fundamental tenet of both the Left and the Right.[2] The remark is a judicious one concerning the ideological positioning of Eurasianism, which was similar to several of the groups with fascist leanings at the time. In this chapter I continue the discussion begun by Leonid Luks in 1998 and Martin Beisswenger in 2004[3] and explore how the Eurasianist founding fathers broached the main themes related to fascism in the broad sense of the term. Setting out from what for them was one of the most controversial themes, namely German racialism and anti-Semitism, I proceed to the most agreed-upon—namely, the call for an organic political regime and the merging of the theories of the Third Way and the Third Continent. I do not investigate the personal and institutional interactions that occurred between Eurasianist groups and those representing the German Conservative Revolution, which Martin Beisswenger explores in chapter 4.

THE CATEGORICAL REJECTION OF GERMAN RACIALISM

The unequivocal rejection of German racialism by Eurasianist theoreticians is rooted in the longstanding academic rivalries between European, mainly Germanic, and Russian scholars in the late eighteenth century and throughout the nineteenth century. German racialist discourses were largely structured around the denunciation of Slavs and/or Russians as inferior on the basis of their so-called Turanian or Turkic-Mongolian origin.[4] Like its European neighbors, Russia had its own science of race, which was developed through ethnological studies of conquered autochthonous peoples,[5] but many Russian intellectuals also sought to refute Germanic racialism's theoretical underpinnings.

At the beginning of the nineteenth century, several German linguists attempted to prove that Slavic languages were close to those categorized at that time as Tatar or Mongolian. This linguistic hypothesis was undermined by Franz Bopp (1791–1867), who revolutionized the understanding of Indo-European languages and confirmed the Slavic language family's proximity to Persian and Sanskrit.

It then fell to physical anthropology to classify Slavs as an Asian race. German anthropologist Gustav Klemm (1802–1867) made the radical claim that "although white, Russians have the qualities of Negroes."[6] In his *Ethnologische Schriften: Nach dem Tode des Verfassers gesammelt* (1864), the Swede Anders Retzius (1796–1860), a professor of anatomy at the Medical Institute in Stockholm, turned craniology into the master science of racial questions. He divided Europeans into two races according to craniometric criteria, classifying peoples as either dolichocephalic or brachycephalic. Slavs were determined to be brachycephalic peoples, with brown skin and small size, like the Tatars and the Mongols, while the Aryans were dolichocephalic.[7] These classifications were reinforced by subsequent historical analyses. For figures such as German nationalist author Ernst Arndt (1769–1860) or Austrian anthropologist and linguist Karl Penka (1847–1912), who advanced the Nordic origin of the Aryans,

Russians were essentially descendants of the Scythians, who were themselves considered Mongols in origin.[8] These authors thus attempted to symbolically expel the Slavs from Europe, asserting that they had not arrived on their current territory until the sixth century, well after the great barbarian invasions and the fall of the Western Roman Empire. The Slavs, they alleged, were the last people to settle in Europe and had retained several inferior cultural and physical traits from their Asian origins.

These theories were challenged by the Slavophile school. From 1845, only two years after the publication of the first volume of Gustav Klemm's work, Aleksei Khomiakov (1804–1860), the founding father of Slavophilism, sensed the importance of racial argumentation in the rejection of Russia. He thus accused Westerners of bias in their view of Russia: "It seems that we are of Indo-European blood and of Indo-European language, and how so! This language [Russian] is the purest, almost Indian; and yet we are not the brothers of our neighbors."[9] Khomiakov states that the best-known branch of the Aryans is the "Germanic family," whereas the Slavs "unquestionably take second place."[10] However, the future Germans can by no means lay claim to the descent of the purest branch of the Aryan world, since "the German language ... does not contain the signs of a complete intellectual development like Sanskrit or the Slavic languages."[11]

The Eurasianists similarly rejected German racialism in the name of linguistics. However, some ambivalence was noticeable in the 1920s in some Eurasianist texts, where use of the terms "race" or "blood" was common. For instance, in 1927 Nina Vernadskaia-Toll (1898–1986), George Vernadskii's sister, published an article that used "blood types" to situate Eurasia between Europe and Asia. At that time, the Eurasianists wanted to reduce the philosophical emphasis of Eurasianism and develop more empirical research. Vernadskaia-Toll's article addressed the point by stating that Russians were closer to Asians than to Europeans, according to blood groups. However, rising German racialism was becoming more and more of an issue for the Eurasianists, who decided not to publish her second article on "Jewish blood."[12]

Confronted with the rise of Nazism, the movement's great figures, such as Prince Nikolai S. Trubetskoy (1890–1938) and geographer Petr N. Savitskii (1895–1968), openly opposed racialism, which they condemned as the "barbarization of Europe."[13] Trubetskoy denounced racialism as an extreme form of anthropological materialism: man cannot be free if some determinism runs in his veins. Divine predestination no longer has any sense if genetics overrides it in the process of creating mankind's fate.

German racialism is founded on anthropological materialism, on the conviction that human will is not free, that all the actions of man ultimately depend on his physiological specificities. . . . Eurasianism, because it rejects economic materialism, sees no reason to accept anthropological materialism, the philosophical foundation of which is even weaker. In these questions of culture, which constitute one of the domains of expression of human freedom, the last word must be given not to anthropology but to the sciences of the mind such as sociology and psychology.[14]

Eurasianists dismissed the concept of "Aryanness" as a frame for understanding Russia because, according to them, Russia's identity is Eurasian, that is, a mixture of Slavic and Turkic-Mongolian populations. More generally, they rejected the idea of formulating identity in genealogical terms. In 1936, at the famous Linguistic Circle of Prague, Trubetskoy held a conference on the "Indo-European problem."[15] He deemed this Indo-European problem to be as purely linguistic and devoid of either ethnic or cultural grounding: the existence of an Indo-European primitive people cannot be demonstrated and archeological and ethnological research on this question is superfluous. He argued that a single Indo-European language has never existed and that this particular linguistic family was formed through convergence—the reciprocal influence of languages of dissimilar origins. Moreover, like Roman Jakobson (1896–1982), he believed that the agglutinative character of Turkic-Mongolic languages was superior to the declension aspect of Indo-European languages. Trubetskoy also rejected the possibility of situating some primitive cradle of mankind in Iran and India,[16] thus dissociating himself and Eurasianism in general from their Slavophile predecessors, who believed in Russia's direct ties to the original Aryan cradle.[17]

Racial approaches were therefore opposed to the fundamental idea of Eurasianism, which asserted the preeminence of milieu over origin, a harbinger of Russian and Central European structuralism.[18] For the Eurasianists, it was more important to know the destination—not the origin—of peoples and languages.[19] Hence, if the languages of the Eurasian space are heterogeneous, they are nonetheless all going in the same direction; the issue here concerns not linguistic kinship but solely geographical contiguity. As affirmed by Jakobson, "The origin of the site of development predominates over the origin of genetic proximity."[20] Affinity between languages is not a state but a dynamic process occurring through spatial contact. Any desire to explain the world and national identities on the basis of a genealogical or genetic basis is therefore considered inadequate, since it looks to a bygone past.

Despite a certain geographic determinism and a devalorization of the individual against the collective, the Eurasianists upheld a discourse that eschewed racialism; they vaunted the Russian people as being a mixture of Slavs and Turkic-Mongols, but also of Jews, Roma, Blacks, and Caucasians (people of the Caucasus region).[21] The accusations of racism leveled at Eurasianists by opponents such as Pavel N. Miliukov (1859–1943)[22] indicate the difficulty Russian liberals had in distinguishing the culturalist and civilizationist narratives of Eurasianism from racialist stances. While both posit the preeminence of collective destiny over individual choice, they draw from differing philosophical principles.

ANTI-SEMITISM VERSUS "EURASIAN JEWISHNESS"

Whereas all the fascist or fascist-leaning movements promoted overtly anti-Semitic discourses that identified Jews with liberalism and cosmopolitanism, the Eurasianists advanced far more nuanced positions, sometimes even philo-Semitic ones. They denounced the crude anti-Semitism of prerevolutionary Russia, the pogroms that victimized the Jews of the Empire, and the adoption of anti-Semitic theories by the White movement in emigration.[23]

Yet the Eurasianist discourse about Jewishness remained ambivalent. In his 1935 text on racism, Trubetskoy reaffirmed that Jews most certainly share certain specificities, but these are of a cultural, not genetic nature. He thereby adopted a culturalist anti-Semitism in which "positive" Eurasian Jews are separated from the "negative," Western-integrated ones. The Eurasianists considered, for example, that the Jews of Poland and of Austria-Hungary played a major negative role insofar as they were a conduit of socialism. Citing the Bund in Russia and Austro-Marxism in Central Europe, the Eurasianists at least partly blamed these Jews for the success of communism in Russia and for its propagation throughout the rest of Europe. The Jews thus stood condemned for their internationalism and their cosmopolitanism. The Eurasianists also blamed Jewish elites for a far greater sin, namely instilling in the Jewish diaspora the myth of a Western-style nation-state—Israel.

The Eurasianists believed that the Jews should have instead participated in the global movement to reject the European identity pattern and joined forces with the Russians. This pro-Eurasian Jewishness was propagated by Iakov A. Bromberg (1898–1948), who proudly presented himself as the "Jew of the movement."[24] For him, Jews had been Europeanized and endured the same evolutions as Christians: secularized at the end of the eighteenth century under the influence of Protestantism and the rationalist schools of thought, they subscribed to the Western utopia of a terrestrial paradise and its false messianism. Nonetheless, he claimed that Westernism was incapable of providing a solution for the Jewish world, but instead left it deadlocked, leading to the European heresy: "The twelfth hour is approaching, where the eastern Jewish people will be forced to confront a tragic dilemma: either to dissolve themselves definitively in the European fold, or into another faith and into non-being without God, like the great majority of their Western fellows, or else, with a sharp rigor, to renounce all misleading utopias and the discord that reigns among its current 'ruling class,' which is entirely won over to the harmful spirit of superficial Europeanization and scientific and progressivist ignorance."[25]

For Bromberg, the future of the Jews was therefore not in Palestine—an Arab land—but in Eurasia. He believed Eurasia offered Jews something like "a new Israel and a new Rome at the same time."[26] He insisted that Jews had been an integral part of Eurasian history: they had had influence in the Kievan principality of the ninth century, where Prince Vladimir decided not to convert to Judaism; they had proselytized in medieval Russia through the movement of the "Judaizers"; they had contributed to world culture with the Hassidic Jewish world in Russian-occupied Poland in the nineteenth century; and many Jewish writers had participated in the Eastern and anti-rationalist trends of Russian thought. Bromberg was proud that many Russian intellectuals held in esteem by the Eurasianists were known for their philo-Semitism: Vladimir Soloviev, Nikolai Berdiaev, Petr Struve, Nikolai Leskov, and others. He thus held Judaism to be "the best representative of the Asian principle in Europe,"[27] a cultural parallel to the way that, geographically speaking, Russia embodies Asia from within Europe.

The Eurasian brand of Jewishness promoted by Bromberg and the Eurasianists found its chief legitimation and ideological expression in the Khazar khanate, a Jewish state that had existed on Eurasian territory in the eighth and ninth centuries. The Eurasianists never specified whether they considered the Jews to be a nation or a faith. They merely advanced the idea of an "attraction between the Turkic psyche and the Semitic psyche"[28] to explain why Khazaria had been the only site of a massive conversion of non-Semites to Judaism. They thus claimed that the Kingdom of Jerusalem was realized for a time in Eurasia, not in the Semitic world: "Judaism there [in Khazaria] accomplished the most essential attempt to confirm its universal reality in the framework of an earthly kingdom."[29] This historical experience justified, in the eyes of the Eurasianists, the important place accorded to Jews within the future Eurasian Federation and their disengagement from the Middle East. Khazaria thus represented far more than a simple moment of Eurasian history: its eminently religious character heralded the key role of Eurasia in biblical revelation; it made it possible to legitimize the natural eschatology of the Russian territory. In this way, Eurasianism sought to reconstruct a genealogy of Eurasian Judaism so as to appropriate and "Eurasianize" Jewish messianism.

Other Eurasianists promulgated even more ambiguous discourses. In a rather polemical text published in a 1926 issue of the famous literary journal *Versty*, the religious philosopher and medieval historian Lev Karsavin (1882–1952), then part of the Eurasianist movement, classified Jews into three identity categories: those who felt themselves to be Jews (highly appreciated), those who were fully assimilated into another ethnicity (including Russian), and those who were poorly assimilated. In creating a category of "poorly assimilated Jews," Karsavin aimed at denouncing the internationalists, socialists, and other cosmopolitans; for him, such Jews no longer belonged to any culture. As he put it: "Denationalized Judaism . . . represents our eternal enemy, the one against which we ought to fight as it fights against our national cultural values."[30] Hence, Karsavin called for an understanding between the Jewish and Russian worlds against their "common enemy,"[31] and proposed various solutions: The Russians should help reinforce the national and religious sentiment of Jews; show them their place in Russia as equal members of the future Eurasian Federation (with rights to self-determination, to a territory, to a culture, and to their religion); and make Palestine, were it to become a Jewish land, a protectorate of Russia.

Eurasianism, however, did not limit itself to elaborating a political program for a Russo-Jewish alliance. It pursued the ambiguous goal of converting Jews to Orthodoxy. For Karsavin especially, Judaism was the main rival of Christianity, since there cannot be two chosen peoples. However, this competition could be attenuated by showing Judaism its proximity to Orthodoxy, which ought to lead to the creation of a Jewish Orthodox Church, similar to the Greek and Serbian ones. The theological contradictions would then be settled by preserving the national character of Jewishness and removing from it all religious aspects that run counter to the Orthodox world—a kind of Jewishness without Judaism. In contrast to Karsavin, Bromberg endorsed a more pragmatic religious rapprochement between Orthodoxy and Judaism. According to him, Orthodoxy had remained close to the Gospels and preserved a national, rather than universalist, character, two elements that left a place for dialogue with Judaism. Further, Eurasianism, as the ideology of the future Russia, was alone capable of understanding the mystical and metahistorical depth of the Jewish tragedy. The Russo-Jewish alliance in Eurasia had the distant goal, then, of the "voluntary entry of Jews into the Christian truth, without rejection, but rather inclusion, of the Old Testament."[32]

The role granted to Jews in Eurasianism was supposed to confirm Russia's historic destiny. In contrast with traditional Russian, anti-Judaic messianism, the millenarianism of the Eurasianists sought to join forces with the Jewish world, to receive a religious legitimation from it. So no longer was there to be any competition between two peoples chosen by God, but instead an intimate collaboration between them. Russians and Jews were held to be the real representatives, the national embodiments, of one and the same entity that had actually been chosen by God: Eurasia. Eurasianism's position with respect to the Jewish world thus turns out to be complex and somewhat contradictory. Without being anti-Judaic or anti-Semitic, the Eurasianists nonetheless have an ambivalent attitude; Jewishness is only appreciated when it serves the Russian people and its Eurasian destiny, either by associating it with Jewish messianism or by dispossessing Jews of their religious specificity through conversion. In its non-Eurasian accounts, Jewishness remains the hated symbol of modernity, liberalism, and cosmopolitanism.

THE SEARCH FOR AN ORGANIC IDEOCRATIC STATE

While the Eurasianists denounced German racialism and did not share the classic and widespread anti-Semitism of the time, many other aspects of fascism attracted them. They were embedded, for instance, in the discourse about the shipwreck of the West and the demise of Enlightenment. The influence of Oswald Spengler (1880–1936), whose first volume of *The Decline of the West* was published in the summer of 1918, was one of their major references. For Spengler and the Eurasianists alike, Europe was at an impasse, which was confirmed by both the intra-Western rifts of the First World War and the October Revolution that was its child. Many pages of Eurasianist publications are thus devoted to reviews of books about the slow death of Europe, its intellectuals, and its ancient culture, as well as books about the appearance of new telluric forces, of masses needing to be led and disciplined, and so forth.

The Eurasianist movement was severely critical of Western democracies and liberalism, but as an eminently modern phenomenon, it sharply rejected monarchy too[33] and denounced the sterile nostalgia of the White emigration. Even if figures such as Savitskii were close to the White army at the beginning of their exile, they quickly became critical of the Whites' inability to accept the Bolshevik Revolution as a point of no return. According to Trubetskoy, acceptance entailed a positive overcoming of the Revolution, not its negation.[34] According to the art patron and Eurasianist Petr Suvchinskii (1892–1985), "Hitherto, the emotional counter-revolution has not succeeded in being a conscious and voluntarist reaction."[35]

By seeing itself as fundamentally postrevolutionary, Eurasianism deemed it necessary to make peace with the Revolution and see it as a redemptive cataclysm, for "the interpretation of the Russian Revolution is the interpretation of Russian history and vice versa: by explaining the meaning of the revolution, we explain the meaning of history."[36] The Revolution thus embodies the historical contradiction in which Russia had lived for two centuries: it is both the peak of its Europeanization—because Marxism is a Western-centric ideology born of the Industrial Revolution—and at the same time its exit from the Western frame of thought, the self-dissolution of imperial Russia and its European values. While Eurasianists reject Marxism, they perceive Bolshevism as eminently Russian.

The Eurasianists thus called for the creation of a new type of Eurasian post-Bolshevik republic, not a democratic but a "demotic" (*demoticheskii*) and autocratic one. As Suvchinskii argued, "It is necessary to seek new forms of Russian statehood in the principle of a popular autocracy, [which is] the best way to unite the nation's sovereignty with the power of the people. Only by uniting these two principles in a single state can a strong and organic power be created."[37] Following the German Romantics inspired by Hegel, of whom the Eurasianists are direct descendants, the state is conceived as the ideal sphere, the theoretical site of the totality, an encompassing whole that does not differentiate society from its government. State is the essential milieu of man.[38]

As the state is a spiritual entity embodying the essence of the nation, politics is conceived as organic: the Eurasian demotic state will transcend social classes and offer an organic popular representation through medieval-type professional guilds; councils of elders; and ethnic, religious, and territorial communities.[39] According to Trubetskoy, the Eurasian state will be an ideocracy, as "the ideocratic state possesses its own system of convictions, its guiding idea, and in virtue of this it has itself actively to organize and control all aspects of life."[40] The Eurasian ruling class will therefore be guided by a monist ideology. A Greek concept, monism attributes oneness or singleness to a concept and claims that a variety of existing things can be explained in terms of a single reality or substance. The Eurasian state thus should combine law, morality, and faith into one ideology; it does not differentiate among the different powers, gives no autonomy to justice, and recognizes no private right capable of opposing it. According to Karsavin, "In the sphere defined by it, all power is absolute, for otherwise it would not be power."[41]

Given such philosophical principles, Eurasianism can certainly be linked to fascism in several respects. First, as an ideology it is structurally revolutionary and calls for a complete break with the past: "By perishing, Russia is spiritually resuscitated,"[42] in Suvchinskii's words. Second, it rejects both Marxism and communism but not the Bolshevik experience, and it seeks to combine what seems contradictory; in the event of the democratization of the USSR, Eurasianism would become a political party that would situate itself "not on the right but on the extreme left wing."[43] Third, it views the nation as an organic community that would be reflected in a specific autocratic, totalitarian regime.

However, Eurasianists can be distinguished from fascist movements on several issues. First, they do not promote an aesthetic of violence and war as the sole means to regenerate societies and create a new mankind. Second, they make no calls for an individual leader shaped by a cult of personality, as they believe in a collective and anonymous leadership embodied in the national collective essence. Third, they remain very traditional in the positive appreciation of Christianity and reject any type of secular or neo-pagan occult narrative.

Buoyed by their vision of politics, the Eurasianists could not avoid being attracted to fascist ideologies. In 1925, a member of the movement, Iakov D. Sadovskii, commented positively on Italian fascism, arguing that, if realized in practice, the Eurasianist project might look similar to the Italian example.[44] In 1932, another Eurasianist, Nikolai A. Perfil'ev, studied the programmatic documents of some Italian and German fascist groups for the movement's almanac *Evraziets*.[45] Italian fascism was criticized for its so-called practical errors (divinization of the Italian people and rudimentary nationalism) but not for its basic principles; rather, fascism was a crude realization of ideocracy that required reworking. Yet, for the Eurasianists, Italian fascism constituted "the most serious attempt to go beyond Europe's cultural and political crisis without exiting the framework of plurinational capitalism."[46] Several Eurasianist texts confirm the movement's awareness of the proximity between fascism and Eurasianism concerning both the nature of the questions raised and the solutions put forward: extreme statism, a mass movement, a new ruling class, a new corporatist social organization, and organicism. "Despite the profound differences," it was argued, "there are to be found in fascism a good number of essential connections with Russian Bolshevism."[47] Thus in the 1920s, nascent Italian fascism was perceived as revolutionary before being classified as "rightist."

In contrast with this attraction to Italian fascism, the majority of Eurasianist publications did not mention German Nazism. At the time Hitler came to power, the movement was in its death throes. The last texts of the Clamart-based Eurasianists all rallied to the cause of the Soviet Union. Aleksandr Antipov (1895–1945), branch president of the Eurasianist Committee of Prague, a representative of the movement at the end of the 1920s and very active during the subsequent decade, acknowledged in a 1933 article on Hitler's rise to power that Nazism was interesting for the questions that it raised, and even for its social and national responses, but that it had to be condemned for its pan-Germanic and Aryan discourse, which stood opposed to Russia.[48] He nonetheless argued, in a discussion with Savitskii, that "there are more talented races and less talented races,"[49] therefore showing that Eurasianists were not immune to the widespread clichés of the time.

THIRD REICH, THIRD WAY, THIRD CONTINENT

Another critical point of convergence between the different fascisms and Eurasianism is the notion of a Third Way, a key concept for the German Conservative Revolution. Eurasianism itself also aimed at being an intrinsically Third Way theory. First, the notion of a specific Russian Way, or *Sonderweg*, was a classic theme of nineteenth-century Russian thought, once again inspired by German philosophy. Second, Eurasianism emptied Marxism of its materialist content and replaced it with different forms of voluntarism and vitalism. It laid claim to the Marxist dialectical version of a Third Way in proposing that Russia had "capitalism as the thesis and communism as the antithesis and was going toward Eurasianism as a synthesis."[50] Third, on an economic level, Eurasianism called for a middle way between capitalism and communism: it endorsed a centralized and autarkic economy that would be under state control with a limited private market. Fourth, Eurasianism sought to promote a type of socialism while also advocating that the nation, not class, was the engine of world history. Last but not least, Eurasianism merged Third Way political theories with the geopolitical theories of the Third Continent. In this incarnation, the movement becomes the direct but undeclared heir of early twentieth-century *Geopolitik*, whose founders were the Germans Friedrich Ratzel (1844–1904), Karl Haushofer (1869–1946), Friedrich Naumann (1860–1919), and later Carl Schmitt (1888–1985), as well as the Swede Rudolf Kjellen (1864–1922) and the Briton Sir Halford Mackinder (1861–1947).

One of Eurasianism's main goals was to deconstruct the classic geographical representations of Russia, which was conventionally seen as a two-part space divided by the Urals.[51] For the Eurasianist movement, Eurasia was a Third Continent, neither European nor Asian; a unique, peculiar space that affirmed simultaneously its internal cohesion and its differentiation from the rest of the world. As stated in a collective Eurasianist work, "Russia's culture is neither a European nor an Asian culture, nor is it the sum or mechanical combination of elements of the one or the other."[52] This perception of a Third Continent was not entirely the invention of the Eurasianists; similar concepts had been advocated in the tsarist period by Vladimir Lamanskii (1833–1914), Vasilii Dokuchaev (1846–1903), and the economist Petr Struve (1870–1944), who was Savitskii's professor in Saint Petersburg. However, the Eurasianists were the first to conceive of the Third Continent in such an explicit way.[53]

This Eurasian Third Continent was understood as a unique totality defined by its geographical specificities and geopolitical features (a continental and autarkic destiny), but whose peculiarities were also linguistic (all the languages of Eurasia would move in the same direction and finally merge) and ethnological (Eurasia as the community of destiny of Eastern Slavs and Turkic-Mongol peoples). Geographical unity, then, subsumed the unity of civilization, and vice versa. The Eurasian territory was understood as a living participant in history, an entity embodying the unity between historical human life and that of nature and the cosmos. Both in Eurasianism and in German *Geopolitik*, the state is envisioned as a living organism, tied to the soil and symbolizing the interaction between the natural and human worlds. The Eurasianists also laid claim to the interplay between a state and its geography, because "the correspondence between the borders of a specific cultural world and a specific geographical region cannot be random."[54] There are, however, notable differences between the German anthro-geographers and the Eurasianists: for the former, the spirit of the people is uniquely a product of their geographical framework; for the latter, there is no direct causality but a reciprocal symbiosis.

Eurasianism thus projected itself as a Third Way that was not simply one political movement among many in interwar Europe. Rather, it was the ideology of a unique civilization-continent, Eurasia, which was to embody the Third Way. Here is where the messianism of the Eurasianists began, why they thought that Eurasia would show the rest of the world the path to decolonization from the European model. Eurasianism indeed condemned the West's "epistemological imperialism." By applying its own concepts to the rest of the world, Europe had obfuscated the diversity of civilizations and established a benchmark for measuring political and economic backwardness. However, Europe, the Eurasianists claimed, did not represent a *level* of development that all nations must reach, but instead a specific and irreproducible *mode* of development. This messianic agenda had already been formulated in an early Eurasianist publication of 1920, Prince Trubetskoy's *Europe and Mankind* (*Evropa i chelovechestvo*); while Trubetskoy had not yet advocated the idea of Eurasian unity, he did endeavor to deny the West any universal value.[55] By merging the Third Way with the Third Continent, Eurasianism opened the door to a narrative on successfully liberating the rest of the world from Western influence.[56]

CONCLUSION

Eurasianism may rightly be considered as the Russian version of the German Conservative Revolution, which was itself part of the tradition of intellectual fascism (as distinct from fascism as a political regime). The Eurasianists rejected German racialism—which was specific to Nazism and not to generic fascism in its Italian archetype—and offered a complex position on the "Jewish question." Unlike fascist movements, they renounced the aesthetics of violence and the cult of the leader, and they celebrated the Christian heritage of Europe. Setting these important elements aside, they nevertheless shared the main tenets of the rightist revolutionary movements of their time, in particular the determination to combine "socialism" and "nationalism" as well as calls for an organicist, totalitarian, and ideocratic state.

By transforming the *political* theories of the Third Way into *geopolitical* theories of the Third Continent, they created a new school of thought destined for a bright future in the post-Soviet decades, and they unwittingly opened an avenue for the international positioning of contemporary Russia. Despite its undeniable European heritage, Eurasianism considered itself to be born solely of the Russian experience and to be propagating a non-European ideology for Russia. But even while disavowing German culture, it remained steeped in the *Naturphilosophie* of the Conservative Revolution, proof, if any were required, of the Europeanness of Russian intellectual history, even among the most brilliant defenders of its irreducible national specificity.

Yet there are notable differences between Eurasianism and the German Conservative Revolution. While the main leaders of the Conservative Revolution were schooled in socialist circles before becoming fellow travelers of fascism and, for some, of Nazi Germany, Eurasianism proceeded

in the reverse direction, going from the "right" to the "left." The main
Eurasianist founding fathers fled Russia after the Bolshevik Revolution
before promoting a reconciliation with the Soviet Union. Eurasianism
found in Marxism its desire to combine theory and practice and recognized in Bolshevism a totalitarian approach that matched its ideals. This
right-to-left trajectory was later reflected in the destinies of Eurasianist
leaders. In contrast with numerous representatives of the White emigration, none of the Eurasianists would rally to the Nazi regime in the hope
of overturning communism. The only exception was a minor figure of the
movement, Alexandr Meller-Zakomelskii (1898–1977), who abandoned
Eurasianism for National Socialism. He became one of the main activists
of the Russian People's Liberation Movement (ROND), editor of the ROND
newspapers, and then worked for the Nazi anti-Comintern propaganda
department targeting Soviet-occupied territories.

Many other Eurasianists became pro-Soviet figures. However, all
would pay dearly, either for backing Moscow or for rejecting both totalitarianisms: those who returned to Soviet Russia, such as Prince Dmitrii
Sviatopolk-Mirskii (1890–1939), perished during the great purges of the
late 1930s; Savitskii, who remained in Czechoslovakia, languished in the
Stalinist camps from 1945 to 1956 and then in the prisons of Communist
Czechoslovakia; Karsavin, a professor at Kaunas University, was arrested
when the Soviets arrived in the Baltic countries and disappeared into the
camps in the 1950s. As for Prince Trubetskoy, he suffered a fatal heart attack in 1938, shortly after the Gestapo searched his apartment.

At the end of the twentieth century, Eurasianism's rebirth in the form
of neo-Eurasianism intensified the ideological interactions with the heritage of the German Conservative Revolution. The latter's historical figures have indeed become the main inspiration for Aleksandr Dugin, who
presents himself as the founder of a so-called Fourth Political Theory—an
almost direct copy of Conservative Revolution theories.[57] The Russian
geopolitician asserts, "The concept of the Third Way was almost always
correlated to the concept of the Russian Way."[58] He goes much further
than Eurasianism's founding fathers in integrating historical fascism
and some elements of Nazism, in particular its esoteric tendencies, into
his eclectic ideology—a move that none of the movement's founders would
have accepted. In this, Dugin betrays the legacy of classical Eurasianism
by destroying the subtle balance that the founding fathers had achieved,
and he has pushed Eurasianist ambiguities to their extreme by siding
more enthusiastically with the fascist regimes of the twentieth century.

CHAPTER 4

A FAILED ALLIANCE

The Eurasianist Movement and the German
Conservative Revolution in the Early 1930s

Martin Beisswenger

In the past two and a half decades, ideas of "Eurasianism" have occupied a prominent place in Russia's political and intellectual discourse. Although contemporary Eurasianist ideas are obviously related to the search for a unifying national idea in post-Soviet Russia and other Soviet successor states, neither the term "Eurasianism" nor the idea of Russia's uniqueness vis-à-vis the Western world is new. These concepts were initially developed in interwar Europe by Russian émigré intellectuals who formed an intellectual and political movement now commonly described as classical Eurasianism. This movement was founded in Sofia in 1921 and soon gained considerable popularity among Russian exiles in the 1920s and 1930s. The Eurasianists of the interwar years redefined Russia as Eurasia based on its geography, history, culture, and Orthodox religion; they rejected modern "Western civilization," capitalism, individualism, and the political system it gave birth to, in particular liberalism and democracy; and they extolled a unique Eurasian civilization to which the future belonged. Unlike most postrevolutionary Russian émigrés, the Eurasianists accepted the October Revolution, which they interpreted as a "healthy" reaction against the "erroneous" Europeanization of Russia. Ultimately, their goal was to transform the Soviet Union into a Eurasian federation and to replace the Communist ideology with a Eurasianist one.

No doubt, the classical Eurasianism of the interwar years and its post-Soviet neo-Eurasianist revival show obvious parallels, in particular a common emphasis on Russia's uniqueness. These parallels have prompted contemporary scholars to study both variations of Eurasianism primarily within a Russian cultural and political tradition, going back to such thinkers and writers as Nikolai Ya. Danilevskii, Fedor M. Dostoevskii, and Konstantin N. Leontiev.[1]

Yet the ideas of classical Eurasianism were also strongly related to another intellectual context that has received far less attention from scholars—namely, the ideas of various anti-democratic political and intellectual groups in interwar Europe. The classical Eurasianist doctrine shared with them—and in particular with the most well-known of these interwar movements, the so-called Conservative Revolution in Germany—a desire for an "ideocratic," essentially corporatist, state and society, as well as an organization of the economy that was neither capitalist nor Communist, and that contained strong elements of a planned economy.[2] Like the Eurasianists, the Conservative Revolutionaries propagated the rejection of liberal political and cultural values, arguing that these had lost their contemporary relevance. Instead, they demanded the renaissance of a strong and independent Germany on the basis of genuinely German traditions and in the form of an "organic" and "national" statehood. They argued that this new Germany should reject the fatal principles of capitalism and organize its economy within a framework of autarky. Although their individual views differed significantly, the representatives of the Conservative Revolution shared anti-democratic and anti-capitalist predispositions. By propagating these ideas widely among the German public, they contributed to the destabilization of the Weimar Republic's political system. Thus, they carry a certain degree of responsibility for the ultimate demolition of German democracy in 1933 and for the National Socialists' rise to power.[3]

Although the dissemination of the Eurasianists' ideas (in Russia or elsewhere) did not have such lethal political consequences, the obvious similarities in the anti-Western, anti-democratic, and anti-capitalist rhetoric of the Eurasianists and the German Conservative Revolutionaries were noted by some historians, who raised the question of mutual influences. The German historian Otto Ernst Schüddekopf, for instance, assumed that the Conservative Revolutionaries were strongly influenced by the Eurasianists' political ideas, in particular by their views on the Soviet Union. He did not, however, support this claim with any substantive evidence.[4]

A more convincing argument was developed by Leonid Luks, who examined Eurasianists and Conservative Revolutionaries within their intellectual and political contexts.[5] Both movements, Luks showed, emerged in the wake of catastrophic events—the First World War and the Bolshevik Revolution. Both were active during the 1920s, when the political situation in both countries was unstable and appeared to be ideally suited for "ideocratic" movements that strove to transform the world by means of ideas. According to Luks, both movements were a rebellion of the youth against the ideas of the older generations and were organized internally following elitist principles; both supported the ideal of a "harmonious" or "organic" state vis-à-vis an "internally torn" and "mechanical" West; and both attempted to capture a powerful totalitarian party from within.[6] In a broader sense, Luks argued, both movements reflected a widespread European sense of cultural pessimism.[7] Their cultural and ideological similarities, according to Luks, stemmed from a common political and social context rather than from direct engagement with each other's ideas. As Luks summarized, there were "parallels without points of contact."[8]

Luks's observations are convincing and correctly reflect the lack of relationships between Eurasianists and Conservative Revolutionaries throughout the 1920s. But a close examination of the Eurasianists' unpublished personal papers reveals that in the early 1930s they did make systematic attempts to forge contacts with ideologically similar movements in Europe. These attempts started in early 1932, when the Eurasianists first established personal contacts with groups of French rightists, the so-called nonconformists, who in turn invited them to the European Youth Congress held in Frankfurt am Main in February 1932.[9] A Eurasianist representative duly attended the congress and there encountered representatives of several German Conservative Revolutionary groups. In the following months, the Eurasianists attempted to establish close contacts with those groups whose ideas they found most congenial; one Eurasianist even dreamed of a broad cooperation and the creation of a "Fourth Ideocratic International."[10] Even after the Eurasianists realized that most of the German groups not only were not interested in such contacts, but openly expressed anti-Russian sentiments, they continued to monitor the activities of German Conservative Revolutionaries in order to gain a better understanding of Soviet Russia's possible future enemies.

The relationships between Eurasianists and Conservative Revolutionaries in the early 1930s, which remain virtually unknown in historiography, clearly went beyond simply being "parallels without points of contact."[11] Based on the Eurasianists' personal archival papers as well as periodical publications of the Eurasianists and other conservative groups, this chapter discusses the following questions: Why exactly did the Eurasianists become interested in the Conservative Revolutionaries? With which German groups did they attempt to establish relations and what goals did they want to pursue? And why precisely did these contacts take place in the early 1930s? The answers to these questions will contribute to a better understanding of how Eurasianism fits within the European intellectual tradition and to what extent their anti-Western sentiments and claims for Russia's uniqueness were a product of their time and mirrored similar ideas of other far-right groups in interwar Europe.

CONSERVATIVE REVOLUTIONARIES

Although the Eurasianists expressed a broad interest in anti-liberal movements throughout interwar Europe, they were primarily interested in those in Germany, whose humiliating defeat in the First World War led to the emergence of particularly militant anti-liberal sentiments. Judging from the Eurasianists' internal correspondence and memoranda, as well as from their publications, their interest focused mostly on four German Conservative Revolutionary groups: Gegner (Adversary), Die Tat (The Deed), Schwarze Front (Black Front), and Widerstandsbewegung (Resistance Movement). What ideas and principles of these groups attracted the Eurasianists' attention? Before discussing the Eurasianists' attempts to establish contacts with them, this section will briefly review these groups' intellectual and political profiles.

Quite obviously, the Eurasianists' curiosity was attracted by the most prominent and active representatives of the Conservative Revolution and those who also published influential journals. Furthermore, these four groups had a particular interest in Russia and the Soviet Union, an interest that oscillated between fascination and fear. In this sense they were part and parcel of interwar Germany's complex and ambiguous attitude toward Russia and "the East."[12]

The Gegner Group

The Gegner group formed around the journal of the same name in early 1932, when Harro Schulze-Boysen, the intellectual leader of the group, became the journal's editor.[13] Discussing the journal's new theoretical agenda, he stressed its fundamental openness and pragmatism and claimed: "We don't have a program. We don't know incontrovertible truths. Only one thing is sacred to us: movement."[14] Still, a number of central ideas propagated by the members of the group were easy to identify: they opposed capitalism, yet insisted that the struggle against it should not be waged through the existing workers' parties, such as Germany's Social Democratic Party (SPD) or the German Communist Party (KPD). Rather, it was an "order of the socialist revolution," that is, a chosen minority that should lead the struggle.[15] Schulze-Boysen propagated an "inward" revolution that would lead to the creation of a "new man," and ascribed a particular role to the young generation, the so-called "third front." This third front, in his opinion, would stand above all political parties and express the people's will.[16] This front could be joined by people of divergent political views and belonging to different political parties. As Schulze-Boysen declared: "We . . . must stand together against the old dogmas. For a new life. *Adversaries* from all camps, unite!"[17]

In the economic sphere, the authors of *Gegner* were in favor of socialism, which they understood as planned economy, economic autarky, and redistribution of property. In the political sphere their ideal was a state built on the basis of national unity (*Volksgemeinschaft*). Unsurprisingly, Schulze-Boysen and his associates were deeply impressed by the alleged social and economic successes of the USSR, which they believed had successfully connected the mobilization of the people and the integration of the country on the basis of a planned economy. In the USSR, they were convinced, the national and socialist revolutions coincided, resulting in a total mobilization of all social forces and economic resources. They regarded the Soviet Union as an example to learn from, and they spoke out against any plans to overthrow the Soviet regime with the help of foreign intervention.[18]

The fundamental openness of *Gegner* to cooperation with other political groups explains why the journal initially did not publicly oppose the National Socialist Party (NSDAP), and even in early 1933 claimed it was possible to "accelerate" the Nazi "revolution" toward a genuine socialism. Nevertheless, the German police considered the authors of *Gegner* radical Communists, and in April 1933 the journal's editorial office was vandalized by Nazi storm troopers. One staff member was killed and Schulze-Boysen was arrested and severely beaten. This attack, as well as Schulze-Boysen's sympathy for the Soviet experiment, may later have prompted him to join the German resistance against the National Socialists. During the Second World War he became the leader of the so-called Red Orchestra and transmitted intelligence information to the Soviet secret service. In 1942 he was arrested by the Gestapo and executed.[19]

Die Tat

The group of Conservative Revolutionaries that emerged around the journal *Die Tat* differed from *Gegner* in that they had a more concrete economic and political program, as well as practical political goals.[20] The leading figure of *Die Tat*, the journalist Hans Zehrer, became the journal's de facto editor in October 1929, and already at that time was considered a champion of Germany's "spiritual renewal." Other prominent authors of *Die Tat* were Ferdinand Fried (pen name of Ferdinand Friedrich Zimmermann) and Giselher Wirsing. These three constituted the inner core of the Tat Circle (*Tat-Kreis*) that soon emerged around the journal. The group rapidly gained broad public attention. Still, the Tat Circle never attracted many members; in fact, it consisted almost exclusively of the journal's authors.

The journal's popularity greatly increased in the early 1930s, when the editors were able to strike a chord with a broad audience by presenting ready-made answers to the most disturbing contemporary questions.[21] Initially, the journal featured sharp criticisms of the contemporary situation and outspokenly declared its noninterference in concrete political matters. Yet, over time, *Die Tat*'s own program became more detailed and pronounced, and their involvement in politics increased.[22]

The essence of *Die Tat*'s critical agenda was a passionate denunciation of the economic and political system of the Weimar Republic. Characterizing the current situation in terms of crisis, catastrophe, or chaos, the authors criticized the politics of the "Weimar system," which they regarded as synonymous with liberalism. The Tat Circle also connected Germany's political crisis to the overall crisis of capitalism that was undermining the entire existence of the middle class, the *bürgerlicher Mensch*. For the journalists of *Die Tat*, the beginning of the Great Depression in 1929 signaled the imminent end of private capitalism.[23]

The positive agenda of *Die Tat* was based on a fusion of irrational myths, abstract concepts, such as faith, and a cult of youth and "the powers of the future." Particular political significance was ascribed to a supposed middle layer of society that was to become the bearer of political power. The future state was to be governed by "the best," represented by upper-middle-class intellectuals, or the *bürgerliche Intelligenz*, whose historical calling was the creation of a "national socialism." The journalists of *Die Tat* envisioned a national unity (*Volksgemeinschaft*) within an authoritarian state and hoped for the construction of a powerful German empire. To achieve this goal, Germany had to eliminate its political and economic dependence on the West. In their plans to change the world order, *Die Tat* authors ascribed a particular role to Russia as a strategic partner, existing outside the "Versailles system." At the same time, their imperial ambitions were directed toward Eastern and South-Eastern Europe, which they considered Germany's natural sphere of influence, and where they saw an escape from Germany's political and economic encirclement by Western powers.[24]

Over time, the journalists of *Die Tat* intensified their political propaganda as well as their attempts to interfere in current politics. This activism culminated in their support for the conservative general Kurt von Schleicher and efforts to bring him to power. The authors of *Die Tat* regarded his tenure as chancellor beginning in December 1932—with the support of President Paul von Hindenburg—as the incarnation of their own ideal of political power, based on principles of Roman Law: a unity of presidential authority (*auctoritas*) and military power (*potestas*). Although their ideal was soon swept from power by Adolf Hitler, they quickly reconciled themselves to the new situation and several members of the Tat-Kreis, such as Fried and Wirsing, went on to have accomplished careers in the Schutzstaffel (SS).[25]

Schwarze Front

Ideologically close to the Tat Circle, although considerably less influential, was the conservative movement Schwarze Front.[26] Its leader was Otto Strasser, an army lieutenant, lawyer, and former member of the SPD, who in 1925 became a member of Hitler's NSDAP. A fighter for a "genuine" national socialism, Strasser came into conflict with the party leadership, in particular with Adolf Hitler, and was expelled from the party in 1930.[27] After that he founded the Kampfgemeinschaft Revolutionärer Nationalsozialisten (Fighting Community of Revolutionary National Socialists), and in 1931 tried to organize a more inclusive movement, called Schwarze Front. The name of the movement reflected Strasser's concept of two dualistic and antagonistic political fronts: the "reactionary" front that united "conservative" and "liberal" forces; and the "fronts of revolution," which combined the "red" (Communist) and "black" (national revolutionary) fronts.[28] Strasser's movement and his journal, also named *Schwarze Front*, aimed to propagate the idea of the "black" front and to unite several national revolutionary organizations that stood in opposition to Hitler's party. Despite Strasser's ambitions, the Schwarze Front never expanded beyond a small group of former NSDAP members, activists of Strasser's group, and was of only marginal political importance.[29]

The program of Schwarze Front, which was published in August 1931 in the form of a sweeping manifesto, shared many ideas with the platforms of other rightist groups, in particular *Die Tat*. It called for a "total revolution," which was meant to be simultaneously "socialist," "national," and *völkisch,* and was destined to reshape Germany's economy, politics, and culture. This revolution would initiate a "return" to the origins of being, nature, history, fate, and god.[30] Like those published in *Die Tat,* the authors in *Schwarze Front* decried a general crisis, called for national unity (*Volksgemeinschaft*), and sympathized with the ideas of autarky, property based on the principle of fiefdom, and a corporate state. The connections between Schwarze Front and Die Tat were underscored by close personal contacts between Otto Strasser and Hans Zehrer: the latter even attended the founding congress of Schwarze Front in October 1931. These contacts were discontinued, however, when in 1932 Zehrer moved from the field of revolutionary ideas into actual politics.[31] In his turn, Strasser, as a personal opponent of Hitler, was forced to leave Germany in 1933. Still, as analyzed in Patrick Moreau's article in this volume, he continued to conduct propaganda against Hitler after he emigrated, first to Austria, and later to Switzerland and Canada, and had a certain influence in postwar Germany.[32]

Widerstandsbewegung

The fourth group of Conservative Revolutionaries with whom the Eurasianists tried to establish contacts was the so-called Widerstandsbewegung (Resistance movement), a circle that emerged around Ernst Niekisch and his journal *Widerstand* (Resistance).[33] In 1919, Niekisch had played a prominent role in the Bavarian Council Republic in Munich, and later became a member of the SPD, which he soon left due to political disagreements. In 1926 he founded the journal *Widerstand,* which became a mouthpiece for his political concept of resistance against the Treaty of Versailles. He called for the "liberation" of the German working class, which, in his opinion, would be impossible without Germany's liberation from the obligations imposed by the Versailles treaty. According to Niekisch, this liberation was to be achieved not by an open struggle but by a growing mood of resistance among the population.[34]

Niekisch offered a detailed description of his political and philosophical ideas in one of *Widerstand*'s programmatic essays, published in April 1930 under the title "The Politics of German Resistance." Revealingly, his concept of resistance extended not only to rejection of the contemporary liberal state but also, more broadly, to repudiation of the ideas of 1789— that is, of enlightenment and humanism. He believed that these values found their expression in individualism, in bourgeois understandings of the world and the economy, and in Marxism, parliamentarism, and democracy. Although the bearers of the ideas of 1789, in his opinion, were primarily the Romanic states—France and Italy—where these concepts were supported by "political Catholicism," Germany, too, was now forcefully subordinated to these states and their ideas through the "Weimar system."

In its resistance to the victors of the First World War, Germany was to draw upon support from Russia, where Bolshevism had become the most radical form of protest against the ideas of humanism and the values of civilization. In contrast to the "West," contemporary Russia was, in his mind, neither individualistic nor liberal, and it valued politics more highly than the economy. Believing that Germany should develop its own ideas to counter the ideas of 1789, Niekisch demanded that the country should abandon the "West" and turn toward the "East," leave the global economic system, reduce its industry to a minimum, implement de-urbanization, and introduce import tariffs in order to protect its agricultural sector. Germany would create a system of camps where young people would engage in obligatory service that would teach them discipline and instill a "will to poverty" and a frugal lifestyle. In Niekisch's opinion, the establishment of an authoritarian and highly disciplined lifestyle would elevate the country's defense capabilities. Niekisch also advocated the abolition of private property as it emerged from the tradition of Roman Law, and declared a new principle of property that would be granted only for service performed for the people and the state.[35]

Niekisch's philosophical views were summed up in his so-called "Potsdam idea." This idea amounted to an idealization of Prussia during the reign of Friedrich II and served as the historical and philosophical foundation for his political conception of resistance. Niekisch wrote: "The meaning of the Bolshevik Revolution lay in the fact that in the moment of deadly danger, Russia embraced the Potsdam idea and drove it toward an extreme, an almost excessive degree. Russia created a purely military state, where even everyday life is subordinated to the rules of a military camp and where citizens are capable of extreme forms of austerity and military action whenever it is needed, and where all manifestations of life are charged with the will to defense."[36]

He thought that the Germans had to learn this "will" from Russia and suggested that German legions should be dispatched to the East in order to join the "Russian regiments."[37] The Germans had to retrieve the "Potsdam idea" from Moscow and adopt Russia's Communist forms of social organization. Since "German substance" was of "higher" quality than "Russian substance," adopting these structures would not pose any threat to Germany's character. Eventually, he believed, "Potsdam will be the Rome and Paris for the new Eastern world that will stretch all the way to the Pacific Ocean."[38]

Niekisch's fascination with the Soviet experience was in no small measure stimulated by the allegedly outstanding successes of the Five-Year Plan and the collectivization of agriculture. In Berlin, Niekisch joined the Working Group for the Study of the Soviet-Russian Planned Economy (ARPLAN) and as one of its members visited the Soviet Union in 1932.[39] After Hitler's rise to power, which he met with undisguised hostility, his journalistic activities were significantly restricted. In 1937 he was arrested by the Gestapo for organizing illegal political circles and sentenced to life imprisonment. After his liberation in 1945 by the Red Army he joined the KPD. He later became a professor of political science at Humboldt University in Berlin and served as a deputy of the German Democratic Republic's parliament until he was convicted of "objectivism" and "idealism" in the early 1950s and forced to retreat from active politics.[40]

TOWARD AN ALLIANCE

The four abovementioned German Conservative Revolutionary groups differed in certain programmatic principles and in their degree of involvement in current politics. Still, they all shared a complete rejection of liberalism and democracy in the political sphere, and of capitalism in the economic sphere. They also exhibited a certain degree of interest in Russian affairs, in particular the Soviet system of planned economy. The affinity of many of these ideas with the Eurasianists' principles facilitated the latter's rapprochement with these groups in the early 1930s. The reasons why these contacts happened exactly at that time may be explained by the changing political and economic situation in Europe as well as by internal problems that beset the Eurasianist movement itself.

The general background for the contacts between the Eurasianists and German Conservative Revolutionaries was provided by the beginning of the Great Depression in 1929. For many intellectuals throughout the world, this social and economic crisis demonstrated the inherent instability of the capitalist world order and the necessity of searching for new forms of social and economic development beyond capitalism and democracy.[41] The Eurasianists had developed similar views almost a decade earlier, but in the early 1930s intellectuals in many European countries came to similar conclusions and competed with each other in their search for a new world order. It is telling that the Eurasianists were primarily interested in the plans for a new order developed by the German Conservative

Revolutionaries rather than in their critique of the old system. And the Eurasianists approached only those German groups whose political and economic concepts for a future ideocratic state were congenial to their ideals.

More importantly, at the end of the 1920s and the beginning of the 1930s the Eurasianist organization experienced a serious internal crisis that prompted one faction of the movement's leadership to start looking for allies to reinvigorate the movement. At that time, the Eurasianist movement consisted of several groups that were based in different European cities. Already at the end of the 1920s, the group based in the Paris suburb of Clamart, which included several prominent Eurasianists, such as Petr P. Suvchinskii, one of the founders of the movement, the philosopher Lev P. Karsavin, and the literary scholar and critic Dmitri P. Sviatopolk-Mirskii, were increasingly falling under the spell of Marxism and had begun to propagate pro-Communist and pro-Soviet views. These became particularly explicit after the foundation of the Eurasianist weekly *Evraziia*. The shift to the left alienated other Eurasianists, who sympathized with some Soviet innovations but remained ardently anti-Communist. In reaction to this shift, another leading Eurasianist, the linguist Nikolai S. Trubetskoy, declared his resignation from the movement in January 1929. But by 1930 the Clamart group, too, ceased to exist.[42] As a result, in the early 1930s only a fraction of the earlier Eurasianist leadership remained in the movement, and only one of the movement's founders, Petr N. Savitskii, continued to actively promote the Eurasianist cause.

As head of the more conservative and nationalist wing of Eurasianism, which was based primarily in Prague, Savitskii tried hard to consolidate the remnants of the movement. In early September 1931, the First Congress of the Eurasianist Organization was held in Brussels with delegates representing Eurasianist groups from Prague, Paris, Brussels, Latgalia, London, and Belgrade.[43] On this occasion, the movement's program was updated and systematized by the Eurasianist legal scholar Nikolai N. Alekseev and published in Prague in early 1932 as *Eurasianism: Declaration, Formulation, Theses* (*Evraziistvo. Deklaratsiia, Formulirovka, Tezisy*).[44] This new program, similar to the programs of German Conservative Revolutionaries, was strongly anti-capitalist, and offered as an alternative a mixed state–private economic system. The Eurasianists emphasized the importance of centralized planning and, at least in theory, supported the Soviet model of industrialization. At the same time, again much like the German Conservative Revolutionaries, they opted for economic autarky. Concerning the future political organization of the state, the Eurasianist program demanded the creation of an "ideocracy," in which the selection of the ruling elite would be conducted according to their loyalty and devotion to the Eurasianist idea.[45]

Soon after the Brussels Congress and the publication of the new program, the Eurasianists focused their attention on various European radical rightist movements. In early 1932, Nikolai A. Perfil′ev, a young member of the Eurasianist group in Brussels, studied programmatic documents of some Italian and German groups and made them available in Russian translation to a larger Eurasianist audience.[46] Soon he also published Russian translations of excerpts from the program of the German Schwarze Front.[47] At this point, the Eurasianists' interest in political and ideological movements in Europe looked rather similar to their earlier comments on contemporary European politics. But throughout the 1920s, despite such publications, Eurasianists made no attempts to enter into a direct relation with any European far-rightist groups. Then, in 1932, the situation changed fundamentally when Eurasianists suddenly initiated contacts with German Conservative Revolutionaries.

The decisive event took place in early 1932, when the now undisputed Eurasianist leader Petr N. Savitskii came from Prague to Paris for a brief visit. In the French capital the Russian-Baltic philosopher and Eurasianist Vasilii E. Sezeman (Sesemann) introduced Savitskii to members of the French nonconformist group that was centered around the journal *Plans*. And one of the leaders of the group, Alexandre Marc (pen name of Aleksandr M. Lipianskii), informed Savitskii of the upcoming European Youth Congress that was being organized by *Plans*. This congress was to be held in Frankfurt am Main in early February, and Marc invited one or two Eurasianists to attend. In late January 1932, Savitskii discussed this invitation with the Eurasianist group in Prague, and it was decided to send Aleksandr P. Antipov to the congress.

Antipov, a law scholar and member of the Prague Eurasianist group, was well suited to the task of forging contacts with European nationalist groups, as he himself sympathized with attempts to synthesize national and socialist ideas. In the Russian case, he believed this synthesis would make it possible to transcend the division of Russians into pro-Bolshevik "Reds" and anti-Bolshevik "Whites."[48] Henceforth, Antipov would be the Eurasianists' expert on and liaison with the German Conservative Revolutionaries. In Frankfurt, Antipov was granted the non-binding status of an observer. Still, the Eurasianists regarded his presence there as highly important. As Savitskii suggestively remarked, at the congress "there will also be representatives of German national socialist groups."[49]

Quite revealingly, Savitskii described all German participants in the congress as national socialists. At this time the National Socialist German Workers' Party (NSDAP) was only one among many German far-rightist groups, but Savitskii was using the term in a literal sense, denoting all groups that tried to fuse national and socialist ideas. The actual NSDAP, which the Eurasianists called "Hitler's party," was at the time not really of interest to the Eurasianists, and they dismissed it as ideologically and programmatically shallow.[50]

Therefore, Eurasianists did not regret the absence of the NSDAP at the European Youth Congress in Frankfurt and tried to forge connections with other groups. Antipov attended various presentations and general discussions, and also established personal contacts with representatives of some of the groups. Moreover, he used the opportunity to speak about the Eurasianist movement and its ideas in front of over one hundred French, Belgian, and German delegates. Antipov's presentation took place at the end of the first, introductory session of the congress on February 7, 1932. In his speech, delivered in German, Antipov expressed the Eurasianist party's support for joint organized activities with the youth of Europe. He characterized the Eurasianist movement as "anti-capitalist but non-Communist," explained the Eurasianists' economic system that combined a planned economy with individual economic initiative, and called for the "primacy of the spiritual" against a predominant materialist philosophy. He described the Eurasianist teaching as ideocracy and gave the USSR as the example of a country already governed by an idea. Finally, he even "hinted at the desirability of creating a Fourth Ideocratic International in the future"; in his mind, it would be a global coalition of all "national socialist" youth movements that would overcome and replace the Third Communist International.[51]

Later that day, Antipov was approached by a number of French delegates, some of whom confessed their full agreement with Eurasianist ideas. According to Antipov, they were happy to receive the Eurasianist theses, which had been specially translated from Russian into French and German for the event. The German delegates, Antipov admitted, were more reluctant to establish contact with him and he had to make some effort to approach them. He explained this by the fact that most of the German groups at the congress conceived of Germany as a self-contained entity, and they also suspected him of being some kind of "semi-Bolshevik." The Jungpreußischer Bund (Young Prussian League), represented by Jupp Hoven, and Niekisch's Widerstand were more interested in Eurasianism, but even with them he found it difficult to find a "common language." Antipov decided to contact those German groups he found most interesting after the congress; in particular he singled out Niekisch's Widerstand ("perhaps the most interesting of them all") as well as Otto Strasser's Schwarze Front.[52]

Overall, Antipov was quite enthusiastic about his participation in the Frankfurt congress, which had given him the opportunity to introduce Eurasianist ideas to the German groups and to learn about their programs. He found that the Eurasianists shared certain ideas with some of these groups, in particular with Widerstand, Die Tat, Strasser's Schwarze Front, Umsturz (Subversion), and Vorkämpfer (Spearhead), and he advocated approaching these in order to establish regular contacts.[53] Whereas the first three groups would continue to figure in the Eurasianists' writings, the latter two were never mentioned again.

Immediately after his return from Frankfurt to Prague, Antipov contacted Otto Strasser's Schwarze Front and Niekisch's Widerstand. The latter group responded immediately and sent Antipov their program, asking for the Eurasianist's opinion.[54] We may assume that during the weeks after his return from Frankfurt, Antipov carefully studied the journals and programmatic documents of those German groups he had become acquainted with at the congress. The result of this study was a memorandum, "On the Prospect of Relations with German Groups," presumably written in late spring or early summer 1932 and addressed to the Eurasianist leadership. At this point, Antipov focused on three German groups: Gegner, Die Tat, and Widerstand.[55]

Harro Schulze-Boysen's Gegner group was discussed first in Antipov's *Memorandum*. Schulze-Boysen had been co-organizer and chair of the Frankfurt congress, but his journal and group were organized only after this event. In Antipov's view, Gegner was the most inclusive among the various German groups, yet programmatically it was rather weak. Antipov mentioned that, according to Gegner's program, it was imperative to create a minority "organized in the form of an Order" that would transcend all existing classes. It would be formed by "all those sympathetic to this idea" regardless of their political orientation. Antipov explained that Gegner had no further ideas "except this idea of a 'ruling elite' and the rejection of capitalism."[56] He mentioned that Gegner was "sympathetic" toward religion—an important point in the Eurasianists' own teachings. Overall, Antipov concluded, the program of Gegner was still in the making; their "forces are young [and] inexperienced." Still, he underscored that the group's outlook was quite broad, "without national narrowness and prejudice," and that there was nothing in their writings that from a

Eurasianist perspective would be "unacceptable." He therefore recommended the following approach to *Gegner*: "We have to focus all our efforts on establishing the closest possible relations with them. We have to try to nourish them with our ideas and attempt to publish [Eurasianist] articles in *Gegner,* and our final goal would be the joint publication of a common journal (*Gegner* or another one)."[57] Thus, the fundamental ideological and political openness of the journal prompted the Eurasianists not only to forge contacts with *Gegner,* but also to try to influence the group's ideas.

Antipov's efforts soon bore fruit. In August 1932, Harro Schulze-Boysen responded with great interest to an earlier letter from Antipov that had contained Eurasianism's program and an outline of the movement's history.[58] Schulze-Boysen found both documents "extremely interesting" and discovered "much that was related" to his own ideas. He interpreted Eurasianism as evidence that the "Russian" (*russischer Mensch*) was moving away "from Edison and Marx" and was in the process of rediscovering his genuine identity. Furthermore, Schulze-Boysen invited the Eurasianists to contribute a brief article on Eurasia and the Eurasianist movement to the next issue of *Gegner,* which would have a special focus on Europe and was to appear at the end of September 1932. Schulze-Boysen admitted that "so far the concept of 'Eurasia' was [in Germany] almost unknown," and therefore such a publication "might be interesting" to "the German public." He revealed that the general purpose of the special issue was to provide an explanation of why the German people had rejected "Pan-Europe," which was Richard Nikolaus von Coudenhove-Kalergi's rival project of European unification, based on democratic and pro-capitalist principles.[59] Schulze-Boysen was convinced that Coudenhove-Kalergi's ideas emerged from a "West that embodies capitalism pure and simple" and that was culturally alien to Germany. It was imperative to seek an entirely different approach, for an anti-Western, anti-capitalist, and explicitly pro-revolutionary form of European unification. And in these efforts, the Eurasianists, Schulze-Boysen implied, would be the *Gegner*'s valuable allies. He confessed that he would be "sincerely pleased if [he and the Eurasianists] could remain in permanent contact" and concluded his letter "with comradely regards."[60]

In early September 1932, Petr N. Savitskii responded to Schulze-Boysen's letter, reprociating the "comradely regards," and sent the invited essay on "Eurasia."[61] However, the essay failed to appear as planned in the September issue of *Gegner.* Instead, the journal published a short editorial notice on "Eurasianists." It informed its readers that the journal had received Eurasianism's program and characterized the group as a "postrevolutionary émigré movement . . . that calls itself anti-capitalist but not Communist." It also mentioned that the Eurasianists strove toward autarky and an "ideocratic state system." At the same time, *Gegner*'s editors expressed scepticism toward Eurasianism's ideocratic plans as well as toward any state structure that was based merely on an idea. Still, *Gegner* considered the appearance among the Russian émigré community of a circle of "anti-interventionists with a predominantly positive attitude toward the USSR" a remarkable event. The editors promised to soon publish a more detailed report on the Eurasianists if circumstances allowed.[62] But the journal was closed by the Nazis in 1933, putting an abrupt end to all contacts between the Gegner circle and the Eurasianists.

The Tat Circle was the second Conservative Revolutionary group discussed in detail in Antipov's *Memorandum*. But his attitude to Die Tat was more skeptical. The group's more sophisticated programmatic principles made it difficult to influence its ideology or even to establish effective mutual relations. In his *Memorandum* Antipov underscored that in contrast to *Gegner*, this group was less interested in general questions of ideology but rather was focused on more concrete issues related to German reality. He stressed that in Germany Die Tat was influential and occupied a "place of honor." But he cautioned that the group "continues in new forms the old German policy (in disguise) that attempts first to subordinate Central Europe, with the further goal of subordinating the East, i.e., Russia." Antipov concluded that the politics of Die Tat were "potentially hostile to Russia." Still, he noted that many programmatic principles of Die Tat were close to those of the Eurasianists.[63] As Antipov would explain in a later article, these included the idea of a mixed "state–private economic system," as well as a concept of an "organic" statehood organized on the basis of corporative structures and administered by a "ruling elite" that was selected according to a certain ideological principle.[64]

The obvious proximity of the political and economic concepts of Die Tat to those of the Eurasianists prompted Savitskii to study this German group's ideas in greater detail. His unpublished notebooks from November and December 1932 contain lengthy excerpts of numerous articles published in *Die Tat* during that year.[65] Savitskii studied the political journalism of Hans Zehrer, in particular his declaration of the end of the contemporary political system and his call for replacing it with a corporative state organization. In *Die Tat*'s economic publications Savitskii noted Werner Sombart's concept of a planned economy and Ferdinand Fried's statements regarding the inevitable establishment of economic autarky and Germany's economic expansion to the East. Savitskii was also interested in Giselher Wirsing's views on international relations and his calls for political collaboration with the USSR in a joint struggle against the Treaty of Versailles.[66]

Although the imperialist aspects of Die Tat ideas were incompatible with Eurasianist concepts, the Eurasianists still found it desirable to establish some kind of contacts with the group. Antipov was primarily interested in the possibility of publishing Eurasianist articles in the journal *Die Tat*. After the journal's February 1932 issue published an article by the Russian émigré Boris Izhboldin on "Bolshevism as an ideocratic economic system and its ideological challengers," the chances of having Eurasianist publications appear there as well looked quite good.[67] However, Antipov's attempts to contact the group directly did not elicit any response. In early summer 1932 he complained that the German journal still had not responded to his letter containing a German translation of the Eurasianist program, which he had sent to *Die Tat* soon after the Frankfurt Youth Congress. Antipov assumed that this lack of response was related to the journal's particular nationalist character: "This journal is very German and very political, and dealing with something outside this focus, in this case engaging in common action with [Eurasianism], is not something it will do; now, for us, moreover, this is not desirable either, due to [the journal's] traditional-German character." Obviously, Die Tat was not interested in relations with the Eurasianists. Furthermore, as one of the authors of the journal revealed in a conversation with the Eurasianist Vasilii E. Sezeman, the circle considered contacts with any ideologically similar groups of "secondary" importance.[68]

The Eurasianists' opinion of Ernst Niekisch's Widerstand movement was even more ambiguous than their attitude toward *Die Tat*. On the one hand, this group, in Antipov's words, advocated a "rejection of the West," hailed "Russian étatist ideas," supported the Soviet regime, and fought against interventionist tendencies. On the other hand, the Eurasianists were appalled by Widerstand's explicitly anti-Russian "national chauvinism." Russia, according to the group, "together with Germany must constitute one entity under the leadership of Germany." Widerstand's national chauvinism, Antipov argued, superseded by far even the chauvinism of Hitler.[69]

It is hardly surprising that of all the German Conservative Revolutionary groups, the Widerstand circle was seen by the Eurasianists as the least desirable candidate for collaboration. As Antipov noted: "It is, of course, outside our interests to strengthen in any way the positions of 'Widerstand,' but we might use this movement's journals [...] with the goal of making our own ideas better known.”[70] Interestingly, despite their reservations, the Eurasianists eventually managed to establish some contact with Niekisch. In Savitskii's notebook from November–December 1932 we find clear evidence that Niekisch had responded to the Eurasianists' advances, although the nature of his response remains unclear.[71] It is worth mentioning that Savitskii continued to be interested in Niekisch's historiosophy in the following years; he widely read and excerpted Niekisch's works, in particular his 1930 book *Entscheidung*.[72]

In analyzing the possibilities of establishing contacts with the German Conservative Revolutionaries, Antipov cherished no illusions. He concluded his *Memorandum* with a sober final statement: “Collaboration with German groups is entangled with difficulties of a special kind. Namely, Germany is currently living too much of a tempestuous life; Germans are unable to engage in anything that has only an indirect relation to the German reality. Moreover, those German groups that are of particular interest for us are predominantly nationalist, and Germany is located too close to Russia for the national aspirations of the former not to collide with those of the latter. Nevertheless, [...] opportunities for the establishment of relations do exist.”[73] But the events of the following months made even this careful assessment of possible future contacts sound too optimistic.

KNOW YOUR ENEMY

As 1932 drew to a close, the already limited opportunities for the Eurasianists' to cooperate with the German Conservative Revolutionaries dwindled even further. In the previous months, German politics had become dramatically more radicalized, with the NSDAP doubling its vote count and gaining the most votes of any party in the July general elections. Now, even Antipov, who continued to follow the publications of the German conservative groups, did not see many prospects for cooperation. In a survey article published in November 1932, Antipov reassessed the ideas of the four groups he had earlier considered potential allies. At this point, however, he was not primarily interested in an alliance with them; his analysis rather followed the principle “know your enemy.”

Even the title of Antipov's article, “New Radical Movements in Germany,” signaled a shift in the Eurasianists' attitude toward the German Conservative Revolutionaries.[74] Departing from his earlier *Memorandum*, where he had merely spoken about “German groups,” Antipov now explicitly called them “radical.” He no longer grouped the movements according to their desirability as possible allies for the Eurasianists but, first and foremost, considered the orientation of their foreign policy programs. He distinguished three main tendencies: the first was represented by Die Tat and Schwarze Front, which both "see Germany's future in Central Europe, where the hegemonic role should belong to the German people." The second tendency, "characterized by an orientation toward the USSR," was represented by the Widerstand group. The Gegner group was a representative of the third tendency: it sought "rapprochement with anti-capitalist elements in West European countries in order to create a pan-European federation based on non-capitalist principles." Despite their differences, all the groups, Antipov explained, strove to "pursue a violent change of the existing order"; only Die Tat advocated changes through "gradual evolution."[75]

Revealingly, Antipov now added to his analysis a discussion of the ideology of the Schwarze Front. No doubt the reason was that the Eurasianists perceived these views as extremely dangerous for Germany's neighbors. Although ideologically under the spell of Die Tat, Antipov explained, "in its economic views Schwarze Front is less radical than Die Tat." Yet its foreign policy program worried him greatly: the group's "Pan-German tendencies are emphasized to the extreme and have a defiantly aggressive character." Antipov also stressed that in contrast to Die Tat, Schwarze Front accepts only "revolutionary" forms of social and political change, and its program "includes the demand for a new war."[76]

Antipov's overall conclusion was disillusioning. Although the German groups he reviewed still had many ideas in common with the Eurasianists, he admitted that the creation of a "Fourth Ideocratic International" was currently impossible: "All the German groups, except Gegner, are to one or another degree aggressively nationalist; and this is not a suitable basis for international collaboration."[77]

After Hitler came to power in Germany in January 1933, the Eurasianists continued to follow the actions and writings of the German Conservative Revolutionaries with growing concern. In yet another survey that was published later in 1933, Antipov again offered an assessment of the ideologies of the German youth movement, now within the context of the new National Socialist Germany. He claimed that the National Socialist movement was "broader than the National Socialist Party of Adolf Hitler," and that almost all German youth movements at that time in one way or another shared "national socialist" ideas. Even though many of the "Conservative Revolutionaries" had joined the Nazi party after Hitler's victory, Antipov still expressed confidence in the potential influence of Conservative Revolutionary ideas. The

Eurasianists asserted the ideological weakness of the actual National Socialist Workers' Party and assumed that "Conservative Revolutionaries" could and would influence Hitler's party from within.[78] But now it was the ideas of these German groups themselves that worried the Eurasianists.

On the one hand, returning to the ideologies of the Tat Circle and Niekisch's Widerstand, Antipov reconfirmed that many of their ideas resonated with those of the Eurasianists, in particular the German groups' call for the establishment of a mixed state–private economy and an "ideocratic" political system. Furthermore, after Hitler's rise to power the Conservative Revolutionaries were in a position to join the new National Socialist state and turn their ideas into reality by shaping the German state and economy.[79]

On the other hand, Antipov could not fail to notice that the ideology of the Conservative Revolutionary groups would influence the foreign policy of Hitler and the National Socialists, particularly with regard to the East, including the Soviet Union. Without much difficulty, Antipov discovered in the writings of the German Conservative Revolutionaries the old idea of *Mitteleuropa*, a concept of German hegemony over Central and Eastern Europe that went back to the nineteenth century.[80] And the re-emergence of this idea was an alarming signal to "those peoples whom the Germans want to integrate." Antipov, who lived in Prague, noted that while the immediate implications of *Mitteleuropa* might relate to Central and Eastern Europe, German ambitions stretched even further to the East, to the "eastern space from the Arctic Ocean down to the Black Sea," in which the journalists of *Die Tat* had expressed particular interest. Antipov discovered the same worrisome tendencies in the writings of Ernst Niekisch and the Widerstand group. Although the "idea of Potsdam" was inspired by the Russian and Soviet example, Niekisch assumed that after having shed the harmful influence of the West, Germany would struggle and compete with Russia over hegemony in the East.[81] Needless to say, in Antipov's article of 1933 there was no further talk about possible collaboration between the Eurasianists and the German Conservative Revolutionaries.

Still, the Eurasianists made one final attempt to test the waters and establish contact with representatives of the German Conservative Revolution. In April 1933, a few weeks after Hitler had become Reichskanzler of Germany, the young German Heinrich Stammler, who at the time was studying in Prague with Petr N. Savitskii and had joined the Eurasianist movement, traveled to Berlin.[82] On this occasion Stammler, who was a grandson of the famous philosopher of law Rudolf Stammler and was sympathetic to the ideas of the Conservative Revolutionaries, visited *Die Tat*'s editorial office, obviously with Savitskii's authorization. There, however, he found no interest in the Eurasianists' ideas. In a letter to Savitskii he relayed his conversation with one of the journal's junior staff members, noting that his reaction was rather "cool" and "displayed this kind of distrust that is now widespread in Germany against all kinds of 'émigré' movements."

But even more importantly, Stammler conveyed his overall gloomy assessment of the Conservative Revolutionaries' situation after Hitler's rise to power: "Generally, in the near future all these circles do not have any real prospects, unless they are able to integrate themselves into the NS-DAP. The Gegner, Otto Strasser's Revo[lutionary]-Nazi-Movement and, in all its perplexity now also the 'Tat-Kreis' have demonstrated that they are in a pretty shaky position."[83] Thus the Eurasianists' insistent attempts to build contacts with ideologically similar German groups came to a close in early 1933 when these groups themselves were rapidly disintegrating.

CONCLUSION

In the early 1930s, the projected alliance between Eurasianists and German Conservative Revolutionaries was pursued by the Eurasianist leaders with considerable effort and dedication. But this alliance failed. The political differences between the two movements were insurmountable, and in the Eurasianists' view, the Germans' aggressive nationalism and plans for territorial conquest in Eastern Europe and Soviet Russia were too dangerous. Furthermore, the German Conservative Revolutionaries were firmly convinced of their own ideological importance and originality; their attitude toward the Eurasianists' rapprochement ranged from indifference to dismissive arrogance. Only with Harro Schulze-Boysen's Gegner circle, the group that had the vaguest and most inclusive political program, were the Eurasianists able to establish some relations.

Yet despite the evident failure of any large-scale collaboration between Russian Eurasianists and German Conservative Revolutionaries, let alone of the idea of establishing a Fourth, "Ideocratic" International, the contacts between the two camps are highly instructive.

First of all, study of these contacts allows us better to contextualize the Eurasianist movement within modern European intellectual history. The Eurasianists, like all other so-called "postrevolutionary" Russian groups, were part and parcel of a pan-European anti-democratic and anti-liberal movement of the interwar period. This movement included the German

Conservative Revolutionaries, but also the French and Belgian nonconformists. It is astonishing how easily the Eurasianists found a common
language with their German counterparts when they spoke about broader
ideological principles. Even in the literal sense of the word, as their correspondence was conducted in German, this ease of communication was
quite striking. No less surprising is the affinity of their programmatic
principles, such as rejection of the "West" and of liberalism, individualism, democracy, and capitalism. Their positive programs also had much
in common: while both Eurasianists and Conservative Revolutionaries
were anti-Communist, they called for a significant role of the state in the
economy and the establishment of economic autarky, favored corporatist
models of state and society, and proposed an "ideocratic" political system
ruled by a chosen elite.

At the same time, the failure of the Eurasianists' plans for an "Ideocratic International" very clearly demonstrated the limits of international
cooperation among rightist and nationalist movements. Such cooperation
was possible as long as purely intellectual projects were being discussed
and plans against a common enemy were developed. Yet when some of
these intellectuals gained real or alleged political influence, as happened
with the journalists of *Die Tat*, cooperation turned into confrontation.
Aggressive nationalist movements in real politics are incompatible, even
if they share basic ideological principles.

Finally, the rapprochement of Eurasianists and German Conservative
Revolutionaries in 1932 provides an interesting historical backdrop to
similar efforts currently underway to forge cooperation between neo-Eur-
asianists and the New European Far Right.[84] Whether these contemporary efforts turn out to be more successful than the similar attempts in
the early 1930s remains to be seen.

PART III

THE WAR EXPERIENCE: COLLABORATIONISM AND THE SOVIET UNION

CHAPTER 5

THE SOVIET UNION, RUSSIA, AND THEIR PEOPLES AS PERCEIVED BY FRENCH VOLUNTEERS IN GERMAN UNIFORM, 1941–1945

Jean-Yves Camus

On July 8, 1941, two weeks after Nazi Germany attacked the USSR, the Legion of French Volunteers against Bolshevism (LVF) was founded in Paris.[1] Some of the group's combatants, after training in the General Governorate of Poland, went to Smolensk and then Viazma.[2] They headed to the front at Kriushino in December 1941, with the firm intention of triumphantly marching to Moscow.[3] This plan was never realized.

On May 2, 1945, after several changes of name and assignment, the last French volunteers of the 33rd Waffen Grenadier Division of the SS Charlemagne Regiment surrendered to Soviet troops in Berlin. In his classic study of French volunteers in German uniform, General Albert Merglen estimates their number at about 10,000,[4] which is fewer than the number of French volunteers deployed in Spain as part of the International Brigades (15,400). Pierre Giolitto puts the number at closer to 30,000, which is probably inflated because it includes all French people who engaged voluntarily in the units of the Nationalsozialistische Kraftfahrkorps (NSKK), the Luftwaffe, the Kriegsmarine, the Todt Organisation, the Speer Legion, and the diverse units of the Waffen SS,[5] principally the Walloon Legion led by Léon Degrelle.

This chapter examines the varying ways that French people fighting in German uniform perceived the USSR (generally using "Russia" to apply to the entire Soviet Union), the peoples comprising it, and the Communist

ideology driving it, both during their military service and in the postwar
period. Why take an interest in the ideas of a few thousand soldiers who
represent merely a marginal, if radical, form of collaboration with Nazism?
There are at least two reasons: First, these men were practically the only
French collaborators who were in direct contact with the Soviet territory
and its peoples.[6] Second, many of these former combatants, both those who
were punished post-liberation[7] and those who fled France to escape repri-
sals, resumed their extreme right-wing militant and intellectual activities
during the Cold War decades.[8] This group helped create and perpetuate an
inspirational myth: namely the "European combatant" whose engagement,
transcending narrow French nationalism, makes him the intellectual
ancestor of a variety of European nationalism that, as this volume demonstrates, emerged on the Extreme Right during the postwar period.[9] In 1998,
former officer Henri Fenet,[10] who was the key public figure of the Truppen-
kameradschaft,[11] the association of former LVF members, expressed the
ideological continuity as follows: "We also fought for a united and communitarian Europe and for several years the European people have awaited
the birth of this united Europe, hoping that it will not be a miscarriage. We
planned the path of independence for our self-determination and now the
Europeans are taking the path that we paved back then. Instead of thanks
we have reaped legal prosecutions."[12] Throughout the mass of apologetic
pseudo-historical postwar literature, the image of the French Waffen-SS
combatants is featured as the ideal that radical nationalist militants should
emulate, both for their military "exploits" and their emblematic representation of the figure of the "reprobate" in France from the *épuration* until the
present day. They therefore compete symbolically with the figure of the *milicien*, the Vichy regime's paramilitaries who bore arms against the French
Resistance, and usually embody the prototype of "traitor" and "accursed."
All these terms were repackaged by those to whom they were applied and
their admirers. Today they have come to form a sort of "revisionist history"
that glorifies the pariahs of the "system" established by the victors of 1945.

This literature, which has its own publishing houses[13] and confidential
bulletins, is devoted to the reenactment of Second World War battles,
describes visits to the places where they occurred,[14] and even includes its
own cartoons.[15] Before migrating to the marginal subculture of the Far
Right in the 1960s and 1970s, this literature was produced by mainstream
publishers, thus ensuring the leading works of the genre a widespread distribution. These works include the trilogy written by Marc Augier, alias
Saint-Loup;[16] the numerous works by Jean Mabire;[17] and Christian de la
Mazière's book, *Le rêveur casqué* [The Helmeted Dreamer].[18] Thinly dis-

guised fictional accounts of the actions performed by French volunteers in German uniform have become an integral part of the intellectual heritage of the Extreme Right, from the times of Europe-Action until present-day neo-Nazi, revolutionary-nationalist, and European-nationalist milieus. This literature recounts the history of the combatants who fought against "Bolshevism," but who also were deployed in Russia and Belorussia and/or came up against the Red Army, whether in Galicia, Pomerania, or Berlin. Confronting this army gave them a new, alternative view of Russia; namely, as a powerful state that combined the dangers of both communism and the Asian racial peril encroaching upon Europe.

DEPLOYMENT OF THE FRENCH VOLUNTEERS IN RUSSIA

Before advancing to the front, the LVF trained at the Deba camp in Sub-Carpathian Poland. The LVF arrived at the eastern front during the terrible winter of 1941–1942, where it fought in extreme weather conditions that left a lasting impression on the survivors and significantly shaped their vision of Russia. Arriving via Smolensk, the advancing LVF troops were stopped by Soviet troops near Dyutkovo at the edge of Narskyi Prud and the Nara River, sixty kilometers from Moscow. They endured significant casualties, and by December 7 the surviving troops who were still fit for combat had decided to retreat to the town of Kruszyna in the Radom region of Poland. This evacuation was not solely due to the losses: it was approved by the German Chief of Staff, which sought to end the Legion's internal political quarrels. The Legion had been infiltrated by the Parti populaire français of Jacques Doriot, who had been at the front since October 1941. In addition, the Germans planned to replace the Legion's inept leader, Colonel Roger-Henri Labonne (1881–1966), who was also a Doriot supporter. By spring 1942, the surviving remnants of the division had been dispatched to hunt down partisans in the Briansk region and to the north of Gomel.[19] From June 1943 to March 1944, they were stationed on both sides of the highway from Warsaw to Moscow, between Borisov in the west and Tolochin in the east. The Bobr battle of June 1944 marked the culmination of the Legion's activities inside the USSR. It ended in defeat and the Legion retreated to Minsk, via Kaunas, in early July. The soldiers were then evacuated to Greifenberg (present-day Gryfice in Poland) and Danzig.

In accordance with the law of July 22, 1944, the Vichy government had authorized the engagement of French citizens in the Waffen-SS, thereby endorsing a new step toward total collaboration. This decision was in response not only to the SS's growing need for men, as it had been decimated fighting on the Russo-Ukrainian front, but also to the Reich's desire to bring French volunteers, including the *miliciens*, under a single German command. After training, first in annexed Alsace and then in Bohemia, the unit called the Waffen-Grenadier-Brigade der SS Charlemagne became operational in July 1944. It arrived in Turka, in present-day Ukraine, on August 5, 1944, then fought on the Galician front in the border region of Sanok (Poland).

The operation in Turka, which was reached after passing through Munkàcz, then part of Hungary, was the only large-scale French contact with Ukraine. There were some individuals who reached Ukraine; they had volunteered for the Belgian Walloon division on an individual basis, in many cases attracted by the personal prestige of Léon Degrelle and his heroism in the battles of Kuban (1942) and Cherkassy (1944). The famous book of memories by cartoonist Dimitri (Guy Mouminoux, alias Guy Sajer), *Le Soldat oublié* [The Forgotten Solider, 1976],[20] has been erroneously regarded as the testimony of a member of the Waffen-SS, when in fact the author was an Alsatian conscript (a *malgré-nous*) who had been assigned to the Grossdeutschland Division of the Wehrmacht, which advanced as far as Kharkov and Voronezh on the Don.

After retreating from the Sanok front in Poland, the French volunteers would never again fight on Soviet territory. They would beat a retreat westward in step with the advancing Red Army, going via the then-Polish Voivodeships of Pomerania and the Baltic coast to Kolberg-Korlin, ultimately fighting in Berlin until May 2, 1945.[21] The LVF's knowledge of Russia is therefore far more fragmentary than that of the Walloon volunteers who fought in Donetsk in 1941, in Kuban in 1942,[22] and again in Ukraine and Estonia (Narva) in 1943–1944.

AN ESSENTIAL MOTIVATION: ANTI-COMMUNISM

In the foreword to his book *Les volontaires*, Saint-Loup characterizes the LVF as "international brigades that mobilized out of political ideology." When profiling the unit's first volunteers, he deliberately highlights a former member of the Marty Brigade, which fought against Franco in Spain, and another volunteer in the Durrutti Brigade.[23] Both individuals, it turns out, became disenchanted with the ideology that they were defending.

The militant wing of the fascist Parti populaire français, whose members often came from the Communist Party, was the most active political supporter of the Legion. Jean-Paul Cointet rightly identifies the PPF as "the veritable inspirer of the Legion."[24] After 1943, the PPF sharpened its anti-Communist rhetoric, and several recruiting posters clearly show the omnipresent "crusader" mindset against Bolshevism. One poster offers a message from Marshal Pétain, which begins: "By participating in the crusade that Germany is leading. .. you are contributing to removing the Bolshevik peril." Another poster announcing a public meeting in Dinan, Brittany, on June 20, 1943, promises testimonies from soldiers who have returned from the front line and who will use film to explain "What we ought to think of the paradise of the Soviets and of Bolshevism in general."

The slogan at the time was to "save Europe from Bolshevism" by all means possible, including joining the LVF.[25] Instead of analyzing the anti-communism found in the discourses of Collaboration, which has already been done in all the classic works on the period,[26] I want to underscore here that Doriot was not the only LVF protagonist with first-hand experience of the USSR. The LVF had not simply arrived in a country that was totally unknown to them.

One of these well-informed men was the Legion's chaplain, Mgr Jean de Mayol de Lupé[27] (1873–1955), a monk-soldier with legitimist monarchist, anti-Communist, Catholic, and pro-Nazi convictions that formed a highly dubious syncretic model. Mayol de Lupé was deployed as a chaplain in the Armée d'Orient after the armistice of 1918, serving in Bessarabia where, in early 1919, General Berthelot, fighting for Romanian territorial claims, assigned him to fight against the Bolsheviks at Kishinev, Bender, and Tiraspol.

Colonel Roger Labonne, of the Colonial Infantry, may have proven to be a mediocre tactician, but he had relevant experience after serving as a military attaché in Ankara and as an intelligence officer in Constantinople.[28] In these posts and then later in China, he studied USSR-Turkey relations and developed his own views on the need to control the Pacific theater.[29]

Journalist and writer Jean Fontenoy (1899–1945), another Communist defector to the PPF, brought a unique perspective on Russia as well. Fontenoy had been Tolstoy's translator and director of the Moscow office of the Havas news agency. After being wrongly accused of spying and expelled from the USSR, Fontenoy volunteered for the Finnish Army in 1940 and was decorated by Baron von Mannerheim. While serving on the outskirts of Moscow in 1941, he was promoted to lieutenant and made head of the LVF propaganda division. He was known for writing a 1938 brochure published by the PPF, *Frontière rouge, frontière d'enfer*, in which he rages about the alleged monopoly of the Jews in Ruthenia. On November 6, 1937, he wrote to Otto Abetz: "The French are mistaken. They believe that since

Stalin killed Zinoviev, etc. . . . , Russia knows anti-Semitism. In fact, the Jews reign supreme here."[30] Fontenoy committed suicide in Berlin at the end of April 1945, as Soviet troops entered the city.

This anti-Semitic obsession, which groups the Jews together with the Bolshevik Revolution or Communism and presents them as the true masters of the USSR, is shared by other LVF sympathizers. Pierre-Antoine Cousteau (1906–1958), the author of *L'Amérique juive* (1942), was known mainly for his prewar columns analyzing the USSR in the weekly *Je suis partout,* and as the co-translator of Ivan Solonevitch's book *Barbelés rouges: Trois russes s'évadent des bagnes soviétiques.*[31]

The great paradox of the LVF volunteers is that they are driven by a fierce anti-Communist fanaticism but ultimately, as Jean Mabire writes, "All the volunteers turn out to be more or less fascinated by Russia."[32] They are all torn, as we shall see, between their revulsion toward the Soviet regime and its most prominently politicized elements (the political commissars) and their fascination with the country itself. They often revered Russia's inhabitants for preserving the customs and attitudes of an idealized Russian people who had survived key historical events, including the 1917 Revolution and the Stalinist regime, without having essentially changed their nature.

However, the French volunteers never realized that the Nazis intended to eliminate the Russian people, or at the very least consign them to a form of serfdom after a series of massive population displacements. For the pan-Germanists of the Waffen-SS, the "territories of the east," at least as far as the Urals, were to be colonized by Germans, even if the minister in charge of these regions, Alfred Rosenberg, envisioned mobilizing Slavs, Balts, and Caucasians in the service of the Reich, using their anti-Russian nationalism to serve the aims of Germany's war. An examination of the map of future Europe drawn up by the European-ethnic faction of the Waffen-SS proves even more interesting. The theoretician of this faction was the Swiss officer Franz Riedweg, whose views would be embraced by the two main champions of the French SS, Saint-Loup and Jean Mabire. Published by Saint-Loup in the appendix to his book *Les SS de la Toison d'or,*[33] the map divides former nation-states into provinces according to ethno-linguistic criteria and draws a line consigning many peoples to be "outside Europe"; this line corresponds exactly to the current eastern borders of Poland, Slovakia, Hungary, and Romania. Some people were not duped: Philippe Martin subscribed to the Spenglerian conception according to which communism is "the combination of Russian expansionism and the immense human reservoir of Central Asia"[34] against which it is necessary to bring to bear "a revolution of absolute violence, ignoring all political, biological and moral barriers." He points out that "In Hitler's work the East returns as a leitmotif: Alexander the Great led his phalanges toward the East, followed by the first Crusades and the Teutonic Order. But Hitler's east has nothing legendary about it: it is endless space, horizons without limits, the abundance of the breadbasket of Ukraine, the oil of the Caucasus, a sort of agricultural Arcadia matching the industrial Walhalla in which Germany flails . . . Germany's survival depends on east-ward expansion."[35] The Führer's perspective did fool some Frenchmen. For example, Lucien Rebatet, a contributor to the newspaper *Devenir*, an organ of the French SS, wrote: "This Russia, which escapes all our notions, debonair one day, savage the next, with its hallucinatory or ignoble climate for nine months, but the paradise of its summer, its enormous lifeblood, its people who were so able to get along well with the French and would have doubtless ended up at Europe's side if Pan-Germanism had not blinded Hitler."[36]

FOLLOWING IN NAPOLEON'S FOOTSTEPS

The LVF's legionaries, at least according to their revisionist account, had another reason to volunteer to fight in Russia: they thought of them-selves as "the last *grognards*"[37] and sought to emulate Emperor Napoleon I and his Russian campaign of 1812. This is a rather ambiguous point of reference since this campaign ended in French defeat, and, furthermore, the passage of Napoleonic armies through the "residence zone" led to a loosening of the constraints on the Jews confined there, not to increased persecution.[38] Nevertheless, following the Nazis' defeat, many volunteers found it comforting to place themselves alongside Napoleon, confirming their belief that they had restored some of France's military glory.

After the war, taking uncertain facts and testimonies on faith, some authors even asserted that descendants of French soldiers of the Grande Armée were still living in the villages through which LVF legionaries had passed. Thus, in 1974, the novelist Jean Raspail relates, in the chapter titled "Les Hussards of Katlinka" from his *La Hache des steppes,* that in the spring of 1942 members of the 638th infantry regiment (the LVF's official identity) "went into a village in the Mamajevka Forest in south Smolensk, its appear-ance different to the usual village encountered in the Russian countryside."[39] There, 133 years after Napoleon's campaign, the LVF volunteers "came across traces of our Napoleonic *grognards*, three to four generations down the line." For them, manifestly, this village "of about twenty homesteads" was not entirely Russian since, "when they caught sight of it through the curtain of trees, they immediately had the impression that they were seeing something *different,* something never before seen among the collectivized

farmers," namely "the well-maintained roofs and walls of the *izbas*, the careful alignment of the single main street, the piles of snow geometrically arranged in the square, the stables and henhouses that were just as well-maintained as the *izbas*, not one shutter of which was hanging loose on its hinges."
As if to confirm the legend, "after some days of rest and contact with the
natives," the volunteers discovered graves and "a small diamond-shaped
rusty tin plate, with eroded edges, about 8 cm in height, on which could
be read an engraved numeral: 6," the number that the soldiers of the Sixth
Hussars "still wore in 1812 on their black shako, just below the cockade."[40]

In addition to the LVF members who saw themselves as "Napoleonians,"
there likely were some volunteers, notably those officers from the nobility
and those, also of noble origin, from the French *milice*, who had an entirely
different view of Russia. They saw a country that had welcomed royalists
fleeing the French Revolution of 1789 far more warmly than the English
had. An example was Bernard de Polignac, a sergeant in the LVF, who died
near Bobr in 1943 in an attack by partisans. He was a descendant of Prince
Jules de Polignac, the last president of the Charles X Council of Ministers.
His father had been able to begin rebuilding the family fortune thanks to the
lands granted them in Ukraine by Catherine II. Also in this category was
Victor de Bourmont (1907–1945)[41] (named for his forebear, Marshall Louis
Auguste Victor de Ghaisne, count of Bourmont), who had served Napoleon
despite his royalist sentiments, betrayed him at Waterloo, and had served
as a minister in the Polignac government. This view of Russia was likewise
held by all the volunteers whose names recall the old landed nobility (rather
than the court nobility), people who remained loyal to the senior branch of
the Bourbons and for whom nineteenth-century Russia represented the
defense of the Counter-Revolution. They felt obliged to come to Russia's aid
when the opportunity arose to get rid of the Communist regime. But these
volunteers had evidently forgotten the declaration of the Marquis de Roux,
the leader of Action française, who wrote in his book *La Restauration*: "The
Emperor Alexander underlines in all ways possible that he is continuing
the treatment of the Count of Lille out of pure humanity. In all of political
Europe, only Joseph de Maistre, minister in Petersburg of the King of Sar-
dinia, persists in thinking that the King of France remains the centerpiece
of the European system."[42] The LVF volunteers were to be, similar to the
Belgian Rexist volunteers, convinced by their time in Russia that the people
remained attached to the old order, the Orthodox religion and the imperial
family. One of them expressed it as follows: "In the region that we are crossing, the inhabitants have remained very devout and very attached to the
family of the tsars. Yesterday, we visited a house made of clumps of earth

and the family living in it had buried the icon of their emperor. They have just unearthed it and lavished it with all sorts of attention."[43]

VOLUNTEERS FROM THE RUSSIAN DIASPORA IN FRANCE

The volunteer ranks also included men from the so-called White emigration; that is, Russian opponents of the Bolshevik regime. Their presence was a direct result of the emphasis placed on anti-Bolshevism in the recruitment drives for the LVF and the Charlemagne division. For some young people of the emigration, getting involved was a way to contribute to the anti-Communist ideological war, and also, if a German victory resulted, to put an end to the despised regime governing the USSR. Several volunteers of Russian origin who joined the LVF during "actions" of the combatants on the eastern front are particularly noteworthy. The best known of these figures, probably due to his self-proclaimed noble title, was the Oberjunker Serge Protopopoff (1923–1945), a former *milicien* born in Nice. He joined the LVF in 1943 and was assigned to the Waffen-SS. He fought in the Pomerania campaign before dying in the Battle of Berlin, in which he reportedly destroyed Soviet tanks.[44]

Serge Krotoff (1911–1945) is remembered for his summary execution at Bad Reichenhall (Bavaria) on May 8, 1945 by French soldiers of the Leclerc Division. He and a dozen comrades had been handed over to the division the day before. In a fairly complete biography, Grégory Bouysse[45] describes a man who was hardly a model soldier. The grandson of an interpreter at the Russian embassy in France whose family converted to Catholicism, Krotoff, a mediocre Navy officer, was put in charge of the Montpellier office of the General Commission for Jewish Questions (CGQJ) in January 1942. Later that year, he was made director of the Police for Jewish Questions in Toulouse, and lastly, in spring 1943, an agent of the Sicherheitsdienst (SD), first in Toulouse and then in Paris.[46]

Other LVF volunteers with a White Russian émigré background include Corporal Georges Stogoff, the division's interpreter. Wladimir Hall (1919–2006) enlisted in 1941 but soon realized that fighting alongside the Germans was not compatible with his anti-Communist convictions. He requested his repatriation to France nine months later.[47] Georgian émigrés who had dreamed of freeing their native land from Communism with the help of the Germans, such as Sergeant Georges Sikharoulidzé (interpreter) and Constantin Amilakvari[48] (flagbearer), also realized that the alliance with the Nazis was a bad choice. The Office of Russian Émigrés seems to have played an important role in disseminating Nazi propaganda among the Russian community to get young people to volunteer. Laurent Joly describes this propaganda office as follows: it was "led by Iurii Gerebkoff,[49] a genuine German agent, tasked with listing the Russian refugees, with supervising them, etc. . . . It published and distributed a Russian-language newspaper, with collaborationist leanings, *Russkyi Vestnik* (*Le Messager de Paris*), among the Russian community in Paris. The Office refused to grant Jews its legitimation card." [50] The Office carried out surveillance and recorded information in an effort to identify possible Soviet agents and Jews of Russian origin. Gerebkoff's second-in-command, Paul (Pavel Nikolaevitch) Bogdanovitch, also published the newspaper *Parizhskii vestnik*[51] and played a significant role as an "expert" on race-related issues, serving as an advisor to the Commissariat general aux questions juives (CGQJ) on such issues as the Jewishness of the small Karaite and Subbotnik communities, and more generally on the "racial" status of émigrés from Eastern Europe.[52] A CIA report claims that, from spring 1941 until the liberation of Paris, the Office played a role in "engaging Russian émigrés in the German army, the Todt Organization, the Speer Legion,[53] and voluntary labor in Germany," with its activities including "interceding on behalf of Russians arrested by the Gestapo or under its suspicion, on the condition that the victims sign up to being engaged on the eastern front."[54]

This claim has not been thoroughly examined. In any case the Office, under the guidance of an agent his opponents named "The Russian Führer of Paris," seems to have quickly exceeded the role of representative for the German Occupation authorities that it played beginning in 1940, when a Russian representative committee was founded by members of ROVS (General Union of Russian Combatants), the RSNUV (Russian National Union of Participants in the War, led by General Anton V. Turkul), and the NTS (National Union of Russian Solidarists). The committee's program called for "absolute intransigence against the Judeo-Marxist International and freemasonry; a struggle against all forces that prevent the rebirth of national Russia; by considering that Orthodoxy played a decisive role in the creation of the Russian government, as it inspired the Russian imperial idea, within the faith of God, the pledge of the rebirth of our Fatherland."[55] Besides those who were drawn to collaborationism by the Office, some others decided to work for the Nazis simply because they believed it could further their aspirations to play a role in the Russian émigré community. The best known case is that of Foulques de Baillard Lareinty-Tholozan, an authentic French count who had been adopted by the second husband of his mother-in-law, one Prince Kotchubey, and had added the title "Prince Kotchubey" to his own name. Killed in 1944 as a German sympathizer, he had a son, Honoré-Louis, who disappeared in Pomerania in 1944 and who, according to several sources, had enlisted in the LVF in part due to his family's economic collapse and in the hope that a German victory in Russia would enable him to reclaim his distant family's ancestral lands.[56]

THE CRUELTY OF RUSSIA AND THE GENEROSITY OF ITS PEOPLE

The LVF volunteers provided candid accounts of the harsh realities that they experienced in Russia and on the Pomeranian front, facing the advancing Red Army, which they viewed as the forward guard of the Asian conquest of white Europe. Mabire writes: "The same cry resounded everywhere. Nothing seems to be able to stop this invasion of the innumerable Asian hordes. In the far north, the third front of Belorussia is pushing its offensive toward Königsberg. On its left, the second front of Belorussia is heading toward Danzig and seeming to gain hold of Tannenberg. The former empire of the Teutonic Knights will suffer the harsh law of revenge. The Slavs want to settle a secular account with the Prussians."[57] Gilbert Gilles, another volunteer who fought at Diwenov in Pomerania, recalled "those young girls, those mothers and those grandmothers [who] must have been serially raped by the victors" and then "had their throats cut or been disemboweled, according to the methods dear to the Mongols, the Kyrgyz, and all the savages of Asian Russia."[58] This description of the military opponent is in line with the lived experience of the battles of the "first winter" of 1941–1942, during which the LVF suffered tremendous losses.

At this point, the battles fought on Soviet territory were so devastating that all written memories, whether direct, indirect, or fictionalized, tend to portray the victims as heroic figures assailed by exploding Russian shells and land mines. These maimed warriors would have their bodies touted as symbols of Russo-Soviet cruelty. The key figure here is the Breton Jean Bellec, alias Jean Benvoar (1920–1982),[59] whose wartime godmother was a Galitzine princess[60] who visited him when he was being treated at the Hospital Foch de Suresnes and aided him financially upon his prison release. Benvoar, immortalized by Saint-Loup in *Les nostalgiques*,[61] lost both legs and four fingers on his left hand near Brest-Litovsk in 1941. Jacques Benoist-Méchin reports in *De la défaite au désastre*[62] that he visited him along with General Galy, the General Commissioner of the Legion, who awarded him a Médaille Militaire. Benvoar was widely photographed by the press, driven to the Arc de Triomphe for a ceremony at the Eternal Flame, and after the war came to settle in Lenggries (Bavaria), where he was visited by young militants from the neo-Nazi movement.

A local Swiss newspaper announced his death: "My Honour is named Fidelity. The friends and comrades of Jean Benvoar, seriously maimed in the war, Croix de Fer, Médaille Militaire, Croix de Guerre avec palme, announce, with great sorrow, his death at Lenggries (Bavaria) on November 19, 1982 at the age of 59."[63] In 2006, some survivors of the Second World War and their youngest admirers were still paying visits to his widow after stopping at the "sacred sites" of Braunau and Berchtesgaden.[64]

Belgian volunteer Henri Moreau (alias Paul Terlin) entered the ranks of the heroes when a French publisher released his autobiography. On August 25, 1944, near Narva, Moreau had both of his arms blown off by a Soviet shell. He resumed his political activities postwar, not only in Belgium, where he promoted the ideas of Social Credit, but also in Canada, where he collaborated with the newspaper *Vers demain,* in which the Pèlerins de Saint-Michel, an ultra-conservative Quebecan Catholic movement, published their ideas of social creditism.[65]

If the enemy was harsh, so was the country. Russia's cruelty comes through in its coldness, its iciness, which inspired the title of Mabire's work, *Par moins 40° devant Moscou.*[66] The facts mentioned in this work are accurate: the winter of 1941–1942 was exceptionally severe, the division's equipment was insufficient or inappropriate, and flawed military instruction increased the losses. As for Saint-Loup, he states in his work *Les volontaires*[67] that: "The First Battalion had yet to see an enemy and already Russia had defeated it, simply confronting it with the organized emptiness of its infinite spaces and its medieval channels of communication, which were wiped out by the snow and the deep winter ice."[68] He went on to describe "a cadre reduced to silence in the stupefying stasis of a universe that was frozen by temperatures as low as –40° C."[69]

Combined with the extreme weather conditions, the misery of the villages and villagers helped reinforce this negative image of Russia. Pierre Rusco, passing close to Brest-Litovsk in early May 1942, noted: "I would never have thought that humans beings could live in such conditions. . . . Men and women walked barefoot in the frozen mud, and my surprise was ever greater upon reaching the station, where we were greeted by swarms of destitute but friendly children dressed in ragged clothes, who would offer us an egg in exchange for a cigarette or bread."[70] However, according to the volunteers, Russia had some positive features, especially the "infinite spaces," which caused apprehension during wartime but instilled optimism about the country's potential within a rearranged European geopolitical space.

The French were most affected by encounters with their Russian allies, who were deployed alongside the Reich in "ethnic" or reserve units called Hiwis. One volunteer, a French-speaking Swiss, wrote: "I recall an evening in the company of a considerable group of Cossacks, who came to visit us a few kilometers from Taganrog. . . . The Cossacks were fierce adversaries of the Bolshevik regime and we formed entire divisions with these valiant combatants."[71] The Russian peasants that Rusco encountered near Borisov "showed us not the slightest hostility"[72] and, in another place, they were even, he writes, "particularly welcoming," especially the young women, who "went into the forest to gather strawberries and blueberries [for us]."[73] Whereas Russia's winter, and then its thaw, was terrible for the men, its "violent and brief summer"[74] fascinated the French volunteers, as did, ultimately, the country itself. Saint-Loup's mythical hero, Le Fauconnier, the prototype of the fanatically national socialist officer dedicated to a Europe of ethnicities rather than to pan-Germanism, declares: "One can only come to adopt Russia by marrying it. Russia cannot be occupied against the will of the Russians. You cannot move across Russia as you do along the motorway from Munich to Salzburg."[75]

MEMORY, AFTER 1945

At the war's end, and as amnesty laws restored their freedom, the erstwhile volunteers strove to keep alive the memory of their engagement and to help each other with the difficulties of social reintegration. These collaborators faced a form of ostracism that was far harsher than that faced by the "economic collaborators" and the many police auxiliaries, who had often been wise enough to play both sides with the Resistance, at least at the very end of the war. The LVF volunteers were hated either because, as *miliciens*, they had fought against their fellow countrymen on French soil,[76] or, as *légionnaires*, they had fought in German uniform on the eastern front. For a perspective on this issue, see the often semi-apologetic literature from Saint-Loup and Mabire, which gave rise to a specific counter-narrative or counter-history. There is no space in the present study to deal with the actual militant trajectories of the survivors from 1945 to the present day.

However, in terms of Russia, the main question that arises is that of returning, to visit either the battle sites or the graves of the fallen. While such trips were almost impossible during the Communist period, since the early 1990s return has been an option open to the "forcibly enlisted," namely, those from Alsace-Lorraine in France, and in particular for those interned by the USSR at the Tambov camp.[77] They are considered to be victims of Nazism who acted against their own will. Thanks to organizations such as the Association Pèlerinage Tambov, founded in 1995, these veterans can visit Russia in a public and organized manner. Representatives of the local Alsace-Lorraine authorities frequently accompany them on these journeys and are welcomed by their Russian counterparts upon arrival. These trips, which are often intergenerational, aim at keeping alive the memory of forced enlistment in the annexed *départements*, an aspect of the war that was never understood by French people living outside these regions, who scarcely distinguished between the volunteers and the forcibly conscripted *malgré-nous*.[78]

The situation of the survivors of the LVF and the Charlemagne division is obviously different. No archive has been found so far that confirms that none of the volunteers and conscripts, voluntarily or not, remained in the USSR after being liberated from the camps. This scenario is not entirely a fantasy: the last *malgré-nous*, Jean-Jacques Remetter, returned to Strasbourg on April 15, 1955. Prior to his death in 1984 he testified to the main daily newspaper in Alsace[79] that at the end of 1954 he had been given a choice between remaining in the USSR with an annual stipend of 5,000 rubles or returning home but never speaking of his experiences in the concentration camp system in Tomsk and the Tashkent region. Geneviève Herberich-Marx and Freddy Raphaël report that "Following the testimony of Jean-Jacques Remetter, some members of the Association des Anciens de Tambov claimed in turn that they knew horrible things about the Soviet repressive system but were unable and unwilling to speak about it. . . . If we had said all that we know, explained their president, it would be terrible" (i.e., it would have been interpreted as pro-Nazi propaganda). The president of the association also claimed that "some former prisoners were only freed because they agreed, upon return, to engage in espionage and supply intelligence." Herberich-Marx and Raphaël explain: "Patrick Meney's work, *Les mains coupées de la taïga* (1984), revived hope in the many families that never resigned themselves to the death of a son who had gone missing in the vastness of the Russian continent. The work of mourning could not be carried out. Claims from the leaders of the Gaullist-inspired Association des évadés et incorporés de force (ADE-IF) that Alsatians are highly unlikely to be still prisoners in a camp are opposed by the testimonies of the members of the rival association, the Anciens de Tambov."[80] To my knowledge, no former volunteers have taken any organized or publicized pilgrimage to Russia or Belarus. Former volunteer Pierre Rusco (real name: Ruscone, 1921–2005), claims that he consulted the available archives in Minsk for his work *Stoï!* If this is correct, he did so in an individual capacity.

Another issue is the upkeep of the volunteers' graves. This work is carried out across the entire territory of the former USSR by a German association entrusted with this mission, the Völksbunde Deutsche Kriegsgräberfürsorge e.V. However, its role does not extend to the graves of foreign volunteers buried outside of German military cemeteries. Private French and Polish associations carry out excavations seeking missing soldiers and arrange appropriate burials for remains found at digs or construction sites across Central and Eastern Europe, and they do so without distinguishing between Allied or Axis prisoners of war, or the forced or free laborers who perished on one of the eastern fronts. The Verein zur Bergung Gefallener in Osteuropa e.V, for example, has carried out expeditions in Russia and Ukraine and has found unidentified French volunteers in Polish Pomerania.[81] It is also possible that these searches are still being carried out on former Soviet territory by Verein, though that remains unconfirmed. Furthermore, while associations of French volunteers or French groups of historical "re-enactors" with extreme-right political leanings continue to gather for commemorative ceremonies in Germany (Bad Reichenhall), Austria (in Ulrichsberg, Carinthia), and occasionally elsewhere (Neveklow in the Czech Republic, a training site for SS recruits),[82] they do not do so in Russia.

We know more about how volunteers have communicated their experiences to later generations. During the Cold War, many former French volunteers of the Waffen-SS mobilized against communism, whether as protestors or as soldiers. In May 1948 the French army, engaged in Indochina against the Vietnamese Communists, agreed that collaborators sentenced to less than fifteen years in prison could be released upon assignment to a special unit, the Overseas Light Infantry Battalion (Bataillon d'Infanterie Légère d'Outre-Mer—BILOM).[83] A vague promise of amnesty was made to some 800 volunteers, but no guarantees were given and their service in BILOM was an essential condition. Some took advantage, possibly to continue their careers in the French army, in some cases in Algeria. Others refused the offer because France post-1945 seemed to them to be preparing for a Soviet alliance: Grégory Bouysse[84] mentions the conflicting choices of two PPF militants, Pierre Laurion, who volunteered for BILOM, and Christian Martrès, who refused. So even if the former volunteers' attitudes toward the USSR remained rooted in anti-communism, that fact did not necessarily translate to a call to Atlanticism.

However, beginning in the 1950s, some extreme-right wing militants who were trained in the ideological school of the Waffen-SS, while they also repudiated communism, clearly differentiated between opposition to the Soviet regime and Marxism, on the one hand, and the necessity of including the Slavs, and therefore the Russians, in their plans to construct a "Third Way" Europe, on the other.[85] This school, which René Binet called "European socialism," interpreted the Russian Revolution of 1917 through an ethnic paradigm: it underscored that, at least in its beginnings, the Revolution occurred in European Russia, that it was hijacked by "a clique foreign to the country" that enforced its model against the "democratic socialism of the Nordic and European peoples,"[86] and that some of the Slavic peoples of the USSR will naturally be stakeholders in the war for the survival of the white race, as soon as they are rid of communism. Binet's tireless political activity, his role, along with Amaudruz and Bardèche, in the creation in 1951 of the European Social Movement (ESM) and the movement's biological racism have already been widely studied.[87] I will delve here into the lesser-known parts of this Europeanist neo-fascism (or neo-Nazism), which sought to look beyond the temporary division of the European continent into west and east, and speculated about what some of the peoples in the USSR could contribute biologically, demographically, and politically to a reunified and communism-free Europe.

In 1949, Pierre Clémenti (1910–1982), a minor leader of the Collaboration, issued *La troisième paix*, which recalls his discovery, on the eastern front, of a "magnificent Russian people, healthy, vigorous and good,"[88] a people that, according to him, would come to contribute to the implementation of "national socialism." Clémenti had already founded the French National Communist Party (PFNC) in 1934, which he renamed "national collectivist" in 1940 at the request of the Germans. Although he had only a few militants following him, they included such notables as Eric Labat (1921–1964),[89] Christian de la Mazière, and Pierre Vigouroux,[90] all authors of postwar memoirs. Clémenti remained politically active until the 1970s, publishing a periodical titled *Le combat européen* and heading diverse activist groups, including the Comités d'action européenne, while at the same time rallying to the Ordre nouveau movement (1969–1973). Other former volunteers joined Jeune Nation (1954–1958), a strictly French nationalist and Pétainist movement led by a former member of the Parti Franciste, Pierre Sidos (b. 1927). The first issue of the newspaper *Jeune Nation* (January 5, 1958) carried an article by Jean Malardier,[91] then one of the group's leaders. Others made the equally anti-Communist but pro-European nationalist decision to support the journal *Europe-Action* (1963–1966). In addition to articles by Marc Augier and Pierre Bousquet,[92] the second issue's table of contents lists an article by Pierre Lamotte, the pseudonym of the very discreet Robert Blanc,[93] who to this day continues to pass on the volunteers' ideological legacy.[94] Jean Mabire was *Europe-Action*'s chief editor.

Beginning in 1948,[95] Mabire had pursued the goal of forming a phalanx of youth dedicated to promoting the "Europe of Ethnic Fatherlands" so vaunted by Saint-Loup.[96] Pierre Vial, Clémenti's godson, spent his ideological apprenticeship at the journal. First and foremost, *Europe-Action* was the brainchild of Dominique Venner, the former Jeune Nation activist who played a pivotal role in the transition from French nationalism to European nationalism. Venner's long bibliography reveals his fascination with the White armies,[97] his revulsion to communism, and his apology for the Freikorps actions in the Baltic states and Weimar Germany. But at the same time, this is a man who, as editor of the journal *Enquête sur l'histoire*, in winter 1994 devoted an entire issue to the theme "Russia: A thousand years of enigmas" and in his editorial signaled his certainty that Russia was engaged in its "social reconstitution along with its empire's," an empire destined to become a great power again, which ought to be a "friend" of Europe, and can succeed insofar as it has the ability to make "countless borrowings from the outside world, but to adapt them and in so doing remain itself."

Persuaded that Russia would help Europe contend with "American hegemonic power and Islam,"[98] Venner thus revives and updates the idea of a union of "white" peoples made possible by the fall of the USSR. This vision of a Europe founded on a fundamentally anti-Semitic "scientific and biological racism" resembles the thought of Marc Augier (Saint-Loup). It clearly raises a significant problem; namely the multi-ethnic character not only of the former USSR but also of the current Russian Federation. All the former volunteers, as we have seen, noted the role of the "Asian" combatants in the Red Army. Even in their postwar writings some volunteers continued to hold that "the USSR, like Europe, America, and South Africa [is] consumed from the inside by Africans and Asians," an idea originated by the above-mentioned Robert Dun (alias Maurice Martin).[99] The contradiction between the necessary alliance with White Russians and the multi-ethnic reality of Russia can only be resolved through one of two opposing discourses that still divide extreme-right groups: Eurasianism or Eurosiberianism.

For a number of years, the French Extreme Right considered the possibility of integrating the ethnically European part of the USSR into a unified continent free of communism. The idea was promoted by the journal *Le Devenir européen*, published in Nantes by Yves Jeanne[100] with the assistance of Léon Colas, both of whom adopted a European-ethnicist and neo-Evolian line. The journal endorsed a "united-European-ethnicist federation made up of Slavic, Celtic, Latin, Nordic, and Germanic confed-

erations,"[101] but it never defined the borders it would take. However, Yves
Jeanne had previously[102] written about his key interest in the USSR's
evolution, claiming that its leaders would cast off Marxism on the way
to making Russia a "pan-Slavic and national state, such as Tsarist Russia was capable of being," a Russia that would embrace the transition to
anti-Zionism and anti-freemasonry, especially in the vein of the famous
Russian anti-Semitic essayist Valerii Emelianov.

The journal *Militant*, founded in 1967 by European nationalists who
clamored for "national socialism" with reference to Proudhon and the Paris
Commune, took a different approach.[103] Headed by three men who had volunteered for the eastern front—Pierre Bousquet (1919–1991, a former member
of Parti Franciste), Jean Castrillo (1922–2012, a member of the PPF in 1938),
and Henri Simon (1919–1997)—*Militant* served as the National Front's official organ from 1973 to 1975. Bousquet was the NF's first treasurer in 1972
and *Militant* was the voice of the party's European-nationalist and overtly
anti-Semitic inclinations until the party decided to split in 1980, on the
ground that the NF had become too moderate. Strongly opposed to *Devenir
européen* and a prisoner to his anti-Communist experience, Bousquet did
not reject the market economy, and he expressed concern about the tendency in some nationalist milieus to "yield to the subtle and sly KGB operation
of brainwashing" designed to fool people into believing that the Soviet
leaders are "dyed-in-the-wool national socialists and scorn the *bougnoule*
[*sic*]."[104] The question nonetheless remains, he continues, as to "what is better: a century or two of Marxism that preserves Western civilization despite
it all or an advanced liberalism that causes it to disappear completely?"[105]

Militant continues to be published today. It was published independently until 1983, when it became the organ of the Parti Nationaliste
Français (PNF), a very small neo-fascist group. The PNF gained strength
when, between 2013 and 2015, it absorbed Oeuvre française and Jeunesses nationalistes, two Sidos-inspired movements banned by the French
government. In 2015 PNF elected its new Chairman, Jean-François Simon,[106] whose ancestry was a clear signal that the volunteer's legacy was
not forgotten. *Militant* then took a very distinct Russophile turn and came
to consider "Russia [as] the stumbling block of globalization"[107] and that
"the new opposition between Russia and the West desired by the latter is,
rather, a conflict between two models of society and civilization." This
conflict can be summed up as follows:

> Two conceptions stand opposed: on the one hand, Russia, which founds its
> future on its 1,000 year-old tradition including Christian Orthodoxy; on the

other, the United States and the E.U., which aim to establish a subverted, constructivist, amoral social order, based on the principle that the artificial conceived by man can be substituted for the authentic. In a healthy fashion, Russia privileges the endogenous renewal of generations, where the West aims at the replacement of white populations through immigration, denying the vital role of ethnic and cultural specificity, and presenting men as interchangeable. Russia is the country, then, that combats the inversion and perversion of mores illustrated by the "marriage" of homosexual couples and gender theory—ideas endorsed by the West and presented by it as being the new obligatory norm. In truth, Russia, which for seventy years was the seat of global subversion and a criminal regime of which it was the first victim, asserts itself today as the current haven of our millennial civilization, whereas the West has become synonymous with barbarism." [108]

Another of the journal's original ideas lies in its assertion that "the Georgians and Armenians are part of the European and Christian camp." Above all, *Militant* presents the unique case of a group whose mastermind, Jean Castrillo, after being "imprisoned by the Russians, became Slavophil[e] and converted to Orthodoxy."[109]

CONCLUSION

The experience that French volunteers in German uniform had of Russia is known mainly through the literary genres of novels and military history. Jean Mabire, for instance, the author of a number of important works on this topic, did not read German. His works are not historical accounts; rather, they create an inspirational myth, similar to the works of Saint-Loup. They include a Romantic dimension that ought not be taken lightly and that adds to the commercial aspect. The neo-rightist Belgian intellectual Christopher Gérard rightly considered Mabire's works on this subject to have been done "for hire"—that is, to make a profit—perhaps as a testimony "to the memory of his comrades during the terrible years" or even as a way of "remaining faithful to his adolescent rebellion." The memories of former volunteers constitute, according to the same source, a particular "Eastern genre," a sort of "Manichean epic that has confined some of the volunteers within forms of nostalgia that are as murky as they are incapacitating." Gérard is no less severe in his appraisal of Saint-Loup, who he describes as "an enlightened member of the Collaboration," someone who "excelled in elaborating an *a posteriori* mirage, that of an idyllic Europe under the guidance of Seductive Supermen, pure knights in battle against the gnomes of Asia." The reality,

however, "was less exalted [and included]: deportations, pillages, forced en-
listments," not to mention the "abyssal scorn of the Third Reich for the Balts,
to say nothing of the fate reserved for the Slavs and other 'sub-humans.'"[110]

One would be hard-pressed to express this any better. Moreover, there is
a world of difference between the description of the Waffen-SS as a "grand
European army" and the reality of the ideology taught to recruits in the
training camp at Sennheim (Alsace). In memoirs titled *Siegfried et le Ber-
richon*, Léon Gaultier bluntly reports that his *Weltaanschauung* instructor
told him: "National socialism is not an International. Its limit is the white
zone of humanity and more particularly the gathering and the destiny of
peoples of Germanic origin."[111] From February to July 1944, the journal of
the French Waffen-SS, *Devenir*, tried to make last-minute French recruits
of the Charlemagne Division believe that the goal of the "Black Order" was to
grant each and every country taking part in its fight equal status with Germany in the Europe-to-come. That was, of course, only wishful thinking.

These "fringe" authors of the Extreme Right, like the survivors whose
militant positions in the European-national ranks I have traced, played an
important role in the contemporary rehabilitation of Russia's role as the
chief actor in the Eurasianist geopolitical and/or Eurosiberian project,
so dear to today's identity-politics fundamentalists. Even rewritten and
reinterpreted, the memories of the "former volunteers" have helped forge a
new European imaginary. The transmission of the experience of the eastern front took place through written texts, and its militant sociability was
developed through its meeting places and sites of commemoration. Major
portions of the history of this ideological testimony remain to be written,
particularly with regard to the young members of the neo-national socialist
movement who nurtured the idea of a Europe of ethnicities, following in the
footsteps of Mabire and Saint-Loup. Such is the case with the Basque-speak-
ing poet and writer Jean (Jon) Mirande,[112] known and recognized on both
sides of the Bidassoa, who belonged to the Groupe Collaboration and the
Jeunes de l'Europe Nouvelle (JEN) led by Marc Augier,[113] and who became
prized by the New Right; and Mirande's friend Georges Pinault (alias Goul-
ven Pennaod)—himself from the Breton autonomist milieus and the JEN.

As Stéphane François and Nicolas Lebourg emphasize, one of the major
ideological mutations of the extreme Right in the second half of the twentieth century in fact lies in its transference of German nationalist conceptions of *Kulturvolk* (people of culture) and of *Schicksalsgemeinschaft*
(community of destiny) onto the European frame of reference.[114] The testimonies of former French volunteers, fictionalized or genuine, have broadly
played their part in it, by adding Russia into their nationalist imaginary.

CHAPTER 6

THE RUSSIAN NATIONAL SOCIALIST VIKING PARTY IN THE SOVIET OCCUPIED TERRITORIES

Boris Kovalev

Hitler's rise to power in Germany was cause for hope among a large number of Russian émigrés. Many people who fled Russia after the Bolshevik revolution of 1917 embraced the political changes happening in Berlin as a victory of anti-Communist forces: as they saw it, "an entire group of nations have won with their White Idea—Italy, Portugal, Germany, and Hungary."[1] In the Soviet Union itself, some individuals welcomed the advance of German troops, in the hope that they would be freed from the Soviet regime. Works by Aleksandr Kazantsev, Wilfried Strik-Strikfeldt, and Catherine Andreyev[2] have argued that some patriotic Russian intellectuals initially saw the Nazi invasion as a "liberation from the hated Bolshevism" and were therefore ready to assist the Third Reich.

While the story of General Andrei Vlasov's army is famous, this chapter focuses on a less-well-known case, that of Konstantin Voskoboinik (1895–1919) and his Viking People's National Socialist Party of Russia (PNSPR), located in the Briansk region, on the border with today's Belarus and Ukraine. Voskoboinik published a first collaborationist manifesto in the journal *Golos naroda* (Voice of the People) in November 1941, and the Viking party was officially launched in 1942, after his death, under the leadership of his disciple Bronislav V. Kaminskii (1899–1944). It did not take a solid institutional form until March 1943, and ceased to exist as soon as Soviet forces retook the territories in 1944. This research is based on the very detailed testimony of his wife, Anna V. Kolokoltseva-Voskoboinika. On

May 24, 1945, the Soviet Department of Counterintelligence ("Smersh") of the Thirteenth Army arrested her. The warrant for her arrest stated:

> Have examined the material submitted on Anna Veniaminovna Kolokoltse-va-Voskoboinika, born in 1899 in the city of Kazan, Russia, citizen of the USSR. Member of the National Labor Party of Russia, has secondary education and is qualified as a draftsman, comes from a family of servants, her father is a teacher of Russian language. Kolokoltseva-Voskoboinika, who lived in areas temporarily occupied by German troops, actively participated in the organization of an anti-Soviet political party, the National Labor Party of Russia. As a member of the central organizing committee of the party, Kolokoltseva-Voskoboinika pursued anti-Soviet activity, and therefore was subjected to arrest and search.[3]

During her interrogation on September 5, 1945, Anna Voskoboinika wrote a long statement. Obviously her sincerity can be questioned as we do not know under what conditions she wrote her testimony, being well aware that she would not escape punishment. Nevertheless, this document uniquely highlights the trajectory of her husband, a man who would become one of the most famous ideologues of Russian collaborationism.

THE CIVIL WAR, ORIGIN OF AN ANTI-SOVIET STANCE

Konstantin Voskoboinik was born in 1895 in the city of Smelak, Kiev province. His father was a railway worker. This category of workers, in comparison with the majority of the population of the Russian Empire, had a privileged position. For the family, the first Revolution of 1905 was a life-changing event. During the revolution Voskoboinik's father took part in a strike committee, and he was therefore subjected to repression by the tsarist government: he was dismissed from the railway service and excluded from future public positions. The family's income deteriorated significantly. Only after the Bolshevik revolution could his father find work on the railroad, and he died of typhus in 1922.[4] At that time, Konstantin Voskoboinik held leftist political views. He sympathized with the then-illegal Socialist Revolutionary (SR) Party. Despite the outbreak of First World War in 1914, he enrolled in the law program at Moscow University, but he dropped out in 1916 to volunteer for the front. In 1919 Voskoboinik fought in the civil war on the side of the Reds, proving himself a good soldier. In 1920, just after he married his wife Anna, he was wounded and discharged from the Red Army, found unfit for military service.[5] Afterward he was sent to work as a secretary at the Khvalynsk military commissariat.

Although an absolute majority of the intelligentsia enthusiastically welcomed the February revolution and the overthrow of the autocratic regime, their attitudes toward the Bolshevik revolution were, if not hostile, then wary and negative. In January 1918, the Bolsheviks dissolved the popularly elected Constituent Assembly. July 1918 was a key date in the final formation of the country's one-party dictatorship, since by then the representation of the so-called "petty-bourgeois democrats"—SRs and Mensheviks—had greatly diminished in the Soviet councils. The civil war and war communism, along with the idea of permanent revolution, led to the devastating impoverishment of the majority of Soviet citizens. Peasant uprisings erupted throughout the country, driven by the despair and utter destruction that resulted from the policy of the new government, which was robbing villages to finance an enormous Red Army and the urban proletariat.

Sympathetic toward the Left SRs and their peasant slogans, Voskoboinik strongly supported these uprisings. In spring 1921, he joined the ranks of the SR forces that were operating in the area of the Saratov province under the leadership of Kirill Vakulin and then of his successor, Fedor G. Popov, and was assigned to operate a machine gun. [6] In the region under his control, Vakulin had "canceled" the dictatorship of the proletariat and given full power "to the people, not divided into classes and parties." He asserted that the idea of a multi-party communism had "a great future." In his opinion all parties, except for the monarchists-reactionaries, had the right to coexist in a Soviet parliamentary republic. The new revolutionary government declared free trade "as a transitional stage to socialist cooperation and dismissed any kind of a state monopoly on key products and manufactured goods." Vakulin-led rebels seized granaries and handed out bread and weapons to peasants, under slogans such as: "Long live Soviet power without Communists and commissars!" and "Long live the free people and free trade!" [7] The rebels recognized a right to small private property, but they would oppose big capital and "avoid the concentration of capital and land in the hands of cooperatives and cooperative organizations." Popov intended to break the blockade of the Soviet Republic by opening relations with the democracies of Europe and America. According to the rebels, the Bolshevik desire to dominate the world was the greatest of all crimes. [8]

Tellingly, at that very time, the Bolsheviks succeeded in sealing their victory in the civil war in the European part of Russia. Finally, peace came. Many members of rebel movements such as the one in which Voskoboinik fought were not supporters of the restoration of the monarchy or of the White army. Rather, in their policy documents, they claimed that the Communists had abandoned the ideals of the revolution. One of the rebel leaders, Grigorii S. Maslakov—who just six months earlier, in July 1920, had been admitted to the ranks of the Bolshevik Russian Communist Party, RCP(b)—wrote in a leaflet-manifesto:

> Comrades! We are not against Soviet power, that is what we are fighting for. ... We are not against the people, we are against the dictatorship from the top, as we are now ruled by dictators.... We want the people to dictate, not one man. We are not against our fellow Communists who follow the right path and work for the good of the people, we are against paper Communists. We promised ourselves and vowed not to lay down our arms until these reptiles are fully destroyed.... Long live free soviets, but these soviets should be properly elected by the people, not appointed from above. Down with all dictators, no matter who they are![9]

The report prepared by the regimental assistant chief in Saratov district, M. T. Molostov, to be sent to the Provincial Committee of the RCP(b) on June 8, 1921, explained the reasons for the success of the anti-Bolshevik rebel groups: "The sentiment of the population of the district, who have all suffered the burden of the campaigns on both sides during three years of civil war, and more than 50 percent of whom are reactionary and sympathetic to the bandits' movement, was apparent in the support that people provided to Vakulin with all means necessary for the bandits."[10]

Anna Voskoboinika would later say about these events:

> In any case, my husband was hostile to the October Revolution and so when in the spring of 1921 Khvalynsk was taken by Popov's White squad,[11] which if I'm not mistaken was drawn from the Volga peasant rebels, my husband joined the squad and left Khvalynsk (which the squad held for two days).
>
> Knowing that I would be very much against such an act, as by that time I had no political beliefs and no hostility to the Bolsheviks, my husband did not inform me about his departure and I learned about it from my colleagues at work, who saw him driving off with the squad.[12]

Anna Voskoboinika remained in Khvalynsk without her husband and then left for Gorky to join her parents. She recorded her husband's disappointment with the rebel movement: "He often told me afterwards that the squad was like a gang because of the poor discipline and the behavior that prevailed there."[13] Indeed, the insurgency in the early 1920s was doomed to failure. The rebel forces were scattered and poorly coordinated, and they engaged in systematic plunder. On April 5–10, passing through the Agkarsk county, the

Vakulin–Popov brigades "caused a lot of destruction to the economic life of the county." In almost every village, they robbed and killed. They took horses, seed grain, fodder, harnesses, clothing, and linens. Not only Communists died at the hands of Popov's brigades, but also ordinary townsfolk.[14] Naturally, people in the Saratov province viewed the insurgents as enemies.

AT PEACE WITH THE SOVIET REGIME: THE NEP YEARS

As a consequence of his time as a rebel, Konstantin Voskoboinik was under constant suspicion by the Soviet authorities. On all questionnaires, including employment applications, he had to answer in the affirmative to the questions: "Have you ever served in the army or institutions of the White governments (White armies)? In which ranks (positions), and where?" and "Have you or your parents lived in the areas occupied by the Whites? When, where, how long, and what was your and your parents' occupation at that time?" On his way home, Voskoboinik seized the documents of a fisherman-farmer named Ivan Ia. Loshakov, born in 1888 and a native of the village of Zolotoe in Saratov region. Under the identity provided by these documents he went downstream to Astrakhan. There he was able to get permission from the People's Commissariat to make a trip to Moscow University and he traveled with the documents to Gorky, where he was sure he would find his wife staying with her parents.[15]

This new stage in the life of Konstantin Voskoboinik, with new documents under a new name, coincided with major changes taking place in the country. The Bolsheviks virtually abandoned their plans to undertake a "cavalry attack on capitalism." The New Economic Policy (NEP) led to a rapid recovery of the economy, which had been almost destroyed during the course of seven years and two wars—the First World War and the civil war. Now Soviet Russia allowed private markets and various forms of ownership, attracted foreign capital in the form of concessions, and implemented a monetary reform. At that time Voskoboinik decided to move to the capital with his wife. As Anna Voskoboinika recounted:

> At this point, his mood was not anti-Soviet, as he was disappointed in the White movement, and only the fear of retaliation made him change his name and start living under a false name. After having spent two or three days in Gorky, my husband went to Moscow, where he got a job as a hunting instructor in the People's Commissariat. (That year, he was unable to enroll in the university.) That fall I too went to Moscow, where I was registered for the second time along with my husband under the name of Loshakova, which I used until 1933.[16]

The stolen name of Loshakov saved them from possible prosecution for participation in the anti-Soviet insurgency. Although Voskoboinik himself came from the family of a railroad worker and was therefore a proletarian, the documents of the fisherman likewise did not assign him to the "the former exploiting class." Consequently, he enjoyed full rights, including the right to higher education, of which he successfully took advantage. His family enjoyed a period of relative stability. From the testimony of Anna Voskoboinika: "In 1922, my husband enrolled in the Plekhanov Institute of National Economy in the electro-industrial department, and I continued to work as a typist in the People's Commissariat. The first years of my husband's studies coincided with the period of the NEP, which kept my husband in seemingly complete agreement with the Soviet authorities. As for myself, I felt absolutely no hostility to the Soviet regime at that moment."[17]

During the NEP years, the Bolsheviks flirted with their former political opponents from other socialist parties, at least with those who were ready to accept their hegemony and join the ranks of the RCP(b). Apparently, Konstantin Voskoboinik was not averse to fitting into this new Soviet system. The need to keep a low profile and not attract excessive attention greatly irritated him and caused him discomfort, but he avoided any conflicts with state authorities for ten long years. Then, in the late 1920s, the Bolsheviks started curtailing the NEP. In 1929 Stalin launched the Great Turn or Great Break, moving the Soviet economy toward total collectivization, and embarked on attacks against the intelligentsia, with campaigns against the so-called "Industrial Party," the "Worker Peasant Party," and the "Federal Bureau of the RSDWP (Mensheviks)." Probably in these circumstances, the best option for Voskoboinik would have been to hide, perhaps even to go somewhere far away from Moscow, where state security control would be weaker and relationships between people were easier and more patriarchal. However, Anna and Konstantin thought differently:

> Being determines consciousness. And so gradually, even imperceptibly, there was more and more resentment toward someone or something. We were living under false names, which meant perpetual fear. This fear created a sense of alienation and distrust of our surroundings.
>
> By nature, my husband and I are very sociable, energetic, and my husband with his level of maturity and determination was an above-average student. At the same time, in view of the circumstances, my husband found it necessary constantly to restrain himself, not to stand out, as he was "vulnerable to exposure." This fear led my husband to become distrustful, morbidly suspicious, and unhappy with everyone around him.

The more he found strength, the more these forces had to be restrained, and the more the dissatisfaction and discontent grew.[18]

A SURVIVAL STRATEGY DURING THE 1930S

Voskoboinik was clearly unhappy with the pace of his career development: "By the time of graduation, while working as a head of the electric measurement workshop in the Chamber of Weights and Measures, by spring of 1931, his sentiments were clearly not on the side of the Soviet government. Rather they took the form of dissatisfaction with life and more. He felt a great desire to work honestly and not at half-capacity, but to make full use of his experience, knowledge, and accumulated energy. To work in this way would only be possible with a legal status."[19] In the spring of 1931, the Voskoboiniks came to a decision that they could no longer continue to live with their current status. In March 1931, Konstantin turned himself in to the NKVD. At that time, Soviet newspapers would devote their front pages to stories about criminals who came to the police to confess. It was said that such people often were not even punished. For example, the famous writer Leo Scheinin, who also served in the Prosecutor's Office, wrote in *Izvestiia*: "Most of the people who came to confess were sent to various cities to work. The Moscow criminal investigation office began sending former offenders to work."[20]

Anna would explain their decision fourteen years later:

What did we hope for? First, we thought that perhaps everything would end well: some restrictions, positive assessment of his work, voluntary recognition, and if he were convicted, it would be better to serve a one-time penalty than to suffer all his life. . . . As a result, my husband was sentenced to three years' imprisonment in a concentration camp. And now I can say with certainty that these were the most peaceful years, both for me and for my husband, despite the fact that throughout these that years he spent in the camps, I had to do a lot of work, and we were not together. But we both knew, and I knew in particular, that these years would pass, and everything would be new again, as it should be.[21]

However, Soviet propaganda and the realities of life in Stalin's Soviet Union were two different stories. Repentance did not bring relief. Although his wife hoped for a while for a favorable outcome, the prisoner himself did not share her optimism. Anna relates:

In 1932, I took time off to visit my husband in the camp, and spent a month with him. And there I noticed the sharp differences that emerged in our moods. If I had full confidence that now our life would improve, my husband thought otherwise. He said that now he would never be trusted, that now everything would be even worse than it was before 1931. He began to criticize the regime bitterly.[22]...

In 1933, in the fall, my husband returned from the camps. I continued to work in Moscow, while my husband applied for a job in Gorky. In Gorky, he could not get a resident registration until he got a job, but he could not find a job (although they said that they needed a worker like him) until he received permission from the NKVD.

So a month passed. He could not find a job. After Moscow, he arranged a job through Narkomtiazhprom in Krivstroi [the metallurgical plant in the city of Krivoi Rog] as a shift engineer in an electrical shop. It was difficult for him to adapt to work at first, given the widespread distrust toward former convicts. But everything gradually smoothed out, and in 1935, work returned to normal.

Then the NKVD called. A few days later my husband was fired from work on the grounds that there was a need for layoffs. Again, he was wandering in search of a job, in search of a corner to live. I left the city and got a job in Gorky, and after a three- or four-month interim my husband got a job in Orsk. There it was the same pattern of distrust. We had to live somehow.[23]

Abiding by the rules did not lead to a positive result. Voskoboinik, who had once had a neutral attitude toward the Soviet government and the Communist Party, had now become a staunch opponent. Konstantin was able to save himself during the great terror by deciding to falsify documents once again and change his residence:

My husband did not see a way out. He found it easier to again live illegally. Around 1936–1937, my husband invented a new biography that concealed his criminal record, and under new personal documents he got a job as a teacher in the Lokot settlement at a college of forestry.[24]...

What had he achieved over the last five years? Instead of Moscow, we now lived in a remote province, held far less interesting and low-paid jobs, and had problems within the family. The situation did not get any better, but instead became much more serious and dangerous. Now, if he were exposed, he would be subject not only to imprisonment, but also to the death penalty.

In those years from 1933 until 1937, my husband developed a hatred of the Bolsheviks that pushed him into active resistance in 1941. Between 1933 and 1937 we lived together only part of the time, so he did not have such a strong influence on me then. After 1937, from the time that he accepted the job at the forestry college, we lived together all the time and were very isolated. My husband was tired of struggling with life. He was unhappy with everything and perceived it all in a very gloomy light.[25]

In the late 1930s, Soviet society existed in two dissociated worlds—the world of the regime's propaganda, and the real world. Newspapers, books, radio, and films all reported on the great achievements in building socialism. The 1936 Constitution guaranteed Soviet citizens freedom of conscience, freedom of speech, freedom of the press, freedom of assembly, freedom to organize protest parades and demonstrations, inviolability of the home, privacy of correspondence, and more.[26] In practice, everything seemed to be the opposite. During their wanderings around the country, the Voskoboiniks had to face the dark side of life in Soviet society. It was not just about personal grievances:

> We were unhappy with life and unhappy with the government. That was clear to me. But my husband said that half of the population was like us and I was beginning to believe him, to be sure that the people were against the Soviets.
>
> Collectivization. We were against collective farms. I myself was opposed not so much to the collective farms themselves, as I thought that collective farms are in essence not a bad thing, but I was against that cruel, in my view, policy that went along with collectivization.
>
> People were without clothing and without shoes. I resented that now, in the twentieth year of the revolution, no one could organize the production of light industry, that they were too obsessed by world issues, world revolution, and that they did not want to care about people, about individuals. They thought only about war. I did not understand it.
>
> And besides, there was a complete absence of freedom of speech, freedom of the press, freedom of opinion.[27]

During this period of history, Soviet propaganda had become extremely militarized, stressing the inevitability of armed confrontation with the capitalist countries. Although the Soviet Union portrayed itself as a peace-loving state, future war was viewed quite optimistically.[28] The Voskoboiniks, however, not only had strong antipathy to Soviet realities, but they also feared that the country was weak and unable to defend itself. The outbreak of war between Nazi Germany and the Soviet Union on June 22, 1941, showed that the vaunted combat capability of the Red Army was a myth. In the first weeks of the war, the Wehrmacht successfully advanced, capturing large territories of the Soviet Union.

THE BIRTH OF THE VIKING PARTY, OCTOBER 1941–JANUARY 1942

The outbreak of war was unsuccessful for the Soviet Union, not only militarily, but also ideologically. German propaganda was no less successful than the Wehrmacht advance. The need to fight ideologically, against the promotion of Nazi ideology, was underestimated by the Soviet leadership. Due to the atmosphere of spy mania of the late 1930s the Soviet Union lacked experienced propagandists: several prominent members of the All-Union Communist Party and the Comintern, who had practical experience in fighting National Socialism in Germany and fascism in Europe more globally, had been arrested. Soviet propagandists of the new generation focused on combating only the symbols of Nazi Germany, such as uniforms and paraphernalia, and while they criticized its anticommunism and anti-Semitism, they did not develop a well-argued position against fascist theories. This propaganda was served in very primitive forms, not only in the media, but also in military academies and higher party schools. After September 1939 and the Ribbentrop–Molotov nonaggression pact, even this inadequate anti-Nazi propaganda practically disappeared.

At the same time, in spring–summer 1941, the Nazi war machine had been well equipped for the war against the Soviet Union. German propagandists enjoyed great freedom in their work and could respond quickly to any enemy action. According to the instructions of Goebbels on June 5, 1941, propaganda against the Russians should be as follows: "no anti-socialism, no return of tsarism; no talk about dismantling the Russian state (otherwise we would embitter the army, which wants Great Russia); against Stalin and his Jewish henchmen; land should be returned to the peasants, but the collective farms should be maintained to secure the harvest. Sharp critique of Bolshevism, we should expose its failures in all areas. The rest can be adjusted in the course of events."[29]

During the second half of 1941, German propagandists made some minor adjustments to these points: for the population of the occupied territories and the soldiers of the Red Army, the war should be presented as a liberation mission, with Germany fighting against Bolshevism. Hitler and his associates had decided to put an end to the barbarity of Stalin and the Communists against their own people and inspire the peoples of the Soviet Union. The success of the Wehrmacht was inevitable not only because it was the strongest army in the world, but also because the Red Army was neither willing nor able to fight for the interests of the Anglo-American capitalists and the All-Union Communist Party. A few days before the attack on the Soviet Union, in a directive addressed to the Wehrmacht,

Alfred Rosenberg stated that, "The use of all means of active propaganda promises more success in the fight against the Red Army than in dealing with all the other enemies of Germany." [30]

Nazi propaganda in the initial period of the war was *"blitz* propaganda," but it was aimed at achieving long-term results. Every citizen of the Soviet Union was supposed to hear what he or she wanted to hear. A representative of the national republics would be offered a promise of independence and prosperity for his or her nation; a farmer, a promise to dissolve the collective farms; a worker, a sharp increase in living standards; the intelligentsia, freedom to act and speak freely.

In her interrogation, Anna Voskoboinika stated that although her husband was full of anti-Soviet feelings, he was not participating in any anti-Soviet activities at that time. "Before the arrival of the Germans, neither I nor my husband (with the exception of his participation in the Popov gang) had undertaken any active efforts against the Soviet regime." [31] Their personal situation dramatically changed with the arrival of Nazi troops. Anna proposed to Konstantin that they should evacuate, but he replied with a categorical refusal:

> Even before the arrival of the Germans in Lokot, I argued with my husband about evacuating. I did not want to remain in occupied territory, and my husband did not want to leave. I was already aware of all the contradictions that we had to contend with against the Germans. The Germans were the enemies of my country, but they were also allies in the struggle against Bolshevism. It tormented me. My husband said that they were temporary, necessary allies. He was sure that the war would provide the necessary external impetus that could easily and quickly topple the Soviet regime. [32]

The events of the first few months of the war, when the Red Army was in rapid retreat, had convinced Voskoboinik that the Russian people were opposed to the Soviets. According to his wife, Konstantin had never thought that Germany could defeat the Russian people; he was convinced the Soviets would collapse, and a new Russian regime would emerge that would then fight against the German troops with real popular support. They thus stayed in Lokot, which was occupied by Wehrmacht on October 4, 1941. The Nazis were very serious in their intentions to attract representatives of the local community to their side. One of the first men to offer them his services was Konstantin, who was trusted not only because he initiated contact with the Germans, but also because he actually had a past history of fighting against the Bolshevik regime in the early 1920s.

On October 20, Voskoboinik received a German-issued certificate appointing him as a prefect. Immediately, under German orders, a local self-government for Lokot city was formed, along with an armed group of volunteers to serve as a public militia squad. From that moment, Konstantin started active work on several fronts. He led both administrative and political initiatives. He rebuilt a local hospital and organized aid donations for the wounded.[33] At the same time, he attached the greatest importance to ideology, propaganda, and political and educational work. As a first order of business he rebuilt a local printing press, as he could not imagine working without the printed word. He wrote a manifesto-appeal, published as Order No. 1, under a pseudonym, Engineer Earth (*Inzhen'er zemlia*). It was printed in large quantities and distributed over the entire Orlov and Kursk regions in areas occupied by the Germans.

The manifesto proclaimed:

On today's date, the People's Socialist Party of Russia has launched its work.

The People's Socialist Party was founded in the underground of the Siberian concentration camps. The shorter name for the People's Socialist Party is Viking (Knight). The People's Socialist Party takes responsibility for the fate of Russia. It is committed to establishing a government that will provide peace, order, and all conditions necessary for the peaceful flourishing of labor in Russia, to maintain its honor and dignity. In its activities, the People's Socialist Party will be guided by the following program:

(1) Complete elimination of the Communist system and the collective farm system in Russia.

(2) Ownership of all arable land to be transferred to the peasantry free of charge to be held by the heirs in perpetuity, with the right to lease and exchange plots, but without the right of sale. (One citizen is entitled to one plot of land.) Plot size is about 10 hectares in central Russia.

(3) Free allocation to every Russian citizen of use of a household plot to be held by the heirs in perpetuity, with the right to exchange, but without the right of sale. Plot size is about 1 hectare in central Russia.

(4) Free development of private initiatives, with individuals permitted to engage freely in all business activities, trade, crafts, and industry. The amount of privately held capital is limited to five million gold rubles for every adult citizen.

(5) Entitlement to a two-month annual leave for all sectors of production, to use for work on one's own household plots.

NOTE: leave extends to four months for workers in hazardous occupations.

(6) All citizens are entitled to receive free timber from state reserves to build homes.

(7) State ownership of forests, railways, natural resources, and all main plants and factories.

(8) Amnesty for all Komsomol members.

(9) Amnesty for all unranked Party members who were not involved in violent practices against the people.

(10) Amnesty for all Communists who participated in armed attempts to overthrow the Stalinist regime.

(11) Amnesty for Heroes of the Soviet Union.

(12) Ruthless extermination of the Jews who served as former commissars.

A new political order in Russia will be constructed on the basis of freedom for workers, private property within the limits established by law, state capitalism complemented and corrected by private initiative, and civil courage.

This program will be carried out after the war ends, and after the accession of the People's Socialist Party to power. The first to receive all benefits will be those citizens who, taking up arms, not sparing their own lives, have acted in the construction and strengthening of the new system. All parasitism and theft must be met with fierce opposition.

Our party is a national party. It remembers and appreciates the best traditions of the Russian people. It knows that the Vikings, with support from the Russian people, created the Russian state in ancient times.

Our country has been destroyed and devastated under the rule of the Bolsheviks. A senseless and shameful war, caused by the Bolsheviks, has reduced many thousands of cities and factories in our country to ruins.

But the Viking party believes in the power and civil courage of the Russian people, and vows to revive the Russian state out of the Bolshevik ruins.

With the spirit of St. George, the Russian army fought and defeated enemies in days gone by, and it will do so again, and therefore our national flag is a white banner with the image of St. George and the St. George Cross in the upper left corner.

Every citizen who shares the program of our party must keep a record of people who want to join it.

Committees of the Viking party should be organized in all regional and district centers.

The People's Socialist Party sends greetings to the courageous people of Germany, who have destroyed Stalin's serfdom in Russia.

Leader of the People's Socialist Party,

ENGINEER EARTH (KPV)[34]

In evaluating this document, we basically agree with Sergei Drobiaz-
ko, who notes a socialist character in the economic part of the program.[35]
Recalling the words of Voskoboinik's wife that "in the NEP period, my
husband seemingly reached complete agreement with the Soviet authorities," it becomes clear that the economic views of the manifesto's authors
were influenced by that economic liberalization, which lasted from 1921
until 1929. Elimination of the collective farm system, free allocation of
all agricultural land to the peasantry, allowing for private initiative while
maintaining state ownership over the primary means of production, and
limitations on private capital—all this, according to Voskoboinik and his
companions, could best address the aspirations of the broad masses of the
population and, above all, the peasantry.[36]

The central political notion of the program is the revival of a Russian
state. In combining socialist but anti-Communist measures with the promotion of Russian nationalism, the leaders of the Lokot self-government
were undoubtedly developing a Russian version of National Socialism,
inspired by its German equivalent. The party's platform makes clear the
need to distinguish the Communist *nomenklatura*, who must be held accountable, from unranked party members, Komsomol members, and Heroes of the Soviet Union, who should be amnestied. The program's strong
anti-Semitism, calling for "ruthless extermination of the Jews who served
as former commissars," could only please the Nazi occupiers, and prefig-
ures late Stalinist anti-Semitism and its fight against cosmopolitanism.

A year later, the collaborationist newspaper *Golos naroda*, which was
printed in Lokot, published an anniversary article about the launch of the
Manifesto: "On the morning of November 25, 1941, the new head of the
printing house, Aleksandr I. Boiarov, received an order from Voskoboinik
and his team to print 'The appeal to the people of Lokot on the beginning of
a new life in liberated Russia,' and to appeal to partisans to abandon their
forest lairs and return to their families and build a new happy life."[37] In
those busy days, Boiarov worked as both typesetter and printer, quickly
and accurately. On November 26, the printing house received a second
document to print, the "Manifesto of the People's Socialist Party of Russia," intended to reach the populations of other liberated areas.

Voskoboinik and his associates, Bronislav V. Kaminskii and Stepan
Mosin, declared with assurance that their movement was all-Russian. The
manifesto was distributed in the Orel, Kursk, Smolensk, and Chernigov/
Chernihiv regions. When bidding farewell to his followers setting off on
promotional trips to these regions, Voskoboinik would tell them: "Do not
forget, we are working not for the Brasovsk district but for all of Russia.

History will not forget us."[38] As stated in the anniversary article, "Thanks to the personal involvement of Kaminskii and Mosin, a manifesto printed in a one- to two-week timeframe was distributed among the population of Orel, Smolensk, Kursk, Chernigov, and other areas. Now the populations of all the liberated areas could read and appreciate the Manifesto of the People's Socialist Party of Russia, signed by Engineer Earth."[39]

Anna Voskoboinika later admitted that: "The manifesto signed by 'Engineer Earth' was born before the party was established. The manifesto was written on November 25, 1941, all of December was spent on its technical design and distribution, and on January 8, 1942, my husband was killed. Therefore, my husband wrote neither the party platform nor the statute. The party itself had not been formally established as an organization. In the event, the release of the manifesto marked the end of the first phase of the 'Viking' party, which later became the NSTPV—the National Socialist Labor Party."[40]

The manifesto's announcement of the beginning of the "new era" and its calls to join the new party were met with indifference by a vast majority of residents of the occupied territories. There was no significant increase in the party's ranks. But the Soviet leadership was far from indifferent, and decided to physically eliminate Voskoboinik and his associates. To do this, they called on Soviet partisan units operating in that area under the command of Aleksandr Saburov.[41] On the night of January 8, 1942, a consolidated partisan unit on 120 carts entered Lokot without a shot and attacked the barracks and the house of the prefect. The partisans had underestimated the strength of the enemy and the first attack was repulsed. After some time the besieged Vikings received some reinforcements. Sensing that victory was near, Voskoboinik came out onto the porch of his house and called on the partisans to surrender, but he was struck by machine-gun fire. Taking advantage of the confusion of the enemy, the partisans were able to freely leave Lokot. Badly wounded, Voskoboinik could not be saved despite the efforts of German doctors who flew in from Orel, and he died on the operating table. According to partisan sources, Voskoboinik's last words were: "And I was going to play a role in history."[42]

VOSKOBOINIK'S LEGACY IN SOVIET LITERATURE

His death was mythologized both by Soviet historians and writers and by supporters of Voskoboinik. It could be interesting to take a short detour to see how Voskoboinik's name was spread in both Soviet and anti-Soviet literature.

Arkady Vasil'ev, a former security officer, the public prosecutor in the trial of Sinyavskii and Daniel, and author of best-sellers, described the day in his novel *V chas dnia, vashe prevoskhoditel'stvo* (At one in the afternoon, your honor):

> On January 8, 1942, Voskoboinik left the house—he was on his way to dine with a German officer in the town council. Voskoboinik was approached by a man in a shaggy fur cap. Two others were standing a little to the side, talking peacefully with security guards.
>
> The one in the fur hat politely stopped:
>
> "Allow me, Mr. Mayor . . ."
>
> "What do you want?" Voskoboinik hastily replied. "Speak," and he opened the car door.
>
> "I was asked to tell you that you are sentenced to death for treason to the Motherland."
>
> Voskoboinik was speechless with fear. The partisan calmly continued, "I have been entrusted to enforce the judgment!"
>
> And he discharged a trophy pistol into the traitor. Two of his companions ran toward the car and threw a grenade at the guards. The guards did not even try to interfere—those who survived the explosion took to their heels.[43]

This description is a complete fiction. General Aleksandr Saburov's memoirs, published in large editions in the Soviet Union, also mentioned Voskoboinik's story. In his *Sily neischislimye* (Countless forces), Voskoboinik got only one paragraph: "Lokot held the headquarters of the so-called All Russia National Socialist Party, which was headed by Voskoboinik, hiding under the pseudonym Engineer Earth. Our scouts found out about this party and tracked down its leaders to their hiding place. We considered how best to neutralize this hornet's nest. In January, our forces raided the Lokot district commander's office. The infamous party and all of its central committee were eliminated."[44]

In Saburov's second book, *Otvoevannaia vesna: partizanskie zapiski* (Recaptured spring: Notes of a partisan), Voskoboinik's story got further attention. Saburov wrote that his intelligence officer Burovikhin had told him that "in the district town of Lokot, people had organized an All-Russia National Socialist Party and that the core of the party was made up of tsarist officers and émigrés, headed by Voskoboinik—pen name Engineer Earth—and that in connection with this party, Burovikhin came to the attention of a certain "important person."[45] This "important person" was a German officer who gave him the task of "gaining the confidence of the party leadership and quietly finding out whether Voskoboinik had any relatives in America."[46] The official warned that in Lokot, Burovikhin would perhaps hear words that would not entirely correspond to his natural respect for the greatness and purpose of the German Reich, but that he should look the other way and report everything to him personally."[47] At a meeting of the partisan commanders, the following information was reported: "Voskoboinik's guard consists of old, experienced tsarist officers. They come from all over—from France, Czechoslovakia, and Poland. This is their core. And even if people did not come to them, in Lokot they have gathered all the scum who had nothing to lose in life."[48]

According to Saburov, Voskoboinik mentioned to Burovikhin that he chose Lokot as his residence because of its historical significance, but also because the city stands on the edge of the Briansk forests—a partisan stronghold.[49] The Soviet partisan commander viewed Voskoboinik as a mere puppet in the hands of the Gestapo Colonel Sperling. "Sperling is about sixty years old. Unlike the majority of Gestapo officers, he is educated, cultured, and well read; has an excellent knowledge of French and English and is fluent in Russian. He has traveled the whole world: he has been to Asia, America, the German African colonies, and lived for several years in Russia."[50]

Partisan scouts even suspected him of playing a game of his own: "Maybe Sperling and the whole company are involved in some conspiracy against Hitler? Maybe they are planning a 'palace coup' in Berlin?"[51]

At the end of this fictional plot, it turned out that Sperling was an agent of the U.S. special services, and was courting Voskoboinik and supporting the creation of his party on behalf of American business interests, which wanted to gain access to the deposits of manganese ore in the area.[52] Saburov depicted the operation to eliminate Voskoboinik as a complete and relatively bloodless victory for the partisans: "The order was given to eliminate Voskoboinik—and Lesha Durnev took him out with a gun. We received orders to crush the officers' guard, this core of the 'party'—and there we also did well; hundreds of enemies were killed. However, all this was achieved not without cost... four of his comrades were killed."[53] Obviously Voskoboinik's companions described this event quite differently. The newspaper *Golos naroda* as of January 8, 1943 published a quite emotional article under the title "A Year without Konstantin Pavlovich":

A year ago, on January 8, 1942, Stalin's brutal gang of thugs attacked the administrative center of the Brasovsk district—Lokot city. The bandits hoped that with one stroke they would take the city and strangle the new people's power, but the enemies had miscalculated. A genuine son of the people led a reviving power: the hero of our time, Konstantin Voskoboinik, whose name inspired and encouraged people to fight Stalin and Jewish slavery.

It was frosty early morning when more than 250 bandits broke into Lokot and surrounded the headquarters. With the first shot Konstantin Pavlovich was on his feet and personally led the fight with the bandits.

It is hard to believe that eighteen soldiers, led by this man of genius, managed to repel the bandits' attack. But they did. Everyone knew that he was fighting for a new, happy life without Jews and commissars. Every soldier knew that where Konstantin Pavlovich is, there is victory. Indeed, the bandits could not withstand the brutal fire of the heroic squad and fled.

But although the gang ran, the dear life of Konstantin Pavlovich ended. He was severely wounded and on the morning of January 9, 1942, he died. However, the idea that he fought and died for did not die; the people held fast to it as they languished under the yoke of Stalin's slavery. From the ashes of Konstantin Pavlovich, new civil leaders, militia fighters, and the people vowed revenge for the bloodshed. The power organized by Konstantin Pavlovich passed into the hands of Bronislav V. Kaminskii, a staunch fighter for a happy future for the people. The People's National Socialist "Viking" Party, organized by Konstantin Pavlovich, took responsibility for the fate of the Russian people.[54]

THE FATE OF THE POST-VOSKOBOINIK NATIONAL SOCIALIST LABOR PARTY

After the defeat of the German troops near Moscow in the spring of 1942, the Wehrmacht and the German intelligence services actively lobbied to change people's perception of the war in the occupied territories, and to step up propaganda in order to consolidate popular support. However, the leadership of the Third Reich, including Hitler, were not convinced of the need to gather more local support and categorically opposed such initiatives.[55]

In April 1942, the collaborationist newspaper *Golos naroda* published the program of the People's National Socialist Viking Party of Russia (PNSPR) and sought to portray their movement as equal to the NSDAP. In the introduction, they stated: "Our party is confident that the great German people would render further help and that the ideas tested in the battles of the German People's National Socialist Party, with its immortal leader Adolf Hitler, are dear to our hearts."[56] In essence, the PNSPR turned into a reduced version of the All-Union Communist Party, with Nazi colors. It honored the cult of the dead leader (Lenin for the Communists, Voskoboinik for the PNSPR), and the cult of the living leader (Stalin, Kaminskii). On the sidelines there was the wife of the dead leader (Nadezhda

Krupskaia, Anna Voskoboinika), megalomania (the Bolsheviks' project to build a Palace of Soviets, Kaminskii's plan to build an enormous monument to Voskoboinik on the model of the "Monument to the Battle of the Nations" in Leipzig, Germany[57]), and changing place names (Petrograd to Leningrad, the town of Lokot to Voskoboinik).

The German leadership was distrustful and suspicious of any political associations in the occupied territories if they were not created with the direct involvement of Nazi intelligence agencies. The attempt by Kaminskii and his colleagues to develop the PNSPR was thus severely restricted. Not until March 22, 1943, did the chief prefect of the Lokot district municipality announce the need for a practical solution to a "completely fair and long overdue" issue—the formation of the National Socialist Party of Russia (called in some documents the National Socialist Workers' Party of Russia).[58] The manifesto of the Russian National Socialists stated that national salvation could be achieved only by combining all the honest people in Russia into one powerful organization. The leader of the party was to be "the head of the new government B. V. Kaminskii."[59] The PNSPR's main agenda declared the following:

1. Overthrow of the bloody Stalinist regime in Russia.
2. Creation of a sovereign state to unite the peoples of Russia.
3. Recognition of the right to self-determination for different nationalities in Russia that are ready for existence as independent states.
4. Elimination of the class-caste strife artificially created by the Bolsheviks, by the establishment of an equitable social order in New Russia.[60]

One point of the agenda stated: "All property rights of the former landowners and capitalists (both Russian and foreign) are considered forfeit." When Russian citizens asked what was meant by foreigners, NSRP activists responded that these were Germans. But when the German leadership asked the same question, the answer was different: "These are the Anglo-American Jewish capitalists, to whom Stalin has sold Russia."[61] Proclamations would usually end with a slogan: "Long live free Russia without Jews and Communists!"[62]

After Voskoboinik's death, his widow was urged to keep a low profile. She acknowledged that,

> After the organization of the Lokot local government, I worked first as chief of staff, then as the head of the general department of self-government. As the head of the general department, I was responsible for all correspondence

(with the exception of the legal department) and registration of the admission and dismissal of employees, and I personally reported to Kaminskii on all requests from the civilian population. In my work, I never spoke publicly. Only two of my articles were printed in the newspaper: "Obituary," on the anniversary of the death of my husband, and a note with recollections of Kaminskii's joint work with Voskoboinik. So my work proceeded until January 1944.[63]

The party was occupied primarily with the situation on the war front. In 1942, the followers of Kaminskii actively fought with the partisans. At that time the Lokot government had a fairly high degree of autonomy. As partisans posed increasing threats to the rear of the German army, Kaminskii continued the militarization of the area. The "Russian People's Liberation Army" was being formed. At the same time, Voskoboinik and his policy documents were remembered only on the pages of newspapers and during solemn speeches. In August 1943, under pressure from the Red Army offensive, the Lokot municipality, with the Kaminskii brigade, moved to Lepel, in the Vitebsk region, in Belarus. There began the second period of the Viking party, which can better be described as the formation of the NSPR party.

Judging by the words of Anna Voskoboinika, Kaminskii was less interested in the ideological aspect of the struggle against Bolshevism than her husband had been:

> The manifesto was released again, only this time signed by members of the central organizing committee (COC): Mosin, Bakshanskii, Vasiukov, Veshilo and Khomutov. After the death of Voskoboinik, when both self-government and the brigade were taken over by Kaminskii, the party work immediately stalled, or rather entirely ceased to exist. Kaminskii directed all his attention to the building and strengthening of the brigade. Whether it was his personal desire and he considered it feasible, or it was done on the orders of the Germans, I do not know. Many of us thought that Kaminskii was not interested in the political work, and so he did not care about it at all.
>
> Anyway, I will say one thing: the brigade completely lacked a proper political-educational program. Such a program did not exist at all, and Kaminskii would always stall when it came to the organization of the party and its design.[64]

On February 15, 1944, the Kaminskii brigades were redeployed from Lepel to Diatlovo in Grodno region, in western Belarus. A few members of the People's Labor Union (PLU) also went there. One of them, Boris Bashilov, described their work: "Kaminskii has long wanted to create a political organization, the idea of which originated from Voskoboinik. The Ispolbiuro of PLU sent him an engineer, Khomutov, who managed to gain Kaminskii's confidence and persuaded him to set up, without the consent of Hitler, a Russian National Socialist Party. Kaminskii, who at that time did not care (this was in Lepel), approved Khomutov's plan. Khomutov 'designed' a party program. In reality, it was an exact replica of the program of the PLU."[65] In her testimony Anna Voskoboinika spoke of Khomutov very positively: "The reason that I switched to active party work should be attributed to my acquaintance with Khomutov. Khomutov made an excellent impression on me. He was energetic, brave, honest, and ideological. He and Bakshanskii are actually the members of the central organizing committee (COC), who wrote the program and the charter of the party, and it is to Khomutov that the party owes its existence, as neither Mosin nor Vasiukov nor Bakshanskii was able to achieve what Khomutov managed to achieve."[66]

At this time, the newspaper *Boevoi put'*, in its article "Our Brigade Commander," in honor of Kaminskii's forty-fifth birthday, declared that "B. V. Kaminskii picked up and fulfilled the idea of K. P. Voskoboinik to organize the Russian National Party. . . . With their concerted efforts a manifesto was laid out, along with a program and charter for the party that reflected the aspirations of the broad masses of the Russian people both on this side and on the other side of the front."[67] Thus, a major party-building process began only three years after the launching of the war. This Russian party was active mainly on the territory of Belarus. *Golos naroda*, which was published in Diatlovo, openly contended that Russians, Ukrainians, and Belarusians were one people. This lasted for nearly half a year.

Starting in Diatlovo, the party proceeded to practical work. It pursued policy and educational work in the brigade, the newspaper *Golos naroda* was taken over by the COC, book stalls selling literature were opened, work was done to disseminate the new ideas, and new members were enrolled. New branches of the COC were opened in Minsk, Polotsk, Dvinsk, and Lepel. The COC organized a Mutual Aid Society and the Russian Union of Youth. During the months of April, May, and June 1944 party work increased, until the evacuation of Diatlovo in July–August 1944. The departure from Diatlovo ended the work, and effectively ended the existence of the party itself.[68]

The most ideological members of the party were PLU adherents. At the time of the evacuation from Diatlovo, only Khomutov decided to stay in the re-Sovietized territories to conduct anti-Soviet propaganda. Boris Prutkov and a group of eight or ten people accompanied him. Khomutov's desire to stay and work on the other side of the front was discussed at a meeting of the COC. All the members of the committee were against it, because they believed that the party should operate on German territory, and that Khomutov himself would be of more use there, especially as there had been no preparation for this transition, and everyone understood that this enterprise was at high risk. However, Khomutov's decision was irrevocable. He believed that in Germany, the Russian party could not exist, that there would be nothing to do there, and the only thing that he could do was to work in Russia, stay underground, and conduct ideological propaganda work.[69]

In July 1944, the brigade, along with the COC, was evacuated to Germany. In September of that year, after the death of Kaminskii, the COC met on German territory in the town of Shemrats, where the brigade was stationed, and it became clear to all that it was both impossible and useless to continue the work of the party. The party was disbanded and its members scattered. Those who were within the reach of the Soviet secret police were arrested. On October 4, 1945, Anna Voskoboinika was sentenced to ten years in prison. She fully—once again, we do not know the conditions under which she wrote her testimony—recognized her responsibility, stating:

> To sum up the work of the party, I must say the following: the party sought to prepare people brought up in the anti-Bolshevik spirit.
>
> The party sought to forge people into active fighters to overthrow the Soviet regime. The party conducted its primary activity within the Kaminskii brigade, which led an active struggle against the partisans and participated in the battles against the regular units of the Red Army. The brigade worked in full contact with the Germans; it worked for the Germans. The party supported the brigade, and therefore the party, even if it is hard to write, worked for the Germans.
>
> Once again it must be emphasized that the political struggle could not take place in a time when the homeland was in a state of war, when the homeland was in danger, and that this fact alone already signifies betrayal of the people, since it undermines the unity of effort and aids the enemy. It is an even greater betrayal when your ally is an enemy of the homeland.[70]

CONCLUSION

The life of Konstantin Voskoboinik is a history of delusions and lies. Although inspired by the ideas of the Bolsheviks, he felt disappointed by them after he began to fight in the civil war on the side of the Soviet authorities. Then he joined a rebel group that had nothing more to offer than smuggling and looting. Voluntary surrender to the NKVD brought him none of what he had hoped for. Finally, the Nazis were willing to accept his idea of a Russian National Socialist Party only in close connection with the anti-partisan movement. Voskoboinik's trajectory is an instructive example of how many Soviet citizens who chose to collaborate with German troops were not genuinely convinced by Nazi ideology—though many of them shared the Nazis' anti-Semitic views. Their main objective was to overthrow the Stalinist regime, even if some were obviously also attracted by the revolutionary genocidal logic of Nazism.

On the night of August 30, 2009, in the village of Lokot in the Briansk region, a group of citizens erected a memorial sign in the form of an Orthodox grave marker at the burial site of Konstantin Voskoboinik. A few hours later the cross and a wreath in front of it had been destroyed. The memory of the conflicts in the former occupied territories is far from being erased even some seventy years after the events.

PART IV

THE POSTWAR EUROPEAN FAR RIGHT'S DRAW FOR THE SOVIET EAST

CHAPTER 7

PRO-SOVIET GROUPS IN THE COLD WAR EUROPEAN RADICAL RIGHT

Nicolas Lebourg, Jean-Yves Camus, and
José Luis Rodriguez Jiménez

Understanding the pan-European nationalism of the postwar period requires that one go back to 1942, when the Third Reich began to make use of the theme of a "new Europe" as embodied in the foreign volunteers of the Waffen-SS fighting on the Eastern front.[1] This idea of pan-European unity under the Nazi umbrella became a key propaganda theme that combined a military strategy for the "Black Order" (getting more and more troops) and a political tactic for the Nazi regime (convincing the populations living under the rule of the Reich and its allies that Nazi rule was not inspired by pan-Germanism). This theme of a "new Europe" created a real ideological divide between German nationalists and pan-European ethnicists. Some of the former, in particular General Gottlob Berger, accepted, though somewhat unenthusiastically, the incorporation of native non-Germans,[2] as it was a useful way of keeping up SS troop numbers to compensate for the heavy losses on the battlefront.[3] By the war's end half of the 900,000-strong Waffen-SS was comprised of non-Germans. The Wehrmacht, on the other hand, stuck to the idea that the German Army should only include Germans (either German nationals or *Volksdeutsche*) and showed disdain for the pan-European idea.

From the start of the postwar period to this day, one of the most powerful mobilizing myths of the European extreme Right has been the epic of those foreign volunteers of the Waffen-SS, deemed a kind of prelude to the emergence of a pan-European national consciousness that would surpass the narrow nationalism specific to nation-states. The myth was propagated through more or less apologetic literary productions situated midway between historical tales and novels, and whose main French representatives were, for instance, Marc Augier (alias Saint-Loup) and Jean Mabire, whose works were published in the 1960s and 1970s by major mainstream publishing houses such as Presses de la Cité, Fayard, and Balland, and sold in the tens of thousands. To acquire political viability after 1945, the extreme Right groups that considered the framework of the nation-state obsolete and promoted a pan-European nationalism had nonetheless to strip the latter of its neo-Nazi coating. They turned it, in the context of the Cold War, into a story about Europe being torn between the two world powers, the United States and the Soviet Union.

This pan-European extreme Right held various, often conflicting views when it came to the future shape of Europe. They were also in disagreement on the links European nations should build with the Soviet Union and, subsequently, with Russia. This variability was compounded by the complex interplay of relationships, especially in France and Belgium, between the New Right that emerged from the GRECE group (Groupement de recherche et d'études pour la civilisation européenne) and the so-called National-Revolutionary and National Bolshevik movements. These three movements have also influenced the esoteric neo-Nazi Spanish underground, born of the neo-Nazi movement CEDADE (Círculo de Amigos de Europa Español), which was launched at the time of the Franco regime. This article analyzes these three ideological trends, which have all displayed, at different levels and with slightly different interpretations, an attraction toward the Soviet Union, Russia, or the socialist bloc.

Since the collapse of the Axis, pan-European nationalism, or Europeanism, has remained the core value for a key segment of neo-fascism that considers the framework of the nation-state to be obsolete or irrelevant. The combined dreams of constructing a united Europe and a pan-European party are deeply linked to the history of Belgian Jean-François Thiriart (1922–1992, known as Jean Thiriart). His life and the history of his movement, Jeune Europe (Young Europe), are difficult to chronicle. The biographical details Thiriart has provided in his numerous writings must be taken with caution, as their author often indulged in mythomania in order to magnify his influence. Moreover, the Parti communautaire national-européen (PCN), which was founded in 1984 and claims to be Jeune Europe's legitimate successor, has produced a series of pseudo-historical texts that present Thiriart and the group as left-leaning, anti-imperialist, and even philo-Communist.

In fact, the history of Jeune Europe, from its inception in 1965 until its demise, through its changes and numerous splits, is first and foremost a story of subversion during the Cold War, and then of an evolving European nationalism aimed at superseding the nation-state. The influence of Thiriart is not restricted to his activity with Jeune Europe, however. He also conveyed some of his ideas to the French group Europe-Action, which was the progenitor of the French New Right as embodied in the GRECE movement, and to its foremost thinker, Alain de Benoist. The topic of Thiriart's activity and ideology is rendered even more complex by the intertwined relations between the French and Belgian extreme Right, as well as by the relationship between the New Right and the national revolutionaries in both countries.

YOUNG EUROPE, JEAN THIRIART, AND THE DREAM OF A EURO-SOVIET EMPIRE

The postwar French extreme Right has had some difficulties in positioning itself with regard to the Soviet Union and the Eastern bloc. During the Nazi occupation years, a staunch anti-Communist stand was the trademark of Marshal Philippe Pétain's regime, but a part of its base found his nationalism too narrow-minded and reactionary and opted to support a Nazi "New European Order" with its focus on Eastern Europe. When the Eastern front was opened up in the summer of 1941, those radical collaborationists came to the conclusion that the fight against the Soviet regime and its ideology had to be fought alongside the Germans, even if, as Jean-Yves Camus has shown previously in this volume, many French volunteers in the Légion des Volontaires français contre le Bolchevisme (LVF), and later on in the Waffen-SS, were sympathetic to the Russian people living under the Soviet regime, whom they saw as the guardians of the lifestyle and values of "eternal Russia," unspoiled by materialism and the influence of the West. This call to arms was exemplified by Jacques Doriot, a former high-ranking member of the Communist Party trained by the Comintern, who in 1935 turned his back on his former ideology and founded the extreme Right Parti populaire français (PPF), which later became the spearhead of pro-Nazi collaborationism. One should also mention the ideological evolution of René Binet (1913–1957), for it is symptomatic of the ambiguities of the postwar extreme Right: a former Communist Youth member (1930), he switched to the Trotskyists (1935), later to fascism, and finally enlisted in the Waffen-SS. While he was one of the most active far-right radicals after the Second World War, he first called for reconciliation between former collaborationists and Communist Résistance fighters, urging them to unite in order to build a socialist Europe separate from the two major blocs.[4] He subsequently showed sympathy for Titoism, describing Marshal Josip Broz Tito as a "Slav Doriot."[5]

Binet participated only marginally in the slow reconstruction of the postwar French extreme Right. However, he inspired many of the groups that emerged in the 1960s, including the Europe-Action experiment led by Dominique Venner, which involved the young Alain de Benoist (b. 1943), the future theoretician of the French New Right. Largely inspired by Lenin's *What Is to Be Done?*, Venner's pamphlet *Pour une critique positive* (1962) advocated a new direction in the ideological and strategic views of French extreme-right radicals, calling on them to drop the tradition of political and military putsches, to build an international alliance of nationalists, and to give up French nationalism in favor of a European nationalism grounded in Binet's belief in the entitlement and supremacy of white people.[6] After 1945, with the threat of communism looming, the remnants of the reactionary extreme Right in France had no reason to feel an attraction to the USSR: the Communists were ousted from the French government in 1947 for fear that they were going to take over the country; France had become a world power again, holding one of the five permanent seats on the UN Security Council; and in any case, the reactionary Right continued to see Marxism, or Bolshevism, as an absolute evil. However, there still existed a minority, with Thiriart as an intellectual reference, who chose the opposite direction and preferred a Euro-Soviet empire to a U.S.-led Europe.

Thiriart launched the Parti Communautaire européen (PCE) in 1965. He considered the United States to be the number one economic, political, and strategic enemy of Western Europe. The new "collabos" (a French popular word used to describe the pro-Nazi collaborationists) were those who were undermining the European community by rechanneling the European project toward the formation of a "plutocratic republic extending from Frankfurt to San Francisco." From then on, the main issue for Thiriart and his group was to engage in a "global struggle against U.S. imperialism," and therefore to draw from the leftist repertoire of the socialist camp.

In its publication *La Nation européenne* (launched September 1967), the PCE did not hesitate, for instance, to publish an article from the Cuban press agency, thereby exemplifying Carl Schmitt's definition of the essence of politics: identifying the main enemy and acting accordingly.[7] The group adopted positions that, while heretical for the extreme Right, were not disconnected from the evolution of public opinion between the 1940s and the 1960s. In France, opinion surveys from the 1960s testify that the image of "eternal Russia" was strongly associated with that of the USSR, whose approval ratings fell from 37 percent in 1964 to 9 percent in 1967.[8] Moreover, the idea that nations could be superseded by a European unity also met with some success, especially among higher social classes. The project for creating a "European nation directed by a central government" had a 29 percent approval rating at that time (rising to 39 percent among managers and professionals).[9]

The evolution of Maoist China led Thiriart to think that a confrontation between China and the United States was inevitable, and that this conflict would enable East Europeans to drive out the Russian occupier from the Warsaw Pact countries. It was thus deemed necessary to work toward an alliance with the Chinese state. This strategy by no means indicated approval of Maoism (which Thiriart thought was barbaric in the primary sense of the term) nor even a real understanding of it (in the official PCE organ, it was said that the "Chinese way" to Marxism started in 1952, a statement that demonstrates a clear ignorance of the facts).[10] For Thiriart, communism was a total failure as a state doctrine, but it had proved a complete success as a religion and mode of management of the masses.[11] Yet in order for a national-communitarian Europe, "that is to say a non-Marxist Europe," to come into being, Western nationalists and Eastern Communist leaders were going to have to reach an understanding. It would be necessary for China to adopt a "united front" policy (sometimes called the "Front National") against the USSR and the United States, to support European nationalists, and ultimately to become an ally of a communitarian Europe. In the meantime, "anti-American subversion, of a paramilitary character, and then in the form of a military one, [required] the use of inviolable sanctuaries, bases for rest, for training," which China could provide. Thiriart's new position therefore did not, as has often been claimed, advocate the establishment of a dialogue with the Left, much less a conversion to Maoism. His ideology remained perfectly summarized by an image on the front page of an issue of his newspaper: a Communist flag being pulled back to reveal a Celtic cross. The headline reads "A European National Communism?"[12]

Nevertheless, Thiriart forged links with the East; in the summer of 1966 he published an article in the official Yugoslav magazine *Medunarodna Politika* and allegedly met with Zhou Enlai in Bucharest. Relations were in any case good enough at the time that, after having met in Francoist Spain in 1966, the PCE envisaged holding its 1967 summer camp in Romania.[13] According to Thiriart, he asked the Chinese prime minister to commit to launching a "quadri-continental" war against the United States, and to include in it that "richest colony of the United States," Europe. The aim was, of course, to weaken U.S. military forces by stretching their resources, but also to provide a "rear base" for the guerrillas and spur them to action.

Thiriart also built increasingly solid contacts with the Arab-Muslim world. The Syrian and Iraqi ambassadors as well as Palestinian and Algerian leaders were all interviewed in *La Nation européenne*,[14] a newspaper distributed in Algeria, which specialized in reprising Soviet propaganda and also promoted Arab and Palestinian nationalist ideas that equated Zionism with Nazism. It was claimed that Jews as a whole were united with Israel and the proposal was made to move the European Jewish population to the United States.[15] However, the newspaper also published a "pro-Zionist" article from "our correspondent in Israel," stating that the Jewish genius could develop only in Israel, which would welcome Jewish immigrants from the world over.[16] It then accused the Jews of controlling the West and of attempting, via Israel, to extend their domination around the world. Thiriart also met with the Iraqi head of state, Ahmed El Bakr, after his coup d'état in July 1968. Some weeks later, Thiriart was received in Libya and in Egypt, where he participated in a congress of the Arab Socialist Union. *La Nation européenne* featured advertising by the League of Arab States and the Palestinian Liberation Organization (PLO). Indeed, it seems to have been the support of the PLO that enabled Thiriart to stay afloat financially; in 1967, when Yasser Arafat replaced Ahmed Shukeiri at the head of the organization, both the newspaper and the PCE disappeared.[17]

Connections with the Arab world were considered so close that Portuguese secret service documents accused the PCE "of being linked with the secret services of certain Arab countries."[18] Among his Arab nationalist partners, Thiriart again tried to promote collaboration in the framework of his so-called quadri-continental guerrilla warfare. He proposed that they train European brigades who would lend their support to a war for the destruction of Israel, and would use that combat experience to acquire the military skills needed to form a "Popular Liberation Army of Europe." In support of this engagement, Thiriart's ideological heirs claimed that the first Europeans to die fighting against Israel was Roger Coudroy, one of the PCE's militant members who had been trained by Fatah.[19] In the fall of 1967, Gérard Bordes, one of Jeune Europe's leading French members, allegedly sent a memorandum to the Algerian authorities proposing the establishment of an anti-Zionist and anti-American intelligence service in Europe. He also asked the Algerians to provide terrorist training to European nationalist militants.

In order to counter the United States, Thiriart invited Europe to rethink its relationship with the Soviet Union. He contended that European culture could only continue to exist with help from the USSR, as "a Weltanschauung of the 'homo novus' might possibly emerge from communism, but not from the bric-a-brac of American metaphysics." Thiriart therefore stopped denouncing the "Mongolian hordes crouched behind an Asian Bolshevism," but instead recognized in the USSR some pan-Slavic leanings and an ethnically European character.[20] From the 1980s until his death onNovember 23, 1992, Thiriart became an ever stauncher supporter of Russia. A theoretical text that he wrote in 1983, after fourteen years of political inactivity, shows his increasingly positive evaluation of the USSR.[21] At the same time, he had come to the conclusion that "there is a real will to make the USSR collapse" among Jewish American and "Zionist American political leaders."

Consequently, he felt that an alliance between Europe and the USSR was needed, with Europe permanently shutting down U.S. military bases on its soil and the USSR recognizing that Africa and the Middle East should remain in Europe's zone of influence (evidence of Thiriart's unrepentant "Eurafrican" theories from the late 1950s–early 1960s). At that stage of his career, Thiriart explicitly believed that Russia was part of Europe, and that the idea that Russia was intrinsically Asian was purely a Nazi misconception. According to him, both the USSR and Western Europe could agree on a kind of Monroe doctrine based on "Europe for the Europeans," an idea that had already been proposed by Belgian collaborationists[22] and several Nazi dignitaries at the end of the Third Reich (although it would be more accurate to see this as the postwar pro-Nazis' attempt to reinterpret their writings as support for an enlarged Europe rather than an imperialistic Germany).[23] Thiriart believed that this partnership could ultimately lead to the building of a Greater Europe "from Dublin to Vladivostok."

While working with the Spaniard José Cuadrado Costa, he came around to the idea that only Russia could serve as the cornerstone of a "Greater Europe." In 1984, in the journal of the Parti communautaire national-européen (PCN), Cuadrado Costa introduced references to the Russian National Bolshevik movement—specifically to Nikolai Ustryalov, its founder in the 1930s—and got the endorsement of Thiriart, who highly praised his article and recommended it as a must-read "intended for a highly educated readership."[24] Thiriart saw the USSR (later the Russian Federation) as the new frontier of the imperial European dream.[25] He began writing a book (never finished) on the "geopolitics of the Euro-Soviet empire." He also started to work on a book with Cuadrado Costa, to develop the concept of a "totalitarian" political system to be implemented in the empire, a kind of "hyper-communism purged of Marxism."[26] It should be remembered that this approach was much more pro-Russian than pro-Soviet. When Thiriart was dreaming of a merger of the USSR and Europe in order to regain power over Africa, he was actually plowing his usual furrow. As with many French Nazi collaborators, his call for a "Eurafrican" union was only a way to establish white supremacy on the African continent and exploit the natural resources of Africa in the interests of Europe. While forcefully quoting Mao, Lenin, and Stalin, he argued that economically the new Europe should be based on "communism without Marx," which the leader of the PCN, Luc Michel, had compared to the New Economic Policy (NEP).[27]

It is therefore not surprising that Thiriart, whose publications in the 1960s already indicated his knowledge of the German Conservative Revolution, now claimed to be a "European National Bolshevik," favoring a Jacobin empire from Reykjavik to Vladivostok. The duty of European nationalists was thus to prepare for the invasion of Europe by the Red Army.[28] Thiriart called for a European Communitarian Party that would be "transnational, with cells from Dublin to Vladivostok, intended to draw on the best of the [Communist parties] as it was also important to create a transnational right party. . . . Finally, the project of a Greater Europe, a Greater European Republic, is likely to interest the industrial community."[29]

This ideological change occurred after Thiriart and his followers, at the end of the 1960s, had rediscovered the ideas of Ernst Niekisch, as they were now disseminated by German national-revolutionary groups such as the Sache des Volkes–Nationalrevolutionäre Aufbauorganisation (SdV–NRAO). The SdV–NRAO asserted that the political struggle should follow the motto "For the Cause of the People and the Nation," which refers to an expression of Lenin: "Make the people's cause the cause of the nation and the cause of the nation will be the cause of the people."[30] The motto was used for the first time on the extreme Right by Arthur Grosse, in an article in the *bündisch*[31] journal *Das Junge Volk* (published by National Bolshevik Karl-Otto Paetel) in 1929. Grosse became a National Bolshevik agitator, and in this article he endorsed the concept of class struggle.

From then on, the motto became very common in the National Bolshevik movement. François Duprat first used the expression in France in his weekly *Les cahiers européens* (1973–1978), and within a few years, it became an essential marker of the nationalist-revolutionary movement. Indeed, the motto was quoted in each manifesto, printed repeatedly, and became a slogan throughout nationalist-revolutionary Europe. Anyone using the motto from a right-wing perspective was labeled a national-ist-revolutionary. It should be noted that the nationalist revolutionaries did not achieve any ideological synthesis, since at the same time they claimed affiliation to the nationalist declaration of the German Communist Party (1931), which Lenin in his time had sharply rebuked for "nationalist infantilism."

The SdV–NRAO served widely as an example for non-German movements. Breakaway members of the SdV–NRAO criticized it for being a reactionary organization, and merged with Maoist dissidents to found joint cells within the environmental movement and to advocate for neo-Soviet councils there. Only about thirty militants participated in this split, but the operation took on symbolic importance and generated a militant mythology among some German nationalist revolutionaries at a much later stage, playing a leading role in the agitation surrounding the euro-missiles crisis.[32] This pattern of pretending that Far-Leftists had joined the national revolutionaries in a common fight likewise unfolded within the PCN (as well as in the SdV–NRAO), which still claimed to have been born, in 1984, from the common opposition of nationalists, Maoists, and environmentalists to Pershing missiles. The PCN clearly put forward this would-be trans-ideological nature of its program at the European level when in 1993 it sought to replace the European Liberation Front (ELF, a self-proclaimed National Bolshevik pan-European network set up in 1991 under the influence of Thiriart and Aleksandr Dugin) with what it called a Black–Red–Green Front.[33]

Thiriart's ideas were popularized in Russia by Aleksandr Dugin in 1992, the year Thiriart traveled to Moscow to meet the so-called national-patriotic opposition. He died shortly thereafter, but his disciple Luc Michel tried to build on this legacy. The first issue of the publication launched by the PCN after its break with the ELF presents an editorial titled "Leader" accompanied by a photograph of PCN leader Luc Michel standing under a portrait of Lenin. The head of the PCN declares: "For National-Communism, or European National Bolshevism, which we prefer to call 'communalism,' the Battle of Moscow is a landmark. From now on, European National Communism is no longer just an activist praxis in some vanguard organizations like the National-European Communitarian Party or the Russian National Salvation Front. It is above all a community of activists, a reality of flesh and blood, sacrifice and hope."[34] There was clearly an idea here that Russia could serve as an "external base" for European nationalists' actions, along the lines set out by Thiriart. This alliance also held out the possibility of providing a left-wing and Eastern aesthetic for Western Europe's radical Far Right that would allow it to escape the shadow of the fascist regimes.

The trajectory of Jeune Europe and its heirs raises a number of unresolved issues. The first is Thiriart's yet-to-be-written biography, since, as it stands, his path as a militant owes as much to legend as to reality. The second is the muddle of accusations made against a number of the movement's cadres that they were agents, or even double agents, of intelligence services with opposing interests in the fight against communism and the USSR. It is also a possibility that the ideological reversals of Jeune Europe cannot be attributed to organized counter-subversive measures typical of the 1960s, but can be explained instead by the organization's mutations in response to geopolitical changes in Europe.[35] Research is still needed into the nature and scope of the contacts between Thiriart and his Arab, Romanian, and Chinese contacts, since we have little to go on other than the version provided by Jeune Europe on this topic.

Jeune Europe remains a unique example of a centralized pan-European nationalist extreme Right movement. Its originality and its contribution to promoting a European geopolitical space in the form of a single united nation-state are beyond question. The movement, even if small in numbers, was a training school for several key contemporary figures, among them the member of the European Parliament from the Northern League, Mario Borghezio, the respected Italian medievalist Franco Cardini, and Vlaams Belang's former regional councilman, Ludo Monballiu. A number of extreme-right groups have continued to spread Thiriart's work and ideas. Particularly noteworthy are Christian Bouchet in France, with the Nouvelle Résistance movement, and Juan Antonio Llopart Senent in Spain, with the Movimiento Social Republicano (MSR). In contrast, Luc Michel and his PCN (which published a single issue of *La Nation européenne* in June 2005) espouse a National Bolshevik orthodoxy that denies all connections with the extreme Right and currently engages in supporting Russia through Michel's nongovernmental organization, the Eurasian Observatory for Democracy and Elections (EODE).[36]

THE FRENCH NEW RIGHT AND THE THIRD WAY MOVEMENT

Thiriart's ideas also influenced the premises of the New Right and inspired the launch of the French journal *Europe-Action*. In the wake of the political disaster experienced by supporters of French Algeria when President de Gaulle decided to grant independence to this former French territory (1962), *Europe-Action* reaffirmed the neo-racist views of Binet and of the American Francis Parker Yockey (1917–1960) regarding the unity of the white world. But it did not adopt the positive approach to the USSR developed by Yockey, who believed the neo-fascists would have to form an alliance with the Soviet Union if they wanted to break the alleged "Jewish-Israeli" yoke under which the West lived.[37] During the ideological transition from French to European nationalism, several fringe groups of the French extreme Right, including Jeune Europe, tried to temporarily join the Left, not adopting socialism, but hoping to further their cause by allying with the left wing in its opposition to the conservative Right. This initiative included a call to join François Mitterrand's Federation of the Democratic and Socialist Left, praise for Tito's independent policy after 1968, and even hopes of uniting with the anarchist movement.[38] These tactics, however, ran into a structural problem of the extreme Right, namely its misunderstanding of leftist ideological concepts. The same issue of *Europe-Action* could, for instance, paint a rosy picture of Titoism (with its "own path to socialism that would not have been repudiated by Proudhon") and claim that the "legacy of Stalin" was the establishment of a "national communism" transplanted to the West,[39] without perceiving the obvious contradictions. This inconsistency testifies to the limits of the far-right attempt to co-opt leftist narratives.

Changes in the portrayal of the USSR on the French extreme Right were due less to developments in the Soviet Union itself than to the cultural transformations of French society. First, the French intellectual scene rediscovered the legacy of the Conservative Revolution. In 1972, the left-wing philosopher Jean-Pierre Faye published *Les Langages totalitaires*, a book analyzing the German Conservative Revolution, with particular attention to Otto Strasser and Ernst Niekisch. The book also popularized the concept of the "horseshoe," according to which political ideologies should not be represented as a Left–Right spectrum with the extreme Left and the extreme Right at opposite ends, but instead should be shown with left and right coming together like the two ends of a horseshoe and thus able to join a common fight against "the System." The same concept was disseminated by the Paris-based German journalist Armin Mohler.[40] A few years later, in 1978, the historian Louis Dupeux published his doctoral dissertation on the history of German National Bolshevism, thus providing the French public with in-depth knowledge of this previously little-known political ideology.[41] The German National Bolsheviks had a profound impact on such national revolutionaries as Christian Bouchet, Luc Michel, and Yves Bataille, who acknowledged a debt to those authors for helping them break away from their previous conceptions of Europe.[42]

Finally, in 1984, the historian Patrick Moreau published an article on Strasserism that significantly influenced extreme Right perceptions, as the author made analogies to Albania, the Khmer Rouge, and Maoist China. When Armin Mohler died in 2003, the French national-revolutionary press stated that his model for the Conservative Revolution had "a fundamental influence (along with those of Louis Dupeux and Jean-Pierre Faye) on the redefinition of the national-revolutionary orthodoxy."[43]

In 1981, for the first time since the beginning of the Fifth Republic, France experienced political change with the election of François Mitterrand, a Socialist, as president. Mitterrand's Cabinet included four Communist ministers. At the same time, and despite that change, which stirred up considerable fear within the ranks of the conservative Right and the traditional extreme Right, GRECE changed its views on the USSR. A *völkisch* leader of GRECE, Pierre Vial, who came from Europe-Action, had been influenced by Binet, and was the godson of the collaborationist Pierre Clementi. He stated that the USSR was the embodiment of the eternal Russian empire, "which probably holds the key to the future of the world." A year later, Alain de Benoist went even further by stating that the USSR was "much more Russian than Marxist" and that, compared to the United States, it was "objectively less inclined to universalism, to egalitarianism, and multiculturalism."[44] However, GRECE still positioned itself as belonging to the rightist camp. The 1981 annual forum of the New Right examined the question of "an alternative to socialism" and GRECE explicitly presented itself as a contender for political influence on the right. In 1983, at the GRECE conference on the "Third Way," Alain de Benoist declared that he was providing ideological ammunition for the parliamentary Right in their collective struggle against the Left, which had come to power in May 1981 and, at that time, included Communist ministers in the Cabinet. Pierre Vial, however, admitted to being extremely disappointed by the parliamentary Right. The same year saw several failures in a row in GRECE's strategy: the termination of links between GRECE and the Hersant media group, influential among the right-wing government parties; a sharp drop in sales of the New Right flagship journal *Éléments*; the closure of the Copernicus publishing house; and the departure of many GRECE members who joined the Front National.

In 1984, the GRECE discourse shifted more openly to the left and to the East. At the movement's annual conference, Alain de Benoist declared, "some are not resigned to the idea that one day we will wear Red Army caps. Indeed, this is not a pleasant prospect. But we cannot stand the idea of having to spend the rest of our lives eating hamburgers in Brooklyn."[45]

Pierre Vial attacked the "bourgeois system" by glorifying Che Guevara, the Red Brigades, and the Baader-Meinhoff group; he called for a "common front between revolutionary leftists and revolutionary rightists" to overthrow the system. Finally, in the columns of the *Partisan européen*, a journal linking the New Right with a *völkisch* and nationalist-revolutionary tendency, Alain de Benoist proclaimed his sympathy for the Eastern bloc and declared that he had voted for the French Communist Party, which had become an expression of "national populism."[46]

Should these assessments be seen as a sincere move to the left or a shift to the East? Probably not. In fact, this philo-Communist detour led ultimately to a modernization of revolutionary-conservative views, which took place after the failure of relationships with various components of the rightist camp, when the New Right saw its political and intellectual space narrowed by the first electoral successes of Jean-Marie Le Pen's Front National.[47] At that time the Front National promoted a free-market economy, and the shift toward an anti-capitalist narrative was a way for GRECE to dissociate itself from Front National and maintain its ideological specificity. Moreover, GRECE had come into the media spotlight during the summer of 1979, when the mainstream press accused it of recycling Nazi ideas within the conservative Right. It may also be asked whether pro-Soviet proclamations by GRECE, following the entry of Communist ministers into the Mitterrand government, may have fueled the criticism of Stalinism as "a fascism of the Left," a controversial strategy followed by the New Right–inspired Club de l'Horloge, and subsequently co-opted by various parts of the mainstream Right.

In the political space ranging between the New Right and the national revolutionaries, it is worth mentioning the writing of Jean Parvulesco, a Romanian-born émigré who was close to the New Right but had a distinct esotericist doctrine that later influenced Dugin. Parvulesco was inspired by the geopolitics of Halford Mackinder and by Julius Evola's Nazi-inspired "spiritual racism." He argued that Stalin's policy was aimed at creating a "Eurasian continental unity, the occult goal of which was to launch a world revolution from the center of the Earth, and to work toward the goal of the Polar thinkers, that is, the transhistoric pursuit of the Heartland, at the end of the last age of Darkness."[48] According to Parvulesco, Eurasia should become the zone of dialectical confrontation between the United States and the Soviet Union, ending in "a new unity of civilization [within] the same community of civilization, of being and destiny."[49] This geopolitical-esoteric formulation of Europe-Action's ideology means that the fate of the white world is that of the Eurasian continent. It is the forerunner of the theories developed in the post-Soviet period by "identitarian" figures like Pierre Vial and Guillaume Faye. Parvulesco was one of the first to assert that the Soviet Union's destiny was to save the white race.[50]

National Bolshevism ideology also found a second revival on the periphery of the New Right. One should particularly mention the publication *Vouloir,* run by the Belgian neo-rightist Robert Steuckers, a follower of Thiriart who also espoused a *völkisch* ideology. In two articles published in 1986, Thierry Mudry, a proponent of a pan-European ethnic nationalism who was close to the PCN and to Nouvelle Résistance, reminded his comrades that the concept of a "Third Way" was also present in Niekisch's texts.[51] Mudry and Steuckers then went on to work with Guillaume Faye, an important theoretician of GRECE who regularly worked with national revolutionaries. The three of them launched the periodical *Le Partisan européen*, which played the role of a lexical-ideological laboratory for the radical Right. All kinds of hybrid trends were inspired by Mudry and Steuckers, who introduced both the National Bolshevik eagle emblem and the ideas of Niekisch in France and Belgium.[52]

The economic model promoted by the French and Belgian National Bolsheviks was inspired by Strasserism, though its doctrine was based on the notion of autarkic racial empires. Using Patrick Moreau's article mentioned above, *Le Partisan européen* paid tribute to the supposedly "pro–small farmer nationalist socialisms" of the Khmer Rouge, Mao, and the Albanian regime. According to Thierry Mudry, Mao, Pol Pot, and Enver Hoxha were "nationalist revolutionaries" who rejected the homogenizing character of Marxism in favor of *völkisch* approaches: "Marxism-Leninism, in its Stalinist version, is a form of nationalism with an ethnic foundation (based on ethnic identity and purity) and a historical one (the Communist Party, and especially the supreme leader taking control of the Albanian, Chinese, or Khmer state)."[53] In the same publication, Alain de Benoist too proclaimed his support for the Oriental versions of communism.

A third step in the revival of National Bolshevism took place in 1991 with the collapse of the Soviet Union. Seeing that Jean-Marie Le Pen was not willing to accept the return of a national-revolutionary tendency in the Front National, and having read an article on the concept of the "periphery" in the Conservative Revolution under Weimar, Christian Bouchet launched Nouvelle Résistance, a National Bolshevik group that drew on the ideology promoted in *Partisan européen* and the work of Jean-Pierre Faye. After the fall of the USSR, National Bolshevism was held up as a new horizon for European radical nationalism, and from this point of view,

Nouvelle Résistance influenced its counterparts in several European countries. Neo-rightists and European national revolutionaries came together in the European Liberation Front (ELF), which positioned itself as a continuation of Jeune Europe. Niekisch was deemed a prophet by Alain de Benoist. Stalin was venerated by Nouvelle Résistance as the "visionary figure of the complete revolution of the twentieth century," because his achievements were anti-capitalist, anti-individualist, anti-Western, anti-Zionist, and communitarian in the sense that he had worked toward a *Volksgemeinschaft* (People's Community), a national community transcending class divides and grounded in a mystical belief in the national interest being put above the individual's rights. In this context, Robert Steuckers went so far as to proclaim in the press of the European Communitarian Party that "anti-Stalinism is a variant of the globalization discourse."[54]

National Bolshevism thus came to the rescue of the French and Belgian extreme Right, which was in search of its own political space, lexicon, and vision. Still, the ethnic question remained central for them. Nouvelle Résistance stated it was campaigning for "the power of the councils ... a type of political organization ... known in Europe since the appearance of Indo-Europeans,"[55] explicitly referencing the Nordic (Viking) popular assembly, a reference that really has nothing to do with the self-proclaimed "Leninism" of the group. This idea was in fact drawn from the National Bolshevik intellectual Paul Eltzbacher (1868–1928), who tried to reconcile the *Volksgeist*[56] theory with that of the people's councils. According to Eltzbacher, National Bolshevism was the antidote to Marxism because the Soviets were an "organic construction" that introduced "the ordered dictatorship of the entire working people." Nouvelle Résistance also took inspiration from another representative of the German Conservative Revolution, Karl-Otto Paetel (1906–1975), who proposed a revision of the Nazi Party program to include an alliance with the USSR and a *völkisch* Aryan "people's state of councils." Paetel recognized the existence of the class struggle, and believed that the nomenklatura of the socialist countries should be destroyed along with the bourgeoisie in order to establish a Proudhonian-style socialism.[57] A similar pattern of National Bolshevism can be observed in the Spanish Far Right as well.

SPANISH NEO-NAZI CEDADE AND ITS NATIONAL BOLSHEVIK TEMPTATIONS

Following the defeat and unconditional surrender of the Third Reich and its allies, postwar Spain became a refuge for a large number of officials of the SS, Wehrmacht, and other Axis armies, as well as leaders of various fascist parties. During the early years of the postwar period, some subgroups of Spanish fascists, primarily those belonging to radical factions on the periphery of politics, revived relations with neo-fascists and neo-Nazis from other European countries. This allowed an electorally very weak Spanish extreme Right to play an important role at the European level in promoting neo-Nazi narratives.

The Origins of Neo-Nazism in Spain

The first predecessor of Spanish neo-Nazism was the Spanish delegation of Jeune Europe. Jeune Europe continued the work of the European Social Movement (ESM), a pan-European nationalist group created and maintained by an international neo-Nazi network. ESM was founded as a rival to the New European Order that aimed to take advantage of discontent in Belgium following the loss of colonial territories in the Congo; meanwhile, their contacts with the extreme Right in France were connected to the paramilitary OAS (Organisation de l'armée secrète). These associations functioned as an international platform, with national delegations and an array of publications dedicated to critiquing decolonization in Asia and Africa, defending the superiority of whites over blacks, and claiming the superiority of European culture over all others. Their goal was to restore the "old continent," which was in decline after the two world wars, as a viable alternative to the powers of the United States and the Soviet Union.

Jeune Europe opened an office in Madrid in October of 1962, and a second in Zaragoza shortly thereafter. Its members were radical Falangists, activists, and intermediary units of FET-JONS (the Franco-led Spanish Traditionalist Falange of the Juntas of the National-Syndicalist Offensive) under the direction of Antonio Méndez García. Their activity was limited, consisting of sending one representative to the organization's meetings in European cities, along with editing and distributing a series of memoranda and promoting or participating in political acts—for example, some worked on commemorating the anniversary of the death of the Romanian fascists Ion Moța and Vasile Marin on the Madrid front during the Spanish Civil War. It is possible that funding for all of these activities was granted by FET-JONS. Though Jeune Europe was supported by its political affiliation with the Falangists, who were accustomed to ultranationalist Spanish ideals in the form of National Catholicism, the organization's statutes established the study and development of "united European thought" as an objective. However, they did not specify what that meant;

their documents presented anti-Semitic, anti-Communist, and anti–North American content.[58] In any case, Jeune Europe had a limited impact outside of Belgium, and the Spanish delegation ceased operations in 1963.

During the following years, there emerged other groups that declared Nazi principles or expressed admiration for neo-fascist and neo-Nazi groups operating in Europe at that time. These groups appeared in Barcelona. Radical Falangists had settled in that city, some of them former combatants in the Blue Division that had been sent by Franco to support the Wehrmacht on the Russian front. This faction generally held a highly critical view of the official party apparatus. Some of these Falangists made use of the ample funds available for the dissemination of propaganda and the functioning of presses dedicated to propagating the ideology of Hitler's Germany and Fascist Italy, in many cases through accounts of the war. It is likely that these Falangists received funding from the party even as they criticized it, and also were supported by Nazi émigrés.

It can be supposed that the Belgian Léon Degrelle, who owned estates in Spain, also assisted these groups, along with the Austrian Otto Skorzeny, who directed an engineering company, and the Croatian fascist leader Ante Pavelić, who owned a press in Valencia. Most of the more notorious Nazis and fascists lived at least partially in hiding. People became more aware of this situation when the rumor spread that Israeli agents or a Jewish militia from Belgium had attempted to kidnap Degrelle, and that Pavelić had survived two assassination attempts at the hands of agents of the Yugoslav government during his stay in Argentina. Nonetheless, there were various Nazis who contributed money for the production of books, for travel abroad, and for the organization of political actions in Spain.

The Rise of CEDADE

In 1965, several groups of Spanish fascists held a meeting in Barcelona to discuss the creation of an association in Spain that would be based on Nazi ideology. Their first step was to establish a society dedicated to the appreciation of Richard Wagner,[59] and next, to obtain status as a political organization, which was permitted under the law of associations implemented the year before. In September 1966, Círculo Español de Amigos de Europa (Spanish Circle of Friends of Europe, or CEDADE) was officially established. During the initial stage of CEDADE's existence, the association was in the hands of individuals associated with the Falange such as Ángel Ricote and Pedro Aparicio. However, after first using premises lent by FET-JONS, from 1968 onward CEDADE occupied a property in Barcelona and dissociated itself from actions linked to the Falangists' political agenda. The constituents of the executive junta declared themselves to be pan-Europeanists and Catholics, showing respect for Franco's regime and, in large measure, for FET-JONS. While they also held positive views of the Spanish fascist party, they reserved their true admiration and enthusiasm for Nazism.

Beginning in January 1967, CEDADE circulated an information bulletin whose early editions were produced using the cyclostyle duplicating process. The bulletin included information about local activities as well as news from abroad about other neo-Nazi organizations. It praised the apartheid laws in South Africa and the statements of politicians like George Wallace, an American Independent candidate in the 1968 presidential election who strongly promoted racial segregation in schools. There was no shortage of derogatory statements directed at Roma, Jews, and dark-skinned races in general. One of the identifying characteristics of CEDADE's bulletins was denial of the Holocaust, a theme that also showed up in the publications of the Falangists, but on a smaller scale. The Nazi fugitives Skorzeny and Degrelle came to play a particularly relevant role in the history of CEDADE.

In 1970, CEDADE had relatively small operating groups in Barcelona and several nearby areas in Catalonia, as well as in Madrid, Alicante, Málaga, Murcia, Zaragoza, Seville, and Valladolid. In all, there were approximately 200 active members.[60] In February of that year, Jorge Mota gained the presidency of CEDADE, and from then on emphasized the Nazi orientation of the organization, although they strategically maintained links with Falangists and the ideology of the Falange party, founded by José Antonio Primo de Rivera during the 1930s.[61] This was the only logical option given the limited number of CEDADE members as compared to the thousands of people who attended Falangist rallies and public meetings.

The emblem adopted by CEDADE was an eagle sitting upon a yoke with a torch rising behind its back. In this design, the eagle symbolized both Germany and Spain (the Spanish eagle of San Juan). The yoke was taken from the Falange ensign; the eagle and the torch came from Nazi imagery. These elements appear inside a Celtic cross or solar cross, a symbol that was adopted by Jeune Europe and utilized by neo-Nazi and neo-fascist groups throughout Europe. The Nazi and Falangist symbolism represented the inexorable victory of youth, as it was the incarnation of light and order in the European culture and race. CEDADE's inspiration and its sources of political authority were not sought inside Spain, but rather abroad, particularly in the work and movements directed by Adolf

Hitler, Léon Degrelle, and Corneliu Codreanu. It is also possible to trace in CEDADE's publications the influence of Jean Thiriart, Julius Evola, and Alfred Rosenberg, the biological racist arguments of Arthur de Gobineau, and the works of Richard Wagner and the poet Dietrich Eckart. However, in relation to race and racism, CEDADE managed to offer a "moderate" account of its ideals and aims, without falling into the virulent racism of its predecessors. This may have been because CEDADE's leadership knew that the Catholic Church and members of the Francoist party had confronted this theme during the 1940s, and in this and other topics relating to ideology and social customs, the Church had emerged triumphant. The document "Project for the Foundation of a New Europe" (1970) contained features that were common to the generalizing tendencies of other neo-Nazi organizations that managed to offer a version of "light racism." For example, it stated: "We conceive of the idea of a people as the conjunction of individuals united by a single mission and by demonstrated cultural, historical, and racial unity that shapes them as a nation. The white ethnicities of Europe conform to this political, cultural, and biological [understanding of] unity."

After Franco's death in 1975, Spain began a transition from dictatorship to democracy. At that time, Falangist and neo-Francoist associations transformed into political parties and captured a share of the vote from those who retained positive memories of the former regime and its dictator. In that climate, CEDADE was dismantled as a political party. Nonetheless, the organization retains importance as the principal Spanish neo-Nazi organization and the one that lasted the longest, from 1966 to 1993. It was also one of the principal actors in the dissemination of Nazi material in Europe. The importance of CEDADE and the publishing enterprises established by its leaders lies in their work of exporting Nazi material abroad and in their persistent efforts to extend negationist ideas, to disseminate publications and films with racist content, especially anti-Jewish, and to deny the responsibility of the Third Reich in initiating the Second World War and the Holocaust in Europe.

Adapting Aleksandr Dugin to the Spanish Context

In the 1990s, various leaders and members of the defunct CEDADE joined other organizations and collaborated in the creation of new parties. Given the demise of the Far Right in Spain, the principal objective was to find a workable formula for a political program and rhetoric that would be capable of winning voters as some of their European counterparts had succeeded in doing. While neo-Francoism, based ideologically on National Catholicism, continued to be the dominant trend, those who endeavored to resurrect the Far Right in Spain attempted to introduce the ideas of the French New Right and, subsequently, those of National Bolshevism.

It was in the political context of the rise of the conservative and Christian Democratic People's Party and the disappearance of the Far Right due to its repeated failures that a number of Spanish neo-fascists and neo-Nazis decided to experiment with National Bolshevik propaganda. The imitators of Alain de Benoist in Spain believed that they would find the solution to their political problems by trying to adapt the discourse of the Russian nationalist Right to the Spanish case. Would the Russian mix of nationalism and communism, post-CEDADE far-right leaders wondered, serve as a way to create righteous indignation in Spain, awaken the masses against liberal democracy, and earn them sufficient political support to gain access to the state's institutions?

Among Spanish neo-fascists, one of the first who paid serious attention to Russia was the singer, writer, and agitator Fernando Márquez. In April 1986 in Madrid, Márquez launched Proyecto Bronwyn, labeling it an "alternative social movement" that would develop his work in the "double-faceted space of music and politics."[62] In 1993 he produced the first issue of *El corazón del bosque: Revista para otra gente* (The Heart of the Forest: A Journal for the Other People), in which he gathered texts and ideas from the radical Right of the 1920s and 1930s and other articles that focused on the elections in Russia. In one article, Márquez defended the ideas of Vladimir Zhirinovskii, specifically his position against neoliberalism and the global dominion of the United States.[63] In the following issue he published an interview with Aleksandr Dugin, who interested him due to his past as a singer and songwriter as well as his political action at that time. Márquez expressed admiration for Dugin, in whom he saw "a Russian rightist," which he understood as an adherent to traditionalism along the lines of Julius Evola, in contrast to conservative Western liberalism.[64] By 1992 Dugin's book *Mystery of Eurasia* had been translated into Spanish as *Rusia: Misterio de Eurasia* by the Madrid publishing house Grupo Libro 88, while the nationally circulated daily paper *El Mundo* had published two of his articles.[65]

Márquez and other fascists were pleased to read that Dugin had declared himself an anti-Communist, and that after traveling through Western Europe he had described that part of the world as being under occupation by the United States and its ideology, which he defined as "totalitarian capitalism." Above all, his Spanish followers were interested in his definition of his political projects as national and patriotic opposition, and intrigued that he had called for an alliance between communists and anti-liberal nationalists to fight together against liberalism. Márquez wrote along similar lines, and it should come as no surprise that by that point he had a regular column in *Próximo Milenio* and often praised the work of Isidro Juan Palacios (b.1950), a prolific and popular writer who belonged to CEDADE and was active within the People's Party, and who was the editor of periodicals conveying the ideas of the New Right. In his reflections, Márquez imagined that an invention of his called Frente Ibérico de Salvación (the Iberian Salvation Front) would join forces with a re-established FE-JONS (Spanish Falange of the Juntas of the National-Syndicalist Offensive), with factions of the Far Right that were "prepared to progress toward the Third Position," and with sectors of the Left, mainly "hardline Communists."[66]

The figure of Dugin and the theories of National Bolshevism were attractive to other Spanish neo-fascists and neo-Nazis, possibly due to Márquez's influence. This affinity is implied by the activities and texts of Alternativa Europea, a group based in Barcelona and directed by Juan Antonio Llopart during the latter half of the 1990s. This group was the official branch of the ELF in Spain. Alternativa Europea was attentive to Dugin's ideas in their official publication, *Tribuna de Europa*, which featured the names of Nazis such as Ramón Bau and declared itself "in opposition to Yankee-Zionist imperialism." Its articles praised *Hespérides*, considered the best Spanish-language publication that was "alternative in character," comparable to *Krisis*, which was edited by Benoist, and to *Trasgresioni*, edited by Marco Tarchi. *Tribuna de Europa* printed interviews with Dugin in two of its issues,[67] published an article by Christian Bouchet on the topic,[68] produced a recompilation of texts with the title "Dossier: The National Communist Temptation," and published an editorial by Llopart titled "National Bolsheviks?" The response to that leading question was in the affirmative: "We believe in daily labor and in fidelity to our principles, and our synthesis of those principles is sound and decisive. That is none other than to anticipate the social and national revolution of Europe: National Bolshevism."[69]

Subsequent issues of *Tribuna de Europa* included several calls to national revolutionaries, National Bolsheviks, and ramiristas (members of a radical trend in Spanish fascism, following Ramiro Ledesma). These calls were meant to inspire participation in a new political project that would be "national revolutionary." The group continued to publicize its aims to its Russian comrades,[70] and Alternativa Europea maintained a close relationship with Nouvelle Résistance. The editors of the neo-Nazi journal *Resistencia*[71] were also attracted by National Bolshevism. So too was the National Republican Party, which made as much known in its bulletin *La III República*, which began publication in 1996 under the direction of Juan Colomar. Another source of information about National Bolshevism in Spain was Juan Antonio Aguilar, whose influence can be seen in *Disidencias*, the Aurora Project, *Hespérides*, and FE-JONS party bulletins. When Aguilar took over the editorship of the FE-JONS bulletin *Nosotros somos quien somos* in 1996, that publication also paid homage to Dugin.[72]

Hence the tradition for Spanish neo-fascist groups to develop a pro-Russian narrative, a paradox in the context of Spanish history, where Russia does not play an important role and where the memory of Soviet support to the Left during the Spanish Civil War had shaped far-right history.

CONCLUSION

The West European extreme Right's tendency to lean to the East, from Yugoslavia to China through the Soviet experience, raises several points. First, the use of ideological markers that were meant to be associated with the European Left—for instance the call for a union of "proletarian nations" according to the formula invented by Enrico Corradini in Italy after the First World War—was an aesthetically effective ideological oscillation during the Cold War decades. However, it did not allow Thiriart, the New Right, and diverse National Bolshevik groups to break free from the extreme margins of politics or to connect with leftist-oriented movements. It was effectively impossible to move beyond the historically legitimated association of fascism with anti-communism and communism with anti-fascism, and to offer a plausible combination of Right and Left.

Second, the extreme Right's attraction toward the East was an attempt to stop and possibly roll back the influence of the United States in the postwar world, with the aim of reconstructing what Europe had had (including what it had outside of Europe) before the First World War. For Thiriart especially—and today for the "identitarians"—looking to the East was intrinsically connected with the hope for a revival of "Euro-Afrique" as the final geopolitical conception of a white Europe dominating its "natural" sphere of influence. The "proletarian" narrative was therefore always, openly or implicitly, linked to a racial presupposition of white superiority. The existence of a transnational ideological market born from the Waffen-SS call for pan-European unity was maintained during the

Cold War decades and revived with the collapse of the Soviet Union. This transnational ideology demonstrates the existence of a common cultural space in which extreme-right radicals try to present themselves as the vanguard of European national unification, and update their pro-Soviet/pro-Russian stance by supporting the narrative of today's Russian state.

Third, it would be a mistake to draw an uninterrupted ideological line between the German Conservative Revolution of the interwar period and contemporary National Bolshevik figures. Whether in Belgium, Germany, France, or Spain, neo-fascists from the 1970s to the 2000s were seeking a new ideological posture, not ideological continuity with the German founding fathers. They built their position by adopting certain aspects of a Conservative Revolution that they came to know primarily through the way it has been modeled historically. Christian Bouchet and Luc Michel both discovered the work of Ernst Niekisch through that of Jean-Pierre Faye, and referred to it only when they thought it was useful to their stance. Robert Steuckers, one of the key promoters of National Bolshevism, acknowledged this bluntly: "As for the Niekisch movement, I believe it never existed. We tried to rediscover this author, but then the international situation changed and his ideological utility faded."[73]

In many aspects, the extreme Right of the Cold War era was desperate to increase its level of militancy and its political leverage, and therefore was ready to co-opt any new lexicon that would help it stay in tune with the times. The notion that the USSR could be a *Volksgemeinschaft* is certainly orthodox in the National Bolshevik terms of the interwar period. However, it cannot be interpreted as a move to the left, as it was based on applauding the USSR's betrayal of Marxism. Following its failure to recruit disaffected members of the French Trotskyist Lutte Ouvrière and the French Communist Party, Nouvelle Résistance asserted straightforwardly its attachment to the extreme Right, not the Left: "Let's be clear, we see ourselves as red-brown, National Bolsheviks, National Revolutionaries, Strasserians, etc.. .. we are primarily fascists as defined by fascism before the Lateran Treaty and the Republic of Salo."[74]

CHAPTER 8

STRASSERISM IN GERMANY

In Search of an Anti-Western Alliance with Stalin's USSR and Putin's Russia

Patrick Moreau

T he Weimar Republic was born of the German defeat of 1918. It struggled for legitimacy amid the "stab in the back"[1] myth, a profound climate of hostility toward the reparations to be paid to the Allies,[2] and shock over the loss of territories.[3] It was in this poisonous atmosphere that the fragile Weimar democracy, experiencing the full force of the great crisis of 1929,[4] had to contend with vigorous opposition coming both from the Communist Party of Germany (KPD), the darling of Lenin and subsequent object of attention of Stalin and the Comintern,[5] and from the National Socialist German Workers' Party (NSDAP), or Nazis, as well as various groups of nationalists and monarchists. The Far Right spanned a wide array of opinions, from the Young Conservatives, *Völkisch* racialists, the Peasant Movement, Bündische, supporters and ideologues of the Conservative Revolutionary movement, to the National Socialists, National Bolsheviks, associations of war veterans, and the Freikorps. In this diverse political kaleidoscope, the so-called leftist National Socialists, and especially the Strasser brothers, Otto (1897–1974) and Gregor (1892–1934), constitute a fascinating case of blending ideological repertoires. Ernst von Salomon's book *The Questionnaire* offers a humorous portrait of this "nationalist-revolutionary," anti-Western, anti-systemic, and frequently (self-proclaimed) socialist world.[6] In 1960, in his publication of the same name, Otto-Ernst Schüddekopf characterizes this current as a grouping of "left-wingers from the right" (*linke Leute von rechts*).[7] In this chapter I focus on the socialist current within the NSDAP, and explore the political heritage of these anti-Hitler Strasserist movements through the tumultuous history of Germany to the present day, as well as the place of Russia in it.

LEFTIST NAZISM AGAINST HITLERISM (1925–1938)

The history of National Socialist leftism in Weimar is primarily the story of its leader, Otto Strasser, and his older brother, Gregor. Otto Strasser was born in 1897 into a family of Bavarian officials of the Christian, national, and social tradition. He enlisted in August 1914. He was decorated for his acts of military valor and attained the rank of officer in 1918. In June 1919, while Gregor Strasser was getting involved with nationalist agitation and meeting Adolf Hitler for the first time, Otto was on his way to Berlin, where, while studying economics, he joined the German Social Democratic Party (SPD), and was elected to the student parliament as the founder of the "university association of socialist veterans." An occasional contributor to the SPD newspaper *Vorwärts* (Forward), he helped to lead the Red Hundreds' (Proletarische Hundertschaften) resistance to the Kapp Putsch.[8]

Otto Strasser broke with the SPD in April 1920. He accused the party of betraying the Ruhr workers' uprising, which in fact was abandoned by the Social Democratic government to be put down in a military action led by General von Watter with Freikorps participation. Back in Bavaria, he met Adolf Hitler in October 1920. There was an immediate antipathy between the two men, and Otto refused to join the nascent National Socialist movement. Later, at the Halle Congress of the left-wing Independent Social Democratic Party (USPD), Strasser met Grigory Zinoviev, who seems to have convinced him of the validity of the Bolshevik revolutionary experience, its utility as a model of action for Germany, and the necessity of rapprochement between Germany and Russia.[9]

In late 1920, Strasser thus mixed many theoretical influences: revolutionary socialism, nationalism, social Christianity, moderate anti-Semitism, and a pro-Bolshevik sentiment that was more Romantic than ideological. He tried to integrate many of these facets into his subsequent theoretical works and political practice. Between 1920 and 1925, Strasser earned his doctorate and became a business executive. In his free time he deepened his political knowledge, particularly by frequenting young conservative and nationalist circles, but especially through critical reading of books and articles by Oswald Spengler[10] and Arthur Moeller van den Bruck,[11] while refusing to participate in any organization. Through exposure to the thinkers of the Conservative Revolution, he sketched a first draft of a doctrine that was nationalist, socialist, and, in the international field, supportive of emerging nations such as Russia.[12]

Meanwhile, his brother Gregor had left Bavaria for northern Germany, where he became the organizer and propaganda head of the Deutschvölkische Freiheitspartei (German *Völkisch* Freedom Party).[13] The return to economic order seemed to permanently reduce the chances of a National Socialist protest movement and compelled various National Socialist trends to join forces. Hitler's release from prison on December 20, 1924 gave the revived NSDAP its natural leader. However, the mutation of the National Socialist movement, gathering putschists into a mass party, raised serious programmatic problems. Gregor Strasser, through his facilitating activities in the election campaigns of 1924, was fully aware of the difficulty of developing an essentially racialist and nationalist movement in the economic and social conditions of northern Germany. There, a large industrial proletariat solidly organized by the SPD and the KPD formed an unfavorable environment for National Socialist expansion.[14]

The ideological program of the NSDAP from 1920 was clearly inadequate to win over the middle class or penetrate the working class. Gregor Strasser, more an organizer than an ideologue, had the idea of asking his brother to help develop a transformed and revamped National Socialist ideology to reflect the new political and economic environment. Otto Strasser, having been converted to the ideas of Moeller van den Bruck, enthusiastically accepted. The brothers divided the tasks according to their nature and talent. Otto became "the North German ideologue" and wrote articles and speeches for and under the name of his brother.

In 1926, at the Congress of Hanover, the leaders of the National Socialist left presented a program. It specified the economic, administrative, and diplomatic guidelines of the "working group" and presented the framework of a doctrine that would remain essentially unchanged until the annihilation of the leftist current in 1934. From 1930 to 1938, it was disseminated through the ideological theses inspired by Otto Strasser. The National Socialist Left recognized the validity of the NSDAP's twenty-five points of 1920, but also insisted on nationalization, the limitation of private property, and the necessity of a German–Soviet alliance in a war of national liberation against the Western imperialist powers.

Between 1926 and 1930, Adolf Hitler, convinced of the need to get rid of the "Bolshevik" Strasser brothers, maneuvered to weaken the Left and undermine the solidarity of the Strasser brothers without endangering his North German organization. Otto Strasser found himself with only a handful of associates to defend his socialist program. Meanwhile, all higher-ranking party officials who were leftists, including the Gauleiters of Silesia, Pomerania, and Saxony, were excluded from the NSDAP and replaced. The 1929 crisis definitively tipped the balance of power between National Socialist tendencies. In this new social and economic context, Hitler defined the strategic outlines of his party's policy: respect for institutional legality and elective principles, limitation of anti-capitalist rhetoric, greater openness toward conservatives and the Catholic Church, intensification of the anti-Marxist struggle and anti-Semitic agitation, and the systematic use of street violence.

Against these strategic concepts and the reconciliation between the NSDAP and the German National People's Party (DNVP), Otto Strasser could only repeat tirelessly in his writings that Hitler had betrayed socialism in favor of reactionary attitudes, and that the "foundation of a Third Reich" necessarily involved a revolution that was both national and socialist if German Marxists were to be convinced of the uselessness of class struggle.

The inevitable rupture occurred in the summer of 1930. On July 4, the socialists left the NSDAP and founded the Combat League of Revolutionary National Socialists (Kampfgemeinschaft Revolutionärer Nationalsozialisten, or KGRNS). Despite Gregor Strasser's appeal to members of the NSDAP to remain faithful to their leader, the KGRNS developed much more quickly than envisioned in Munich. One can distinguish roughly two phases. The first covered the months of July and August 1930, when an influx of NSDAP defectors provided the KGRNS with cadres. The second, from September until December 1930, was a period of consolidation and strengthening of the party's activist potential. Otto Strasser, Herbert Blank, and Bruno Ernst Buchrucker, the former organizer of the Black Reichswehr, led the KGRNS. In December 1930, the group reached 5,000 members and brought on board the Gauleiters of Brandenburg and Danzig, Hitler Youth and Stormtrooper (SA) cadres, and many leaders of local NSDAP groups in Thuringia, Saxony, Brandenburg, Schleswig-Holstein, and the Ruhr. In late May 1931, after an organizational consolidation phase, the KGRNS resumed its recruitment and managed to bring together 6,100 members divided into ninety local groups. It also produced the weekly *Die Deutsche Revolution* (the German Revolution, circulation 10,000 copies) and a theoretical monthly, *Nationalsozialistische Briefe* (National Socialist Letters). Furthermore, Strasser's movement enjoyed another success on the occasion of the revolt of the Berlin SA led by Walter Stennes in April 1931.

However, the reformism apparent in certain KGRNS economic tenets was criticized by left-wing National Bolsheviks who supported a planned economy and the radical implementation of social ownership of the economy and means of production. Some of the new KGRNS members rapidly lost faith in the ability of the Strasser group to resist the NSDAP's military power, decided to cooperate with the KPD, and subsequently joined it.[15] Varying in intensity, this trend continued until the banning of the KGRNS in 1933. Thus, Strasser's organization involuntarily played the role of a connecting link between Hitler's National Socialism and communism.

This "National Bolshevik crisis" of the KGRNS, along with its inability to combat Marxist theory intellectually and its military weakness, devastated the organization. Neither the elitist path of "officers and non-commissioned officers of the German Revolution" in 1930, nor the alliance with Stennes, nor the future Black Front of 1931–1933, enabled the Strasserists to resist or even respond to Hitler's terrorist blows. This climate of permanent insecurity, exacerbated by SA attacks against meetings of Revolutionary National Socialist activists, led local KGRNS groups to place themselves under the protection of the Communists. This situation inevitably left the most resolute anti-Hitler elements of the KGRNS in a state of permanent unease. The KPD, by its power and national propaganda, quickly emerged as the only political force capable of physically or intellectually resisting Hitler's terror. The most lucid KGRNS activists could not fail to recognize the impotence of their organization, which left the ideological movement increasingly sterile in its practice and political theory.

By fall 1931, the KGRNS seemed doomed soon to disappear. Strasser decided to organize the Black Front, an informal alliance of the Wehrwolf,[16] some local groups of the Bund Oberland,[17] and the remains of a peasant movement led by Wilhelm Hamkens. Reduced by the end of 1931 to a core of fewer than 800 active militants among 1,500 members, in May 1932, the KGRNS sank into a deep crisis. The NSDAP, then the leading party in Germany on the activist and electoral levels, seemed certain of its accession to power.[18]

The unexpected reluctance of President Hindenburg to give the post of chancellor of the Reich to the "Austrian corporal" led to a major and long-anticipated internal crisis in the NSDAP, pitting Hitler against both Gregor Strasser, who wanted Hitler to reduce his demands to a ministerial post, and Ernst Röhm, who demanded a coup. Hitler's dismissal of Gregor Strasser and call to order of the SA led to a flood of resignations that revitalized a then-lifeless KGRNS. By the end of 1932, it had attracted about 4,000 additional members engaged in the anti-Hitler struggle, but nevertheless was powerless to prevent the inevitable appointment of Hitler as chancellor. Otto Strasser even praised Hitler's appointment as a triumph of legality. Blinded by a belief in his own destiny, he saw the event as the first, reformist phase of an inevitable National Socialist revolution that he would one day lead.

But raids and arrests soon decimated Strasser's troops, and the second-in-command of the KGRNS turned out to be an infiltrator from Heinrich Himmler's SS (*Schutzstaffel*). Between 1934 and 1938, Otto Strasser led a dual national and international resistance, first from Austria in 1934, then from Czechoslovakia until 1938. Meanwhile, his brother Gregor was murdered during the "Night of the Long Knives" (June 30–July 2, 1934) together with the highest-ranking SA leaders. Having sought the support of conservatives such as Edgar Jung, Otto Strasser was able to maintain clandestine groups in Germany through 1935–1936 and feed agitation against the regime. The effectiveness of the repression in 1936–1937 reduced him to near impotence and forced him to flee across Europe and on to North America in order to escape the Gestapo. Until 1949, the Allies largely ignored Otto Strasser. They distrusted him as a crypto-Bolshevik Nazi, an opinion that Douglas Reed described in his book *The Prisoner of Ottawa*.[19]

STRASSERISM'S IDEOLOGICAL FOUNDATIONS

We shall now examine the theses of the Strasser group in comparison with other neoconservative or Hitlerian points of view on foreign policy and Marxist ideology. Inspired by Moeller van den Bruck, the Revolutionary National Socialists believed in the unstoppable rise of the "young" German people, to whom fate had accorded the role of creator and designer of Europe and bearer of the torch of nationalism in the world, supporting all ethnic struggles of national liberation in the colonies, and allying with Russia in a war against the "old" peoples of the West.

Thus Germany's Lebensraum should not be enlarged by conquering the nations to the east. Germany instead ought to devote its future to colonizing and developing historically German lands—hence the inclusion of all German minorities in the Reich. The vital renewal was targeted at the bourgeoisie as well as the proletariat. Otto Strasser, like Ernst Jünger, dreamed of a new worker, but of a particular peasant type, be it the peasant worker, peasant intellectual, or peasant soldier. His vision included many facets of a social upheaval created by the collapse of industrial society, partial dismantling of factories, reduction of urban populations, and forced resettlement of citizens to work the land, as a purification process of the whole people.

Strasser's objective was to achieve a socialization wherein the community and all its members could benefit from the land and the means of production, through the disappearance of heavy industry structures and their dispersion and management in small, decentralized units in rural communities that would bring together peasant workers. Strasser advocated the necessary adoption of a spartan lifestyle, wherein consumption is reduced to the satisfaction of primary needs, with near-autarky on the local level, a medium-term reduction of the production of consumer goods, and a contraction of the remnants of capitalism, already weakened by workers' participation in decision-making, management, and the ownership of capital.

Banks would remain for a transition phase that would lead to their gradual replacement by a national, and later international, institution of a kind of barter economy. The 1932 plan included a Japanese-style co-prosperity sphere for certain raw materials and resources located in Eastern Europe, Asia, and Africa. In this concept, the Soviet Union was considered an objective ally for the new Germany.

Much more representative of the spirit of the Conservative Revolution, the Strasser group seems ambiguous in its relationship with the political actors of the Weimar Republic. Although Strasser proclaimed that he had broken with liberalism and Marxism (the two ultimate enemy fronts of the National Socialist Revolution), a tactical alliance with the KPD and partial semantic adoption of some Communist theories was seen as tolerable, even necessary. This arrangement implied a discourse of a strategic alliance with the Soviet Union and a tactical one with the Communist Party. The KPD's Programmatic Declaration Concerning the National and Social Liberation of the German People provided a theoretical bridge.[20]

In August 1930, the NSDAP and the KPD were on the verge of a historic political breakthrough, which took place during the legislative elections of September 14, 1930. The NSDAP won 18.3 percent of the vote (+15.7 points) and 107 deputies, and the KPD won 13.5 percent (+2.5 points) and 77 deputies. With a view toward these elections, the KPD newspaper, *Rote Fahne* (Red Flag), had published the Programmatic Declaration on August 24, 1930. At the time, political commentators highlighted the surprising importance the Communists gave to the national question, which was clearly at odds with the strategic direction agreed upon at the Sixth Congress of the Comintern in 1928.[21]

The Comintern's official policy announced the emergence of a "third period of global development after the war and the Bolshevik Revolution." After the "relative stabilization" of the capitalist world between 1923 and

1928, capitalism was supposed to be in a new phase characterized by the intensification of class struggle, during which the Communist parties had to fight for the proletarian revolution, the dictatorship of the proletariat, and, in the case of the KPD, for "Soviet Germany."[22] This vision identified a major enemy, the Social Democrats, who were accused of "social fascism," echoing Zinoviev's 1924 analysis.[23] The Communist line was a "United Front at the base," with the goal of driving a wedge between the Social Democratic workers and their "social fascist" parties. While National Socialism was still weak in organizational terms, the Communist Party engaged in a militant policy of violent confrontation with the Nazis, relying on its combat organization, the Alliance of Red Front Fighters (Roter Frontkämpferbund, or RFB).[24]

However, the Comintern could not overlook its failure in the German context since 1929. From the second half of 1929, the NSDAP won many elections and grew into a mass movement. With its very aggressive SA, it was more and more frequently the clear winner of street battles with the Communist fighters. At the same time, Hitler's strategy of rapprochement with conservative national forces caused discontent in the left wing of the NSDAP, which resulted in the Strasserist crisis in June–July 1930.

The KPD's Programmatic Declaration Concerning the National and Social Liberation of the German People sought to respond to these new realities. The party primarily targeted workers and the unemployed, whom they promised a better world—seven-hour workdays in a four-day workweek, a massive reduction in all prices, and so forth—in a Soviet Germany. Beyond this traditional clientele, the KPD addressed "all those who work." Behind this vague formulation, it sought middle-class support, and to achieve this, developed a nationalist argument. It rejected the Treaty of Versailles, reparations, the Young plan, and interest on "imperialist loans." The KPD declared itself to be the only true defender of nationhood; it alone would be capable of uniting all non-capitalist strata of society (workers and poor peasants as well as salaried employees and middle-class workers) under the dictatorship of the proletariat, in order to "overthrow the power of capital" and any foreign or domestic attempts to oppose it. The KPD's patriotic militancy briefly broke with Marx and Lenin. Until his death, Vladimir Lenin—along with Karl Radek, with him and after him—was radically opposed to any abrupt denunciation of the Versailles treaty by the German Communists.[25] The KPD program and its temporary separation from Lenin must be understood in the context of domestic politics.

In 1930, the leaders of the KPD could only note the failure of its militant policy of confrontation with the SA and the growing electoral power of the

NSDAP. These two factors prompted the KPD to consider that Nazism was, in fact if not in theory, "the main enemy" of the moment, but also "the negative face of a highly positive phenomenon." In this vision of a dialectical process, Nazism was "the counterpart of the revolutionary upsurge, the inevitable secondary manifestation of a revolutionary situation."[26]

Suddenly, Nazism became objectively useful, because it helped to break bourgeois society for the ultimate benefit of the Communists, and also because it radicalized hitherto moderate social strata. Nazism would "pave the way" for the revolution, making it a sort of "father of the revolution." This explains why, in 1930–1931, in KPD texts and the speeches of Communist deputies in the Reichstag, we find the term "the two armies of the revolution"; in other words, the proletarian "vanguard," and the "rearguard" or "reserve" momentarily attracted by Nazism "but bound to join the vanguard before long, because the attacks of the capitalists radicalized into fascism harm not only the proletariat, but also the middle classes and all the petty bourgeois."[27] The KPD considered itself the natural "heir" of fascism once it succumbed to its contradictions.

Hitler's problems with the left wing of his party allowed the KPD to believe that significant National Socialist proletarian fractions were naturally destined to join the "proletarian front." The scale of opportunities offered by the crisis of the NSDAP and the SA revolts led the KPD Central Committee, meeting in plenary session over January 15–17, 1931, and considering "the increasing radicalization of the class situation," to "make the slogan of 'popular revolution' (*Volksrevolution*) the main strategic slogan of the party." It was not until the fall of 1931, with the worsening economic and social crisis and the Harzburg Front unifying the opposition of the NSDAP and the DNVP, that doubts appeared among Communist ideologues. Although "Liberation Policy" remained the KPD's official line, the party reoriented its action toward a "United Front at the base," albeit with timid attempts at a United Front "at the top" with joint meetings with Strasserists and National Bolsheviks (the KPD security service protected Strasserist meetings). This practice would eventually be abandoned, but led to many former Nazis joining the KPD. Still, until 1934, Hitler's hatred of Strasser was the reason for his benevolent neutrality toward the KPD and Stalin.

Undoubtedly one of the most modern aspects of Strasser's thought, which formed the basis of his ideological sustainability after 1945, was his vision of nationalism as a detrimental component of the imperialism of "Western powers." The weakening of Germany's enemies, such as France and England, came not only from the strength of all the national liberation movements in the British or French colonies, but also from the bursting apart of pseudo "nation-states," such as France or Belgium. As far as we know, Strasser was the first to have systematically stressed the importance of linguistic and ethnic independence movements, for example among the Bretons, Flemish, Basques, and Scottish. These perspectives would be recovered a decade later by the SS headquarters and fifty years later by European national revolutionaries. For left-wing National Socialists, nationalism was a tool to reorganize Europe along ethno-linguistic lines as well as a political model for all peoples of the world. Strasserist nationalism was the ultimate value for every political action, but unlike Hitler's project, it was not based on racialism.

THE NATIONAL-NEUTRALIST STRATEGY (1945–1974)

The Allies and then the Adenauer government did everything possible to prevent the return of Otto Strasser to Germany.[28] They feared—wrongly, in light of Strasser's activities until his death in 1974—that he intended to unify National Socialists who sought political reorganization. In 1945, from his Canadian exile, Strasser established a network with survivors of his Weimar-era organizations. Then, in October 1948, he decided to found the Federation for the Renewal of Germany (Bund für Deutschlands Erneuerung). This organization of a few hundred followers advocated armed neutrality for Germany.[29]

This position implied an anti-Western and anti-Communist strategy; it required the departure of the Allies, but adopted a very measured tone in the case of Stalin, who saw possible German reunification and neutrality as a means to weaken the Western camp. However, the bulk of the Bund's activities consisted of the legal battle over Strasser's return to Germany. In November 1954, despite the German government's resistance, the Federal Constitutional Court of Germany permitted Strasser to return to the country and restored all his rights to him. This ruling was made possible by expert testimonies, written by historians close to the Communist Party, affirming the anti-Nazi nature of the Black Front. Largely isolated from the West German extreme Right,[30] Strasser sought salvation in the founding of a political party, the German Social Union (Deutsch-Soziale Union, or DSU) in 1956. But the party dissolved in 1962, and from then until his death Strasser focused his efforts on the theoretical journal *Vorschau* (Preview).

The DSU attracted a steady stream of young activists who would become acquainted with Strasser's ideas and then leave the party, which was electorally impotent, divided by ideological conflicts, and paralyzed by Strasser's excessive ego. The importance of the DSU and its divisions, such as the Independent Workers' Party (Unabhängige Arbeiter-Partei, or UAP), lay elsewhere. After the disappearance of the DSU, a few hundred activists trained by Strasser integrated into extreme Right movements and parties like the German Empire Party (Deutsche Reichspartei) and the German Conservative Party (Deutsche Konservative Partei), which would become the seeds of a larger party founded in 1964, the National Democratic Party of Germany (Nationaldemokratische Partei Deutschlands, or NPD). Following the collapse of the NPD in 1969, Strasser's ideas have continued to be associated with extreme-right circles until the present day.

Strasser's message of the 1950s to 1970s can be summarized in four points that remain ideologically relevant to this day.

(1) German Socialism as Solidarism: As far as we know, Strasser is the father of this term, at least in Germany and Europe. It is characterized by a distinctive anti-capitalism and entails the socialization of banks, business concerns, and other means of production for the purpose of redistribution for the benefit of citizens.

(2) Community of the People: Strasser strove for a corporatist state based on the representation of five social groups (workers, peasants, salaried workers and civil servants, self-employed professionals, artisans and business owners) in which Germany would have a presidential system and a "true democracy" liberated from partisan influences.

(3) *Völkisch* Renaissance: The German soul is to be reborn after its release from the "materialist-liberal" spirit.

(4) National Freedom: Germany must be reunified and practice "armed neutrality" and anti-imperialism. Support for all forms of liberation struggles, military or cultural, was to form the basis for the international relations of an autarkic and neutral Germany.

The formation of a Grand Coalition of the Christian and Social Democratic parties (CDU/CSU–SPD) in 1966 sowed the seeds of a political and electoral breakthrough for the National Democratic Party of Germany.[31] The NPD emerged as a party that attended to collective concerns and was one of the only forces opposing the power of the established parties. Polls at the time testify to the population's deep dissatisfaction due to both the economic crisis and fear aroused by the 1968 student revolution. The NPD made the most of the population's political insecurity and fears. In

April 1968, it achieved its best electoral performance in regional polls in Baden-Württemberg, with 9.6 percent of the vote. A charismatic leader and excellent communicator, Adolf von Thadden, was at the head of the NPD. The cadres chosen by von Thadden were hostile to Strasser (who had been concentrating on publishing since the failure of the DSU) as well as the "national revolutionaries."

In this difficult context, the Strasserists split: some of them remained in the Independent Workers' Party (UAP); another faction joined or moved closer to the German New Right; and the rest would become "Trotskyist" infiltrators in the NPD. The presence of countless former SS and NSDAP cadres in the party meant that Strasserists could hold only intermediary or local leadership positions. They still constituted a "left wing," which—small as it was—would play an important role in the breakup of the NPD between 1969 and 1971.

Another reason for NPD cadres' hostility toward Strasserists was that the National Democratic program stood for a "single, corporatist and autarkic party." Supranational European integration was rejected in favor of a Gaullist "Europe of nations" that avoided any acculturation or binding political-economic ties (anti-Americanism, anti-Communism). The NPD advocated no socialist measures or nationalization, and proposed to practice an interventionist and nationalistic "Colbertism." The number of immigrant workers was to be reduced in order to ensure full employment for ethnic Germans. Although "American" capitalism was a vector of moral decadence, von Thadden saw the "correction" of the capitalist system as a panacea for the economic crisis. The NPD also maintained its claim to the "original territories of the German people" stolen after 1945 (Alsace-Lorraine, the Sudetenland, and the former German territories in Poland). For their part, Otto Strasser and a number of Strasserists believed that the crisis was the beginning of the collapse of the capitalist system, which would lead to a social revolution of the unemployed. Ultimately, they stuck by a national-neutralist project that was increasingly unrealistic in the context of the Cold War.

The NPD's ideological recipe actually worked for a time and gave the party a solid electoral base. With only 4.3 percent of the vote at the 1969 Bundestag elections, the NPD missed the threshold to enter the Bundestag. Within months, this failure led to an electoral collapse in regional and local elections in 1970–1971 and the loss of potential supporters. While the Strasserists active in the NPD denounced von Thadden's national-conservative strategy of 1969, the party leadership was torn over the possible appointment of a new chairman. These disputes further reinforced the NPD's negative image among the population. By the end of 1970, the party was politically finished.

From 1971 to 1993, the NPD experienced a rapid decline and was supported only by a handful of true believers whose intensity could not compensate for the erosion of registered membership. This dual trend of organizational weakening and militant tightening of the party's activist core led to an extremist ideological hardening of the NPD and its gradual shift toward increasingly activist methods. For lack of any other means, they favored spectacular actions (marches, provocations, violence) attracting high media attention. From 1976 on, this negative publicity constituted the party's main means of propaganda. On the eve of communism's collapse and Germany's reunification (1989–1990), the NPD drew increasingly close to neo–National Socialism.

The Strasserist "New Right" from the Environmentalist Front to Leftist Nazism

The emergence of a new intellectual and then also organizational right in West Germany was the work of figures such as Henning Eichberg, Uwe Michael Troppenz, Wolfgang Günther, Lothar Penz, and Wolfgang Strauss.[32] From the late 1960s, they pursued a syncretic ideological approach, proposing a new language and different strategies from those of the old German Right.

This New Right took shape between 1969 and 1971. Outside the NPD, there existed nuclei of national revolutionaries who shared an anti-imperialist sentiment against both Soviet territorial expansionism and American cultural colonization, German nationalism favoring reunification, policy principles of "bio-humanism" organized around the contemporary findings of genetics, eugenics, and ethology, and ecological awareness. Additional common elements included support of state socialism and planned economy, a fascination with revolutionary activism inspired by Leninist organizational principles, and intellectual roots in the ideological traditions of the Weimar-era Conservative Revolution. The preferred approaches of the leaders of these small groups could be found in the columns of the magazine *Junges Forum* (Young Forum) and a series of brochures called Junge Kritik (Young Critique).

Despite its intense political and literary activities, the membership and means of the New Right still remained very limited. In 1970–1971, it consisted of some forty members around *Junges Forum* in Hamburg, and about fifty other members of the Extra-Parliamentary Collaboration (Außerparlamentarische Mitarbeit, or APM) in Berlin, which published three theoretical journals and leaflet series: *Ideologie und Strategie* [Ideology and Strategy], *Rebell* [Rebel], and *Berliner Nachrichtendienst* [Berlin Information Service]. Adding to these meager forces were a dozen "national-revolutionary base groups" at universities or on the margins of the NPD, which were content to propagate national-revolutionary theses within the Young National Democrats (Junge Nationaldemokraten, or JN). At this time the two main activist components were Friedhelm Busse's Labor Party (Partei der Arbeit, or PdA) and the Independent Workers' Party (UAP), both based in North Rhine-Westphalia.

Busse, the former head of the NPD trade-union committee in North Rhine-Westphalia, was excluded from the party late in 1970 after participating in an attack on the Soviet embassy in Bonn with members of the German Social Action group (Deutsch-Soziale Aktion). In June of the following year, he founded his Labor Party with Krefeld as its base. Leading about seventy members and publishing the bimonthly magazine *Dritte Republik* (Third Republic), with a circulation of 1,000 copies in 1971, Busse organized his party on the Communist model by referring to "democratic centralism" and aspiring "to combine the legal struggle of elections with active subversion." He used the Maoist slogan of "people's struggle," sought publicity through contact with the Communists and the extreme left, and even spoke in support of the anarchists of the Baader-Meinhof Gang. Busse blithely mixed a hodgepodge of ideological theses from Eichberg and his personal mythology populated by the feats of Gregor Strasser and the head of the SA, Ernst Röhm. Despite some spectacular provocations, the Labor Party stagnated organizationally until 1972, when it split in favor of the New Right Action (Aktion Neue Rechte, or ANR) (an NPD breakaway) and the UAP.

The UAP had emerged from a split in Otto Strasser's DSU and established itself in the Ruhr. With approximately 100 to 120 members in 1970–1971, the UAP claimed the precepts of Otto Strasser: National Socialism, anti-imperialism, European neutrality, and social revolution. The UAP never considered dissolving and joining a larger national-revolutionary organization that was established throughout West Germany. UAP leaders favored waiting for the collapse of the NPD to recover members and convert them to the revolutionary project. In 1971, the 400 members of the German New Right were divided among twelve groups. By 1974–1975, what was left of the ANR was disintegrating. The organizational development of the New Right and Strasserist elements thus paused while work on Strasser's theoretical model continued.[33]

After the failure of the ANR, the New Right proved unable to reconcile its theoretical contradictions. In the 1980s, it divided into five movements, only one of which achieved some organizational success, by infiltrating the new environmentalist protest movement. With about 1,000 members in 1973 and 1974, 800 in 1975, and only 600 in 1976, the New Right was moving toward organizational insignificance, while continuing to attract NPD sympathizers who, for the most part, after a few months of activism, left these tiny dogmatic groups in further pursuit of an impossible revolution. The political legacy of the New Right nevertheless weighed heavily on the future development of the German extreme Right.

Between 1974 and 1976, some half-dozen groups were founded and gradually moved from the New Right to the neo-Nazi scene. The first was the Rightist Bloc for Workers, Peasants, and Soldiers (Rechtsblock für Arbeiter, Bauern und Soldaten), established in Ludwigsburg. It published the magazine *Fanal* (Beacon), was led by a former NPD/ANR leader, and had at most thirty or forty members. Friedhelm Busse's Labor Party (PdA), reconstructed after its split with the ANR in 1973, struggled with only a dozen members until 1975, when it transformed into the People's Socialist Movement of Germany/Labor Party (Volksozialistische Bewegung Deutschlands/Partei der Arbeit, or VSBD/PdA), based in Munich. These organizations, plus at least five other mini-factions, all used the slogan of "people's socialism," like their ideological forebears, the Strasser brothers. They were reserved with regard to Hitler, whom they criticized for his "betrayal of socialism" and his lack of interest in the wave of European volunteers[34] who had fought against Bolshevism and were championed by Heinrich Himmler and some SS circles. The members of these small factions nevertheless grew increasingly close to the "Hitlerian" circles that were forming in West Germany in 1975–1976, with the merger becoming complete in 1980. For at least one of its components, the decline of the New Right concluded in neo-Nazi activism, active anti-Semitism, anti-Zionist anti-imperialism in support of the Palestinian cause, and finally domestic terrorism.

The formation of the Cause of the People/Organization for the Construction of the National Revolutionary Movement (Sache des Volkes, or SdV/Nationalrevolutionäre Aufbauorganisation, or NRAO) and the Solidarist People's Movement (Solidaristische Volksbewegung, or SVB) as rigid cadre schools led some members of grassroots groups to favor a "spontaneous" and autonomous approach. On this path, they came across splinter elements of Maoist groups, in particular the Communist Party of Germany/Marxists-Leninists (Kommunistische Partei Deutschlands/

Marxisten-Leninisten, KPD/ML), and in 1976 formed cells that, beginning in 1978, incorporated themselves into the environmental movement.

At least four such groups formed, the most important of which was the Laser group in Rhineland-Palatinate. It published the journals *Laser* and later *Aufbruch* [Awakening] and in the 1980s, the periodical *Wir Selbst* (Ourselves). The Solidarists (SVB) and the NRAO almost completely disappeared from the organizational scene by the early 1980s. There were several reasons for this accelerated decline. The first was the competition from leftist neo-Nazi groups, which revived the anti-imperialist argument and actually engaged in revolutionary terrorist action. Another was the emergence of the Thule Seminar, a German organization similar to Alain de Benoist's Research and Study Group for European Civilization (GRECE), which was ideologically much more sophisticated than "thinkers" such as Lothar Penz. Finally, the environmental movement moved more clearly to the left and began a witch hunt to root out national revolutionaries in its ranks.

THE 1980S: REPUBLIKANER AND NEO-NAZISM

For domestic and geopolitical reasons, Strasserism was barely visible in German politics in the 1980s. No one in Europe, let alone Germany, expected the demise of communism and the reunification of Germany. In a climate of rising military tension, the arms race, and Communist and pacifist agitation, national neutralism had little appeal. Very discreet contacts with the Soviet Union had gone wrong and the Strasserists' adherence to the formula "better red than dead" was an embarrassment. Anti-imperialism, especially the support for Palestinian terrorism and guerrilla movements in Latin America and Europe, had largely migrated to the left and the extreme left. Anti-Americanism had become widely popular in Germany. Strasserists had nothing new to offer ideologically and found themselves irrelevant in the context of a second "New Right," the Thule Seminar, a strong neo–National Socialist current, and a new party, the Republicans (Republikaner, or REP), which absorbed almost all of the Right's potential activists.

Former members of the Christian Social Union (CSU) who wished to revitalize the national-conservative tradition founded the REP in 1983. In 1985, Franz Schönhuber, a television presenter well known for his big mouth, and a former member of the SS, took control of the party. Closely linked to Jean-Marie Le Pen beginning in 1988–1989, Schönhuber wanted to make the REP a new "German national front." In 1986, the party obtained only 3 percent of the vote in elections to the Bavarian Landtag and did not seem to have a future. However, the emergence of an economic crisis in the mid-1980s following the oil price shock of 1979, reminiscent of the one that had helped the NPD breakthrough in 1966–1967, allowed the REP to jostle the established parties. On January 28, 1989, Schönhuber, who was leading a remarkable anti-immigration media campaign, won 7.5 percent of the vote in West Berlin. In June 1989, at the European elections, the REP obtained 7.1 percent of the vote and six seats in the European Parliament.[35]

Ideologically, the REP was an updated copy of the 1960s-era NPD, but with a central propaganda message that had a promising future: the fight against immigration. New themes emerged, such as the rejection of globalization, a stance that was anti-capitalist and anti-American, as well as strongly ecological. The REP completely rejected any national-revolutionary strategy as well as the nationalization of banks and industry. But the demise of communism and the reunification of Germany, along with West Germany's relatively successful overcoming of the economic crisis, finished the REP. At the first elections for the reunified Bundestag, on December 2, 1990, the party received only 2.1 percent of the vote. In 1994, the REP lost its European representation with only 3.9 percent of the vote. Unable to establish itself in the reunified East, the REP is today only a ghost party.

Some references to the Strasser brothers were still cultivated within the global white power, militarist, and racist skinhead movement, but without any clear ideological content. The neo-Nazi formations of the 1980s were more of an SA–Röhm or paramilitary type. Some of them were involved in the extreme-right terrorism of the 1980s and also supported Palestinian terrorism. During this period, Friedhelm Busse's People's Socialist Movement of Germany/Labor Party (Volkssozialistische Bewegung Deutschlands/Partei der Arbeit, or VSBD/PdA) was the only small group claiming the ideology of the Strasser brothers.

The last major player in the neo-Nazi movement was Michael Kühnen, who served several terms in prison. A brilliant communicator, Kühnen managed to reassemble many banned militant groups into his Action Front of National Socialists (Aktionsfront Nationaler Sozialisten, or ANS), founded in 1977. The ANS declared itself to be socialist and considered SA head Ernst Röhm the model "political soldier." The group eventually broke up over the issue of homosexuality. Kühnen died of AIDS in 1991.

When communism collapsed in 1989, the neo-Nazi scene in the West picked up the torch and established extensive contacts with neo-Nazis and skinheads in the former German Democratic Republic.[36]

GERMAN REUNIFICATION AND THE RENAISSANCE OF STRASSERISM

German reunification took effect on October 3, 1990. The following decade saw the traditional extreme Right wither in western Germany while the new federal states in the East became a veritable hotbed of extremism.

In the West, Friedhelm Busse led the Free German Workers' Party (Freiheitliche Deutsche Arbeiter-Partei, or FAP) until it was outlawed in 1995. Between 1989 and 1995, it embodied the Strasserist neo-Nazi scene. Its few dozen members were unable to recruit new adherents. Skinhead movements (with Blood and Honor and Hammerskin leanings) developed quickly, but remained much weaker in the West than in the East. The REP and the NPD remained politically and organizationally impotent in the West, where only the German People's Union (Deutsche Volksunion, or DVU) of the nationalist publisher Gerhard Frey achieved a temporary political breakthrough. The DVU was primarily a nationalist and revisionist formation that effectively brought together an older membership with an extreme-right past. Its leader was a multimillionaire who considered the Strasserists Bolsheviks. Early in 1992, the DVU obtained 6.3 percent of the vote in elections for the Landtag of Schleswig-Holstein, but its success was short-lived. In the East (including the eastern part of Berlin), the extreme Right launched a much more successful assault on the political system. Since 1995 it has managed to establish a semi-hegemonic "culture of the Right" in some regions, which has been pervasive among youth. This development has been accompanied by electoral successes in states (*Länder*) and municipalities.

Indeed, reunification remains unfinished and the inhabitants of the new federal states in the East ("Ossis") still suffer from the mistakes made by the political and economic elites between 1990 and 1994.[37] Chancellor Helmut Kohl had promised the East Germans "flourishing landscapes." This formula certainly allowed for a technically successful reunification and for some time created a climate of optimism. However, by 1992, much had deteriorated economically and socially and nearly 40 percent of the population had lost faith in the political system imported from the West. This was not without reason. East German industry had disappeared, unemployment rates were rising, and the voters' ideological and mental disorientation worsened. All of this allowed the neo-Communist successor to the Socialist Unity Party (Sozialistische Einheitspartei, or SED),[38] the Party of Democratic Socialism (Partei des Demokratischen Sozialismus, or PDS), which is now called the Left (Die Linke), to obtain about a quarter of the vote in the East. Since December 2014, it has formed a coalition government with the Social Democrats and the Green Party in the state of Thuringia. The Communist/post-Communist PDS/Left is now seen as the party defending East German identity as well as an anti-capitalist corrective force in an unjust system.[39] To this day, socialism is a strong element of East German identity, and globalization is perceived as a threat. Democratic parties (the Christian Democrats, the Social Democrats, the Greens, and the Free Democrats) are blamed for being cast in the West German ideological mold.

In this context of polymorphic crisis, the German extreme Right has adjusted successfully to the language, standards, and values of the East. According to an NPD slogan, it battles on three fronts: take the streets, take the parliaments, and win over minds. This entails three essential components: violence and extra-parliamentary action, electoral strategies and grassroots organizing, and the ideological penetration of vernacular and youth cultures into mainstream culture. Despite their small number in 1994, Strasserists were well armed for this battle. After 2004, the NPD's electoral results gave the illusion of a renaissance of the German Far Right—first in the context of the new federal states, then in the whole country. [40] But although it is indisputable that the NPD has had some regional and local success, its achievements remain relatively insignificant. In Bundestag elections from 2002 to 2013, the party was barely able to mobilize voters (0.4 percent in 2002, 1.6 percent in 2005, 1.5 percent in 2009, and 1.3 percent in 2013). In the 2014 European elections, the NPD received 1 percent of the vote and one seat in the European Parliament (Udo Voigt). In the regional elections, it was more successful.[41] Because of the 5-percent hurdle, the NPD is currently represented only in the parliament of Mecklenburg-Vorpommern. However, the party has more than 200 elected local representatives in Thuringia, Saxony, and Saxony-Anhalt. These areas are where it has its political roots, and from there it strives to win potential voters.

Former Bundeswehr officer Udo Voigt led the NPD from 1996 to 2011. In our conversations, the party leader adopted a very skeptical attitude toward socialist and national-revolutionary currents. However, the majority of NPD members in the East take anti-capitalist positions, as do the party's official youth organization (JN), the unofficial National Socialist "comradeship" groups on the periphery of the party, and most of the few intellectual members (mostly former members of the former German Democratic Republic's ruling SED). The government had threatened to ban the NPD, but the Constitutional Court stopped this procedure in 2003. New proceedings are underway, the outcome of which remains highly uncertain. Faced with this threat, a wing of the party has advocated a more bourgeois face for the NPD, which brings to mind the de-demonization strategy of the Front National in France. This is why the local level has priority. This wing also wants to officially distance itself from neo-Nazi comradeship groups, "socialists," and skinheads, and to strengthen the ideological efforts of the party to modernize and make itself more attractive in the West. The national-revolutionary and anti-capitalist wing, presently dominating the party leadership, also wants to strengthen the organization, but by absorbing useful personalities from the comradeships and other groups on the periphery. This would heighten the risk of banning, since the police could then rightly refer to the presence of many neo-Nazis in the party's organizational chart.

The JN youth organization (with 350 members in 2014) takes a National Socialist line that is close to Strasserism. The comradeships, after a period of strong organizational growth in the 1990s, especially in the East, have declined since 2001. Affected by multiple bans, prison sentences for numerous activists, and total infiltration by the German police, this model has lost its attractiveness to activists. Before being neutralized by the police, the neo-Nazis (both Hitlerists and Strasserists) began to search for new modes of organization and some made preparations for terrorist action. In contrast, the skinheads remained stuck in their traditional style of organization and their sub-culture (music, fanzines, dress-code, etc.). Just like skinheads, the neo-Nazis emphasized action, violence, and the hunt for foreigners (SA-style). A small percentage of the neo-Nazi groups tried to consolidate their theoretical positions and choose the path of "political soldiers." At this point, some began to criticize Hitlerism and defined themselves as national-revolutionary and anti-capitalist, generally quite close to the Strasser brothers. In the years 2009 to 2016, there were changes on the extreme Right and new political formations emerged. The NPD crisis between 2010 and 2013 resulted in a dual weakening in terms of electoral success and membership (2009: 26,000 members; 2014: 21,000).

The Autonomous Nationalists emerged in 2006, after the dissolution of many neo-Nazi "comradeships."[42] Between 2009 and 2013, this movement gained influence on the neo-Nazi scene in both the West and the East, with 1,000 to 1,500 activists and supporters. However, in 2016, after numerous police actions, there was a noticeable decline. What differentiates the Autonomous Nationalists from the bulk of active neo-Nazis is primarily their style of dress and complete lack of a structured organization. Generally communication and propaganda are conducted via telephone and online. Dressing completely in black, they have copied the look and aesthetics of the autonomous extreme left, who in turn drew their inspiration from the Weimar period. They have also recycled the iconography and slogans of the anarchists. The Autonomous Nationalists march in closed blocks and practice violence against the extreme left and the police. Although there are no theoretical texts for reference, an analysis of their websites shows that these "National Socialist" activists place themselves in the tradition of the Strasserist left National Socialist wing.[43] They call themselves anti-capitalist, anti-imperialist, anti-American, and anti-Israel, and advocate for a national liberation doctrine, "white" Germany, and a Europe of nations. They are pro–Vladimir Putin. The fight against immigration and Islam, together with anti-globalization, is the dominant line of agitation.

The Identitarian movement has also grown in popularity in Germany. These regionalist nativists are actors of the New Right movement and more or less distant heirs of de Benoist's GRECE.[44] The key tenets of their ideology are identity, ethnopluralism with the segregation of racial and ethnic groups, anti-Americanism, and anti-Islamism, and rootedness in the tradition of the rebirth/birth of a new Europe. They make reference to the Conservative Revolution, as well as to the publications of Aleksandr Dugin and Alain de Benoist. Strasserism, on the other hand, is rejected.

An analysis of Strasserist activities online, including Cause of the People[45] (SdV) as well as many blogs addressing questions of German socialism and national-revolutionary strategy, show that the debate is continuing. What is striking is the support for Vladimir Putin and the proliferation of references to Dugin. Several fringe groups draw inspiration from Dugin, among them the Third Way (Der III. Weg), a party founded in 2013 by former NPD members and National Socialist activists, who were joined by members of the banned "Free Network South" Comradeship Network (Kameradschaftsnetzwerk "Freies Netz Süd," or FNS). Mainly based in Bavaria, it has pockets of support in Hesse, North Rhine-Westphalia, Rhineland-Palatinate, and Saxony (200 activists in 2014). The party has adopted the symbols of the Nazi left, declares itself national-revolutionary, and promotes "German socialism" in its ten-point program.[46] It also reveres Putin as an anti-imperialist actor.

The German extreme Right is now divided among more than 230 organizations, parties, study circles, and semi-informal structures that share several ideological foundations. Almost all of these variants (including Strasserism) display anti-capitalist, anti-globalization, anti-American, and predominantly anti-Zionist, xenophobic, and nationalist stances. The nature of radical Islam is certainly a controversial topic, given its anti-Zi-onism and anti-capitalism, but the Islamic state is considered a funda-mental threat to (white) Europe. The only truly new common feature is the unconditional support for Putin's present anti-EU and anti-American policy.

This pro-Russian (and anti-Ukrainian) position has intensified since the annexation of Crimea. The whole German extremist Right describes Ukraine as a country under American command and the Maidan rev-olution as a CIA putsch. Putin and his Eurasian project are seen as an anti-imperialist bulwark and a model for the preservation of Russian identity and Russian culture. The rapidly increasing number of trips by extreme-right cadres to Russia, the international conferences taking place there discreetly (and others elsewhere in Europe), and the numerous contacts of Russian diplomats with activists of the German extreme Right are signs of an active penetration and instrumentalization of the German extreme Right by the Russian services.[47] These activities also extend to the new national-populist and German party, Alternative for Germany (Alternative für Deutschland, or AfD).

CONCLUSION

The rise of Alternative für Deutschland (AfD), a populist, national-con-servative, and anti-European party with about 19,000 members, and the Pediga anti-immigration movement, have greatly reduced the electoral chances of the NPD, which continues to fracture ideologically.[48] At the September 2017 legislative election, AfD celebrated its historic third place success, with 13 percent of the vote—the first time in almost six decades that an openly nationalist party will enter the Bundestag. The party has two wings—one conservative and national-liberal, the other socialistic and anti-system. The latter wing includes some Strasserist activists, but their influence is very limited. The ideological bridge between the two factions is their hostility to the "Europe of Brussels," the fight against immigration, and their pro-Russian attitude.

Competitor parties of the NPD and the AfD, such as the Right, the Citizens' Movement of North Rhine-Westphalia, and the Third Way, are on the lookout for a development strategy that could involve an enhanced dual anti-immigration/anti-globalization campaign. Strasserism, en-compassing the national socialism of Gregor and Otto Strasser and the Weimar-era Conservative Revolution, provides a theoretical framework that feeds the militancy of Autonomous Nationalists and some skinheads and National Socialist comradeships, and inspires one wing of the NPD and also the new party, the Third Way. In this sense, Strasserism and its national-revolutionary strategy are still present in the German political system, and remain devoted to developing a positive relationship with Russia.

PART V

THE QUEST FOR IDEOLOGY IN THE SOVIET NOMENKLATURA AND UNDERGROUND

CHAPTER 9

LEV GUMILEV AND THE EUROPEAN NEW RIGHT

Mark Bassin

The striking affinities that have developed between radical-conservative movements in Western Europe and Russia since the end of the Cold War have been widely noted.[1] Much attention has focused in particular on the example of Aleksandr Dugin, who in the 1990s emerged as one of the most effective and influential progenitors of this movement.[2] Dugin borrowed openly and extensively from the ideological legacy of the so-called European Conservative Revolution—the theories of Carl Schmitt, Julius Evola, Karl Haushofer, and others—in formulating his own extremist vision for Russia, and he actively developed personal contacts with the leaders of the European New Right, inviting them to Russia and disseminating translations of their ideas and their works. More recently, Dugin has come to be appreciated in his own right in the West as an important New Right theorist. His works are available in a variety of European translations, and they are helping to shape the radical right's perception of global affairs. This relates particularly to the role of Russia, which is increasingly understood in terms of Dugin's neo-Eurasianist perspective.[3]

Indeed, the resonances between Russian and European radical conservatism are no longer limited to purely ideological cross-fertilization. One of the more fascinating side effects of Russia's actions in Ukraine in 2014 has been to reveal the political connections that are developing between the Putin regime and radical-conservative tendencies in the West. The Russian government has underwritten the activities of the Front National in France in the non-trivial form of a nine million Euro loan, battalions of young New Right enthusiasts from France and elsewhere travel to eastern Ukraine to fight in the ranks of the Russian-supported separatist army, and Putin has given public indications of his solidarity with the extremist Jobbik party in Hungary and Ataka in Bulgaria.[4] The leader of the UK Independence Party, Nigel Farage, praises the Russian leader's "brilliant" political maneuvering, and no less a stalwart of America's conservative establishment than Pat Buchanan has begun—sensationally—to wonder if Vladimir Putin might not actually be "one of us."[5]

This chapter considers a rather different example of the resonance between Russian and European conservatism, namely the Soviet historian and geographer Lev Nikolaevich Gumilev (1912–1992). Best known for his "ethnos theory" and his Eurasianist perspective on Russian history and identity, Gumilev has become enormously popular and influential in the post-Soviet period, not least of all for Aleksandr Dugin himself, who describes Gumilev as his most important Russian mentor. As with Dugin, there are highly significant similarities between Gumilev and the European New Right in regard to a variety of fundamental assumptions and principles.[6] These similarities are all the more notable in that Gumilev—quite unlike Dugin—had no personal contacts with any European ideologues of his day, was unacquainted with their literature and ideas, and had no apparent interest in or indeed even awareness of their project. Despite this, as we will see, Gumilev and the European New Right developed perspectives that were highly comparable, founded on similar principles and articulated through similar images and allusions. Yet despite the powerful resonances in terms of basic concepts and theoretical orientation, there were nonetheless profound differences in terms of the practical implications for their respective societies that Gumilev and the Europeans deduced from these principles.

THE ALLURE OF ETHNOS

The European New Right began to take its current form in the late 1960s. Inspired by the radical-conservative and fascist movements of the interwar period, it has nonetheless attempted (with varying degrees of success) to modulate the ultra-nationalist and expansionist bellicosity of the earlier period.[7] Today, the New Right describes its concerns as essentially defensive, focused on the protection of the peoples of Europe against various processes of the contemporary world which, it claims, are threatening their existence.[8] Most broadly, these threats emanate from the homogenizing dynamics of modernity, which seek to eradicate vital religious, cultural,

and national differences and reshape all of humanity to fit a single universal model. On a global scale, this drive to standardization is apparent in the
reckless quest for universal integration through globalization and *mondialisme* or "one-worldism," while within Europe it inspires the state-sponsored
project of European integration.[9] Both processes are driven by an obsession
with the rights and entitlements of the individual on the one hand and an
insistence on the unconditional equality and uniformity of all individuals
on the other—an ethos derisively referred to by a leading theoretician of the
New Right, Alain de Benoist, as "individuouniversalism."[10] These developments can have only one result, namely the reduction of the entire population of the world to a uniform and colorless monocultural mass.[11] This
is precisely what is occurring today in Europe, where the indiscriminate
acceptance and integration of immigrants from around the world under the
aegis of so-called multi-culturalism represent an acute threat to the integrity of Europe's indigenous populations. In the face of the integrationist and
assimilationist forces of an inexorably globalizing world, the European New
Right advocates the principle of *différencialisme*, or "differentialism."[12] The
"right to be different," it insists, is a fundamental human entitlement.

To counter the menace of individuouniversalism, the European New
Right seeks to reanimate an older discourse of ethno-politics centered
around the ideal of the *Volksgemeinschaft*, understood in terms of the
Gemeinschaft–Gesellschaft distinction first elaborated in the nineteenth
century by the sociologist Ferdinand Tönnies.[13] In this juxtaposition,
Gemeinschaft represents an essentialized organic and holistic community, not "imagined" or "constructed" but real-existing. In it, individuals
feel an organic sense of belonging and solidarity on the basis of common
origins, common social values, and a common culture.[14] A *Gesellschaft*,
by contrast, is a formalistic and impersonal collection of individuals,
who consent to coalesce for reasons which they believe will ultimately
serve their individual interests. While a *Gesellschaft* always acknowl-
edges the autonomy and prerogative of the individual, in a *Gemeinschaft*
the individual cannot be separated from the group as a whole. It is a per-
sonalistic form of association, developing spontaneously rather than
through deliberate construction. Belonging to a *Gemeinschaft* inheres
naturally, as it were, in an individual's persona; it is not a matter of choice
but rather determined by the existential reality of who they are.[15]

In the past, the term "nation" served as a sort of colloquial equivalent
which could capture the nuances of the *Volksgemeinschaft* concept.[16]
While this usage persists, it is nonetheless problematic in the present
day, for the sense of "nation" is now colored through its association with

the political entity of the modern "nation-state." The New Right regards the latter as a *Gesellschaft* organized along the principles of universalism and equality—an "outdated construct based on assimilation and the destruction of distinction[17]—such that many tendencies within the New Right abandon the term "nation" altogether. In its place, the more exotic concept of the *ethnos* is frequently adopted to refer to "the basic unit of homogeneous cultural energy" that corresponds to the New Right's idealized vision of organic human communities.[18] Since the 1970s, the concepts of nation/nationality have been increasingly supplanted by ethnos/ethnicity—either through combining them (as "ethno-nations") or by discarding the former altogether (as "ethno-cultures" or "ethno-cultural communities").[19] An ethnos is understood as "an organic cultural unity, possessing its own unique spirit and historical background, and existing in the world with its own, particular form of being."[20] The ethnic community takes absolute priority over the nation-state, with ethnocultural belonging having a higher status and value than civic entitlement. Indeed, for the New Right the organic ethnos-*Gemeinschaft* is quite simply the essential (and essentialized) *modus* of human organization, and it is only through membership in it that an individual can realize his or her full existence.[21] An ethnos provides "a sense of identity and . . . a meaningful orientation to the entire world population. It is by virtue of their organic adherence to the society [i.e., ethnos] of which they are a part that men build their humanity."[22]

Gumilev's thinking was shaped by his perception of a threat of homogenization in post-Stalinist society that was similar to that we have just noted in Western Europe.[23] In his case, the agent of this process was neither *mondialisme* nor neoliberal globalization, but rather Soviet Marxism. From the outset, the Soviet project of modernization and development embraced a Marxist teleology of social and economic progress, according to which all of its regions and peoples should eventually attain the same level of advanced "socialist" construction. It was assumed that this process would bring about profound transformations, not the least of which would be the elimination of the ethno-national differences among the many nationalities that comprised the Soviet population. As all Soviet citizens increasingly developed the same economic, social, and cultural standards and norms, so the official dogma maintained, the material basis for their differentiation would gradually disappear, until—in a process called *sliianie*, or "fusion"— they would merge together to form a single, homogeneous Soviet nation.[24]

To be sure, this issue was highly politicized, and the specifics varied considerably from regime to regime. In the Stalinist 1930s and 1940s, for example, the eventuality of *sliianie* was acknowledged but pressed into the very distant future. For the purposes of the present day, Stalinism in fact developed a concept of essentialized ethno-nationality, which corresponded in important respects to the *Volksgemeinschaft* model just described.[25] For the foreseeable future, socialist development would deliver a standard level of high development for all the Soviet peoples, but the latter would remain precisely as *sovetskie natsii*, that is to say socialist ethno-nations. Under Stalin's successor Nikita Khrushchev, however, the official line was inverted dramatically. Ethno-essentialism was abandoned, and it was now maintained instead that *sliianie* was not only already taking place in contemporary Soviet society, but indeed had already progressed to the point of creating a new sociopolitical entity, the *sovetskii narod*, or Soviet nation. Khrushchev called for the acceleration and deepening of this process. While his radical position on the issue of *sliianie* was one of the factors that led to his ousting in 1964, the assimilationist inclination did not go away. On the contrary, the notion of a post-ethno-national *sovetskii narod* continued to enjoy official endorsement down to perestroika in the late 1980s.[26]

Along with many of his compatriots in the USSR, Gumilev was highly uncomfortable with the post-Stalinist project for the *sliianie* of the Soviet peoples, and his opposition to it provided a major stimulus for his theoretical work on the problem of ethnicity, from the 1960s through the 1980s. Like the New Right in Europe, he rejected any notion of universal or pan-human values. There is no such thing as general or universal history, he declared, and "to speak about a history of all humankind makes no sense."[27] The experience of history demonstrates that all attempts to impose "a universal system of values have always collapsed and led only to more bloodshed."[28] The *sliianie* project of the Soviet state, conceived precisely in this universalist spirit, was the cardinal folly of the "political utopia" that the Soviet leaders hoped to create, and could be achieved only through the forcible mixing of the Soviet peoples—"the Ingush with the Baltic peoples in Siberia, and Koreans with Kalmyks in Kazakhstan."[29] The goal, however—to "make everyone resemble yourself"—could have no conceivable justification.[30] "Why should we try to squeeze the behaviour of an Abkhazian and a Chukot, a Lithuanian and a Moldavian all into a single frame? This is pointless and harmful. How can we create a single ethnos for the entire planet [or our country]?"[31] In rejecting the Soviet *sliianie* project, Gumilev echoed the conviction we have just noted in the European New Right regarding the absolute value of the differences between national groups, and he similarly emphasized the imperative to maintain these. He spoke in highly positive tones about the *mozaichnost'*, or mosaic quality, of the multinational Soviet population, and believed that precisely this diversity was one of its most important qualities. Difference and diversity were necessary conditions for humankind to flourish. "If everyone merges and becomes the same," he reasoned, "then there will be no movement, no cultural development, and life will simply cease to exist."[32]

Like the European New Right, moreover, Gumilev's term of preference for the communities making up this mosaic pattern was "ethnos" (*etnos, etnosy*), rather than "nation" (*natsiia; narod*) or "nationality" (*natsional'nost'*). The term *etnos*, it should be noted, had its own history in the USSR, where in the 1960s and 1970s it came into much more general use than in the West. Following the lead of Iulian Bromlei, the Director of the Academy of Sciences' Institute of Ethnography, a phalanx of ethnographers set about elaborating a formal "ethnos theory," and in a sense Gumilev—although no admirer of Bromlei—was part of this movement.[33] But mainstream Soviet ethnography was always careful to describe the ethnos in terms that were not at obvious odds with official policy. This meant most importantly that it could, in principle, be part of the *sliianie* process, in the sense that ethnies could combine to create greater homogeneous entities, described by the ever-inventive Soviet specialists as "metaethnies."[34] Gumilev, for his part, rejected this idea entirely. He opted instead for precisely the same *Gesellschaft-Gemeinschaft* distinction that we have noted above, and argued that ethnies, as spontaneous organic communities, correspond to the latter category.[35] They cohered on the basis not of individual choice or group decision but rather of natural kinship, shared historical experience, and what he called a common "behavioral stereotype" that was unique to each group. Formalized social relations, understood in Marxist categories such as class, did not play any role. For Gumilev, the ethnos was the most fundamental and durable category of human organization. Ethnic belonging was an existential mode of being, an intrinsic and immutable part of the very persona of all individuals which could be neither transcended nor transformed.[36] "No human being can live outside of an ethnos," he affirmed—indeed any attempt to do so would be tantamount to "pulling oneself out of a swamp by one's own hair."[37]

THE ETHNOS AS A NATURAL ORGANISM

The radical-conservative tradition in prewar Europe had commonly conceived of the ethnos-*Gemeinschaft* as a natural organism, fundamentally shaped by the biological-genetic characteristics of its respective race. The so-called *Volksbiologie*, or national biology, developed by the Nazis was resurrected in Germany already in the early 1950s, and this naturalist orientation—eventually rechristened rather more discreetly as "biological realism"—continues to provide inspiration and guidance for significant parts of the New Right down to the present day.[38] According to this perspective, each ethnos represents a "biological reality" determined by its own unique gene pool (*genetische Sammelbecken*) and genotype, which serve to differentiate it biologically from all other groups.[39] Theorists of the New Right repeat the old arguments of German *Rassenkunde* that aggression is a natural feature of interethnic relations, and that the mixing—even intermingling—of ethnies represents a "racial mongrelization" doomed to produce ethnies that are "genetically manipulated" or "biologically imploded."[40] Culture and ethnicity can never exist "entirely independently of race, and, since any significant level of racial miscegenation transforms the basic structure of a racial type, it also transforms ethnic type . . ."[41]

In addition to hard-core racial science, the New Right has also sought to legitimate its biological realism with the apparently more neutral scientific arguments of cybernetics and socio-biology.[42] The systems theory developed by Ludwig von Bertalanffy in the 1960s provided a conceptual framework for understanding the ethnos as a closed natural-organic system or organism, which like all other organisms acted in accordance with universal natural laws.[43] In the same period, biologists such as Konrad Lorenz and especially his student Irinäus Eibl-Eibesfeldt extended the field of ethology—the science of animal behavior—to include human populations as well.[44] This notion of a biology of human behavior, in which genetic inheritance was the "determining factor," proved very useful for the New Right's elaboration of a naturalized model of the ethno-organism.[45]

To be sure, not all tendencies of the New Right embraced these racialist and biological discourses. Appreciating how they serve to undermine any ambitions of broadening the appeal of his project, Alain de Benoist has been particularly outspoken on this point. Downplaying this socio-biological perspective, he emphasizes instead the importance of cultural and civilizational factors in the constitution of ethnies.[46] "I am hostile," he declared, "to interpretations of human reality based exclusively on biology," and he dropped objectionable references to race and genetics.[47] Yet although de Benoist's option to abandon racialism caused considerable consternation for his co-thinkers in the New Right,[48] it did not in fact represent a complete rejection of the principles of biological realism. On the contrary, he continues to affirm the general significance of biology as one of the formative agents conditioning the nature of society.[49] In particular, he explicitly supports the practice of endogamy as a natural means of "defending" the integrity of the homogeneous ethnos against genetic mixing with foreign elements.[50]

One of the most important characteristics of the ethnos-*Gemeinschaft* as a natural organism was its territoriality. Before 1945, the importance of organic *Verwurzelung,* or rootedness in a specific geographical region, and the specific space-need of individual ethnies were conceptualized in notions such as *Blut und Boden* and *Lebensraum.*[51] Using a different terminology, Lorenz and Eibl-Eibesfeldt continued to maintain the significance of this connection as a vital biological nexus for the existence of the ethnos, which functions in human communities as it does in the animal world.[52] In a 2014 polemic, a leading New Right ideologue loudly reaffirmed the principle of ethno-territoriality. "Any talk about people and culture boils down to dealing with the fundamental question of territory. It is a cardinal question that is impossible to avoid, since it opens and closes every debate on identity. In effect, territory is to a people what air is to our lungs. If it happens to disappear, the cultural and biological life of an ethnic group is threatened with asphyxiation (in a very real sense) in a short span."[53]

Each ethnos exists in a dynamic but harmonious and primordial socio-ecological relationship with its geographical homeland, from which it draws spiritual as well as material sustenance. This native territory represents the group's natural patrimony, and no ethnos can long lead a healthy existence beyond its borders. In every case, the attachment to the ethno-region is exclusive to the respective group.[54] Homelands are not and cannot be shared, for the presence of multiple ethnies in one region is necessarily disruptive for all affected.

Gumilev shared the view of the ethnos as a natural organism, and he developed his own version of biological realism.[55] There was a special significance to this in his case, for Soviet ethnography, unlike its Western counterparts, had always strongly resisted any naturalistic perspective on ethnic life,[56] and thus Gumilev's theories in this regard were original in a way that the European New Right—which drew on a rich legacy of racialist "science"—was not. Indeed, Gumilev's natural-biological conception was the most sensational and controversial aspect of his work, and it attracted the hostility not only of professional colleagues, but also of the political authorities in the USSR. "I consider ethnic processes to be purely a part of natural and biospheric processes," he declared.[57] Ethnic existence had nothing to do with Marxist laws of social development; indeed, as a natural—*prirodnyi* or *estestvennyi*—phenomenon, the ethnos was more properly the subject of natural science than sociology.[58] Along with the European New Right, he asserted that ethnicity was a "biological" or "biophysical reality.... Ethnic belonging, which manifests itself in the human consciousness, is not a product of this consciousness," it is "a biological dimension located beyond consciousness and psychology, on the boundaries of the physiological."[59] Gumilev made frequent use of the metaphor of a biological organism, likening the ethnos either to an individual human being—which in a similar fashion "is born, matures (*muzhat'sia*), grows old and dies"[60]—or to aggregate organisms found in the natural world. "Collective forms of existence can be seen in many species of terrestrial animals: ants, herds of hoofed animals, flocks of birds, and so on." For the species Homo sapiens, "the corresponding form [of collective life] is the ethnos."[61] Ethnies represented "biological communities" in an entirely literal sense, which operated in terms of "biological time" (predetermined successions of organic growth, decline, and rebirth) as opposed to historical time (progressive development in a linear fashion).[62]

Gumilev's specific view of the relationship of genetics to race and ethnicity, however, was highly ambivalent. Along with the rest of his Soviet colleagues, he categorically rejected the *Rassenkunde* so popular among his contemporaries in the European New Right.[63] In no way, he maintained repeatedly, is ethnicity racially determined or conditioned, and he explicitly denounced "Social Darwinism" in the West, which sought to apply "biological laws to social life."[64] At the same time, however, he was in fact powerfully attracted to the science of Soviet genetics, which in the 1960s was re-establishing itself after decades of suppression led by the Stalinist agronomist T. D. Lysenko. Gumilev was associated with a number of leading geneticists, among them the internationally acclaimed scholar N. V. Timofeev-Resovskii, and he used their ideas quite extensively in constructing his own theories about ethnicity. Gumilev believed that each ethnos, as a biological or quasi-biological organism, possessed a unique genotype, which had to be protected from exogenic influences if the integrity of the group was to be maintained. On this basis, he stressed the importance of endogamy as an institutionalized group practice.[65] Endogamy served a specifically genetic function in "stabilizing [i.e., protecting] the composition of the gene pool" and thereby helping to consolidate the "sustainability of the ethnic collective."[66] Failure to practice endogamy would lead to *metisatsiia* or interbreeding among different *etnosy*—a process which, he claimed, "creates a mixed (*smeshannyi*) gene pool, which will produce descendants that are inferior (*nepolnotsennyi*)."[67] "Open contact and free love," he declared, "destroy nature and culture."[68] Like the European New Right, moreover, Gumilev was also strongly influenced by cybernetics— von Bertalanffy's writings on systems theory were published in the Soviet Union in the late 1960s and attracted a good deal of interest there[69]—and also by the work of Soviet ethologists and behavioral scientists, in particular his colleague at Leningrad State University, M. E. Lobashev.[70]

Most significantly of all, Gumilev stressed the fundamental importance of ethno-territoriality and the organic emplacement of an ethnos in its own native geographical region in terms very similar to those of the European New Right. All ethnies not only displayed a "close interconnection with their respective geographical landscape," but also represented a "necessary component part" (*sostavnaia chast'*) of this landscape, "interacting with its fauna and flora" to form an *etnolandshaftnaia tselostnost'* or "ethno-landscape totality."[71] Indeed, the natural-geographical landscape acted as a sort of vital platform for ethnic development, one which "shelters and nourishes" the ethnos and defines thereby its most important life-parameters.[72] Gumilev's emphasis on the existential importance of the external environment amounted to a veritable ecology of ethnicity.[73] He characterized this relationship using a term he took from the classical Eurasianists (who similarly emphasized the importance of external geographical factors): *mestorazvitie*, or topogenesis.[74] The ethnic homeland—its "ecological niche"—represents "one of the component parts of that system we call an ethnos."[75] Gumilev drew heavily on the eminent natural-scientific traditions of ecology and landscape science in Russia—above all the work of V. V. Dokuchaev, L. S. Berg, and V. N. Sukachev—as well as the notion of the biosphere and the biospheric circulation of energy developed by Vernadskii.[76] He maintained that the ethnos represented an integral element of the "closed system" that was the natural ecosystem or biocenosis of their native regions, as natural and necessary as any other part of its plant or animal life. The ethnos was connected to its respective niche umbilically, as it were, and its survival in any other region was, under normal circumstances, unthinkable.[77] And like the European New Right, Gumilev believed that any one ecological niche could support only that ethnos which had developed naturally within it. The prolonged presence of a "foreign" ethnos within the boundaries of another group's homeland necessarily led to the degradation and ultimate demise of the indigenous ethnos—a situation Gumilev famously characterized as a *khimera*, or chimera.

ETHNO-PLURALISM, ETHNO-TERRITORIALITY, AND "COMMUNITIES OF DESTINY"

Based on these ideas about the nature of ethnies and the existential threats confronting them in the contemporary world, the European New Right articulated its alternative to the universalization and homogenization of modernity in the form of so-called ethno-pluralism. Ethno-pluralism rejects the "racist" notion that there is any essentialized inequality between ethno-cultural groups, insisting rather on the principled equivalence of all peoples. Ethnies are not developmentally "higher" or "lower," and they are not more or less civilized. All of them have their own rightful position in the global fabric of ethnic life, and they all share the same entitlements to self-expression, self-determination, and, as we have already seen, the "right to be different."[78] Indeed, the mutuality of the principle of difference provides the most genuine basis for interethnic solidarity, to the extent indeed that the New Right is adamant that the defense of the identities of immigrants and foreigners is no less important than that of indigenous Europeans.[79] However, ethnopluralism attaches a critical proviso to this acknowledgment of ethno-cultural equality, namely that ethnies are not merely different but essentially incommensurable. "Divergent cultures cannot reach shared understandings or be judged by common standards."[80] On the contrary, each ethnos represents a veritable closed system, self-sufficient unto itself and functional only to the extent that its homogeneity in all respects is preserved. An ethno-cultural group can define itself only in terms of an essentialized us–them juxtaposition that sets it apart from all other such groups. "Confrontation," de Benoist notes, "makes identity possible."[81] The compromising of this juxtaposition through mixing and integration inevitably undermines the group's sense of itself and with this its very existence. For this reason, ethno-pluralism insists on the need to maintain a strict separation between all ethno-cultural groups. And the most effective means of maintaining this separation and ethnic homogeneity is to mobilize the principle of ethno-territoriality and ensure that the various ethno-cultures are kept physically separate. "Without barriers, without a certain level of separation from other peoples, and without a specific territory on which to live as a distinct people, an ethnic or a racial group would disappear through mixture or assimilation into other groups."[82] Noting the natural inclination toward competition and conflict between ethnies, the ethologist Eibl-Eibesfeldt declared "that the best way to maintain peaceful cooperation between peoples consists in guaranteeing to each of them a territory that each people has the right to administer in its own way, and in which it is permitted to develop itself culturally as it sees fit. . . . Peaceful collaboration between different peoples is [only] possible on the condition that each ethnic group possesses its own territory and can regulate its own affairs without exposing itself to any repressive domination or to territorial amputations."[83] If the ethno-territorial principle is respected, there is no reason that several different groups cannot coexist and prosper within a single state structure, as the example of Switzerland clearly indicates.[84]

Gumilev developed what was effectively an ethnopluralist perspective of his own, which reproduced all of these basic points. Rejecting Marxist teachings about the "progress" of humanity through ever-higher stages of social, economic, and cultural development, he declared that no ethnos was more or less civilized or developed than any other. All were equal, sharing similar organizational patterns and undergoing the same process of natural development. At the same time, however, each ethnos represented a unique, self-contained, and self-sustaining entity. Gumilev placed immense emphasis on ethnic individuality, maintaining that the real-existing differences between groups were reflected in a subjective group awareness of a *svoi–chuzhoi* (us–them) juxtaposition which—precisely echoing de Benoist—provided cohesion and identity.[85] Ethnic individuality means that different groups cannot be combined or merged without injuring their integrity. "It is impossible to unite (*ob"edinit'*) ethnies, for the resulting union will always involve the principle of compulsion. Ethnies cannot simply be made to love each other."[86]

Precisely like the European New Right, Gumilev concluded that the only way to ensure peaceful coexistence was to segregate ethnies physically on the basis of their respective natural homelands.[87] Gumilev considered this arrangement to be the "optimal variant of ethnic contact"—one in which all ethnies live "next to each other but separately (*porozn'*), cultivating peaceful relations and not interfering in the other's affairs."[88] The historical pattern of ethnic settlement in Siberia provided a good example of what he had in mind. Ethnies in Siberia "occupied the different landscape regions that corresponded to their [historical habitation and] cultural-economic patterns, and they did not disturb each other but rather helped them. The Iakuts settled in the broad floodplains of the Lena river, the Evenks in the watersheds of the taiga uplands, and the Russians along the river valleys. The expanses of the steppe were left to the Kazakhs and Kalmyks, and the forests to the Ugrian peoples."[89] This symbiotic variety—a "colorful diversity" (*pestrota*) and "mosaic quality" (*mozaichnost'*)—was an important biological aspect of ethnic survival, indeed "the optimal form for human existence." Organized natural separation helped to minimize competition for resources, and enhanced opportunities for helpful cooperation.[90]

Although an ethnos is a cohesive entity, for the New Right it nonetheless represents only one level on a continuum or hierarchy of ethnic affiliation. Internally, it comprises smaller units of so-called sub-ethnic groups, such as the Bretons or Alsatians in France, or the Bavarians or Swabians in Germany. At the same time, ethnies themselves represent constituent units of yet larger entities, referred to as "cultures" or, rather more loosely, as *Schicksalsgemeinschaften* or "communities of destiny." Despite the clear differentiation of their component ethnies, the latter nonetheless share common interests and experience some sense of common identity.[91] These poly-ethnic aggregates correspond loosely to the notion of *Weltkulturen* or "world civilizations" elaborated by Oswald Spengler after World War I and reanimated in the 1990s by the Harvard political scientist Samuel Huntington.[92] There is an important difference, however: While Spengler and Huntington included the United States as part of *das Abendland* or "the West" (albeit with different nuances), the European New Right explicitly rejects this association. Europe is described as a self-contained civiliza-tional entity unto itself, different from, and indeed opposed to, the United States.[93] Over centuries of cohabitation across a common continental space, the primordial European ethno-cultures have developed similarities and objective affinities, to the extent that certain New Right theoreticians not only view them as "a highly unified population in terms of biology and anthropology" but indeed also argue for the existence of a European—and incidentally also a "white"—racial type, essentially opposed to those that developed on the continents of the Americas, Asia, and Africa.[94]

The New Right today calls upon the European peoples to develop an appreciation of their shared cultural-historical affinities that could serve as the basis for their eventual geopolitical mobilization. As de Benoist ex-plained, "in a globalized world, the future belongs to large cultures and civ-ilizations capable of organizing themselves into autonomous entities and of acquiring enough power to resist outside interference."[95] Practically, a pan-European consolidation could take various forms. De Benoist himself proposes the creation of a European federation, based not on the liberaliz-ing and universalizing foundations of the European Union but rather on the principle of ethno-regionalism. Membership of various peoples in a single political structure would be based on mutual recognition of their similari-ties and common interests, while respect for essential differences would be guaranteed by the institution of ethno-territorial autonomy.[96] Other New Right theoreticians call for a revival of an imperial state—on the model of the ancient Roman or Holy Roman empires—as a strategy for the desired poly-ethnic agglomeration of the future.[97] Such a neo-imperial political structure would represent a "complex 'mosaic' of different European peo-ples,"[98] within the framework of which "ethnocultural groups of all levels and types [would] have the right to live with freedom and separately from others . . . to live autonomously in their own territories and to resist mix-ing."[99] A further difference with Huntington is that the New Right regards Russia as a natural historical part of the European ethno-cultural zone, and considers it to be a vitally important component of any future pan-

European empire. This is an important source of the considerable support for Dugin's neo-Eurasianist project noted at the outset of this essay, and indeed the European New Right has formulated its own trans-continental vision of "a federal, imperial Grande Europe, ethnically homogeneous (that is, European), based on a single autonomous area, and allied to Russia." This continental bloc is often referred to today as "Euro-Siberia," and when consolidated could aspire to become "the premier world power (in a world partitioned into large blocs), self-centered, and opposed to all the dangerous dogmas now associated with globalism."[100]

For his part, Gumilev developed his own elaborate scheme of ethnic hierarchy. Below the ethnos were subordinate entities which he also called "sub-ethnies" (sub-etnosy). These resembled the ethnos in many respects, and were commonly rooted in a particular geographical locality.[101] Within the corpus of the Great Russian ethnos, Gumilev identified Pomory, Cossacks, Chaldony (Russian Siberians), Kriasheny (Orthodox Tatars), and other groups as sub-ethnies.[102] At the other end, ranged above the ethnos were "superethnies" (superetnosy). The superethnos was an assemblage of different ethnies whose mutual sympathy came from the innate quality of what Gumilev called "complementarity" (komplimentarnost'). Complementarity between the members of a superethnos was reflected in the "political, ideological, and religious values" that they all shared,[103] but superethnic coherence was based most importantly on a deep sense of "common historical destiny" (obshchaia istoricheskaia sud'ba) that was basically identical to the Schicksalsgemeinschaft concept of the European New Right.[104] Like the European New Right, moreover, Gumilev located his superethnos concept in the Spenglerian discourse of world-historical civilizations, and he described its ideal internal organization in terms of what can be readily recognized as ethno-regionalist principles.[105] Within the limits of a single superethnos, that is, ethnic life should be "separate but equal," with each ethnos remaining carefully within the boundaries of its respective ecological niche. Repeating the imagery of the New Right, Gumilev described the superethnos as a "mosaic totality," an arrangement which helps to preserve ethnic individuality and restrict the scale and intensity of interethnic conflict.[106] Mixing between the ethnies in a single superethnos was further controlled by the universal observance of the principles of endogamy.[107]

THE NEW RIGHT'S RECEPTION OF GUMILEV

Unlike Aleksandr Dugin, Lev Gumilev was never a well-known figure in the West, beyond academic specialists in Soviet affairs. There was little free

flow of ideas in general between the USSR and the West, and this was especially true in the case of Gumilev's work, which did not enjoy official support
or even approval. But despite this, and the relative paucity of translations
of Gumilev's writings into European languages, he is not an unknown
entity for the European New Right. The latter's discussions of Dugin and
Russian neo-Eurasianism frequently acknowledge the inspirational role
of Gumilev as the spiritual godfather of neo-Eurasianism and as Dugin's
mentor in particular. More specifically, the resonance of Gumilev's ideas
with their own ethno-regionalist principles is also frequently stressed. "For
Gumilev . . . the new Russia must adhere to the principle of ethnopluralism.
It is thus not a question of Russianizing the people of the periphery [of the
Russian Federation] but of making of them definitive allies of the 'imperial
people'"—that is, ethnic Russians.[108] Indeed, in some cases the originality
and distinctiveness of his theories about ethnic life are appreciated in surprisingly fine detail. There is, for example, an awareness of the specialized
concepts and terminology he developed, such as his notion of *passionarnost'*
as the driving force of ethnic development or his model of ethnogenesis as a
life cycle in which each ethnos passes through a set of fixed stages.[109] Alain
de Benoist is particularly taken with Gumilev's ecological explanation of the
connection between the ethnos as a "biologized organic community" and
the natural world. He notes the latter's use of the term *mestorazvitie* with
interest, and clearly feels that Gumilev's understanding of ethno-territoriality corresponds to his own. Gumilev, he summarized quite accurately,
"believed that ethnies were created by the place, by space, by its topographic
and economic characteristics . . . This is why any change to the collective
habitus, any modification of this space and place, alters the destiny of the
ethnos; it can be fatal and lead to its dissolution."[110] A German far-right text
on the concept of ethnos published in 2014 offers Soviet ethnos theory as a
sort of model for the proper understanding of the phenomenon, and includes
a full-page portrait of its most important theoretician: Lev Gumilev.[111]

Beyond these general observations, the New Right deploys Gumilev's
theories and specialized terminology more instrumentally as a legit-
imating conceptual framework for their own ideological and political
priorities. A essay devoted to Gumilev posted on a Swedish New Right
website pointed out how his description of an ethnos as an organic feature
of a natural-geographical landscape and ecosystem provides "an ecolog-
ically based argument against large-scale migration." The Gumilevian
"superethnos" is moreover a useful notion for the purposes of conceptu-
alizing what a poly-ethnic and cohesive community of European peoples
might look like. "In the 1930s, we saw how a European superethnos began

to take form, when so-called nationalists repeatedly wanted to avoid a war among fraternal peoples [of Western Europe], so they could fight together against the Bolshevism of the east." This interwar project to develop a proto-superethnos has been resurrected in the present day, as the "nationalist parties" in the different European countries collaborate in a manner that today can help "create a superethnos out of the European peoples."[112] The ascription of superethnos status to the European ethno-cultural community serves not only to support the solidarity of its members, but also to essentialize yet further their collective incompatibility with all other foreign groups.

This may be kept in mind when considering a European immigration policy that has among other things placed millions of members of the Muslim superethnos in the heart of Europe. Whatever one may think about this, the conflicts that arise are entirely predictable. The complications associated with the integration of the Roma peoples are similar in nature. The Roma "are not a part of the [European] superethnos" and consequently lack "solidarity" with it. It is only because of this lack of superethnic empathy that their "high fertility is seen as a problem"—in the case of any of the genuinely European peoples, it is implied, such a quality would be welcomed as a positive natural advantage and benefit.

DIFFERENCES I: *GEMEINSCHAFT, GESELLSCHAFT,* AND THE STATE

The wide-ranging commonality between Gumilev and the European New Right in terms of orientation and basic concepts begins to fracture, however, in consideration of the more practical political and social imperatives that were and are derived on the basis of their shared ideological orientation. As Rafel Soborski has recently pointed out, "ideological continuity does not mean conservation in fixed ideational structures but rather a state of a dynamic interplay in which highly flexible concepts are able to adapt to, and combine with, new ideas to meet emerging political challenges."[113] Ideas and interpretations are "operationalized," so to speak, in terms of specific historical and political circumstances, and because these circumstances in Western Europe differed in many respects from those in the post-Stalinist USSR, it is unsurprising that the respective political projects differed as well. We can see these differences in regard to a number of major issues. To begin with, although both the European New Right and Gumilev focus on the conceptual juxtaposition of *Gemeinschaft* to *Gesellschaft*, their understanding of what this juxtaposition entails is actually quite different. For the former, the two are seen as intrinsically opposed, indeed mutually exclusive, entities, organized in different ways and on the basis of very different principles. Indeed, one of the major problems of the modern world for the New Right is the fact that ethnies—which naturally represent *Gemeinschaften*—are nonetheless formally organized as political *Gesellschaften*, in the form of nation-states. As we have seen, the New Right opposes the contemporary nation-state system, in which they see embodied the collective evils of modernity: individualism, universalism, and homogenization.[114] The solution they offer is nothing short of revolutionary, in some cases going so far as to call for nation-states to be dismantled altogether, in order to liberate their peoples and enable their ethno-cultural rebirth.[115]

This, they believe, would enable the reanimation of European ethnic life in the spirit of *Gemeinschaft* and the political reassociation of the ethnies themselves—along strict ethno-regionalist principles—into the pan-European federation or empire (or federated empire) discussed above.[116] Moreover, because the familiar forms of nationalism as a collective identity structure developed in the nineteenth and twentieth centuries are closely associated with the institution of the nation-state, certain tendencies in the New Right reject populist nationalism as well. In the contemporary world, nationalism is "founded on a political ideal of State and citizenship" rather than the aspirations for genuine ethnic consolidation, and thus can never be "sufficient to create a common identity."[117]

Gumilev took an entirely different position on these questions—a position conditioned by the deep ambivalence of his relationship to the political status quo in the USSR. Having endured many years of banishment in his youth and the organized obstruction of his subsequent academic career, Gumilev was certainly a bitter critic of the Soviet order. At the same time, however, and unlike the European New Right, he was not opposed in principle to the state structure of the USSR, and he certainly entertained no idea whatsoever of its radical or revolutionary reorganization. Indeed, rather than stifling and subverting the integrity of its constituent ethno-cultures, he believed that across most of its history Russia had offered these peoples the optimal conditions for free development. This had been the case since the earliest formation of the imperial state, and there had at least been an effort to maintain it after the revolution, in the form of the Soviet "Friendship of the Peoples" (*druzhba narodov*) policy, promulgated in the 1930s. Gumilev believed that the principles of ethno-regionalism were already effectively inscribed into this policy, and throughout all of his writings he was unstinting in his support and praise for it.[118] For him, the entire point was not the destruction of the Soviet status quo, but rather the defense and reanimation of those positive elements of it against the challenges mounted by the proponents of the modernizing *sovetskii narod* project. It was against the latter that Gumilev's critique was directed, and not against the constitution or existence of the Soviet state as such. Gumilev was in no way a revolutionary—during perestroika he bristled even at the suggestion that he might be a "democrat"[119]—but rather saw himself as a deeply conservative patriot and thoroughly loyal Russian nationalist. In the same spirit that he accepted the Soviet state as a legitimate geopolitical framework for its constituent ethnies, he did not question the legitimacy of the existing nation-state structure of Western Europe, and he did not believe that it inherently subverted the integrity of the ethnies which it included. Gumilev may have concurred with the New Right that the European ethnies were made up of numerous sub-ethnies, but in contrast to the former he did not see this circumstance as undermining the legitimacy of the European nation-states, and he would never have countenanced the devolution of ethnos status to the sub-ethnos level.

There was a further difference between Gumilev and the New Right in regard to the *Gemeinschaft–Gesellschaft* juxtaposition. Although Gumilev saw the two as fundamentally contrasting categories, they were not mutually exclusive. To the contrary, in his view the two forms naturally coexisted as equally legitimate and necessary categories of human communal existence. *Gemeinschaft* corresponded to the "natural" mode of existence, in other words the "ethnosphere" represented by the *etnos*, while *Gesellschaft* was the "social" mode or the "sociosphere," represented by a *sotsiuum* or *obshchestvo* ("society").[120] Every human individual, he maintained, operated simultaneously in both modes, as a member of society and a representative of an ethnos. The two were very different, but there was no inherent contradiction or friction between them. He likened the distinction between them to the contrast between units of length and weight, that is to say, variables that were "parallel but incommensurable."[121] Here again, Gumilev's understanding reflected his essential ambivalence toward the Soviet status quo, in this case the dogmatics of Marxism–Leninism. While his naturalist model of ethnies as biological and ecological organisms extravagantly contravened the strictures of Soviet Marxism, his description of the sociosphere corresponded quite precisely to the letter of Marxist–Leninist dogma. He accepted the Marxist principle that the historical development of the *sotsiuum* was determined by the growth of the material means of production, and that over history it evolved progressively into ever more developed and "advanced" forms: slave-owning societies evolve into feudalism, feudalism into capitalism, and capitalism into socialism.[122] To the end of his life, Gumilev affirmed his fidelity to this Marxist schematic, and—in contrast to many Soviet intellectuals whose Marxist avowals were made strictly out of censorial considerations—there was no question as to his complete sincerity in this matter. He not only saw no inherent contradiction between the *zakonnomernosti* of dialectical materialism that explained social evolution and the biological–ecological laws that controlled the development of ethnies, but he also believed that with his theories he actually achieved Marx's own unfulfilled ambition of marrying the history of nature to the history of humanity.[123] The ideologues of the New Right, by contrast, simply dismiss Marx in a single voice as a leading prophet of "materialistic Liberalism."[124]

DIFFERENCES II: SEGREGATION AND EXCLUSION

Gumilev's position also diverges from that of the New Right in regard to the practice, as opposed to the theory, of ethnic segregation. As we have seen, ethno-pluralism advocates separation and exclusion based on ethno-cultural criteria. While this principle is valid for all groups, its implementation is imperative above all for the purposes of defending indigenous European ethnies against intruder populations from Asia, Africa, and the New World, who are civilizationally and (as many New Right theoreticians continue to insist) racially foreign.[125] These latter groups represent the most acute threat, insofar as they have overloaded the "capacity for assimilation" of Europe's indigenous population and thus prepare the conditions for its collective *Völkertod* or "ethnic death."[126] "Separation" is used in the New Right discourse in an entirely literal sense, as the physical segregation of groups onto separate, discrete territories. In practice it represents a program for the removal—effectively the ethnic cleansing—of peoples identified as foreign from the European ethno-homelands. Failure to implement such a policy would intensify competition over resources between different ethnies in a single region—precisely Gumilev's scenario for an ethnic chimera which could only lead to the destruction of the host ethnos. "Immigrants are perceived as land occupiers (*Landabnehmer*)," wrote the ethologist Eibl-Eibesfeldt, "They take advantage of the most precious resource available to a *Volk*, namely the land. When this happens, they come to be regarded as invaders, and this more-or-less automatically stimulates a reaction of territorial defence. . . . If one *Volk* allows another free immigration and the development of minority communities [in its ethnic space], then that country begins to decline and inter-ethnic competition begins to develop."[127] It goes without saying that immigration into Europe, which is the principal source of the continent's "problematic" poly-ethnic population, should cease.[128] The real challenge, however, is the question of what to do with those many millions of immigrants who are already in situ. De Benoist considers it "unrealistic" that immigrant communities currently ensconced in Europe will decide to leave, or that it would be possible "to oblige them to leave," and thus he opts for the sort of territorial partitioning of European soil just noted.[129] Other New Right ideologues, however, see no problem with the prospect of enforced repatriation, and rather than countenance the conversion of Europe into a patchwork of indigenous and foreign ethno-territorial enclaves they call for the return of all non-European immigrants to their original homelands.[130]

As we have seen, Gumilev echoed the New Right's fierce opposition to the process of social homogenization—driven in his case by Soviet discourses of ethnic *sliianie* and *sovetskii narod*—and similarly endorsed the principled call for the territorial segregation of ethnies into discrete ethnic homelands. More than this, he described the salubrious effect that the latter principle had had in the historic settlement patterns of Soviet ethnies. Nevertheless, these principles did not in his case translate into anything resembling the New Right's activist program of social exclusion in the present day. To be sure, as a closed political space the USSR remained largely untouched by the in-migration from other parts of the world that affected Western Europe. But across the transcontinental expanses of the Soviet Union itself, closed to the outer world, there was massive internal movement and intermingling of populations whose geographical and ethnic distinctions were in many ways comparable to those of the European West. Indeed, the Soviet state actively encouraged such inter-regional migration, among other things, as part of its program to develop the *sovetskii narod*. Given the entire conceptual thrust of Gumilev's ecology of ethnicity, he might have been expected to denounce these population movements and call for the repatriation of Soviet ethnies back to their original ethno-regions. In fact, however, Gumilev did no such thing. His strident denunciations of official Soviet nationality policy never included any sort of critique of the demographic processes or settlement patterns of his own day. More broadly, and despite his principled insistence on the importance of preserving ethnic distinctions, he gave no indication that he believed the Soviet ethnies posed any inherent danger to each other merely by virtue of their differences, or even by their physical presence in each other's territorial homelands. Certainly he issued no call to separate or exclude any group from the Soviet polity that might correspond to the unrelenting appeals toward this end from the European New Right.

The reason for Gumilev's position relates to his belief described above that the peoples of the USSR were bound together by the same sort of civilizational affinities that the New Right argued were characteristic for indigenous European ethno-cultures. The Soviet nationalities were all joined together symbiotically as part of a single Eurasian "community of destiny," which shared a common historical legacy and for many centuries had formed a single political space. It was not only in regard to the ethnic space of his own ethnos (the Great Russians) that he perceived the potential danger of invasion by foreign groups. Rather, he argued that this threat was equally relevant for all groups. Indeed, he maintained that it was most acute for the indigenous ethnies of Siberia—the so-called little peoples (*malye narody*)—and it was only in regard to them that he ever made an explicit call for the implementation of the strict segregationist and isolationist principles of ethno-regionalism. In order to protect the ethno-national integrity of the *malye narody*, he wrote, "I support the creation of reservations (*rezervatsii*). If the small nationalities of the north are left as they are, then scoundrels—of whom there are quite a few in Siberia—will treat them badly. It is necessary that the government intervene on their behalf. ... Special protective zones should be created for them [on their traditional homelands], which the non-indigenous population would be permitted to enter only with permits."[131]

Gumilev's entirely genuine concern for the welfare of his country's non-Russian peoples—quite unthinkable for the European New Right—was much appreciated in his lifetime by the groups in question, and among Kazakhs, Tatars, Yakuts, Kalmyks, and other nationalities his popularity remains undiminished down to the present day. By the same token, his refusal to prioritize the interests of ethnic Russians and to recognize the other Soviet peoples as a competitive menace attracted sharp critique from the burgeoning Russian ethno-nationalist movement.[132] The only exception that Gumilev—a notorious anti Semite—allowed was for the Jews, whom he explicitly identified as a hostile foreign ethnos (or superethnos, as he maintained) that presented a mortal threat to the Russians and others, both historically and in the present day. In the context of Russia, Gumilev used the term "chimera" almost exclusively in reference to the Jewish people. Because the Jews possessed no natural homeland within Russia, the only solution possible was a radical exclusionism that would remove them altogether from the body politic.

It is also important to note that, while Gumilev and the European New Right both use the notion of supra-national civilizations, the specifics of their respective civilizational schemes are at odds. Embracing a meta-geographical perspective of "Eurasia" which originated in the nineteenth century, Gumilev rejected the traditional notion of an absolute and necessary dichotomy between Europe and Asia.[133] To the contrary, Russian civilization developed as a unique amalgam of European and Asian societies, and represented a sort of third, in-between continent that was clearly set apart from and opposed to the other two. This perspective was elaborated most fully in the doctrines of Eurasianism, developed by nationalist Russian émigrés in the 1920s and 1930s. Gumilev adopted the Eurasianist perspective in all its essentials, famously referring to himself as the "last Eurasianist."[134] For him, as for his predecessors, Europe—and in particular Western Europe—was Russia's elemental and essential enemy, against which his country had always struggled, from the beginning of its historical existence down to the present day. Like the classical Eurasianists, he drew no civilizational distinction between Europe and the United States, and included both of them in his conceptualization of *Zapad*, or the West. For the European New Right, as we have already seen, the calculus is entirely different. On the one hand, they do indeed draw an elemental distinction between the United States—a crass and materialistic hegemon seeking to dominate the rest of the world—and Europe, with its rich historical legacies and unbroken traditions of ethnic life. On the other hand, the New Right generally views Russia itself as an important part of European civilization, which shares with the Western European countries the vital imperative to defend European civilization against the hegemonic predations of the North American superpower.[135] While Aleksandr Dugin may have assimilated elements of this latter perspective, nothing could be further from Gumilev's own views.

A final difference between Gumilev and the New Right involves their attitude toward the imperial legacy of their respective homelands. For all of its fascination with the notion of a European "empire" of the future, the New Right can conceive of such a thing only through contrived fantasies about the ethnophilic virtues of the historically remote Romans or Carolingians. By contrast, in regard to the more recent European imperial experience of the modern period, their judgment is actually very critical. De Benoist develops this point at length in reference to the French empire, asserting that its wanton brutality was dedicated to the dissemination of the same vices of universalism, rationalism, and complete global integration that the New Right opposes today. He consequently rejects any form of imperialist nationalism, French or otherwise, and dismisses associated claims to European superiority over other parts of the world.[136] To the contrary, he aligns his sympathies with the global struggle against "Western imperialism"—directed in the present day principally by the United

States—and declares that the stakes in this struggle are as vital for Europe as for anyone else.[137] Gumilev, by contrast, staunchly defended the formation and development of the Russian imperial state, which he depicted as an essentially harmonious and voluntary process, in which non-Russians were always treated as equal members.[138] He did not deny that Russian expansion had occasionally involved forceful conquest, but this was not its principal feature. "It is clear to anyone with even the slightest superficial knowledge of Russian history that the incorporation (*prisoedinenie*) of Siberia would have been unimaginable without voluntary agreement and mutual trust."[139] This trust was based on the deep natural sympathies between the Russians and the peoples they brought into their imperial structure, and the toleration and respect the former showed their new subjects. All these different ethnies are connected not by a common way of life, kinship, or language, "but by sharing a common historical destiny. They were friends."[140]

Thus the Russian state developed as a voluntaristic joint project, based not on conquest, but on the principles of friendly cooperation and mutual toleration.[141] While this tradition may have been subverted during the Soviet period by a "universal ideology of reducing everyone to the same level," the empire's subjects had at all other times been allowed to maintain their autonomy and traditional internal organization to the maximum extent possible.[142] "In [Russia's] 'prison house of peoples' it was possible [for different ethnies] to live in their own way."[143] The challenge for the present, consequently, was not to struggle against this legacy by destroying the primordial unity of the former empire, but rather to reaffirm the original Russian imperial project by reanimating its original egalitarian and collectivist spirit.

CONCLUSION

Although Lev Gumilev was an intellectual and political product of the Soviet period, the powerful resonances and dissonances between his thinking and that of the New Right in Europe are highly significant in regard to present-day attitudes and ideas. The popularity and influence of his work has grown dramatically since the collapse of the USSR, and many of the ideas emphasized in this essay, such as his biological–ecological perspective on the nature of ethnicity or his notion of the superethnic affinities bonding the peoples of the Russian empire and Soviet Union, are embraced today as they never were before 1991. Indeed, it can be argued that despite Aleksandr Dugin's high visibility, Gumilev is actually the more indicative thinker for contemporary Russian conservatism. The juxtaposition between Gumilev and the European New Right also shines a revealing light on the ideological relationship between Gumilev and Aleksandr Dugin himself. In certain respects, such as his avowal of Russian nationalism and fetishizing of the ethnos, Dugin clearly aligns with Gumilev. But in other regards, notably his Europhilia or his preparedness to identify Russia's deepest geopolitical interests with those of Western Europe, he is clearly operating with an entirely different set of values. For Dugin, as for the European New Right, Eurasianism is a shared greater-European project. Gumilev's Eurasianism, by contrast, defined Russia precisely in terms of its civilizational differences from and historical opposition to the West.

In a more general sense, the resonances and dissonances discussed in this essay allow for some reflection on how we analyze and valorize ideologies, particularly in comparative perspective. Such an analysis properly begins with a close examination of the ideas themselves: how they are constructed and how they fit together into apparently coherent frameworks and perspectives. When different agents or groups profess similar ideas, they may seem to share an ideological commonality. Yet while ideas and sets of ideas do possess a certain internal logic and dynamic that is in a sense autonomous, they nonetheless become fully meaningful only as they are "operationalized" in terms of specific social and historical contexts and political agendas. And because these contexts and agendas can vary greatly across space and time, similar ideas can take on significances, point to imperatives, and have effects that are correspondingly different. One example of this can be seen in the work of Afrikaans ethnographers in apartheid South Africa, who were highly receptive to Soviet ethnos theory and borrowed heavily from it for their own purposes.[144] Nevertheless, these ideas always remained what one specialist calls "European baggage in an African context," and their deployment, shaped by very special conditions, did not necessarily correspond to that of Soviet ethnography itself.[145] The juxtaposition between Gumilev and the European New Right that we have examined provides another example. The similarities between them are extremely significant, but they must also be evaluated in light of the equally important differences between the practical implications that were associated with them.

CHAPTER 10

THE YUZHINSKII CIRCLE

Rediscovering European Far Right Metaphysics in the Soviet Underground

Marlene Laruelle

T he Iron Curtain divided Europe for decades, not only physically, with nearly closed borders and limited opportunities to cross to the other side, but intellectually too. Nevertheless, some individuals were able to continue to read each other beyond the ideological wall: dissident circles in the Socialist bloc found ways to access literature produced in the West, and supportive circles in the West helped them to stay in contact by sending books or journals and by clandestinely exporting dissident culture. An under-studied aspect of this interaction during the decades of the Cold War is the rediscovery of West European far-right literature by some of the dissident figures in Moscow bohemian circles. The main example of this is the Yuzhinskii (or Golovin) circle, which beginning in the 1960s consistently tried to anchor in Russia the religious and philosophical doctrines that had inspired fascism and esoteric Nazism. The circle sought to move beyond the classical discourse on Russia's distinctive destiny by counterbalancing it with broader references coming from European metaphysical and traditionalist doctrines. It combined the discovery by the Soviet underground of both punk culture and European far-right thinking, offering a unique rightist-hipster cultural blend.

The Yuzhinskii circle has been mentioned in works devoted to Aleksandr Dugin's career, including those by Andreas Umland, Stephen Shenfield, Anton Shekhovtsov, and Mark Sedgwick.[1] But the information on it is often sparse, with the circle portrayed only as a kind of "prologue" to Dugin's ideological engagement. In fact, the Yuzhinskii circle deserves a full treatment in its own right as part of the history of the Soviet intellectual underground and its continuing impact today. This chapter hopes to offer a coherent narrative of the emergence and evolution of the Yuzhinskii circle. It explores how members of the group drew upon traditionalist ideas to chart a third course, rejecting both the Westernizing liberals and the Russian nationalists whose struggle constituted the dominant ideological contest within the dissident milieu. It then shows how the circle's preoccupation with esoteric mysticism mutated into an increasing engagement with the ideas of the European Far Right, which enabled the circle to become a crucible of post-Soviet conservative ideology.

In this chapter I divide the circle's Soviet history into three phases: (1) around Iurii Mamleev in the 1960s; (2) around Evgenii Golovin and Geidar Dzhemal in the 1970s; (3) and around Dugin himself in the 1980s. Reconstructing the history of the circle is challenging, with sources consisting mainly of excerpts from memoirs and interviews with key players; as personal histories, they are subject to being rewritten by their authors, who enjoy playing up the circle's provocative image and nonconformist legacy.[2]

YUZHINSKII CIRCLE 1.0: MAMLEEV'S METAPHYSICAL SALON

With the release of nearly 5 million prisoners (*zeks*) from prison camps, de-Stalinization drastically altered the everyday Soviet social fabric in the 1950s.[3] As poet Anna Akhmatova remarked, "Two Russias will be eyeball to eyeball: the one that put people into the camps and the one that was put in them."[4] De-Stalinization—and especially the cultural thaw that followed it—also profoundly transformed Soviet intellectual milieus.[5] The underground groups, hitherto clandestine since participating in them imperiled members and their families, were able to formalize gradually into dissident "circles" or salons. They were open to a larger number of members and could more openly disseminate their meeting place, time, and discussion topic.[6]

The ideological diversity of these circles quickly confirmed the multiplicity of political opinions among Soviet dissidents: liberals who looked to the West; determined monarchists; Leninists or Trotskyists who called for a return to the revolutionary roots of the Bolshevik regime; and Stalinists who denounced Khrushchev's thaw. As the years went by, their discussions focused around two main axes, which can be defined schematically as follows. The first axis focused on questions of human rights and religious freedom, and included a broad ideological spectrum of groups ranging from pro-Western liberals to anarchists; the second axis was comprised of intellectuals who were interested in cultural debates and dedicated to preserving the Russian national heritage. This second axis, too, represented a broad political spectrum, one that stretched from pro-Romanov monarchists to those nostalgic for Stalinism.[7] It was the most ideologically and politically complex, since it maintained close contacts with some official circles inside the state structure, the Communist Party, and the Komsomols. As discussed by Nikolai Mitrokhin in his seminal work, *The Russian Party*, from the late 1950s–early 1960s through the 1980s, part of the Soviet establishment gradually adopted Russian nationalist theories. Under the informal name of the "Russian Party," a group of senior officials enabled nationalist dissident claims to gain gradual acceptance.[8]

In the early 1960s a third, more marginal dissident axis emerged. It brought together the "neither/nor" group—that is, those who were as critical of the "Westernizers" as they were of the "nationalists," and who sought other forms of expression for their opposition to the Soviet regime. This group formed around the writer Iurii Mamleev (1931–2015), who graduated from the Moscow Institute of Forestry in 1956 and taught mathematics in adult education courses. Mamleev became known in underground circles by reading his novels to a narrow group of admirers who met at the Lenin Library in the smoking room and in other locations, including Mamleev's home on Yuzhinskii Pereulok, where up to fifty people would crowd into his tiny one-bedroom flat. After the building was razed in 1968, the group met in the apartments of various other members (mostly Golovin, Dzhemal, and Vladimir Stepanov), but kept the name of the original street, the Yuzhinskii circle. Mamleev's group was ideologically close to another salon run by painter Iurii Titov and his wife, Elena Stroeva, a circle that was equally virulent in its criticism of the Soviet regime and sought nonpolitical means of protest, mainly in art.[9] The Mamleevians gathered regularly at the home of Rubina Arutiunian, who was the muse of the Mayakovka dissident circle in the 1950s and 1960s, and then organizer of underground exhibitions in the 1970s. Arutiunian lived next door to the Titovs.[10]

Other salons called the Mamleevians "Satanists."[11] Indeed, Mamleev's novels criticize the Soviet system through the metaphor of monstrosity: their heroes are characterized by extreme violence, sadomasochism, and satanic practices, and they combine all kinds of psychopathologies.[12] The underlying theme is that extreme experiences are needed to transcend the mediocrity of everyday Soviet life. These experiences grant access to a metaphysical reality revealing the fundamental absurdity of the human condition. Mamleev was sometimes—undeservedly—compared

with Dostoevskii for his pursuit of human complexity and the darkness of
the soul. His cult novel, *Shatuny* (The Sublimes) (1966), is considered to
be a metaphor for the activities of the Yuzhinskii circle at that time and
for a practice the writer dubbed "sexual mysticism."[13] This metaphysical
response to Soviet reality, far from the debates of classic dissidents, was
a revelation for a small sliver of Muscovite underground intellectuals
and artists seeking philosophical principles applicable to their bohemian
spirit and practices. In a 2011 documentary film dedicated to Mamleev,
his early supporters recalled the revolutionary effect he produced when
he appeared on the Moscow scene—some called him the "Soviet Kafka."[14]

The core group of the Yuzhinskii circle did not meet exclusively to read
Mamleev's novels. They also discussed the banned books they could obtain,
in particular those linked to metaphysics, Hermeticism, Gnosticism, Kab-
balah, magic, and astrology—all theories based on the existence of a parallel
reality. According to several accounts, in the latter half of the 1950s and
throughout the 1960s, such Western esoteric works were not classified as
politically subversive and were still freely available at the Lenin Library.[15]
Only later were they relegated to the *Spetskhran* (the "special collection"
of prohibited books). Beginning at the end of the 1950s, the works of Helena Blavatskii, Rudolf Steiner, and Petr D. Ouspensky also began spreading
through some underground salons.[16]

Thanks to the influence of the Yuzhinskii circle and similar underground groups, the works of George I. Gurdjieff (1866–1949) gained prominence during this time. Gurdjieff was the founder of a mystical teaching
called the Fourth Way, which was subsequently elaborated in the works
of Petr D. Ouspensky (1878–1947), particularly *The Fourth Dimension*
(1909). The doctrine claims to address human beings' capacity for inner
development and the possibility of transcendence of the body to achieve
a higher state of consciousness.[17] The rediscovery of Gurdjieff in the
Soviet Union cannot be solely attributed to Mamleev. Fedor P. Verevin
(1901–1968) was also instrumental in circulating the writings of Gurdjieff
and Nikolai Berdiaev even before the Second World War, and continued
spreading them once he returned from the Gulag in the 1950s.[18] In the
following decades, three groups of Gurdjieff followers were active: those
gathered around Boris Kerdimun and poet/painter Vladimir Kovenatskii,
who sought contacts with Sufi orders in Central Asia; those led by Kaliten-
ko and Korshakov; and a major group that came together around Vladimir
Stepanov, a member of the Yuzhinskii circle.[19]

At the start of the 1970s, the political atmosphere in Soviet Union became more constrained and the crackdown on dissident circles intensified.

In 1973 Mamleev decided to emigrate after the Soviet Union passed a law that made sending any *samizdat* manuscript abroad punishable with several years in prison. He managed to leave the country the following year, during the first large wave of emigration authorized by Moscow thanks to the atmosphere of détente. Unlike many dissidents, such as Aleksandr Solzhenitsyn, Mamleev never complained about his American years and is said to have quickly adapted to life in the United States.[20] He settled in Paris in 1983 and became a critical figure in Russian émigré circles and anti-Soviet political groups. He emerged as one of the principal representatives of Russian postmodernism and developed a theory of "metaphysical realism."[21]

Once he emigrated, Mamleev played an important role within dissident circles in distributing the émigré annual publication *Okkultizm i ioga* [Occultism and Yoga], which was funded by Aleksandr M. Aseev (1902–1993). A medical doctor by training who was fascinated by the teachings of Agni Yoga, Aseev started a correspondence with Nicholas Roerich (Rerikh) in 1931.[22] In 1933, he began the *Okkultizm i ioga* publication, which was first published in Belgrade and closely supervised by Nicholas's spouse, Helena Roerich. The journal became famous among émigré groups for publishing correspondence between Aseev and Roerich. After the Second World War, Aseev migrated to Paraguay and resumed publishing the journal, continuing until 1977.[23] Mamleev himself published several articles on Buddhism, Hinduism, and Western New Ageism and helped circulate such teachings in the Soviet Union.

In its first years, the Yuzhinskii circle occupied a unique place in the Muscovite bohemian underground by avoiding the Slavophiles-versus-Westernizers debate that then dominated the dissident space. It provided a limited number of followers with access to a hitherto unknown European pantheon of doctrines and beliefs in parallel metaphysical realities that promised a mental escape from the Soviet regime and way of life. Mamleev is often presented as the first to introduce into the Soviet Union previously unknown European theoreticians of Traditionalism, such as René Guénon and Julius Evola. However, descriptions of these "discoveries" barely exist and seem to be attributable to two of his friends and disciples, Evgenii Golovin and Geidar Dzhemal, who embody the circle's second generation.

YUZHINSKII CIRCLE 2.0: GOLOVIN'S AND DZHEMAL'S DISCOVERY OF TRADITIONALISM

In the mid-1960s a second generation of leading figures emerged within the circle, dominated by the trio of Evgenii Golovin (1938–2010), Geidar

Dzhemal (1947–2016, of Azeri origin), and Vladimir Stepanov (b. 1941). They became the engines of the circle once Mamleev left the USSR. The circle's evening gatherings continued to organize "Dionysian initiations" featuring vast quantities of alcohol and sex that were supposed to grant access to another level of human reality, with Golovin as their primary mastermind.[24] The anti-Soviet creed remained the circle's driving force, and all modes of refusing Soviet normality were welcomed. Some authors who later became famous cut their teeth in the group, including Vladimir Sorokin (b. 1955), Viktor Erofeev (b. 1947), and Viktor Pevelin (b. 1962), as well as the jazz musician Boris Grebenshchikov (b. 1953), Gurdjieff disciple Arkadii Rovner (b. 1940), and painter and film director Valerii Konoplev. As in its early years, the group seemed to attract around fifty regular followers.[25] As many as thirty persons would convene at Dzhemal's dacha or at Sergei Zhigalkin's on weekends.[26]

Golovin himself was a poet, not a systematic theoretician or a political thinker, and worked as a translator and literary critic for the so-called "thick journals" of the time. Under his influence, poetry readings became one of the hallmarks of the circle's evenings; until the 1980s, members faithfully recited Rimbaud and Baudelaire.[27] Golovin also gave new impetus to the circle's musical activities. In the late 1970s and throughout the 1980s, his poems were set to music by Vasilii Shumov and his band, Tsentr; by Aleksandr Skliar and his band, Va-Bank; and by Viacheslav Butusov and his band, Kino. Golovin devoted an entire work to Tsentr.[28] His eccentric views earned him a hero's role in Mamleev's novel *Shatuny*, and saw him represented as the character of the Admiral (a nickname he had given himself) in Konstantin Serebrov's novel *Misticheskii andergraund: Germeticheskaia shkola* [The Mystic Underground: The Hermeneutic School].[29]

Little information has been handed down about the methods that the circle used to obtain banned literature. Soviet control over literature had intensified and the Lenin Library *Spetskhran* became less accessible to anyone outside a select group of privileged people. Working as a translator of West European literature, Golovin could access some of these books. But, like other dissident groups, the circle also developed alternative strategies to obtain Western works. One way was to make contact with Western diplomats in Moscow or with occasional visitors to the USSR. Philologist Mikhail Meilakh (b. 1944), a disciple of Gurdjieff and a specialist in medieval troubadour literature, often visited hotels reserved for foreigners in the hope of obtaining banned works, which led to his being arrested by the authorities on several occasions.[30] Another way was to send requests to Western publishers sympathetic to the dissidents, such as the YMCA

Press in Paris. Vladimir Stepanov, for instance, wrote to several Western publishers to ask for works unavailable in the Soviet Union.[31] He was also in contact with Gurdjieffians abroad such as John Bennett (1897–1974), a British scholar-diplomat and probably a member of Britain's MI6 intelligence service, and Idris Shah (1924–1996), an Indian-born Afghan and a teacher of Sufi traditions. Both Bennett and Shah were convinced that Sufism had inspired Traditionalist higher knowledge. They had met in 1962 and worked together for several years spreading Gurdjieff's teachings in Europe and the Soviet Union.[32] However, there is no information that explains how they made contact with members of Moscow's underground intelligentsia.

Geidar Dzhemal played a crucial role within the Yuzhinskii circle by collecting foreign or banned books and republishing them as *samizdat*. In an interview with Vladimir Pozner in late 2013, Dzhemal mentioned that in 1967–1968, Golovin had owned only one of Guénon's books, but that by 1970, he himself had succeeded in having several of them "sent" from Paris and amassing an almost complete collection, which, however, was destroyed by a fire in his apartment in 1973.[33] Dzhemal's friend Vladimir Videman, a Tallinn-based dissident very active in the *samizdat* world, mentions Dzhemal's home library several times in his memoirs, describing shelves filled with copies of *samizdat*, including texts by Gurdjieff on the "Fourth Theory," banned European works, and Qurans.[34] In the 1980s Dzhemal was also close friends with some French diplomatic personnel who transported forbidden books for him by diplomatic pouch.[35]

With Golovin and Dzhemal, the circle's political orientation became more pronounced; on the path to esoterism the circle encountered all the major fellow travelers of fascism and Nazism, especially Julius Evola. Through his passion for poetry, especially "mystical" poets such as Rimbaud, Mallarmé, Rilke, Lautréamont, and Baudelaire, Golovin had first discovered alchemy and Hermeticism in the mid-1950s, at the early age of sixteen. This was well before he met Mamleev in the second half of the 1960s.[36] In an interview with *Elementy*, Dugin's first journal, Golovin declared, "I didn't have any teachers," thus clarifying that he did not consider Mamleev to be his *maître à penser*. Dzhemal confirmed this by recalling that Golovin considered himself the first to introduce Guénon to the Soviet Union, which implies that Mamleev did not know of him, or at least was not very familiar with his work.[37]

Golovin recounted that he found *Crisis of the Contemporary World* by René Guénon (1886–1951) by chance in the Lenin Library *Spetskhran* in 1963 or 1964. Reading this book, which had been completely unknown to him, had an electric effect. It convinced him that Oriental mysticism, until then the main version of mysticism available in the Soviet Union, should be put aside in favor of Western medieval mystical traditions. But in the early 1970s Golovin became disenchanted with Guénon and moved on to other thinkers.[38] In his last work, *Mifomaniia* (Mythomany), published in 2010, the poet criticized Western Traditionalism, contending that its monotheistic nature made it too rhetorical and schematic, and that only pre-Christian esotericism preserved the very essence of alchemy and magic, that is, a belief in the plurality of realities.[39]

Golovin then discovered Julius Evola (1898–1974), particularly *The Hermetic Tradition*, at the Lenin Library. He said that at first the Italian author seemed less convincing than Guénon and more obscure.[40] Evola is best known for denouncing egalitarianism as a product of the Enlightenment, and decrying the decadence of Western civilization. He appeals for a primordial rebirth of humanity via the original Tradition, which, according to him, combines Hermeticism, metaphysics, sexual mysticism, and many components borrowed from Eastern religions. In Evola, Golovin also discovered a politically engaged Italian author who had refused to follow Mussolini's Fascist party because he found it too centrist. Evola instead promoted a German conception of "spiritual races" that was not supported by the Mussolini propagandists, but was well received by Nazi Germany. After the Second World War he provided ideological support to the extreme right-wing terrorist attacks that shook Italy during the "strategy of tension" of the Cold War decades.[41] No source indicates what information was available to Golovin's circle at that time on Evola's postwar activities.

Through Evola and Guénon, the circle accessed a wide range of Western theoreticians and promoters of occultism from the nineteenth century, such as Eliphas Lévi (Alphonse Louis Constant, 1810–1875), Papus (Gérard Anaclet Vincent Encausse, 1865–1916), and Carl du Prel (1839–1899). Golovin, Mamleev, and/or Dzhemal—it is impossible to identify their precise roles—also seem to have introduced members of the circle to the works of Titus Burckhardt (1908–1984) and Frithjof Schuon (1907–1998), both Swiss-Germans and eminent members of the so-called Traditionalist or Perennialist School, which believed in the metaphysical unity of the great religions.[42]

The circle also had access to *Morning of the Magicians* by Louis Pauwels (1920–1997, an editor at *Le Figaro*) and Jacques Bergier (1912–1978). Published in French in 1960 and translated into English in 1963, *Morning of the Magicians* quickly became a classic for its conspiracy theories about the role of occult societies in world politics.[43] It was one of the first works to describe empathetically the close links between Nazism and occult theories. No information is available on how the circle came across this work, but we do know that the first excerpts of *Morning of the Magicians* available in Russian were published in *Nauka i religiia* in 1966.[44] Since neither Mamleev nor Golovin would have needed to wait for a Russian translation in order to access this text, as both could read French and English, it is impossible to say whether the circle discovered Pauwels through the Soviet journal or before it appeared there. What remains to be investigated are the motivations of the *Nauka i religiia* editorial board for this publication and why they selected extracts specifically concerning the esoteric content of Nazism.

Driven by Golovin and Dzhemal, the second generation of the circle went further than Mamleev in their search for the political ramifications of Western Traditionalism and for counter-ideologies to Soviet doctrine. German philosophers, especially Nietzsche, Schopenhauer, and Heidegger, became must-reads for the circle's philosophical discussions. Dzhemal seems to have played a crucial role in this "German turn." His maternal grandfather, a high-ranking party member, was a German-language professor, and the younger Dzhemal became familiar with a certain number of German authors rather early, thanks to his grandfather's unique library. In his interview with Pozner, Dzhemal acknowledged that, unlike many other circle members, he had arrived at Traditionalism through German philosophy rather than Oriental mysticism.[45] In another interview, he said he had discovered Nazi mysticism through Armin Mohler (1920–2003).[46] Mohler, who was close to Ernst Jünger, was the author of *Die konservative Revolution in Deutschland 1918–1932,* published in 1950, a key work in the post-Nazi ideological overhaul of the Far Right in Germany, which influenced the German New Right movement.[47]

The circle's participants also discovered the previously unknown worlds of the extreme-right regimes during the Second World War, right-wing terrorism during the Cold War, and the experiences of Latin American counter-revolutionaries. Both Golovin and Dzhemal referred to three authors as having a structural influence on their ideological evolution: Claudio Mutti, Miguel Serrano, and Mircea Eliade.[48]

Mutti (b. 1946) is an Italian representative of the New Right and has participated in many pan-European organizations such as Young Europe. Trained as a lawyer, he defended Franco Giorgio Freda, whose conviction in the Piazza Fontana bombing was later overturned for lack of evidence. Mutti then touted the Libyan regime of Colonel Muammar Qaddafi, whom he saw as an Islamic embodiment of Traditionalism, and converted to Islam.[49] Today Mutti remains a major ally and promoter of Dugin in Italy.

Miguel Serrano (1917–2009), a Chilean diplomat, was an important theoretician of anti-modernism. He described his ideology as "esoteric

Hitlerism," inspired by Gnosticism, with anti-Semitic conspiracy theories that he reproduced using elements inspired by Hindu traditions and references to Aryan descendants of the Hyperborea.[50] Serrano returned to Chile after the Pinochet coup in 1973 and criticized the new regime for being too centrist. He maintained correspondence with neo-Nazis in Europe and was an important figure for Nazi sympathizers in Chile.[51]

Mircea Eliade (1907–1986), whose works profoundly influenced the European sociology of religion and myths, in particular concerning the distinction between the sacred and the profane, also developed mythological thinking inspired by Guénon and Evola.[52] Eliade was a fervent supporter of the Iron Guard in 1930–1940s Romania, praised the fascist ideology of the movement, and enrolled in Totul pentru Țară [All for the Country], the political movement of the Iron Guard. During the Second World War he traveled in occupied Europe to support occupation regimes and celebrated the establishment of the Salazar regime in Portugal.[53]

Golovin himself was a provocative figure. He published under the pseudonym Aleksandr Shternberg, probably a reference to Baron Roman von Ungern-Sternberg (1885–1921), a White Army general who liberated Mongolia from Chinese domination, massacred Bolshevik supporters, converted to Buddhism, and called for the revival of the Mongolian empire of Genghis Khan.[54] Declaring that he had been initiated to black magic by his grandmother, Golovin instituted a Masonic-style initiation ritual—with the addition of alcohol—for the circle's members. He appreciated the carnival-like character of the circle's references to Nazism and their provocative tastes in the conformist Soviet Union of the stagnation years: pushing boundaries and refusing conventional norms was at the heart of the circle's activities. As one of the circle's members, Arkadii Rovner, stated later, for Golovin a "Heil Hitler" salute meant "Down with Soviet power."[55]

However, at the end of the 1970s and the start of the 1980s, Golovin moved one step further by organizing the circle as an "SS Black Order," with a strict hierarchy among the members. He wrote a hymn for this Black Order, composed several Nazi-inspired songs,[56] and proclaimed himself its *Reichsführer*.[57] The aim was to denounce the egalitarian ideology of the Soviet regime, which the circle equated with the mediocrity of Soviet life, to question the regime's roots in the Enlightenment, and to call for a return to a pagan and Aryan society where men belonged to fixed hierarchies or castes. At the end of the perestroika years Golovin is said to have edited two issues of a journal, *Blesk solntsa* [*Splendor Solis*/Splendor of the Sun], a title inspired by an alchemical text from the sixteenth century, the initials of which, *SS*, revealed Golovin's admiration for Nazi-inspired occultism.[58]

In his interview with Pozner, Dzhemal acknowledged that he and Golovin considered Mamleev's view to be too aesthetic and literary and incapable of encompassing the full ideological scope of their readings.[59] This second generation, active in the second half of the 1960s through the 1970s, gave more prominence to philosophical and political interpretations of their West European "discoveries." Several factors can explain this politicization. One is the greater access to banned texts, thanks not only to *samizdat* but also to the increasing permissiveness of Soviet censors with regard to nationalist themes and some formerly banned esoteric authors. The topic of Cosmism,[60] for instance, made it possible to make certain prerevolutionary authors, such as Nikolai Fedorov (1828–1903), semi-official, and to rehabilitate the occult side of the space conquest ideology promoted by Konstantin Tsiolkovskii (1857–1935) and Aleksandr Chizhevskii (1857–1964).[61] The anti-Zionist and anti-Semitic propaganda of the 1970s also helped normalize the "rediscovery" of the Aryan past of the Slavic peoples, discreetly promoted in journals such as *Nauka i religiia* and *Tekhnika—molodezhi*.[62] In addition, interaction with Western diplomats working in Moscow increased during these years, and the number of books available to well-organized dissident groups grew. Last, but not least, a provocative atmosphere amenable to prohibited ideologies led younger generations to develop a more political vision of far-right metaphysics.

YUZHINSKII CIRCLE 3.0: DUGIN'S NAZI-STAINED IDEOLOGY

Aleksandr Dugin (b. 1962) represents the third generation of the Yuzhinskii circle, the one that would experience the collapse of the Soviet Union and seek to harness the political mobilizing potential of the circle's ideological repertoire.

It is likely that Dugin met Geydar Dzhemal in 1980 and that the latter introduced the former to the circle. Dugin's presence at the circle's reunions in 1980—he was only eighteen years old—is noted by Vladimir Videman in his memoirs.[63] The following year Dugin published in *samizdat* a German-to-Russian translation of Evola's *Pagan Imperialism*.[64] It is likely that a first version had already circulated among the circle's members and that the translation had been a collective effort compiled by Dugin. At that time Dugin was studying at the Moscow Aviation Institute, but he was expelled in 1981 or 1982, in either his second or third year. The reasons for his expulsion are vague. Some sources mention anti-Soviet poetry, others cite a rumor that he had robbed university apartments with a group of friends.[65] Regardless of which version is correct, Dugin probably benefited from paternal protection—his father, Gelii A. Dugin (1935–1998), a customs officer, is said to have become the general-lieutenant of the GRU (*Glavnoe razvedyvatel'noe uprav-lenie*), the main foreign military intelligence directorate of the General Staff of the Soviet Union.[66] Dugin was subsequently declared psychologically un-stable, which enabled him to escape possible prosecution and excused him from military service. There is scarcely any information about Dugin's activ-ities after he was expelled from the institute. He has said that he worked as a concierge and gave private English and French lessons,[67] while other sources claim that he was a translator for marginal institutes such as the Institute for Information on Trade and the Institute of Economic Forecasts.[68]

There is scant information about the circle's activities throughout the 1980s. A group with similar tastes in music and literature took shape in Leningrad, while two separate currents emerged in Moscow. The first one, led by Dzhemal and Dugin, pushed for a more political reading of Traditionalism and began adopting Nazi symbolism as introduced by Golovin. The second group, led by Stepanov and then by Artur Medvedev (d. 2009), who would found the Traditionalist almanac *Volshebnaia gora* in 1993, was attracted to a nonpolitical Traditionalism, and promoted Guenonian principles. Further divisions also appeared within the first current: Dzhemal became increasingly involved in the Islamic revival in Central Asia and participated in the founding of the clandestine Islamic Rebirth Party of the Soviet Union. He traveled to Dushanbe in 1980 to meet with Islamic clerics and then began printing underground Qurans that were sent to Central Asian republics.[69] Dugin remained the main driv-ing force behind the Nazi-oriented branch. The circle was active until at least 1988, still with the same cocktail of Rimbaud poetry, rock music, and political debate.[70] The group broke up gradually during the last years of perestroika, as the new freedoms of speech and association allowed its key figures to take up professional paths in journalism, arts, music, or politics.

There are more details about Dugin's biography starting in 1988, when, upon the advice of Golovin, he joined the national-patriotic front Pamyat (Memory) alongside Dzhemal. Pamyat was then the "cadre school" of Russian nationalism, an extraordinary incubator of radical ideologies. Pamyat's most direct predecessor was the Vitiazi group (the Valiant Ones), formed in 1978 within the All-Russian Society for the Protection of Historical and Cultural Monuments (VOOPIIK), in order to prepare a dissident celebration of the 600th anniversary of the Battle of Kulikovo.[71] Vitiazi was mainly concerned with "historical tourism" and organized ex-cursions and stays at sites related to Russia's major military victories. In 1980 Pamyat was registered with the Ministry of Aviation Industry as an association of bibliophiles that organized evening events focused on writers, historians, and painters of a nationalist persuasion. These took place either at the House of Culture of the Ministry of Aviation Industry or at the A. N. Ostrovskii Museum, and, later, at the Moscow Metro's Palace of Culture. With Dmitrii Vasiliev's ascendance to the top of the organization in 1984, Pamyat went from being a cultural organization to an engine of anti-Semitic propaganda, obsessed by the "fight against Zionism."[72]

After 1987, the association fractured into multiple competing groups, all of which laid claim to the legitimacy acquired during the movement's first years. Dugin joined Vasiliev's faction, and even had a seat on its central council for several months. Nonetheless, he was quickly expelled from Pamyat, along with Dzhemal, for "Satanism" and "anti-Soviet intentions"[73] at a time when the association had largely reconciled with the then-imperiled regime. The accusation of Satanism probably refers to Dugin's Nazi symbolism and the Black Order rituals of the Yuzhinskii circle. Dugin's joining Pamyat indeed coincided with the first appearance of Nazi symbols within the Russian nationalist movement.[74] But these attempts to propagate Nazi occultism were doomed to fail. At the time, Russian nationalism defined itself chiefly either as a Russian path distinct from that of the West or as the defense of the Soviet Union against the German enemy, thereby marginalizing all those who were promoting pan-European ideologies.

In 1989 Dugin joined a small group, the Movement for Intellectual Conservatives, led by Igor Dudinskii (b. 1947), a journalist and literary critic close to dissident circles. Dudinskii had been a regular participant in the Yuzhinskii circle in the 1960s and was close to Russian émigrés in Paris, especially Vladimir Kotliarov.[75] During the last months of the Soviet Union, Dugin tested out various niches from which he hoped to influence the political scene. In 1991, he tried to take part in the anti-Gorbachev conservative putsch through his contacts with deputy Viktor Alksnis, representing the pro-Soviet group Soiuz (Union). He also began to publish in the main conservative newspaper of the time, *Den'*, in July 1991, and was promoted to its editorial board in December of the same year, thanks to his long-standing relations with Aleksandr Prokhanov. *Den'* was Dugin's main link with the major politicians who dominated the Russian nationalist scene at the onset of the 1990s, especially Gennadii Ziuganov and Vladimir Zhirinovskii. However, the newspaper's focus was too pro-Soviet for it to serve as a vehicle for all of Dugin's ideological precepts.

After the Iron Curtain parted, Dugin pursued his own path of interaction with Western ideologies and ideologists and made contact with the political heirs of Traditionalism. His first trips to France, Belgium, Spain, and Italy between 1989 and 1993, probably organized thanks to Mamleev's networks in Paris, allowed him to meet with members of the French and Belgian New Right, such as Alain de Benoist, Robert Steuckers, and Jean Thiriart, as well as with members of the Spanish Thule group, successor to the defunct neo-Nazi organization CEDADE, and with Claudio Mutti himself in Italy.[76] Dugin had fewer contacts with the German New Right, even if he was drawn to historical figures of Nazi mysticism, such as the famous thinkers of Germanic Aryanism Guido von List (1848–1919) and Jörg Lanz von Liebenfels (1874–1954), and especially to Hermann Wirth (1885–1981). Wirth was the founder of Ahnenerbe, the SS-allied research institute in charge of creating the Aryan ideology for the Nazi regime, which had organized many archeological expeditions in search of *Urkulturen*, the original culture of the first Aryans.[77] Dugin's links with Germany's Far Right would develop only later, in the 2010s.

CONCLUSIONS

The Yuzhinskii circle was the first attempt among dissidents to bypass the traditional divisions between Westernizers/liberals and nationalists/monarchists/Stalinists. Initially it sought a response to the Soviet regime not in a rival political ideology, but in metaphysics and the search for another level of reality. This trend became more powerful in the 1960s and 1970s and was encapsulated by the fashion for Oriental religions and mysticisms, Blavatsky and Roerich, shamanism and Tibetan mythology, UFO-logy and so on—similar in many ways to the New Age wave that swept Western countries around the same time.[78] In this atmosphere the circle distinguished itself by its preference for European mysticism, medieval esotericism, and Western authors who embodied German Romanticism and vitalist ideologies.

This initial path also allowed for the discovery and assimilation of the main advocates of Traditionalism—particularly René Guénon and Julius Evola—and the proponents and political heirs of the German Conservative Revolution in the 1920s, Ahnenerbe-inspired Nazi occultism, and postwar Fascist doctrines in Italy and Latin America. In their memoirs and interviews, Mamleev, Golovin, Dzhemal, and Dugin acknowledged their violent rejection, at that time, of the Soviet reality and official ideology. Discovering powerful counter-narratives, seen as taboo in Soviet society, was irresistibly attractive to spirits in search of nonconformism and provocation. Their spiritual quest as a response to the Soviet regime progressively transformed into a path of assimilating and promoting new political doctrines. In three decades, the Yuzhinskii circle evolved from Mamleev's encounter with metaphysics to Golovin's discovery of the political side of Traditionalism, and then to Dugin's revisiting of Nazi mysticism and his attempts to transform it into an engine for concrete political activism.

The circle's networks survived the collapse of the Soviet Union, and it succeeded in using the new freedoms offered by post-Soviet Russia to continue the mission it had begun several decades prior. Its main leaders played a significant role in introducing the European anti-Enlightenment tradition to Russia, and Dugin continues on this course to this day, for instance in translating Heidegger in order to familiarize the Russian public with the German philosopher's teachings. The circle also developed lines of communication with representatives of the Western European Far Right that have proved to be robust over time. Dugin continues to interact closely with the descendants of Julius Evola in France, Belgium, Italy, and Spain, and his contacts with the European Far Right predate those of the Kremlin.

During the Soviet decades, the circle's philosophical theories were very marginal. Although they fascinated a small number of nonconformist intellectuals, they were too radical and too anti-Russian or anti-Soviet to attract a large number of followers. Today the ideological landscape has changed. The precepts of Traditionalism and the Conservative Revolution faintly echo some of the Kremlin's appeals for a new conservative ideology. Along with the electoral success of populist parties in Western Europe, this change of atmosphere has created a new window for the heirs of Yuzhinskii circle to interact with Europe and to see some of their arguments fruitfully integrated into larger ideological coalitions.

NOTES

Introduction

1. Jeune Nation solidariste, March 15, 1979.

2. I borrow the term "intellectual romance" from Richard Wolin, *The Seduction of Unreason: The Intellectual Romance with Fascism from Nietzsche to Postmodernism* (Princeton, NJ: Princeton University Press, 2006). I would like to express my gratitude to Peter Rollberg for his wise advice on the previous version of this introduction.

3. Marlene Laruelle, ed., *Eurasianism and the European Far Right: Reshaping the Europe–Russia Relationship* (Lanham, MD: Lexington, 2015).

4. The consensus is mostly around Roger Griffin's analysis. See Roger Griffin, *International Fascism: Theories, Causes, and the New Consensus* (London: Arnold, 1998) and Roger Griffin, *The Nature of Fascism* (New York: Palgrave Macmillan, 1991).

5. Walter Laqueur, *Russia and Germany: A Century of Conflict*, updated with a new introduction (New Brunswick, NJ: Transaction, 1990).

6. Leonid Luks, ed., *Zwei Sonderwege? Russisch-deutsche Parallelen und Konstrate (1917–2014)* (Stuttgart: Ibidem-Verlag, 2016).

7. Michael David-Fox, Peter Holquist, and Alexander M. Martin, eds., *Fascination and Enmity: Russia and Germany as Entangled Histories, 1914–1945* (Pittsburgh, PA: University of Pittsburgh Press, 2012).

8. Gerd Koenen, *Der Russland-Komplex: Die Deutschen und der Osten 1900–1945* (Munich: C.H. Beck, 2005).

9. John J. Stephan, *The Russian Fascists: Tragedy and Farce in Exile, 1925–1945* (New York: Harper and Row, 1978).

10. David Brandenberger, *National Bolshevism: Stalinist Mass Culture and the Formation of Modern Russian National Identity, 1931–1956* (Cambridge, MA: Harvard University Press, 2002), 6.

1. Late Imperial Slavophilism in the Context of Fascistogenic Ideas

1. Fascism "was not born in the trenches of the First World War and did not die in the ruins of Berlin" (Zeev Sternhell, "Fascism: Reflections on the Fate of Ideas in Twentieth Century History," *Journal of Political Ideologies* 5, no. 2 (2000): 159). On the project of studying peripheral fascisms, see Roger Griffin, "Decentering Comparative Fascist Studies," *Fascism* 4, no. 2 (2015).

2. Viacheslav Morozov, *Russia's Postcolonial Identity: A Subaltern Empire in a Eurocentric World* (Basingstoke: Palgrave Macmillan, 2015).

3. Jack Balkin, *Cultural Software: A Theory of Ideology* (New Haven, CT: Yale University Press, 2002).

4. Uolter Laker [Walter Laqueur], *Rossiia i Germaniia: Nastavniki Gitlera* (Moscow: Mysl', 1991); Aleksandr Yanov, *Russkaia ideia i 2000-i god* (New York: Liberty Publishing Company, 1988).

5. Uolter Laker [Walter Laqueur], *Chernaia sotnia: Proiskhozhdenie russkogo fashizma*

(Washington, DC, 1994): 17. See also Edward Thaden, *Conservative Nationalism in Nineteenth-Century Russia* (Seattle: University of Washington Press, 1964), 205. See also Semen Liubosh, *Russkii fashist Vladimir Purishkevich* (Leningrad: Byloe, 1925).

6. Hans Rogger, *Jewish Policies and Right-Wing Politics in Imperial Russia* (Berkeley: University of California Press, 1986): 213, 230. See also Sergei Stepanov, *Chernaia sotnia v Rossii, 1905–1914 gg.* (Moscow: Rosvuznauka, 1992): 31.

7. See Martin Blinkhorn, "Conservatism, Traditionalism and Fascism in Spain, 1898–1937," in *Fascists and Conservatives: The Radical Right and the Establishment in Twentieth-Century Europe*, ed. Martin Blinkhorn (London: Routledge, 1990), 135.

8. Mikhail Suslov, "'Slavophilism Is True Liberalism': The Political Utopia of S. F. Sharapov (1855–1911)," *Russian History* 38, no. 2 (2011); Mikhail Suslov, "Neo-Slavophilism and the Revolution of 1905–07: A Study in the Ideology of S. F. Sharapov," *Revolutionary Russia* 24, no. 1 (2011).

9. See Ernst Nolte, *Three Faces of Fascism: Action Française, Italian Fascism, National Socialism* (New York: Holt, Rinehart and Winston, 1966); Zeev Sternhell, *La droite révolutionnaire 1885–1914: Les origins françaises du fascism* (Paris: Éditions du seuil, 1978); Zeev Sternhell, *Neither Right nor Left*. Translated by David Maisel (Berkeley: University of California Press, 1986).

10. Gosudarstvennyi arkhiv Smolenskoi Oblasti (thereafter GASO), f. 121, d. 531, l. 4, 146 (letters to various persons, January 20, 1878, January 26, 1893).

11. Parisien [Sharapov], "U Lui Blana," *Novoe vremia*, no. 693 (1878): 2.

12. Parisien [Sharapov], "U Giugo," *Novoe vremia*, no. 712 (1878): 2.

13. Sternhell, *La droite révolutionnaire*, 33.

14. Sergei Sharapov, [lead article], *Russkoe delo*, no. 15 (1888): 2.

15. Sergei Sharapov, [lead article], *Russkoe delo*, no. 13 (1886): 1.

16. Sternhell, *La droite révolutionnaire, 1885–1914:* 103–12.

17. Zeev Sternhell, "Déroulède and the Origins of Modern French Nationalism," *Journal of Contemporary History* 6, no. 4 (1971): 56.

18. GASO, F. 121, D. 1060, L. 5–18 (letters from Lucien Millevoye to Sharapov, 1887–1888).

19. Sharapov, [lead article], *Russkoe delo*, no. 1 (1887): 4. See also GASO, f. 121, d. 1060 (letters to various persons, in foreign languages).

20. Boris Anan'ich, *Rossiia i mezhdunarodnyi kapital, 1897–1914: Ocherki istorii finansovykh otnoshenii* (Leningrad: Nauka, 1970): 72; GASO, f. 121, d. 7 (an entry in the diary of May 31, 1901).

21. Reprinted in 2001 by the anti-Semitic publishing house Peresvet in Krasnodar.

22. Eduard Driumond [Édouard Drumont], "Revoliutsiia v Rossii," *Russkoe delo*, no. 2 (1905): 7.

23. For example, GASO, f. 121, d. 1060, l. 161–162ob. (letter from Pierre Rocheverre, August 22, 1909).

24. Serge Scharapoff, "L'Allemagne et l'opinion russe," *Le Radical*, January 19, 1911: 1; Serge Scharapoff, "Le Nouveau plan stratégique de la Russie," *L'Opinion*, February 18, 1911: 201–3.

25. GASO, f .121, d. 7, l. 7261 (diary entry, undated, 1905).

26. For example, Andrzej Walicki, "The Troubling Legacy of Roman Dmowski," *East European Politics and Societies* 14, no. 1 (1999).

27. GASO, f. 121, d. 541, l. 157 (letter to an unknown person, February 1, 1894).

28. For example, A. L. Shemiakin, *Ideologiia Nikoly Pashicha. Formirovanie i evoliutsiia (1868–1891)* (Moscow, 1998).

29. For example, John Basil, "The Russian Theological Academies and the Old Catholics, 1870–1905," in *Religious and Secular Forces in Late Imperial Russia*, ed. Charles E. Timberlake (Seattle: University of Washington Press, 1992).

30. Ol'ga Danilova, "Frantsuzskoe 'slavianofil'stvo' kontsa XIX–nachala XX veka," in *Rossiia i Frantsiia: XVIII–XX vv.* (Moscow: Nauka, 2006), vyp. 7: 236–70.

31. Sternhell, "Fascism," 151. Cf. Aleksandr Galkin, "O fashizme—ego sushchnosti, korniakh, priznakakh i formakh proiavleniia," *Polis*, no. 2 (1995): 10.

32. Roger Griffin, "Studying Fascism in a Postfascist Age: From New Consensus to New Wave?" *Fascism* 1, no. 1 (2012); Roger Griffin, *The Nature of Fascism* (London: Routledge, 1993): 240; Griffin "Decentering Comparative Fascist Studies," 103–18.

33. Aleksandr Etkind, *Internal Colonization: Russia's Imperial Experience* (Cambridge: Polity Press, 2011), 17, 140.

34. Michael Freeden, "Is Nationalism a Distinct Ideology?" *Political Studies* 46, no. 4 (1998).

35. Salvatore Garau, "If Liberalism Steps into the Fascist Synthesis: The Diverging Views of Zeev Sternhell and Ishay Landa on the Origins of Fascist Ideology," *Journal of Political Ideologies* 19, no. 1 (2014): 60–77.

36. Thomas S. Fallows, "The Russian Fronde and the Zemstvo Movement: Economic Agitation and Gentry Politics in the Mid-1890s," *Russian Review* 44, no. 2 (April 1985): 119–38.

37. Mikhail N. Luk'ianov, *Rossiiskii konservatizm i reforma, 1907–1914* (Stuttgart: ibidem Verlag, 2007); Aleksandr V. Repnikov, *Konservativnye predstasvleniia pereustroistva Rossii* (Moscow: Academia, 2007).

38. Klavdii Stepanov, [editorial], *Moskovskii golos,* no. 2 (1906): 2; Nikolai Aksakov, "Germaniia i Slavianstvo," *Svidetel',* no. 22 (1909): 31; Sergei Sharapov, "Otkrytie Aksakovskogo obshchestva," *Russkoe delo,* no. 11 (1907): 2.

39. GASO, f. 121, d. 534, l. 382 ob. (letter to I. F. Romanov, February 10, 1890); *Russkoe delo,* no. 52 (1888): 1; Sergei Sharapov, "Moi otvet Miliukovu," *Svidetel',* no. 12 (1908): 48–50; Sergei Sharapov, "Moi dnevnik," *Svidetel',* no. 35 (1910): 78; Mikhail F. Taube, "Slavianofil'stvo i ego opredeleniia," *Mirnyi trud,* no. 6 (1905): 181, 193; Nil Durnovo, *Godina Bozh'ego popushcheniia* (Moscow: Vernost', 1907), vol. 1: 4–6.

40. Quoted from "Perepiska I. S. Aksakova i S. F. Sharapova (1883–1886)," *Russkaia literatura,* no. 1 (2005): 153.

41. Quoted from Tat'iana Kiriutina, *Problemy razvitiia russkoi literatury i zhurnalistiki kontsa XIX–nachala XX veka: S. F. Sharapov.* Cand. of sci. thesis (Smolensk, 2001), 18.

42. Will Kymlicka, *Contemporary Political Philosophy: An Introduction* (Oxford: Oxford University Press, 2002).

43. Sergei Sharapov, "Kievskie vpechatleniia," *Russkoe delo,* no. 42 (1906): 8.

44. Sergei Sharapov, *Diktator (Politicheskaia fantaziia)* (Moscow, 1907), 6; Sergei Sharapov, *Samoderzhavie ili konstitutsiia* (Moscow, 1908), 7.

45. Sergei Sharapov, *Opiat' snachala . . . (Razmyshleniia pered tret'ei dumoi)* (Moscow, 1907), 2.

46. *Ob''edinennoe dvorianstvo. S''ezdy upolnomochennykh gubernskikh dvorianskikh obshchestv, 1906–1916* (Moscow, 2001), vol. 1: 185–86.

47. GASO, f. 121, d. 535, l. 124 (letter to Afanasii Vasil'ev, February 13, 1889).

48. Rossiiskii gosudarstvennyi istoricheskii arkhiv, f. 1617, op. 1, d. 29, l. 9 (letter to Mikhail Andronikov, August 15, 1904). In a letter to V. Plehve of November 6, 1902, he avers that "a hundred nihilists did not manage to do as much harm to Autocracy as [Vladimir] Gringmut and Lev Tikhomirov" (two paragons of conservatism). See GASO, f. 121, d. 1045, l. 38.

49. "Germans are the parents of both Russian liberalism and Russian conservatism" (Sergei Sharapov, "Moi dnevnik," *Russkoe delo,* no. 1 (1907): 11. See also: Sharapov, "Pamiati I. S. Aksakova," in Sergei Sharapov, *Sochineniia,* vol. 3 (St. Petersburg: Tip. A. Porokhovshchikova, 1899): 6.

50. Otdel rukopisei Rossiiskoi gosudarstvennoi biblioteki, f. 265, k. 116, d. 22, l. 8 (letter from F. Samarin to Sharapov, undated).

51. Sharapov, *Sotsializm kak religiia nenavisti* (Moscow, 1907).

52. For example, see Peter Rutkoff, "The *Ligue des Patriotes*: The Nature of the Radical Right and the Dreyfus Affair," *French Historical Studies* 8, no. 4 (1974): 585–603.

53. Sharapov, [Lead article], *Russkoe delo*, no. 1 (1890): 5.

54. Konstantin Odarchenko, *Nravstvennye i pravovye osnovy russkogo narodnogo khoziaistva* (Moscow: Tipo-lit. K.F. Aleksandrova, 1897), 370; Odarchenko, "K voprosu o den'gakh i 'zolotoi valiute' kreditnogo rublia," *Russkaia beseda*, no. 12 (1895): 103; Afanasii Vasil'ev, *Miru-narodu moi otchet za prozhitoe vremia* (Petrograd: I. Kushnereva, 1908), 859; Odarchenko, "Narodnoe khoziaistvo s tochki zreniia nravstvennosti i prava," *Russkaia beseda*, no. 4 (1895): 28–37.

55. Odarchenko, "Otnoshenie proizvoditelei k potrebiteliam s tochki zreniia nravstvennosti i prava," *Russkaia beseda*, no. 4 (1896): 12–20.

56. Sharapov, [Lead article], *Russkii trud*, no. 17 (1897): 3. Cf.: Mikhail Suslov, "The Lost Chance of Conservative Modernization: S. F. Sharapov in the Economic Debates of the Late Nineteenth to the Early Twentieth Century," *Acta Slavica Iaponica* 31 (2012).

57. Sharapov, [Lead article], Pakhar,' no. 4–5 (1906): 10.

58. Martin Malia, *Aleksandr Gertsen i proiskhozhdenie russkogo sotsializma, 1812–1855* (Moscow: Territoriia budushchego, 2010): 541.

59. Sharapov, *Mirnye rechi. Po-russki. Staroe i novoe. Tri sbornika 1900 g.* (Moscow: tipo-lit. A. Vasil'eva, 1901): 207.

60. Sharapov, "Neobkhodimye poiasneniia. Slavianofil'skii vzgliad na finansy," in Rtsy [I. F. Romanov], *K svedeniiu budushchego ministra zemledeliia* (St. Petersburg: Tip. S.N. Khudekova, 1893): 12. See also: Sharapov, *Russkii sel'skii khoziain: neskol'ko myslei ob ustroistve khoziaistva v Rossii na novykh nachalakh* (St. Petersburg: Tip. M. K. Remezova, 1894): 29.

61. GASO, f. 121, d. 535, l. 188 (letter to an unknown person, September 6, 1889).

62. Sharapov, "Dnevnik," *Svidetel'*, no. 29–30 (1909): 71–81.

63. Sharapov, *Izbrannoe* (Moscow: ROSSPEN, 2010): 130.

64. Cf. Sharapov, *Vopl' golodaiushchego intelligenta* (Moscow, 1902): 32.

65. GASO, f. 121, d. 559, l. 38 (letter to Empress Maria Fedorovna, August 16, 1906). See also: "Russia . . . is not an organism . . . but a crowd of 130 million individuals" (Sharapov, "Moi dnevnik," in Sharapov, *Sochineniia* (Moscow, 1901), vol. 6: 49).

66. GASO, f. 121, d. 1054, l. 160 (letter to A. Antonovich, August 13, 1906). See aso *Russkoe delo*, no. 2 (1906): 16.

67. Bruce Pauley, "Fascism and the *Fuehrerprinzip*: The Austrian Example," *Central European History* 12, no. 3 (1979): 272–96.

68. E.g. Robert Soucy, "the Nature of Fascism in France," *Journal of Contemporary History* 1, no. 1 (1966): 47.

69. Sharapov, *Izbrannoe*: 30, 37. Cf. "The Tsar is the embodiment of sovereign Russia, the bearer of its collective moral self" (Sharapov, *Izbrannoe*, 139).

70. Rossiiskii gosudarstvennyi arkhiv literatury i iskusstva, f. 572, op. 2, d. 27, l. 9 (letter from Sharapov to A. Engel'gardt, March 15, 1881).

71. Iurii Bartenev, *Pomrachennyi ideal* (Moscow, 1907): 3.

72. Sharapov, *Diktator* (Moscow: Tip. A. Suvorina, 1907), 98–99.

73. Sharapov, *Ivanov 16-i i Sokolov 18-i* (Moscow: Tip. Russkii golos, 1907): 160–61.

74. Sharapov, *Kabinet Diktatora* (Moscow: Svidetel', 1908): 244, 265; Sharapov, *Ivanov 16-i i Sokolov 18-i:* 159.

75. Sharapov, *Diktator*: 100.

76. Griffin, *The Nature of Fascism*: 26.

77. *Svidetel'*, no. 3–4 (1907): 123.

78. *Svidetel'*, no. 16–17 (1908): 20–21.

79. GASO, f. 121, d. 380, l. 1 (letter to V. M. Purishkevich, February 12, 1910).

80. Cf. Susanna Rabow-Edling, *Slavophile Thought and the Politics of Cultural Nationalism* (Albany, NY: SUNY Press, 2012).

81. Vasil'ev, "Nashi okhraniteli," *Russkaia beseda*, no. 8 (1895): 162.

82. Klavdii Stepanov, [lead article], *Moskovskii golos*, no. 1 (1906): 1.

83. GASO, f. 121, d. 22, l. 7 (letter to the Ministry of the Interior, January 1896); Sharapov, [Lead article], *Svidetel'*, no. 7 (1908): 28.

84. GASO, F. 121, D. 545, L. 16, 17 (letter to K. N. Paskhalov, December 28, 1906); GASO, F. 121, D. 545, L. 21 ob (letter to the editor of an unknown Polish newspaper, December 29, 1906).

85. *Svidetel'*, no. 16–17 (1908): 12–13, 17.

86. Sharapov, [Lead article], *Russkoe delo*, no. 1 (1889): 3.

87. Sharapov, *Cherez polveka* (Moscow, 1902): 50–51.

88. Sharapov, "Moi dnevnik CCCXVI," *Svidetel'*, no. 10–11 (1908): 107–8; Sharapov, "Moi dnevnik CCCLI," *Svidetel'*, no. 13 (1908): 53, 55.

89. Mikhail Men'shikov, "Rasovaia bor'ba" [1911], in Men'shikov, *Pis'ma k russkoi natsii* (Moscow, 1999): 130–32; Men'shikov, "Evrei o evreiakh" [1909], in Men'shikov, *Pis'ma k russkoi natsii*: 53–59. Cf. Sharapov's complimentary correspondence with Men'shikov, undated (GASO, d. 310, l. 4). The racial language gradually made its way to Slavophile and conservative circles at the turn of the century. Cf. Lev Tikhomirov, "Aziatskii vopros," in Tikhomirov, *Khristianstvo i politika* (Moscow, 1999), 312. At that time, racist ideology was still far from eugenics, but it nevertheless represented a meaningful attempt to translate the language of religion, culture, and language into the positivistic language of "blood" and corporal characteristics of the collective bodies.

90. Sharapov, "Zashchititel'naia rech'," in S. F. Sharapov, *Sochineniia* (St. Petersburg, 1892), vol. 1: 114–15; *Russkoe delo*, no. 1 (1906): 7; *Svidetel'*, no. 16–17 (1909): 18. See Heinz-Dietrich Löwe, *The Tsars and the Jews: Reform, Reaction and Anti-Semitism in Imperial Russia, 1772–1917* (Chur, 1993): 8. On Russian anti-Semitism see a recent study by Eugene M. Avrutin, "Racial Categories and the Politics of (Jewish) Difference in Late Imperial Russia," *Kritika: Explorations in Russian and Eurasian History* 8, no. 1 (Winter 2007): 13–40.

91. Kireev, "Neskol'ko dannykh dlia resheniia evreiskogo voprosa," in Kireev, *Sochineniia* (St. Petersburg, 1912), vol. 2: 308–10.

92. OR RGB, f. 265, k. 134, d. 1, l. 12.

93. Aleksandr Shcherbatov, *Obnovlennaia Rossiia* (Moscow, 1908): 56.

94. Sharapov, *Cherez polveka*: 38–40.

95. GASO, f. 121, d. 617, l. 2, 2ob.(a draft of the political program, 1907?); *Russkoe delo*, no. 1 (1906): 7.

96. Talitskii [Sharapov], *Bumazhnyi rubl'* (St. Petersburg, 1895): 14.

97. GASO, f. 121, d. 318, l. 1 (letter to P. Miliukov, undated).

98. *Russkoe delo*, no. 35 (1905): 13.

99. *Russkoe delo*, no. 36 (1905): 4.

100. Sharapov, *Kabinet diktatora*: 71.

101. Cf. analogous "crypto-nationalism" of Vladimir Zhirinovskii's fascist program: Andreas Umland, "Zhirinovskii as a Fascist: Palingenetic Ultra-Nationalism and the Emergence of the Liberal-Democratic Party of Russia in 1992–93," *Forum für osteuropaeische Ideen- und Zeitgeschichte* 14, no. 2 (2010): 189–215.

102. Mark Steinberg, "Melancholy and Modernity: Emotions and Social Life in Russia between the Revolutions," *Journal of Social History* 41, no. 4 (2008); E. Mel'nikova, "Eskhatologicheskie ozhidaniia rubezha XIX–XX vekov: kontsa sveta ne budet?" *Antropologicheskii forum*, no. 1 (2004); E. Newstadt, "Components of Pessimism in Russian Conservative Thought, 1881–1905," (PhD diss., University of Oklahoma, 1991).

103. Anthony D. Smith, *Chosen Peoples* (Oxford University Press Oxford, 2003). Mikhail Suslov, "Krizis messianstva i vopros o budushchem Rossii vo vzgliadakh Sergeia Sharapova (1855–1911)," *Voprosy kul'turologii*, no. 9 (2010): 39–45.

104. E.g., Ivan Kireevskii, "Obozrenie sovremennogo sostoianiia literatury" [1845], in Kireevskii, *Polnoe sobranie sochinenii* (Moscow, 1862), vol. 2, 33.

105. *Ruskoe delo*, no. 1 (1907): 12.

106. *Svidetel'*, no. 1 (1907): 3.

107. GASO, f. 121, d. 536, l. 121; d. 7, l. 319 (diary entry, September 4, 1910). Cf.: d. 1054, l. 156 (letter to A. Antonovich, August 13, 1906); d. 1046, l. 97 (letter to K. Kupalov, October 31, 1906?).

108. GASO, f. 121, d. 533, l. 238.

109. GASO, f. 121, d. 1463, l. 15 (letter to S. Kryzhanovskii, August 21, 1906).

110. Sharapov, "Moi dnevnik CLXXIV," in Sharapov, *Sochineniia* (Moscow 1904), vol. 25: 50.

111. OR RGB, f. 265, k. 157, d. 13, l. 56ob. (letter from Kireev to F. Samarin, October 12, 1908).

112. Sharapov, "Moi dnevnik CCCXXVI," *Svidetel'*, no. 10–11 (1908): 133.

113. GASO, f. 121, d. 1045, l. 18 (letter to K. Pobedonostsev, October 20, 1901).

114. GASO, f. 121, d. 533, l. 239–40. Italics are mine.

115. *Russkoe delo*, no. 22–23 (1906): 4.

116. OR RGB, f. 265, k. 157, d. 13, l. 63 (letter from Kireev to F. Samarin, March 13, 1909?).

117. Sergei Sharapov, "Diary DLI," *Svidetel'*, no. 33 (1910): 82.

118. D. Kh. [Khomiakov], "Revoliutsionnye raznovidnosti," *Moskovskii golos*, no. 27 (1906): 4. Cf. Iurii Bartenev, *Okazennaia Pravda* (St. Petersburg, 1907), 4.

119. Iurii Bartenev, *Pomrachennyi ideal* (Moscow, 1907), 7. Compare with the similar ideas of another neo-Slavophile, Klavdii Stepanov, in "Editorial," *Moskovskii golos*, no. 1 (1906): 1.

120. Richard Saage, "Fascism—Revolutionary Departure to an Alternative Modernity? A Response to Roger Griffin's 'Exploding the Continuum of History,'" *European Journal of Political Theory* 11, no. 4 (2012).

121. Mark Sedgwick, *Against the Modern World: Traditionalism and the Secret Intellectual History of the Twentieth Century* (Oxford University Press on Demand, 2004).

122. GASO, f. 121, d. 7, l. 7021 (diary entry, April 25, 1901).

123. Oleg Platonov, "Missiia vypolnima," in *Putin v zerkale "Izborskogo kluba,"* ed. Maxim Kalashnikov et al. (Moscow: Knizhnyi mir, 2015): 177–78.

2. A Reactionary Utopia

1. Alexei Miller, *The Romanov Empire and Nationalism* (Budapest: Central European University Press, 2008), 4–5.

2. Kiev, which in the mid-nineteenth century was still a city with a Polish-speaking majority, was seen by Russian nationalists as the cradle of Rus' and by Ukrainian ones as the heart of their nation. See the very careful study of Kiev by Faith Hillis, *Children of Rus': Right-Bank Ukraine and the Invention of a Russian Nation* (Ithaca, NY: Cornell University Press, 2013); and Theodore Weeks, *Nation and State in Late Imperial Russia: Nationalism and Russification on the Western Frontier, 1863–1914* (DeKalb, IL: Northern Illinois University Press,1996), 11–14.

3. Dzhiovanni Savino, "Okrainy Rossii i proekt natsionalizatsii Rossiiskoj Imperii," in *Puti Rossii: Sbornik statei*, vol. 21, *Novyi poriadok—vechnoe vozvrashchenie*, ed. M. G. Pugacheva and A. F. Filippov (Moscow: NLO, 2015), 231–42.

4. Zeev Sternhell, *Ni droite, ni gauche : L'ideologie fasciste en France* (Paris: Editions du Seuil, 1983).

5. Dmitrii I. Strogov provides interesting accounts of the rightist salons' influence on key political decisions in "Salon kniazia M. M. Andronikova i sistema vlasti Rossiiskoi Imperii," *Klio: zhurnal dlia uchenykh*, no. 3 (2006).

6. V. L. Velichko, "Strannye pretenzii i 'Adelaida' g. Sigmy," *Russkii vestnik*, no. 4 (1903): 787.

7. *Spisok uchreditelei Russkago sobraniia* (St. Petersburg, 1901), 1–3.

8. *Ustav "Russkago sobraniia"* (St. Petersburg, 1901), 1.

9. *Ustav "Russkago sobraniia,"* 1–2.

10. Staryi Slavianofil, *Chto takoe Russkoe sobranie?* (St. Petersburg, 1901), 8.

11. O. A. Zhuravleva cites the opinion of Aleksei S. Suvorin on Golitsyn's works in the biographical entry "Golitsyn Dmitrii Petrovich," in *Russkii konservatizm serediny XVIII–nachalo XX veka. Entsiklopediia* (Moscow, 2010), 148–49.

12. Don C. Rawson in his work about Russian rightists carefully analyzes the political-cultural profile of the Russian Assembly and the features it had in common with other cultural and charitable societies in St. Petersburg. I partly disagree with Rawson's conclusion that is was a quasi-cultural club, a "respectable haven for monarchists" not engaged in politics: the elitist approach of the Russian Assembly was part of a political choice, and the organization was better suited as a cradle for other organizations than as a party. The future leaders of the URP and other monarchist and national-conservative formations had connections with the Russian Assembly, which in the Stolypin era was a kind of meeting place for different factions on the Right. See Don C. Rawson, *Russian Rightists and the Revolution of 1905* (Cambridge: Cambridge University Press, 1995), 46, 55.

13. Vice president of the Russian Assembly from 1906 until 1914, General Geiden was born into a family of officers devoted to the Romanov dynasty. His salon was a gathering place for many people with national-conservative tendencies, such as Bishop Evlogii. He was arrested by the Cheka in 1918 and soon released. See A. Stepanov, "Geiden Nikolai Fedorovich," in *Chernaia sotnia: Istoricheskaia entsiklopediia*, ed. O. A. Platonov (Moscow, 2008), 137–38.

14. *Spisok uchreditelei Russkago sobraniia* (St. Petersburg, 1901), 3.

15. Iu. I. Kirianov, "Russkoe sobranie," in *Politicheskie partii Rossii: Konets XI–pervaya tret' XX veka* (Moscow, 1996), 535. Based on *Letopis' Russkago sobraniia* of May 1901 and January 1903, Rawson obtains slightly different figures: for the year 1901, government and court personnel made up 32 percent of the membership and military officers 17 percent; in 1903 they were respectively 21 percent and 19 percent (Rawson, *Russian Rightists*, 47). Working on Russian Assembly newspapers and reviews raises the question of how to classify some categories and some people; for example, Golitsyn called himself "poet" when he was working in government administration. See *Letopis' Russkago sobraniia*, May 1901, 32–34, and *Letopis' Russkago sobraniia*, January 1903, i–xliii.

16. Iu. I. Kirianov, "Chislennost' i sostav chlenov Russkogo sobraniia," in *Rossiiskaia imperiia: strategii stabilizatsii i opyty obnovleniia* (Voronezh, 2004), 340.

17. For an analysis of Russkoe okrainnoe obshchestvo and Okrainy Rossii, see Giovanni Savino, "Il nazionalismo russo, 1900–1917: Ideologie, organizzazioni, sfera pubblica" (PhD diss., University of Naples Federico II, 2012), 26–40.

18. *Prazdnik russkago samosoznaniia: otkritie kharkovskago otdela "Russkago sobraniia"* (Kharkov, 1903), 2.

19. Rawson, *Russian Rightists*, 49.

20. A. Kaplin, A. Stepanov, "Viazigin Andrei Sergeevich," in Platonov, ed., *Chernaia sotnia*, 130.

21. I. V. Omelianchuk, *Chernosotennoe dvizhenie v Rossiiskoi Imperii 1901–1914* (Kiev, 2007), 18.

22. 1901: 985; 1904: 1,804; 1905: 2,112; 1906–7: 3,800; and then a progressive decline, with 500 members in winter 1914–15. Kirianov, *Chislennost i sostav*, 340, 344, 362.

23. Iu. I. Kirianov, *Russkoe sobranie 1900–1917* (Moscow, 2003), 247–48.

24. *Programma Russkago sobraniia* (St. Petersburg, 1906), 3.

25. *Vestnik Russkago sobraniia*, January 26, 1907, 3–4.

26. *Vestnik Russkago sobraniia*, January 26, 1907, 3–4.

27. A. V. Repnikov, *Russkoe sobranie* in *Russkii konservatizm serediny XVIII–nachalo XX veka. Entsiklopediia* (Moscow, 2010), 439.

28. *Vestnik Russkago sobraniia,* May 11, 1907, 1.

29. In Petersburg one of the candidates was Platon Kulakovskii. See K. Ia. Grot, *Platon Andreevich Kulakovskii* (St. Petersburg, 1913), 17.

30. *Dom i gimnaziia Russkago sobraniia* (St. Petersburg, 1910), 5–6. *Ustav gimnazii i real'nogo uchilishcha* (St. Petersburg, 1907), 2.

31. Savino, "Il nazionalismo russo," 20.

32. Kirianov, *Russkoe sobranie*, 8–9.

33. Vladimir I. Gurko, *Features and Figures of the Past*, ed. J. E. Wallace Sterling, Xenia Joukoff Eudin, and H. H. Fisher; trans. Laura Matveev (Stanford, CA: Stanford University Press, 1939), 676*n*.

34. B. Nikol'skii, "Dnevnik," *Krasnyi arkhiv* 63 (1934): 80.

35. A. Chernovskii, ed., *Soiuz russkogo naroda. Po materialam chrezvychainoi sledstvennoi komissii Vremennogo Pravitel'stva* (Moscow–Leningrad, 1929), 32.

36. V. Levitskii, "Pravye partii," in *Obshchestvennoe dvizhenie v Rossii v nachale XX–go veka*, ed. L. Martov et al., 4 vols. (St. Petersburg, 1909–1914), 403.

37. Rawson, *Russian Rightists*, 60.

38. A transcript of the visit was published in *Russkoe znamia*, January 9, 1906, 2–3.

39. *Pravo*, January 6, 1907.

40. S. E. Kryzhanovskii, *Vospominianiia* (St. Petersburg: Izdatel'stvo Rossiiskoi natsional'noi biblioteki, 2009), 102–3.

41. The "tragic clown of the Duma," as he was called by Pavel Miliukov, was born in Kishinev in 1870, a representative of the Russified Bessarabian aristocracy. Before the 1905 revolution, Purishkevich was a writer without much success, who was involved in the organization of poetry evenings for the Russian Assembly, and published his far-right views on the national question in the newspaper *Bessarabets*. He was elected to the second, third, and fourth dumas, where he was, together with Markov, one of the better known rightist leaders. Purishkevich was at the center of various scandals during Duma sessions. He came into conflict with Dubrovin in 1907, and left the URP to create the Russian Popular Union of St. Michael the Archangel. During the First World War he criticized the empress Aleksandra Fedorovna. Purishkevich was one of the organizers of the Rasputin murder, in an effort to save the Romanov dynasty. After the October Revolution he was arrested by the Cheka in November 1917 but was released on April 17, 1918. Purishkevich went to Kiev, then to the Don, where he joined the Volunteer Amy. He died of typhus in 1920. See A. A. Ivanov, *Vladimir Purishkevich—opyt biografii pravogo politika, 1870–1920* (Moscow–St. Petersburg: Alians-Arkheo, 2011); S. B. Liubosh, *Russkii fashist Vladimir Purishkevich* (Leningrad, 1925); A. B. Nikolaev, R. B. Romov, "Purishkevich Vladimir Mitrofanovich," in *Gosudarstvennaia duma Rossiiskoi imperii 1906–1917. Entsiklopediia* (Moscow: ROSSPEN, 2008), 509–11;

42. Kryzhanovskii, *Vospominaniia,*105.

43. P. E. Shchegolev, ed., *Padenie tsarskogo rezhima: Stenograficheskie otchety doprosov i pokazanii, dannykh v 1917 g. v Chrezvychanoi sledstvennoi komissii, Vremennogo pravitelstv*, vol. 6 (Leningrad–Moscow, 1924–1927), 184–205.

44. Shchegolev, ed., *Padenie tsarskogo rezhima*, 405.

45. Abraham Ascher, *The Revolution of 1905*, vol. 2: *Authority Restored* (Stanford, CA: Stanford University Press, 1992), 273–75.

46. Sergei Iu. Witte, *The Memoirs of Count Witte*, ed. and trans. Sidney Harcave (Armonk, NY: M.E. Sharpe,1990), 516–17. After 1917, Kommissarov went to Germany, where he joined the Aufbau. See Michael Kellogg, *The Russian Roots of Nazism* (Cambridge: Cambridge University Press, 2005), 36.

47. Nadezhda Kitsenko, *Sviatoi nashego vremeni: Otets Ioann Kronshtadtskii i russkii narod* (Moscow: NLO, 2006), 7.

48. V. Mech, *Sily reaktsii* (Moscow, 1908), 86.

49. *Pervaia vseobshchaia perepis'naseleniia Rossiiskoi imperii 1897 g.* (St. Petersburg, 1897–1905), 8:248–51.

50. Antonii was one of the most influential bishops in the Russian Orthodox Church. Born in an ancient noble family in 1863 as Aleksei Pavlovich Khrapovitskii, he started his vocation as an altar boy in St. Petersburg. As a young man he frequented Dostoyevsky's public lectures. In 1881 he entered the Ecclesiastical Academy in St. Petersburg, where he adopted the monastic name of Antonii. He was bishop of Cheboksary (1897–1899), Chistopolskii, and vicar of Kazan (1900–1902), bishop of Volhynia (1902–1914), metropolitan of Kharkov (1914–1918) and Kiev and Galicia (1918–1919). One of the promoters of the Russian Orthodox Church Outside Russia, he was its first head from 1920 until his death in 1936. See A. Stepanov, "Antonii," in Platonov, ed., *Chernaia sotnia*, 34–36; and Savino, "Il nazionalismo russo," 272–73.

51. N. E. Markov, *Istoriia evreiskogo shturma v Rossii* (Harbin, 1937), 23.

52. Rawson, *Russian Rightists*, 242.

53. Vladimir Bobrinskii was the heir of the Bobrinskii dynasty. His father was the minister of railways Aleksei Pavlovich Bobrinskii. Born in 1867, young Bobrinskii received a European education, with studies at Edinburgh University and the Paris School of Political Sciences. He began his political career as a liberal; he participated in the noble liberal circle "Beseda" and he had contacts with political émigrés. But, after the outbreak of the 1905 revolution, Bobrinskii decided to organize a rightist force in his native gubernia, Tula, where he was for many years a representative of the nobility. The Union for the Tsar and Order (Za tsaria i poriadok) was one of the most important Black Hundreds organizations in the Russian Empire, and Bobrinskii was elected as a deputy at the Second Duma, where he became the leader of the moderate rightist fraction. An exponent of Russian neo-Slavism, Bobrinskii oriented the movement toward more nationalist positions; he headed the Galician–Russian Society from 1905 to 1916, and was declared persona non grata by Habsburg authorities. Bobrinskii was one of the organizers and leaders of the Russian National Union, and in the Third Duma he was a supporter of Russification measures in the western borderlands. During the First World War Count Bobrinskii actively participated in the occupation of Galicia, and, after returning from Lvov in 1916, was involved in the formation of the Progressive bloc. After the 1917 revolution, he emigrated to Germany, then Yugoslavia, and then France, where he died in 1927. RGIA f. 1278 op.1 d.40, d. 537, l.13–14, op. 9 d. 89–90; A. B. Nikolaev, R. B. Romov, "Bobrinskii Vladimir Alekseevich," in *Gosudarstvennaia duma Rossiiskoi imperii*, 58–59; Savino, "Il nazionalismo russo," 320–27.

54. *Kholmskii vopros. Obzor russkoi periodicheskoi pechati s 1 ianvaria 1909 do 1 oktiabria 1911 g.* (St. Petersburg, 1912), 9.

55. *Podolianin*, no. 38, 1910.

56. Stephen M. Berk, *Year of Crisis, Year of Hope: Russian Jewry and the Pogroms of 1881–1882* (Westport, CT: Greenwood Press,1985), 51–55.

57. Lucien Wolfe, *The Legal Sufferings of the Jews in Russia: A Survey of Their Present Situation, and a Summary of Laws* (London: T. Fisher Unwin, 1912), 83–85.

58. Hieromonk Iliodor, *The Mad Monk of Russia, Iliodor: Life, Memoirs, and Confessions of Sergei Michailovich Trufanoff* (New York: Century, 1918), 41–42.

59. Krushevan's family was part of the ancient Moldavian aristocracy, russified after the unification of Bessarabia to the Russian Empire. Pavel Krushevan was noted as local writer and journalist and his stories were published in various journals and reviews. In 1897 he became the editor-in-chief of the newspaper *Bessarabets*, which shifted from a liberal position to a more far right and anti-Semitic one. In the pages of *Bessarabets*, Krushevan was supportive of the Kishinev pogrom in 1903, and he contributed to the spread of anti-Semitism in other media.

In August–September 1903, *The Protocols of the Elders of the Zion* was published in *Znamia*, another newspaper under his leadership. In 1905 Krushevan left *Bessarabets* and started publishing the anti-Semitic newspaper *Drug*, continuing until his death in 1909. He was leader of the Bessarabian Union of the Russian People, and was elected to the Second Duma. See R. B. Romov, "Krushevan Pavel Aleksandrovich," in *Gosudarstvennaia duma Rossiiskoi imperii*, 301–2; M. B. Slutskii, *V skorbnie dni: Kishinevskii pogrom 1903 goda* (Kishinev, 1930).

60. Edward H. Judge, *Easter in Kishinev: Anatomy of a Pogrom* (New York: New York University Press, 1995), 30–34.

61. Monty Noam Penkower, "The Kishinev Pogrom of 1903: A Turning Point in Jewish History," *Modern Judaism* 24, no. 3 (October 2004): 187–225.

62. GARF f. 102, op. 316, d. 999, ch. 39, t. 1, ll. 43–46.

63. Flyers with this slogan were distributed in various parts of the Russian Empire. GARF, f. 102, op. 316, d. 999, ch. 39, t. 1, l. 20.

64. Edward Bing, ed., *Letters of Tsar Nicholas and Empress Marie: Being the Confidential Correspondence Between Nicholas II, Last of the Tsars, and his Mother, Dowager Empress Maria Feodorovna I* (London: Nicholson and Watson,1937),190–91.

65. GARF, f. 102, op. 1905, d. 2000, ch. 2, ll. 1, 3, 7, 22–23.

66. GARF, f. 102, op. 1905, d. 2000, ch. 2, ll. 1, 3, 7, 22–23, 33.

67. Robert Weinberg, "Workers, Pogroms, and the 1905 Revolution in Odessa," *The Russian Review* 46, no. 1 (1987): 53–75.

68. Robert Weinberg, "The Pogrom of 1905 in Odessa: A Case Study," in *Pogroms: Anti-Jewish Violence in Modern Russian History*, ed. John D. Klier and Shlomo Lambroza (Cambridge: Cambridge University Press, 1992), 248–89.

69. Rawson, *Russian Rightists*, p. 136.

70. GARF f.1462, op.1, d.862, l.14.

71. Hans Rogger, "Was There a Russian Fascism? The Union of Russian People," *Journal of Modern History* 34, no. 4 (1964): 413–15.

72. Rogger, "Was There a Russian Fascism?" 407–8.

73. A. I. Guchkov, *Sbornik rechei v Tretei Gosudarstvennoi Dume (1907–1912)* (St. Petersburg, 1912), 20–21.The text of the address is available in *Vestnik narodnoi svodoby*, November 25, 1907, no. 46.

74. Sh. M. Levin, "Materialy dlia kharakteristiki kontr-revoliutsii 1905 g.," *Byloe*, no. 21 (1923): 185.

75. L. Tikhomirov, "Dnevnik," *Krasnyi arkhiv*, no. 61 (1933): 103.

76. G. V. Butmi, *Rossiia na rasput'i: kabala ili svoboda?* (St. Petersburg, 1906), 44.

77. GARF f. 117 (Russkii Narodnyi Soiuz im. Mikhaila Arkhangela); *Proekt ustava* (St. Petersburg, 1908); *Soiuz Mikhaila Arkhangela. Proekt i ustav* (St. Petersburg, 1908).

78. GARF f. 116 (Vserossiiskii Dubrovinskii Soiuz Russkogo Naroda).

79. Savino, "Il nazionalismo russo," 26–61.

80. Daniil A. Kotsiubinskii, *Russkii natsionalizm v nachale stoletiia: Rozhdenie i gibel' ideologii Vserossiiskogo Natsionalnogo Soiuza* (Moscow: ROSSPEN, 2001).

81. D. N. Vergun, *Nemetskii "Drang nach Osten" v tsifrakh i faktakh* (Vienna, 1905).

82. *Voina na Balkanakh: Rechi grafa V. A. Bobrinskago, A. N. Brianchaninogo, d-ra D. N. Verguna, V. V. Karpinskago, prof. P. I. Kovalevskago, prof. R. I. Koshuticha i I. V. Nikonorova* (St. Petersburg, 1912),15–16.

83. Robert Edelman, *Gentry Politics on the Eve of the Russian Revolution: The Nationalist Party 1907–1917* (New Brunswick, NJ: Rutgers University Press, 1980), 200–202.

84. Erwin Oberländer, "The All-Russian Fascist Party," *Journal of Contemporary History* 1, no. 1 (1966): 158–73.

85. Kellogg, *Russian Roots of Nazism*, p. 1.

86. RGVA f.772, op. 3, d. 81a, 19, 24.

87. S. A. Stepanov, *Chernaia sotnia v Rossii 1905–1914* (Moscow: Izdatelstvo Vsesoiuz-nogo zaochnogo politekhnicheskogo instituta, 1992),189–92.

88. Stepanov, *Chernaia sotnia v Rossii*, 65.

89. Kellogg, *Russian Roots of Nazism*, 60.

90. Kellogg, *Russian Roots of Nazism*, 155.

91. Gosudarstvennaia Duma, *Stenograficheskii otchet*, February 9, 1911, col. 1556, 1558.

92. Jack London, *The Iron Heel* (New York: Macmillan, 1908).

3. The "Third Continent" Meets the "Third Way"

1. There is a rich literature on classical Eurasianism. See Mark Bassin, Sergei Glebov, and Marlene Laruelle, eds., *Between Europe and Asia: The Origins, Theories and Legacies of Russian Eurasianism* (Pittsburgh: University of Pittsburgh Press, 2015).

2. Nikolai Berdiaev, "Evraziitsy," *Put'*, no. 1 (1925).

3. Leonid Luks, "'Eurasier' und 'Konservative Revolution': Zur antiwestlichen Ver-suchung in Rußland und in Deutschland," in *Deutschland und die Russische Revolution, 1917–1924*, ed. Gerd Koenen and Lew Kopelew, 219–39 (Munich: Fink, 1998). Martin E. Baissvenger [Beisswenger], "'Konservativnaia revoliutsiia' v Germanii i dvizhenie Evra-ziitsev—tochki soprikosnoveniia," in *Konservatizm v Rossii i mire*, vol. 3 (Voronezh: Vo-ronezhskii gosudarstvennyi universitet, 2004), 23–40.

4. For more details see Marlene Laruelle, "La question du 'touranisme' des Russes. Contribution à une histoire des échanges intellectuels Allemagne-France-Russie au XIXe siècle," *Cahiers du monde russe*, no. 1–2 (2004): 241–65.

5. See Marina Mogilner, *Homo Imperii: A History of Physical Anthropology in Russia* (Lincoln, NE: University of Nebraska Press, 2013).

6. Mentioned by Vladimir Lamanskii, *Ob istoricheskom izuchenii greko-slavianskogo mira v Evrope* (St. Petersburg, 1871), 97.

7. Anders A. Retzius. *Ethnologische Schriften* (Stockholm, 1864), 8–12.

8. See, for instance, Karl Penka. *Origines Ariacae: Linguistisch-ethnologische Untersu-chungen zur älteren Geschichte der arischen Völker und Sprachen* (Vienna, 1883).

9. Aleksei S. Khomiakov, "Mnenie inostrantsev o Rossii," *Moskvitianin*, no. 4 (1845), republished in *Polnoe sobranie sochinenii*, vol. 1 (Moscow, 1878), 4.

10. Aleksei S. Khomiakov, *Zapiski o vsemirnoi istorii*, vol. 2 (Moscow, 1873), 13.

11. Aleksei S. Khomiakov, *Zapiski o vsemirnoi istorii*, vol. 2, 425.

12. Martin Beisswenger, "N. V. Vernadskaia-Toll i stanovlenie 'nauchnogo' evraziistvo," *Ezhegodnik Doma Russkogo zarubezh'a imeni Aleksandra Solzhenitsyna* (Moscow: Dom Russkogo zarubezh'a imeni Aleksandra Solzhenitsyna, 2013): 172–76. I thank Martin Beisswenger for bringing this element to my attention.

13. No author, *Evraziiskie tetradi*, no. 4 (1935): 16. These are actually Savitskii's words in a discussion on the international situation, held as part of the Eurasianist conference in Prague in July 1934. I thank Martin Beisswenger for bringing this element to my attention.

14. Nikolai S. Trubetskoi, "O rasizme," *Evraziiskie tetradi*, no. 5 (1935), republished in Nikolai S. Trubetskoi, *Istoriia. Kul'tura. Iazyk* (Moscow: Progress, 1995), 457.

15. Nikolai S. Trubetskoi, "Mysli ob indoevropeiskoi probleme" (1936), republished in Nikolai S. Trubetskoi, *Izbrannye trudy po filologii* (Moscow: Progress, 1987), 44–59, http://www.philology.ru/linguistics1/trubetskoy-87d.htm#1.

16. Nikolai S. Trubetskoi, "Mysli ob indoevropeiskoi probleme."

17. On the Aryan myth in nineteenth-century Russia see Marlene Laruelle, *Mythe aryen et rêve impérial dans la Russie tsariste* (Paris: CNRS-Editions, 2005).

18. More in Patrick Sériot, *Structure and the Whole (Semiotics, Communication and Cognition)* (Berlin: De Gruyter Mouton, 2014).

19. Roman Jakobson, *Evraziia v svete iazykoznaniia* (Paris: Izdanie Evraziitsev, 1931), 3.

20. Roman Jakobson, *Evraziia v svete iazykoznaniia*, 4.

21. Trubetskoi, "O rasizme," 457.

22. Pavel N. Milukov, "Russkii rasizm," *Poslednie novosti*, December 16, 1926, republished in *Istoricheskaia nauka rossiiskoi emigratsii: 'Evraziiskii soblazn,'* ed. Margarita G. Vandalkovskaia, 331–35 (Moscow: RAN, 1997).

23. The journal *Evraziia* denounced the boycott of Jewish shops in Clamart by Russian émigrés as a symbol of the decline of the Russian petite-bourgeoisie. See *Evraziia*, no. 30, June 29, 1929.

24. For a brief analysis, see Stephen Shenfield, "The Jewish Eurasianism of Yakov Bromberg," May 1, 2012, http://stephenshenfield.net/themes/jewish-issues/jews-in-tsarist-russia/105-the-jewish-eurasianism-of-yakov-bromberg; and Dmitry Shlapentokh, "Yakov Bromberg : The Case of a Russian Jewish Eurasianist in the USA," in *Materialy Piatnadtsatoi Ezhegodnoi Mezhdunarodnoi Mezhdistsiplinarnoi konferentsii po iudaike* (Moscow: Tsentr nauchnykh rabotnikov i prepodavatelei iudaiki v VUZakh, 2008).

25. Yakov A. Bromberg, "O neobkhodimom peresmotre evreiskogo voprosa," *Evraziiskii sbornik* VI (1929), 45.

26. Yakov A. Bromberg, *Rossiia, Zapad i evreistvo* (Prague: Izdanie Evraziitsev, 1931), 139.

27. Yakov A. Bromberg, "Evreiskoe vostochnichestvo v proshlom i v budushchem," *Tridtsatye gody* (Paris: Izdanie Evraziitsev, 1931), 209.

28. Nikolai S. Trubetskoi, "O turanskoi elemente v russkoi kul'ture," republished in *Rossiia mezhdu Evropoi i Aziei: Evraziiskii soblazn*, ed. L. I. Novikova and I. N. Sizemskaia, (Moscow: Nauka, 1993), 71.

29. Bromberg, "Evreiskoe vostochnichestvo," 195.

30. Lev P. Karsavin, "Rossiia i evrei," *Versty*, no. 1 (1926): 73.

31. Lev P. Karsavin, "Rossiia i evrei," 75.

32. Bromberg, *Rossiia, Zapad i evreistvo*, 157.

33. The philosopher of the Right, Nikolai N. Alekseev (1879–1964), rejected, for example, the idea that in terms of political regime. Christianity necessarily called for monarchy. He considered that traditional Russian power had multiple religious references (Asian despotism, paganism). Orthodoxy thus appeared to be compatible with the republican ideocratic regime of Eurasianism. Nikolai N. Alekseev, "Khristianstvo i ideia monarkhii," republished in Nikolai N. Alekseev, *Russkii narod i gosudarstvo* (Moscow: AGRAF, 1998), 48–67.

34. Nikolai S. Trubetskoi, "Nash otvet," republished in Nikolai S. Trubetskoi, *Istoriia, kul'tura, iazyk* (Moscow: Progress, 1995), 339–48.

35. Petr P. Suvchinskii, "K preodoleniiu revoliutsii," *Evraziiskii vremennik* III (1923): 38.

36. "Evraziistvo: Opyt sistematicheskogo izlozheniia" (Paris: Evraziiskoe knigoizdatel'stvo, 1926), republished in *Puti Evrazii. Russkaia intelligentsiia i sud'by Rossii* (Moscow: Russkaia kniga, 1992), 388.

37. Petr P. Suvchinskii, "Monarkhiia ili silnaia vlast'?" *Evraziiskaia khronika* IX (1927): 24.

38. See Judith Schlanger, *Les métaphores de l'organisme* (Paris: L'Harmattan, 1995).

39. Alekseev, "Evraziistvo i gosudarstvo," 169.

40. Nikolai S. Trubetskoi, "Ob idee-pravitel'nitse ideokraticheskogo gosudarstva," in Nikolai S. Troubetzkoy, *L'Europe et l'humanité: Ecrits linguistiques et para-linguistiques*, trans. Patrick Sériot (Liège: Mardaga, 1996), 203.

41. Lev P. Karsavin, "Osnovy politiki," in *Rossiia mezhdu Evropoi i Aziei: Evraziiskii soblazn*, ed. L. I. Novikova and I. N. Sizemskaia (Moscow: Nauka, 1993), 184.

42. Petr P. Suvchinskii, "K preodoleniiu revoliutsii," *Evraziiskii vremennik* III (1923), 33.

43. Alekseev, "Evraziistvo i gosudarstvo," 167.

44. Iakov D. Sadovskii, "Iz dnevnika 'evraziitsa,'" *Evraziiskii vremennik* 4 (1925): 400–404.

45. N. P. [N. A. Panfil'ev], "O fashistskoi ideologii," *Evraziets*, no. 21 (November 1932) (un-

paginated); N. P. [N. A. Panfil'ev] "O national-sotsializme," *Evraziets*, no. 21 (November 1932) (unpaginated). N.[A.] Perfil'ev, "'Chernyi front.' Tezisy germanskoi revoliutsii. Osnovnaia programma natsional'-sotsialisticheskoi i revoliutsionnoi organizatsii," *Evraziets*, no. 19 (February 1932): 24–26; reprinted as: N. P. "Novye politicheskie techeniia. Chernyi front v Germanii. Tezisy germanskoi revoliutsii. Osnovnaia programma natsional'-sotsialisticheskoi i revoliutsionnoi organizatsii," *Svoi put'*, no. 2(6) (April 1932): 14–15.

46. Editor, "K otsenke sovremennosti," *Evraziia*, no. 35, September 7, 1929, 3.

47. F., "Politicheskie ocherki sovremennoi Italii," *Evraziia*, no. 13, February 16, 1929, 7.

48. Aleksandr P. Antipov, "Novye puti Germanii," *Novaia epokha, Ideokratiia. Politika. Ekonomiia. Obzory* (Narva: Izdanie Evraziitsev, 1933), 35–43.

49. Aleksandr P. Antipov, "Novye puti Germanii," p. 11.

50. Nikolai N. Alekseev, *Evraziistvo i kommunizm* (pamphlet) (Prague: Evraziiskoe izdatel'stvo, 1927), 4.

51. Mark Bassin, "Russia between Europe and Asia: The Ideological Construction of Geographical Space," *Slavic Review* 50, no. 1 (1993): 1–17.

52. *Evraziistvo. Opyt sistematicheskogo izlozhenia* (Paris: Evraziiskoe knigoizdatel'stvo, 1926), 32. This text is often attributed to Savitskii but it was in fact written primarily by Karsavin, who incorporated some ideas and corrections by Trubetskoi, Savitskii, and others. I thank Martin Beisswenger for bringing this element to my attention.

53. More in Sériot, *Structure and the Whole (Semiotics, Communication and Cognition)*.

54. Petr N. Savitskii, *Rossiia—osobyi geograficheskii mir* (Prague, 1927), p. 32.

55. Roman Jakobson, ed., *N. S. Trubetzkoy's Letters and Notes* (Berlin: Mouton, 1975), 12.

56. Sergei Glebov, "N. S. Trubetskoi's 'Europe and Mankind' and Eurasianist Antievolutionism: One Unknown Source," in *Between Europe and Asia: The Origins, Theories and Legacies of Russian Eurasianism*, ed. Mark Bassin, Sergei Glebov, and Marlene Laruelle, 48–67 (Pittsburgh, PA: University of Pittsburgh Press, 2015).

57. Aleksandr Dugin, *Chetvertaia politicheskaia teoriia* (Moscow: Amfora, 2009).

58. Aleksandr Dugin, *Konservativnaia revoliutsiia. Tretii put'* (Moscow: Aktogeia, 1994), http://my.arcto.ru/public/konsrev/3way.htm.

4. A Failed Alliance

1. On interwar émigré Eurasianism, see: Marlene Laruelle, *L'Idéologie eurasiste russe ou Comment penser l'empire* (Paris: L'Harmattan, 1999); Sergei Glebov, *Evraziistvo mezhdu imperiei i modernom* (Moscow: Novoe izdatel'stvo, 2010); and *Between Europe and Asia: The Origins, Theories, and Legacies of Classical Eurasianism*, ed. Mark Bassin, Sergey Glebov, and Marlene Laruelle (Pittsburgh: University of Pittsburgh Press, 2015). "Classical" Eurasianism is also dealt with in: Stefan Wiederkehr, *Die eurasische Bewegung: Wissenschaft und Politik in der russischen Emigration der Zwischenkriegszeit und im postsowjetischen Russland* (Cologne: Böhlau Verlag, 2007), and Marlene Laruelle, *Russian Eurasianism: An Ideology of Empire* (Washington, DC: Woodrow Wilson Center Press, 2008).

2. The term "Conservative Revolution" was introduced in 1950 by the right-wing political philosopher and writer Armin Mohler, himself an adherent of this tradition (Armin Mohler, *Die Konservative Revolution in Deutschland 1918–1932: Grundriß ihrer Weltanschauungen* [Stuttgart: Friedrich Vorwerk Verlag, 1950]). This concept was supposed to designate an independent philosophical movement that differed both from National Socialism and from conservative reactionism. The term was sharply and convincingly criticized by Stefan Breuer (Stefan Breuer, *Anatomie der Konservativen Revolution*, 2nd ed. [Darmstadt: Wissenschaftliche Buchgesellschaft, 1993]), who suggested instead the concept of a "new conservatism," as well as by Raimund von dem Bussche (Raimund von dem Bussche, *Konservatismus in der Weimarer Republik: Die Politisierung des Unpolitischen* (Heidelberg: Universitäts-Verlag

Winter, 1998), who suggested the term "conservative utopianism." Still, contemporary "conservatives" insist on the continued viability of the term "Conservative Revolution." See Karlheinz Weißmann "Konservative Revolution—Forschungsstand und Desiderata," in *Stand und Probleme der Erforschung des Konservatismus*, ed. Caspar v. Schrenck-Notzing (Berlin: Duncker and Humblot, 2000), 119–39. I fully agree with the arguments against the distinctive character of the "Conservative Revolution" and the term will be used here for the sake of historiographical convention only. On the economic concepts of the Eurasianists, see Martin Beisswenger, "Metaphysics of the Economy: The Religious and Economic Foundations of P. N. Savitskii's Eurasianism," in *Between Europe and Asia*, 97–112.

3. Kurt Sontheimer, *Antidemokratisches Denken in der Weimarer Republik: Die politischen Ideen des deutschen Nationalismus zwischen 1918 und 1933*, 4th ed. (Munich: dtv, 1994).

4. Otto Ernst Schüddekopf, *Linke Leute von rechts: Die nationalrevolutionären Minderheiten und der Kommunismus in der Weimarer Republik* (Stuttgart: Kohlhammer, 1960), 124 and 189. Schüddekopf merely referred to a French journal article that in fact provided a very general characterization of one conservative German group and only in passing and quite superficially hinted toward a certain similarity of this German group's views with those of the Eurasianists: A. M. Lipiansky, "Pour un Communisme National, la revue 'Die Tat,'" *Revue d'Allemagne* 6 (1932) [October 15]: 849–67 (on the Eurasianists, see 861).

5. Leonid Luks, "Die Ideologie der Eurasier im zeitgenössischen Zusammenhang," *Jahrbücher für Geschichte Osteuropas* 34 (1986): 374–95; Leonid Luks, "'Eurasier' und 'Konservative Revolution': Zur antiwestlichen Versuchung in Rußland und in Deutschland," in *Deutschland und die Russische Revolution. 1917–1924*, ed. Gerd Koenen and Lew Kopelew (Munich: Fink, 1998), 219–39. For a comparative perspective on Eurasianism see now also: Stefan Wiederkehr, "'Conservative Revolution' à la russe? An Interpretation of Classic Eurasianism in a European Context," *Journal of Modern European History* 15 (2017): 72-84.

6. Luks mentioned the following differences: whereas for the Eurasianists religion played an important role, for the majority of the conservative revolutionaries religion was rather insignificant; in contrast to the conservative revolutionaries, the Eurasianists did not aestheticize violence and terror; in the political programs of the German groups the concept of a "leader" was of great significance, while for the Eurasianists a collective "ideocratic" rule was more important; finally, and most importantly, as an émigré movement the Eurasianists were deprived of the opportunity to influence directly the political situation in their home country.

7. Luks, "Die Ideologie," 390–94; Luks, "'Eurasier' und 'Konservative Revolution,'" 228–34.

8. Luks, "'Eurasier' und 'Konservative Revolution,'" 237.

9. On the French nonconformists, see, for example: Jean-Louis Loubet del Bayle, *Les non-conformistes des années 30: Une trentative de renouvellement de la pensée politique française* (Paris: Seuil, 2001) and John Hellman, *The Communitarian Third Way: Alexandre Marc's Ordre Nouveau, 1930–2000* (Montreal and Kingston: McGill–Queen's University Press, 2002).

10. For A. P. Antipov's report on his participation in the European Youth Congress (dated February 12, 1932): State Archive of the Russian Federation (henceforth: GARF), f. 5783, op. 1, d. 456, l. 19.

11. For a brief discussion of these contacts see my earlier publication: M. E. Baissvenger [Beisswenger], " 'Konservativnaia revoliutsiia' v Germanii i dvizhenie 'Evraziitsev'—tochki soprikosnoveniia," in *Konservatizm v Rossii i mire*, vol. 3 (Voronezh: Voronezhskii gosudarstvennyi universitet, 2004), 23–40.

12. On this attitude see Gerd Koenen, *Der Russland-Komplex: Die Deutschen und der Osten 1900–1945* (Munich: C.H. Beck, 2005).

13. On the Gegner group see: Aleksandr Bahar, *Sozialrevolutionärer Nationalismus zwischen Konservativer Revolution und Sozialismus: Harro Schulze-Boysen und der "Gegner"-Kreis* (Koblenz: Verlag Dietmar Fölbach, 1992); and Hans Coppi and Jürgen Danyel, eds., *Der "Gegner"-Kreis im Jahre 1932/33* (Berlin: Evangelische Akademie Berlin, 1990). On Schulze-Boysen's biography see Hans Coppi and Geertje Andresen, eds., *Dieser Tod paßt zu mir: Harro Schulze-Boysen—Grenzgänger im Widerstand. Briefe 1915 bis 1942* (Berlin: Aufbau Verlag, 1999). See also: Schüddekopf, *Linke Leute*, 350–54; Karl Otto Paetel, *Versuchung oder Chance? Zur Geschichte des deutschen Nationalbolschewismus* (Göttingen: Musterschmidt Verlag, 1965), 189–205; Louis Dupeux, *"Nationalbolschewismus" in Deutschland 1919–1933: Kommunistische Strategie und konservative Dynamik*, trans. Richard Kirchhoff (Munich: C.H. Beck, 1985), 383–92.

14. Harro Schulze-Boysen, "Der neue Gegner," *Gegner* no. 4/5 (1932) [March 5]: 2.

15. Harro Schulze-Boysen, "Die Saboteure der Revolution," *Gegner*, no. 7 (1932)[April 5]: 3–4, quotation p. 4.

16. Harro Schulze-Boysen, *Gegner von heut—Kampfgenossen von morgen* (Berlin, 1932) (quoted from Bahar, *Sozialrevolutionärer Nationalismus*, 112).

17. Harro Schulze-Boysen, "Vom kommenden Wir," *Gegner*, no. 1/2 (1932) [July 10]: 3–4.

18. Bahar, *Sozialrevolutionärer Nationalismus*, 118–29. *Gegner* even conducted a survey among representatives of various political groups on the question of a possible foreign intervention in the USSR: "Interventionskrieg—Sowjetunion? Was tun wir?" *Gegner*, no. 11/12 (1932) [June 10]: 6–8.

19. Bahar, *Sozialrevolutionärer Nationalismus*, 135–37, 92. On the ideology see also Hans Coppi, "Harro Schulze-Boysen und der 'Gegner'-Kreis," in Coppi and Danyel, eds., *Der "Gegner"-Kreis im Jahre 1932/33*, 61–62.

20. See: Kurt Sontheimer, "Der Tatkreis," in *Von Weimar zu Hitler 1930–1933*, ed. Gotthard Jasper (Göttingen: Kiepenheuer and Witsch, 1968), 197–228; Klaus Fritzsche, *Politische Romantik und Gegenrevolution: Fluchtwege in der Krise der bürgerlichen Gesellschaft; Das Beispiel des "Tat"-Kreises* (Frankfurt/M.: Suhrkamp, 1976).

21. Fritzsche, *Politische Romantik*, 45–57.

22. Fritzsche, *Politische Romantik*, 58.

23. Fritzsche, *Politische Romantik*, 58–127. The members of the Tat-Kreis differed from other critics of the Weimar Republic primarily in their more authoritative knowledge in the sphere of economics. Their economic views were developed under the influence of the economist Werner Sombart, whose students were Zehrer and Fried. They adapted their main arguments against capitalism from him. The members of the circle later considered him their personal friend and constant comrade-in-arms (Fritzsche, *Politische Romantik*, 53, 81, 353 n. 93).

24. Fritzsche, *Politische Romantik*, 128–236.

25. Fritzsche, *Politische Romantik*, 260–314.

26. Patrick Moreau, *Nationalsozialismus von links: Die "Kampfgemeinschaft Revolutionärer Nationalsozialisten" und die "Schwarze Front" Otto Straßers 1930–1935* (Stuttgart: Deutsche Verlags-Anstalt, 1985); Karl Otto Paetel, "Otto Strasser und die 'Schwarze Front' des 'wahren Nationalsozialismus,'" *Politische Studien* 8, 92 (1957): 269–81. See also: Paetel, *Versuchung oder Chance?* 206–24, and Dupeux, *"Nationalbolschewismus" in Deutschland*, 393–418.

27. Paetel, "Otto Strasser," 271.

28. Dupeux, *"Nationalbolschewismus" in Deutschland*, 402.

29. Paetel, "Otto Strasser," 272–77.

30. "Das Manifest der Schwarzen Front," quoted from Moreau, *Nationalsozialismus von links*, 250–51.

31. Moreau, *Nationalsozialismus von links*, 140–47.

32. Paetel, "Otto Strasser," 279–81.

33. On Niekisch's life and ideas see: Friedrich Kabermann, *Widerstand und Entscheidung eines deutschen Revolutioner: Leben und Denken von Ernst Niekisch* (Cologne: Verlag Wissenschaft und Politik, 1973); Hans Buchheim, "Ernst Niekischs Ideologie des Widerstandes, " *Vierteljahrshefte für Zeitgeschichte* 5 (1957): 334–61. See also: Dupeux, *"Nationalbolschewismus" in Deutschland*, 235–43 and 317–47, and Paetel, *Versuchung oder Chance?* 79–105. On Niekisch's image of Russia and the Soviet Union see: Sylvia Taschka, *Das Rußlandbild von Ernst Niekisch* (Erlangen: Palm and Enke, 1999), and Michael David-Fox, "A 'Prussian Bolshevik' in Stalin's Russia: Ernst Niekisch at the Crossroads between Communism and National Socialism," in *Crossing Borders: Modernity, Ideology, and Culture in Soviet Russia*, ed. Michael David-Fox (Pittsburgh: University of Pittsburgh Press, 2015), 185–220.

34. Kabermann, *Widerstand und Entscheidung*, 27–36 and 57–76.

35. ∴ [Ernst Niekisch], "Die Politik des deutschen Widerstandes," *Widerstand* 5 (1930): 97–99. On the necessity of an alliance between Germany and Russia, see also Ernst Nikisch, "Europa betet," *Widerstand* 5 (1930): 65–72.

36. Ernst Niekisch, "Potsdamer Gesetz [1931]," quoted from: Dupeux, *"Nationalbolschewismus" in Deutschland*, 332.

37. Ernst Niekisch, "Abrüstung?" *Widerstand* 5 (1930): 353–61.

38. Ernst Niekisch, "Das Potsdamer Gesetz [1931]," 334. See also: Buchheim, "Ernst Niekischs Ideologie," 342–43. Ernst Niekisch's historiographical conception was strongly influenced by the views and ideas of Fedor M. Dostoevsky, in particular the latter's image of "Germany as a protesting country" (from *A Writer's Diary*, May/June 1877): F. M. Dostojewski, "Deutschland, die protestierende Macht," *Widerstand* 5 (1930): 72–76.

39. See Dupeux, *"Nationalbolschewismus" in Deutschland*, 330, and David-Fox, "A 'Prussian Bolshevik,'" 204–12.

40. Kabermann, *Widerstand und Entscheidung*, 147–54, 213–20; Dupeux, *"Nationalbolschewismus" in Deutschland*, 346.

41. See, for example, Eric Hobsbawm, *Age of Extremes: The Short Twentieth Century, 1914–1991* (London: Abacus, 1995), 85–108.

42. O. A. Kaznina, "N. S. Trubetskoi i krizis evraziistva," *Slavianovedenie*, no. 4 (1995): 89–95; for a detailed account of the affair from P. N. Savitskii's perspective see: Irina Shevelenko, "K istorii evraziiskgo raskola 1929 goda," *Stanford Slavic Studies* 8 (1994): 376–416. This article contains Savitskii's detailed memorandum on the affair.

43. The proceedings of the congress were published as: *Pervyi s"ezd Evraziiskoi organizatsii. Protokol i materialy* (n.p., n.p., 1932).

44. *Evraziistvo: Deklaratsiia, formulirovka, tezisy* ([Prague: n.p.], 1932).

45. *Evraziistvo: Deklaratsiia, formulirovka, tezisy*, 3–6.

46. N. P. [N. A. Panfil'ev], "O fashistskoi ideologii," *Evraziets*, no. 21 (November 1932) (unpaginated); N. P. [N. A. Panfil'ev] "O national sotsializme," *Evraziets*, no. 21 (November 1932) (unpaginated).

47. N.[A.] Perfil'ev, "'Chernyi front.' Tezisy germanskoi revoliutsii. Osnovnaia programma natsional'-sotsialisticheskoi i revoliutsionnoi organizatsii," *Evraziets*, no. 19 (February 1932): 24–26; reprinted as: N. P. "Novye politicheskie techeniia. Chernyi front v Germanii. Tezisy germanskoi revoliutsii. Osnovnaia programma natsional'-sotsialisticheskoi i revoliutsionnoi organizatsii," *Svoi put'*, no. 2 (6) (April, 1932): 14–15.

48. A. P. Antipov, "Belye i krasnye," *Evraziiskii sbornik* 6 (1929): 59–63. On his biography see: V. G. Makarov and A. M. Matveeva, "A. P. Antipov," in *Obshchestvennaia mysl' russkogo zarubezh'ia: Entsiklopediia*, ed. V. V. Zhuravlev (Moscow: ROSSPEN, 2009), 178–80.

49. GARF, f. 5783, op. 1, ed. khr. 355, l. 386: P. N. Savitskii to T. P. Shul'ts, January 31,1932.

50. A. P. Antipov, "Novye puti Germanii," *Novaia epokha: Ideokratiia. Politika-ekonomika. Obzory*, ed. V. A. Pei'l (Tallinn: Izdanie Evraziitsev, 1933), 35.

51. An official transcript of the congress, presumably authored by *Plans* editor Philippe Lamour, was published as "L'action. La recontre de Frankfort," *Plans*, no.12 (February 1932): 121–22. Antipov's report, dated February 12, 1932, is kept at: GARF, f. 5783, op. 1, d. 456, l. 16–22; quotation on l. 19. An abridged version of the report was published in one of the Eurasianists' mimeographed journals: [A. P. Antipov], "Frankfurtskii s"ezd," *Evraziets*, no. 20 (February 1932): 38–40.

52. GARF, f. 5783, op. 1, d. 456, l. 19.

53. GARF, f. 5783, op. 1, d. 456, l. 22.

54. GARF, f. 5783, op. 1, d. 456, l. 19.

55. Bakhmeteff Archive on Russian and East European History and Culture (henceforth: BAR). Columbia University Libraries, New York. George Vernadsky Papers, Box 7. Memorandum of A. P. Antipov to the Chairman of the Eurasianist Organization's Central Committee [P. N. Savitskii] "On the Prospects of Relations with German Groups."

56. BAR, Vernadsky Papers, box 7: Antipov's Memorandum.

57. BAR, Vernadsky Papers, box 7: Antipov's Memorandum.

58. A draft of a German translation of the program together with a German "History of the Eurasianist Movement," written by N. N. Alekseev has been preserved in GARF, f. 5783, op. 1, ed. khr. 249.

59. Coudenhove-Kalergi's project was outlined in *Pan-Europa* (Vienna: Pan-Europa Verlag, 1923). On Coudenhove-Kalergi's biography and the evolution of his thought see Anita Ziegerhofer, *Botschafter Europas: Richard Nikolaus Coudenhove-Kalergi und die Paneuropa-Bewegung in den zwanziger und dreissiger Jahren* (Vienna: Böhlau Verlag, 2004).

60. GARF f. 5783, op. 1, ed.khr. 471, l. 222: H. Schulze-Boysen to A. P. Antipov, no date [August 17, 1932].

61. GARF f. 5783, op. 1, ed.khr. 355, l. 387: P. N. Savitskii to Harro Schulze-Boysen, September 4, 1932.

62. N. A. "Eurasier," *Gegner*, no. 5/6 (1932) [1.10.1932], 8.

63. BAR, Vernadsky Papers, box 7: Antipov's Memorandum.

64. A. P. Antipov, "Novye radikal'nye techeniia v Germanii," *Evraziets*, no. 21 (November 1932) [unpaginated].

65. Slovanská knihovna Prague (henceforth: SKP), P. N. Savicky papers, box 16, item number 231. P. N. Savitskii's notebook, no. 65 [November–December 1932].

66. In his notebook Savitskii excerpted the following articles: Hans Zehrer, "Das Ende der Parteien," *Die Tat* 24, 1 (1932/33) [April 1932]: 68–79; Hans Zehrer, "Die Etappe Papen," *Die Tat* 24, 8 (1932/33) [November 1932]: 625–34; Werner Sombart, "Planwirtschaft," *Die Tat* 24, 1 (1932/33) [April 1932]: 37–42; Ferdinand Fried, "Welthandelskrieg," *Die Tat* 24, 1 (1932/33) [April 1932]: 42–59; Ferdinand Fried, "Der Übergang zur Autarkie," *Die Tat* 24, 2 (1932/33) [May 1932]: 120–50; Ferdinand Fried, "Deutschlands handelspolitische Einkreisung," *Die Tat* 24, 8 (1932/33) [November 1932]: 634–46; M. Holzer, "Die Tragödie der deutschen Wirtschaft," *Die Tat* 24, 2 (1932/33) [May 1932]: 155–68; M. Holzer, "Der Generalangriff auf den Sozialismus," *Die Tat* 24, 8 (1932/33) [November 1932]: 652–58; G. Wolfgang "Der Weg zur ländlichen Planwirtschaft," *Die Tat* 24, 2 (1932/33) [May 1932]: 150–55; Giselher Wirsing, "Die Siegfriedstellung der deutschen Außenpolitik," *Die Tat* 24, 1 (1932/33) [April 1932]: 14–35; Wirsing, "Doch Kompromiß?" *Die Tat* 24, 8 (1932/33) [November 1932]: 646–52.

67. Boris Ischboldin, "Der Bolschewismus als ideokratisches Wirtschaftssystem und seine ideokratischen Gegenspieler," *Die Tat* 23, 11 (1931/32) [February 1932]: 907–21. This article examined the transition from capitalism toward a new economic system using the example of the Soviet Union and Fascist Italy.

68. BAR, Vernadsky Papers, box 7: Antipov's Memorandum.

69. BAR, Vernadsky Papers, box 7: Antipov's Memorandum.

70. BAR, Vernadsky Papers, box 7: Antipov's Memorandum.

71. SKP, P. N. Savicky papers, box 16, item number 231. P. N. Savitskii's notebook, no. 65 [November–December 1932].

72. SKP, P. N. Savicky papers, box 16, item number 231. P. N. Savitskii's notebook, no. 58 [early 1933].

73. BAR, Vernadsky Papers, box 7: Antipov's Memorandum.

74. Antipov, "Novye radikal'nye techeniia" [unpaginated].

75. Antipov, "Novye radikal'nye techeniia."

76. Antipov, "Novye radikal'nye techeniia."

77. Antipov, "Novye radikal'nye techeniia."

78. Antipov, "Novye puti," 35–36.

79. Antipov, "Novye puti," 38–39.

80. The classical study on the concept of *Mitteleuropa* in German thought and politics is Henry Cord Meyer, *Mitteleuropa in German Thought and Action 1815–1945* (The Hague: Martinus Nijhoff, 1955).

81. Antipov, "Novye puti," 41–42.

82. On Stammler, who later in life was professor of Russian and Slavic literature at the University of Kansas, see Edith W. Clowes, "Heinrich A. Stammler, 1912–2006," *Slavic Review* 66, no. 3 (2007): 600–602.

83. GARF, f. 5783, op. 432, ed.khr. 313–13 verso: Heinrich Stammler to P. N. Savitskii, April 24, 1933.

84. On these efforts see Marlene Laruelle, ed., *Eurasianism and the European Far Right: Reshaping the Europe-Russia Relationship* (Lanham, MD: Lexington Books, 2015).

5. The Soviet Union, Russia, and Their Peoples as Perceived by French Volunteers in German Uniform, 1941–1945

1. Under French law, the Legion was considered an association, not a military unit, since France was not a party to the conflict.

2. Viazma was where Napoleon's Grande Armée was defeated by the Russian Army on November 3, 1812.

3. To cries of "To Moscow, to Moscow" the militants of the Parti populaire français (PPF), gathered by chance in a congress in Villeurbanne on June 22, 1941, the date of the invasion of the USSR, first came to adopt the idea, floated by their leader Jacques Doriot, of creating such a military unit.

4. Albert Merglen, "Soldats français sous uniformes allemands 1941–1945: LVF et Waffen SS français." *Revue D'histoire De La Deuxième Guerre Mondiale* 27, 108 (1977): 71–84.

5. French people were engaged, in an individual capacity, in nearly all the German units. Thus, in their reference work *Entre deux fronts: Les incorporés de force alsaciens dans la Waffen-SS* vol.1 (2007), 168. André Huguel and Nicolas Mengus report a combatant from the lower Rhine being in the infamous SS-Sonderbrigade Dirlewanger. But this Alsatian had been forcibly enlisted. By contrast, in *Les français sous le casque allemand* (1994) Pierre-Philippe Lambert and Gérard Le Marec report the presence of French volunteers in the Leibstandarte Adolf Hitler.

6. The exceptions are former Communist militants in the PPF, such as the future general secretary of the Front National, Victor Barthélémy; or in Marcel Déat's Rassemblement National Populaire, such as Henri Barbé, who had travelled to Moscow and were partly trained there.

7. Several volunteers later worked for an intelligence service in an allied country. In his book *Einsatzgruppen* (Paris: Seuil, 2010, 477), Michael Prazan mentions that the volunteer André Bayle (1926–2010) "left for some years to live in FGR where he did intelligence work for the French services." Prazan recorded two hours worth of interviews with Bayle, who,

until his death, ran the association "Histoire et Traditions" and was the author of several memorial books, including *De Marseille à Novossibirsk: Histoire et Traditions*, 1991.

8. On this topic, we refer the reader to the study by Nicolas Lebourg and Jonathan Preda, "Le Front de l'Est et l'extrême droite radicale française: propagande collaborationniste, lieu de mémoire et fabrique idéologique," in *Références et thèmes des droites radicales*, ed. Olivier Dard (Bern: Peter Lang, 2015), 101–38. Numerous cases other than the ones they cite remain to be studied, including notably: Robert Dun (pseudonym Maurice Martin), an author revered in Nietzschean neo-pagan milieus; Jean-Michel Sorel, a former member of Charlemagne, a combatant in Indochina, the editor of *Liberté du peuple* (1957), a militant of the Phalange française, and a former president of the Syndicat National Populaire; Jean Malardier, the onetime leader of Jeune Nation; and Léon Colas, a collaborator on *Devenir européen* and the founder of the Evola spiritual circle.

9. Thus, the Waffen SS described itself as "the first large European army thanks to the diversity of its recruitment," preface by Bernard Plouvier in the new edition of François Duprat's book *Les campagnes de la Waffen SS* (Déterna, 2014).

10. Henri Fenet (1919–2002), a Saint-Cyrien, a cadre of the milice de l'Ain, and an officer of the Waffen SS from October 1943 to May 1945, came out of the war with the rank of commander. He was part of the Pomerania campaign and fought in Berlin in the last days of the war. He was taken prisoner by the Soviets, imprisoned in France, and freed in 1949. He was the author of *Derniers témoignages* (Editions de l'homme libre, 2015). As with many of this publisher's works, which it publishes after the death of their authors, this work is hard to authenticate.

11. Truppenkameraschaft was the name given until 2011 to the French section of the Hilfsgemeinschaft auf Gegenseitigkeit der ehemaligen Angehörigen der Waffen-SS e. V. (HIAG), a right-wing German association founded in 1951 to assert the legal and moral rights of former SS combatants. Owing to the low numbers of French survivors, these latter formed a joint section with former members of the Division Horst Wessel. The numbers 18 and 33 refer respectively to the eighteenth and thirty-third division of the SS. The HIAG publishes a bimonthly bulletin, *Der Freiwillige*, which appeared in French somewhat irregularly in the 1990s. The TK 18/33 is now the NK 33 and limited to the French publication only.

12. This speech is retranscribed in *Der Freiwillige* 44 (1998): 22.

13. *Les éditions de l'Homme libre* (http://editions-hommelibre.fr/), led by the former head of the GUD William Bonnefoy; les Editions du Lore (http://www.ladiffusiondulore.fr/26-editions-du-lore)

14. For example the fanzine *Trente Trois* no. 1 (2009), *Histoire et Traditions* (edited under the guidance of André Bayle, see infra), or the *Bulletin du Cercle des amis de Léon Degrelle*, published by a former FN candidate, Christophe Georgy, who was excluded in 2011. The Italian military journal, *Volontari*, published by Marvia, continued until 2007 to report the minutes of commemorative meetings held close to Marseille by a small group of survivors living in the southeast of France, a group that was "twinned" with the Unione Nazionale Combattenti Repubblica Sociale Italiana led by Gian Maria Guasti. The minutes of this meeting labelled "the last bivouac" (*Volontari* 17, July–August 2007), is a depiction, with photos, of the "transfer of testimonies" between the generation of survivors and the younger members, notably attended by university professor Isabelle Grazioli-Rozet (université Lyon III), a specialist in the work of Ernst Jünger.

15. See the seven volumes of Godus that have been published since 2006, including numbers 2 (*L'épreuve du feu*) and 3 (*Galicie 1944*). Link: http://unejeunessefrancaise.blogspot.fr/

16. *Les Volontaires* (1963), *Les Hérétiques* (1965) and *Les Nostalgiques* (1967), published by Presses de la Cité.

17. *La Brigade Frankreich* (1973), *La Division Charlemagne* (1974), and *Mourir à Berlin* (1975) are all published by Fayard.

18. (Paris: Robert Laffont, 1972). The author also gave an account of his service some years earlier in a film by Marcel Ophuls, *Le Chagrin et la Pitié*, which was widely acclaimed.

19. On the period of hunting down partisans, see Pierre Rusco (Ruscone), *Stoï!* (Dualpha, 2006).

20. (Paris: Robert Laffont, 1967).

21. For an overall view of the various campaigns, see Krisztiàn Bene, *La collaboration militaire française dans la Seconde Guerre mondiale* (Codex, 2012).

22. Their furtherest point of advance was 35 km north of Maikop. See, Fernand Kaisergruber, *Nous n'irons pas à Touapsé* (1991). Moreover, it was in the Walloon Legion that a former White Russian officer received the highest post of commandment in the entire Waffen SS. The former officer of the Imperial Navy Georges Chekhoff (born in Sukhumi in 1892) was in fact Commander of the Legion from April to June 1942. He lived in exile in Argentina.

23. I consulted the edition published in Paris by Presses de la Cité, 1963.

24. Cointet, *Sigmaringen*, 2014

25. The slogan was used for a poster for volunteers to work in Germany. Poster from 1942, Musée de la Résistance de Champigny.

26. In particular those of Philippe Burrin, Pascal Ory, and Robert Paxton.

27. On this prelate, see René Bail's, *Les Croix de monseigneur de Mayol de Lupé* (1994).

28. See, on this point: *Documents diplomatiques français, 1920–1932*, vol. 3 (Paris: Ministry of Foreign Affairs, 1992), 652.

29. Labonne, "Le Traité de Lausanne et la question turque," in *Revue de Paris* 12 (1924) and *Le Tapis vert du Pacifique* (Paris: Buchet-Chastel, 1936).

30. Memorial Archives of Yad Vashem, Jerusalem. Cited by Gérard Guégan, in *Fontenoy ne reviendra plus* (Paris: Stock, 2011).

31. (Editions de France, 1939).

32. (Jacques Grancher 2003), 242.

33. (Paris: Presses de la Cité, 1975).

34. See, Philippe Martin, *A la recherche d'une éducation nouvelle: Histoire de la jeunesse allemande, 1813–1945* (Éditions du Lore, 2010), 186. The author is a former volunteer.

35. Martin, *A la recherche d'une éducation nouvelle,* 197.

36. *Rivarol*, December 19, 1963.

37. The title of the books of recollections by Jacques Auvray, published in 1999 by Irminsul publishing house, which was close to the movement Terre et Peuple.

38. See Jean Baumgarten, *La naissance du hassidisme* (Paris: Albin Michel, 2006).

39. Jean Raspail, La hache des steppes, Éditions Robert Laffon (1974), 200–222.

40. Eugène Labaume, in his work *Relation circonstanciée de la campagne de Russie* (published at Genoa in 1814), points out on p. 260 that this regiment was engaged within the third division of light cavalry commanded by General Chastel, who was himself beholden to General Grouchy. Napolean's taking of Smolensk occurred on August 18, 1812.

41. Victor de Bourmont was regional head of the *milice* in Lyon, and in this capacity was the hierarchical superior of Paul Touvier, who testified against him during his trial in 1994, but failed to get the case reopened.

42. *La Restauration* (Paris: Arthème Fayard, 1930), 10.

43. Letter from a volunteer of the Walloon division in Daniel-Charles Luytens, *SS wallons: Récits de la 28e division SS de grenadiers volontaires Wallonie* (Paris: Jourdan, 2015).

44. He is presented as the son of a former Consul General of Russia. Forbes puts quotation marks around his title "prince" (see *For Europe: The French Volunteers of the Waffen-SS*, p. 454.)

45. Grégory Bouysse, *Waffen SS français* (vol. 1, *Officiers*) (no publisher, 2011).

46. Annette Wiewiorka and Jean-Charles Szurek, in *Juifs et Polonais: 1938–2008* con-

firms this information. Jean Estèbe, in *Les juifs à Toulouse et en Midi toulousain au temps de Vichy*, as does the inventory of the National Archives for the CGQJ, mentions a so-called Serge Kiriloff who had lived in Montpellier and Toulouse, a marine who, like Krotoff, had been close to the fanatical anti-Semite Joseph Lécussan, one of the fiercest of the *milice*. The historian Laurent Joly, author of a monumental history of the CGQJ, thinks that "these happen to be two different persons, both part of the network of Lécussan, himself a marine and most radical adherent of the Far Right, but Kiriloff was more than ten years older than Krotoff (born in 1911)." Letter to the author, July 25, 2016.

47. See his biography in the newspaper *Jour de Galop*, November 10, 2012.

48. Pierre Montagnon, a historian of the Foreign Legion, cites him as being a former non-commissioned officer of the Legion and a close friend of the lieutenant-colonel Dimitri Amilakvari, Compagnon la Libération, Saint-Cyrien, who died before El Alamein in the ranks of France Libre. See *Dictionnaire de la Seconde guerre mondiale* (Paris: Pygmalion, 2008).

49. Born in Novocherkassk, George (Iurii) Gerebkoff (1908-?) was a dancer in a Russian ballet company. He settled in Germany in 1931, and then became a naturalized German citizen, prior to joining the NSDAP and then the SS. He arrived in Paris in March 1941 with the Russische Abteilung of the Gestapo. He removed the ambassador and member of the Resistance, Basile Maklakoff, from the presidency of the Office of Russian émigrés, which he then placed under the tutelage of the Interior Ministry.

50. See Laurent Joly, *Vichy dans la "solution finale": Histoire du Commissariat général aux questions juives, 1941–1944* (Paris: Grasset, 2006), 545 n.

51. A journalist born in Kiev (1883–1973), an officer of the Imperial Guard, military attaché at The Hague, former scout master and subsequently employed by the CGQJ. He played a high-profile role in the talks undertaken by the Nazis and the Vichy administration to have the Karaites not be considered Jews. He published a brochure on the Karaites in Paris in 1942 (titled *Les Caraïtes*), which can be consulted at the library of the Mémorial de la Shoah. See Mikhaïl Kizilov, *The Sons of Scripture: The Karaites in Poland and Lithuania in the Twentieth Century*, (2015), 326.

52. See Richard H.Weisberg: Vichy Law and the Holocaust in France (New York: Routledge 2013), 225.

53. Pierre-Philippe Lambert and Gérard Le Marec, in *Les français sous le casque allemand* (Éditions Grancher 1994, p.80), emphasize the importance of the recruitment of diverse Soviet peoples into the Speer Legion, which, according to them, amounted to 10,000 men at the end of 1942, a majority of whom were Balts. The French, (totaling about 500), including Russian émigrés, were admitted to the Legion from the summer of 1943 on. Their head doctor was the Doctor Lukachevitch and their commander, according to these authors, was a Russian called Sery.

54. Report no. F-6020 of January 30, 1946. It seems to have been written to provide additional information on Gerebkoff's role as an employee of the United Nations Relief and Rehabilitation Administration (UNRRA) in Bavaria, where he was placed under the protection of the American army.

55. Iurii S. Tsurganov, *Beloemigranty i Vtoraia mirovaia voina, Popytka revansha.1939–1945* (Moscow: Tsentrpoligraf, 2010), 96.

56. Cf. http://kotchoubey.com/select-biographies/a-french-kotschoubey-heir-to-the-ukrainian-throne/

57. Jean Mabire, *La division Charlemagne sur le front de l'est* (Grancher 2005), 73.

58. Gilbert Gilles, *Un ancien Waffen SS raconte: L'ultime assaut* (Gold Mail International, 1989), 195.

59. Saint-Loup, *Jean Benvoar, un héros breton*, Collection: "Les cahiers de la Bretagne réelle," no. 275 b, summer 1969.

60. Benvoar's testimony as reported by Saint-Paulien (pseudonym of Maurice-Ivan Sicard) in *Rivarol*, June 10, 1964, 11.

61. *Les Nostalgiques* (Paris: Presses de la Cité, 1967.)

62. Vol. 2 (Paris: Albin Michel, 1985).

63. See *Courrier du Val de Travers* (Switzerland), January 4, 1983.

64. Report from Philippe Coste in *Histoire et Traditions* no. 3, 2006.

65. H. Moreau died in 2008. On his involvement in creditism, see the foreword to the Italian edition of his book: *La Neve e il Sangue* (Novantico editrice, 2010), 25

66. (Editions Grancher, 2004).

67. Saint-Loup [Marc Augier], *Les volontaires* (Paris: Presses de la Cité, 1963).

68. Saint-Loup, *Les volontaires*, 33.

69. Saint-Loup, *Les volontaires*, 49.

70. Rusco, *Stoï!*, 39.

71. François Lobsiger, *Un suisse au service de Hitler* (Editions Albatros, 1985), 96. The fact can be dated from Spring 1942.

72. Rusco, *Stoï!*, 357.

73. Rusco, *Stoï!*, 144.

74. Saint-Loup, *Les volontaires*, 124.

75. Saint-Loup, *Les volontaires*, 124.

76. Many volunteers had enlisted into the Milice française before joining the LVF. The Milice, set up in January 1943, was an auxiliary police force working with the Nazis against the Résistance that is, against their fellow countrymen. That is why its repressive and bloody actions were so despised by the population.

77. On this point, the reader may consult Florence Fröhlig's PhD dissertation, *A Painful Legacy of World War II: Nazi Forced Enlistment, Alsatian/Mosellan Prisoners of War, and the Soviet Prison Camp of Tambov* (Stockholm: Acta Universitatis Stockholmiensis, 2013); and Régis Baty's book, *Tambov, camp soviétique* (Strasbourg, 2011).

78. The General Council of the Lower Rhine thus dedicated an exhibition, held between October 23, 2010 and November 11, 2011, to the question "What happened at Camp Tambov, 1943–45?" The former minister Philippe Richert, President of the Regional Council of Alsace, visited Tambov from February 25 to 27, 2008 and was received there by the French Ambassador and the Governor of Tambov Oblast, something that would be unthinkable for a visit to the graves of former LVF soldiers in the Smolensk or Moscow regions.

79. "Le calvaire de Jean-Jacques Remetter," *Dernières Nouvelles d'Alsace*, February 27, 1984.

80. "Les incorporés de force alsaciens [Déni, convocation et provocation de la mémoire]," *Vingtième Siècle, revue d'histoire*, no. 6 (1985): 83–102.

81. See the fanzine *Trente Trois* no. 1 (2009), on the digs in Rzecino.

82. See the report of the visit organized in 2006 by *Histoire et Traditions* and the group of historical re-enactors called Vent d'Europe, *Histoire et Traditions* no. 3, May 2006.

83. Here the reader can consult the historical account online (http://www.cdvfe-divisioncharlemagne.com/upload/BILOM.pdf) provided by an association of descendants of former volunteers, the *Cercle des Descendants et amis des Vétérans français du Front de l'Est (CDVFE). This circle sees itself as "taking care at once of the material and moral interests of the descendants and of former volunteers" and makes clear that it "does not define itself through a particular political militancy"* (author's email correspondence with the group's head, Commander G., November 25, 2009). In 1949 BILOM was split into two *Compagnies de Marche du Sud Annam.*

84. *Waffen-SS Français* (vol.1: *Officiers*, 2011), available online at: http://www.lulu.com/fr/fr/shop/gr%C3%A9gory-bouysse/waffen-ss-fran%C3%A7ais-volume-1-officiers/paperback/product-15338972.html

85. René Binet, *Socialisme national contre marxisme* (Montréal: Éditions Celtiques, 1975): 53. The text dates from 1950 and circulated in mimeographed form at the time.

86. Binet, *Socialisme national contre marxisme*, 54.

87. See, in particular, Nicolas Lebourg, *Le monde vu de la plus extrême-droite, du fascisme au nationalisme-révolutionnaire* (Perpignan: Presses universitaires de Perpignan, 2010).

88. (Freiburg: Editions de la Jeune Europe), 54

89. Eric Labat was the author of *Les places étaient chères* (La Table ronde, 1951). A translator by profession, he translated, for the same publisher, *Cosaques sans patrie* by German war writer, Franz Taut, a book devoted to those who fought alongside the Reich.

90. Pierre Vigouroux is the author, under the pseudonym of Mathieu Laurier, of *Il reste le drapeau noir et les copains* (Éditions Regain, 1953).

91. Malardier is the author of *Combats pour l'Honneur, Bataillon d'Assaut Charlemagne* (Paris: Éditions de l'Homme Libre, 2007).

92. A former Francist like Sidos, Pierre Bousquet (1919–1991) was to become one of the leaders of the paper *Militant* (cf. supra).

93. A protestant by confession, and a volunteer in the Milice and then, beginning in November 1944, in the Waffen SS, Robert Blanc (1923–2017) is mentioned by Roland Gaucher as one of the participants in the first winter solstice gathering of former members of the collaboration including the former SS Bernard Laignoux that was held on June 30, 1949 (cf. *Les nationalistes en France, la traversée du désert (1945–1983)*. Published by the author, 1985, pp. 144–45. Blanc gives an account in the French edition of the book by Robert Forbes, *For Europe: The French volunteers of the Waffen SS* (2000), published in 2005 under the title *Pour l'Europe: les volontaires français de la Waffen SS* (Paris: Éditions Aencre), which was "translated by a group of former volunteers," according to the editor; and he contributes to Philippe Martin's book, *A la recherche d'une éducation nouvelle*.

94. In his article "Avenir sombre pour les Etats-Unis" (*Europe-Action*, February 1963) he writes: "Race is in any case the new fatherland, the 'carnal fatherland' which has to be defended with a quasi-animal relentlessness." His pseudonym is validated by the complete bibliography of the works of Alain de Benoist, which appeared in 2009 under the auspices of the Association des Amis d'Alain de Benoist. See p. 20.

95. In Mabire's still unfinished biography, the solstice of Marquemont, June 19, 1948 appears as a key date for the gathering of the Communauté de jeunesse in the Vexin commune, a small group that he had founded in the Wandervogel and völkisch spirit. It is possible that this summer solstice event and the winter one that Gaucher mentioned were produced by the same organizers. On Marquemont: Mabire, *La Varende entre nous*, Éditions Présence de La Varende, 1999. The organizational approach to the Marquemont ceremony is elaborated by Fred Rossaert, a former Flemish militant of Jeune Europe, in the *Magazine des amis de Jean Mabire*, no. 22, 2009.

96. Mabire is said to have participated as the head of a group of Cadets in the camp of the *Mille*, a camp organized in Touraine in the summer of 1943 by Francist Youth. See Antoine Graziani, *Les visiteurs de l'aube, Chemise bleue*, vol. 3, p. 458, Éditions Dualpha, 2009. The author himself is a former militant.

97. Dominique Venner, *Les Blancs et les Rouges: Histoire de la guerre civile russe* (Pygmalion 1997).

98. Editorial "La Russie et l'Europe," *Nouvelle revue d'histoire*, no. 7 (2003).

99. Preface to *Le Grand Suicide*, Le Puy, Éditions du Crêve-Tabous, 1984. Maurice Martin (1920–2002) went via communism and anarchism before engaging in the SS. He collaborated toward the end of his life in the identitarian and revolutionary-nationalist journal *Réfléchir et Agir*, founded en 1993. An eclectic author, this autodidact contributed to several marginal anarchist papers (*L'Or vert*, *L'Anarchie*, *L'Homme libre*), to neo-rightist publications (*Vouloir* or *Le Partisan européen*) as well as to *Courrier du Continent*.

100. Yves Jeanne

101. D.E. no. 13, summer 1980, p. 4.

102. D.E. no. 6, November 1978, pp. 3–4.

103. In 1966, upon the initiative of *Militant* and under the presidency of the ex-Francist René Dayras (deceased in 2008) an Association des amis du socialisme français et de la Commune was established that each year organizes a commemoration at the Mur des fédérés and publishes a bulletin called *Le Communautaire*.

104. Like Ferdinand Ferrand, a key figure of Europe-Action and then of GRECE, Bousquet has become a prosperous commercial representative at the Halles de Paris.

105. *Militant*, November-December, 1978, p.15. *Bougnoule* is a pejorative term used in French to designate an immigrant worker of North African origin.

106. The son of Henri Simon. He was president of the PNF, which became a place of refuge for militants of *Œuvre française* and of the Jeunesses nationalistes, and was dissolved by the state on July 23, 2013.

107. Title of the March 2015 editorial, no. 669.

108. Nicolas Ougarov, "Le Haut-Karabagh, lieu éruptif du conflit Islam-Chrétienté," in *Militant*, May 2015.

109. According to the nationalist encyclopedia online, *Metapedia: fr.metapedia.org/wiki/Jean_Castrillo. Jean Castrillo published a work on the Byzantine Empire in 2006/ Constantinople, la perle du Bosphore* (Paris: Éditions L'Harmattan,), the aim of which is to determine the point at which "Europe ends and Asia begins. That is, which peoples comprise part of our civilizational principles and which belong to other cultures?"

110. Christopher Gérard, "Honnête et fidèle," *Magazine des amis de Jean Mabire* no. 22, p. 3.

111. (Paris: Perrin 1991), 182.

112. A figure whose political militantism is unknown or toned down by the Basque milieus, Mirande was the focus of a study by Txomin Peillen (Dominique Peillen): *Jon Mirande, poète parisien* (Bilbao: Euskaltzaindia editions, 2012), (bilingual Basque/French).

113. *La Bretagne réelle* no. 342, February 15, 1973.

114. See, *Histoire de la haine identitaire* (Valenciennes: Presses Universitaires de Valenciennes 2016), 12.

6. The Russian National Socialist Party Viking in Soviet Occupied Territories

1. Mikhail Nazarov, *Missiia russkoi emigratsii* (Moscow: Rodnik, 1994), 257.

2. Aleksandr Kazantsev, *Tret'ia sila. Rossiia mezhdu natsizmom i kommunizmom* (1st ed. Munich: Posev, 1952; 3rd ed., Moscow: Posev, 1994); Wilfried Strik-Strikfeldt, *Gegen Stalin und Hitler* (Mainz: Verlag Hase-Koehler, 1970), Russian edition V. K. Shtrik-Shtrikfeldt, *Protiv Stalina i Gitlera* (Moscow: Posev, 1993); Catherine Andreyev, *Vlasov and the Russian Liberation Movement* (Cambridge University Press, 1987), Russian edition: Ekaterina Andreeva, *General Vlasov i Russkoe osvoboditel'noe dvizhenie* (London: Overseas Publications Interchange, 1990).

3. Arkhiv Upravleniia Federal'noi sluzhby bezopasnosti Rossii po Brianskoi oblasti (AUFSBBO), File 51, Sheet 1.

4. AUFSBBO, File 51, Sheet 59.

5. Konstantin A. Zalesskii, *Komandirii natsional'nikh formirovanii SS* (Moscow: AST-Press, 2007), 13.

6. Zalesskii, *Komandirii natsional'nikh formirovanii SS*, 11–12.

7. Piotr F. Aleshkin, *Krest'ianskie vosstaniia v Rossii v 1918–1922 gg. Ot makhnovshchinii do antonovshchinii* (Moscow: Veche, 2012), 145.

8. Viacheslav G. Iashchenko. *Antibol'shevistskoe povstanchestvo v Nizhnem Povolzh'e i na Srednem Donu: 1918–1923* (Moscow: Stereotip, 2008), 49.

9. Cited in Aleshkin, *Krest'ianskie vosstaniia v Rossii v 1918–1922 gg.*, 150.

10. *Krest'ianskoe dvizhenie v Povolzh'e. 1919–1922 gg. Dokumenty i materialy* (Moscow: Rossiskaia politicheskaia entsiklopediia, 2002), 724.

11. March 17.

12. AUFSBBO, File 51, Sheet 59.

13. AUFSBBO, File 51, Sheet 59

14. *Krest'ianskoe dvizhenie v Povolzh'e. 1919–1922 gg.*, 709.

15. AUFSBBO. File 51, Sheet 59.

16. AUFSBBO, File 51, Sheet 59–59 reverse side.

17. AUFSBBO, File 51, Sheet 59 reverse side.

18. AUFSBBO, File 51, Sheet 59 reverse side.

19. AUFSBBO, File 51, Sheet 59 reverse side.

20. AUFSBBO, File 51, Sheet 59 reverse side.

21. AUFSBBO, File 51, Sheet 59 reverse side.

22. AUFSBBO, File 51, Sheet 59 reverse side.

23. AUFSBBO, File 51, Sheet 59 reverse side–60.

24. AUFSBBO, File 51, Sheet 60.

25. AUFSBBO, File 51, Sheet 60.

26. SSSR Constitution (Moscow, 1927), articles 118–28.

27. AUFSBBO, File 51, Sheet 60.

28. A song from the Soviet film *If War Comes Tomorrow*, composed by Daniil and Dmitrii Pokras: *Esli zavtra voina*, directed by Lazar Antsi-Polovskii, Georgii Berezko, Efim Dzigan, Nikolai Karmazinskii (USSR: Mosfilm, 1938).

29. Elena M. Rzhevskaia, *Gebbels. Portret na fone dnevnika* (Moscow: AST-Press, 1994), 13.

30. *History of World War II 1939–1945*, vol. 3. (Moscow: Voenizat, 1974), 318.

31. AUFSBBO, File 51, Sheet 60.

32. AUFSBBO, File 51, Sheet 60.

33. AUFSBBO, File 51, Sheet 60.

34. AUFSBBO, File 51, Sheet 14.

35. Sergei I. Drobiasko, "Lokot'skii avtonomnii okrug i Russkaia Osvoboditel'naia armiia," in A. V. Okorov, ed., *Materialy po istorii Russkogo Osvoboditelnogo Dvizheniia* (vol. 2, Moscow: Graal, 1997), 174.

36. Drobiasko, "Lokot'skii avtonomnii okrug i Russkaia Osvoboditel'naia armiia."

37. Aleksandr I. Boiarov, *Golos naroda* [Lokot, USSR], December 1, 1942.

38. Boiarov, *Golos naroda*, 196–97.

39. Boiarov, *Golos naroda*, 196–97.

40. AUFSBBO, File 51, Sheet 60 reverse side.

41. Aleksandr Saburov (1908–1974), commander of a partisan unit, Hero of the Soviet Union (1942).

42. Drobiasko, *Lokot'skii avtonomnii okrug i Russkaia Osvoboditel'naia armiia*, 177.

43. Arkadii N. Vasil'ev, *V chas dnia, vashe prevoskhoditel'stvo* (Moscow: Moskovskii rabochii, 1974), 496.

44. Aleksandr N. Saburov, *Silii neischislimie* (Moscow: Voenizdat, 1967), 32.

45. Aleksandr N. Saburov, *Otvoevannaia vesna* (Ustinov [Izhevsk]: Udmurtia, 1986), 146.

46. Saburov, *Otvoevannaia vesna*, 146.

47. Saburov, *Otvoevannaia vesna*, 146.

48. Saburov, *Otvoevannaia vesna*, 162.

49. Saburov, *Otvoevannaia vesna,* 166.

50. Saburov, *Otvoevannaia vesna,* 166.

51. Saburov, *Otvoevannaia vesna,* 167.

52. Saburov, *Otvoevannaia vesna,* 186, 199.

53. Saburov, *Otvoevannaia vesna,* 176.

54. *Golos naroda* [Lokot, USSR], January 8, 1943.

55. Reingard Gelen [Reinhard Gehlen], *Sluzhba* (Moscow: Terra, 1997), 80.

56. *Golos naroda* [Lokot, USSR], April 15, 1942.

57. State Archive of Briansk Region, Collection 2521, Register 1, File 1, Sheet 8.

58. Andrei F. Iudenkov, *Politicheskaia rabota partii sredi naseleniia okkupirovannoi sovetskoi territorii* (Moscow: Mysl', 1971), 43.

59. AUFSBBO, File 11231, Sheet 70 reverse side.

60. AUFSBBO, File 11231, Sheet 71.

61. AUFSBBO, File 11231, Sheet 77.

62. AUFSBBO, File 11231, Sheet 81.

63. AUFSBBO, File 51, Sheet 60 reverse side.

64. AUFSBBO, File 51, Sheet 60 reverse side.

65. *Nasha strana* [Buenos Aires, Argentina], December 13, 1952.

66. AUFSBBO, File 51, Sheet 61.

67. *Boevoi put'* [Aleksandrovsk, USSR], June 16, 1944.

68. AUFSBBO, File 51, Sheet 61.

69. AUFSBBO, File 51, Sheet 61.

70. AUFSBBO, File 51, Sheet 61 reverse side.

7. Pro-Soviet Groups in the Cold War European Radical Right

1. The German-speaking Swiss citizen, Franz Riedweg (1907–2005) provided the inspiration for the "European fraction" of the Waffen SS. On this point, see Marco Wyss, Un Suisse au service de la Waffen-SS (Neuchâtel: Alphil, Presses universitaires suisses, 2010).

2. That is, citizens of a country other than Germany who also were not ethnically German; the latter were accepted as "Volksdeutsche," or even drafted as such against their will, as in Alsace-Lorraine, Luxembourg, and part of Belgium.

3. See Jean-Luc Leleu, La WaffenSS (Paris: Perrin, 2007).

4. Le Combattant européen, June 1946. This journal published by Binet adopted the title of a periodical issued for the LVF (the Legion of French Volunteers against Bolshevism), the Wehrmacht regiment assembled at Doriot's behest.

5. L'Unité, November 6, 1948.

6. Pour une critique positive (Nantes: Ars Magna, 1997; first edition, 1962).

7. La Nation européenne, September 1967, November 1967.

8. Olivier Dard, "L'Anticommunisme des nationalistes au temps de la République gaullienne," Communisme, no. 62–63 (2000), 145.

9. Direction générale de la sûreté nationale, Direction des renseignements généraux, Bulletin de documentation, August 1963 (AN F/7/15582).

10. La Nation européenne, April 15–May 15, 1966; September15–October 15, 1966; January15–February 15, 1967; and September 1967.

11. A viewpoint that split opinion among the extreme Right of the 1960s, but it was not innovative: for example, it was that of the Bulletin de l'Institut national légionnaire, no. 7, September 1943.

12. La Nation européenne, October15–November 15, 1966; November15–December 15, 1966.

13. Direction générale de la sûreté nationale, Direction des renseignements généraux,

"Les activités du Centre d'Etudes Politiques et Sociales Européennes," Bulletin hebdomadaire. Notes et études, October 5, 1966, 3 (AN 19820599/69).

14. La Nation européenne, January 15–February 15, 1967; February 15–March 15, 1967.

15. La Nation européenne, October 1967; November 1968; February 1969.

16. Jeune Europe, January 3, 1964.

17. See Jean-Yves Camus and René Monzat, Les Droites nationales et radicales en France (Lyon: Presses Universitaires de Lyon, 1992). Gilles Munier, one of the main writers of anti-Zionist articles in La Nation européenne and its correspondent in Algiers, was the president of the Association des amitiés franco-irakiennes. In this capacity, he was among the organizers of the support trip by European nationalists to Baghdad in 2003.

18. Frédéric Laurent, L'Orchestre noir (Paris : Stock, 1978).

19. Born in Belgium in 1935, and a Jeune Europe militant in France, Coudroy worked as an engineer in Kuwait with the French company Peugeot and later joined Fatah in Lebanon under the alias of "Salah." He allegedly died in combat on June 3, 1968, according to a communiqué issued by the PLO on that day. In 1969 the Palestine Liberation Organization's research center in Beirut published his brochure, J'ai vécu la résistance palestinienne. There are no direct witnesses to his death and several contradictory versions of it exist: one is that he died in combat in the ranks of al Assifah (The Storm), a Fatah guerilla group who were trying to enter into Israel from Lebanon; another that he shot himself accidentally while cleaning his weapon; another is that he was eliminated by Fatah on suspicion of being an Israeli agent.

20. Jean Thiriart, Un Empire de 400 millions d'hommes: l'Europe (Brussels: Jean Thiriart, 1964); Jean Thiriart, La Grande Nation, L'Europe unitaire de Brest à Bucarest (Brussels: PCE, 1965).

21. Jean Thiriart, Quel destin pour la Bundeswehr ? Mourir pour Washington ou combattre pour la naissance de l'Europe? (1983), 16 pp.

22. L'Europe aux Européens is the title of a book published by Pierre Daye in 1942. A former pacifist and supporter of European unity in the line of Aristide Briand, a supporter of "Euro-Afrique" who later switched to Degrelle's Rexist Party, Daye believed an international union of workers would emerge from the war launched by the Third Reich against the USSR and its ally, the United Kingdom. See Pierre Daye, L'Europe aux Européens (Brussels: Nouvelle Société d'Editions, 1942).

23. François Genoud was the Nazi Swiss banker who financed the 1959 edition of the conversations between Hitler and Bormann. According to Hitler, "What we want is a Monroe Doctrine in Europe: Europe for the Europeans!" And later: "It is possible that under the pressure of events, the Russians will rid themselves completely of Jewish Marxism, only to re-incarnate pan-slavism in its most fierce and ferocious form. As for the Americans, if they do not swiftly succeed in casting off the yoke of New York Jewry, [...] well, it will not be long before they go under, before even having reached the age of maturity." Adolf Hitler, Le Testament politique de Hitler: Notes recueillies par Martin Bormann (Paris: Fayard, 1959), 74 and 146–48.

24. Jean Thiriart, letter of March 13, 1992.

25. José Cuadrado Costa, "Insuffisance et dépassement du concept marxiste-léniniste de nationalité, " Conscience européenne, no. 9 (October 1984).

26. Interview with Jean Thiriart, Conscience européenne, no. 8 (July 1984).

27. Jean Thiriart et Luc Michel, "Le Socialisme communautaire, " Conscience européenne, undated special issue [1986?], 46.

28. "L'URSS héritière du IIIe Reich," foreword by Yannick Sauveur, "Jean Thiriart et le national communautarisme européen," Revue d'Histoire du nationalisme révolutionnaire, no. 3 (n.d.).

29. Lutte du peuple, January 1993.

30. Louis Dupeux, *National-bolchevisme. Stratégie communiste et dynamique conserva-trice*, Paris, Honoré Champion, 1979, p. 326.

31. The Bündisch movement was one of the ideological streams of the German Conservative Revolution, born in 1890 with the founding of the Wandervogel (Migrating Bird) youth group in Berlin.

32. Patrick Moreau, Les Héritiers du IIIe Reich: L'Extrême droite allemande de 1945 à nos jours (Paris: Seuil, 1994),197–202; Louis Dupeux, National Bolchevism: Stratégie communiste et dynamique conservatrice (Paris: Honoré Champion, 1979), 326; Lénine, Du Droit des nations à disposer d'elles-mêmes (Moscow: Éditions du progrès, 1979 [1916]).

33. See Nicolas Lebourg, "Arriba Eurasia? The Difficult Establishment of Eurasianism in Spain," in Eurasianism and the European Far Right: Reshaping the Europe–Russia Relationship, ed. Marlene Laruelle, 125–42 (Lanham, MD: Lexington Books, 2015).

34. Luc Michel, "Aujourd'hui Moscou, demain l'Europe. Nous sommes l'Europe combattante," Nation Europe, February 1994.

35. See Jean-Yves Camus and Nicolas Lebourg, Les Droites extrêmes en Europe (Paris: Le Seuil, 2015).

36. See Anton Shekhovtsov, "Far-Right Election Observation Monitors in the Service of the Kremlin's Foreign Policy," in Eurasianism and the European Far Right: Reshaping the Europe–Russia Relationship, ed. Marlene Laruelle, 223–44 (Lanham, MD: Lexington Books, 2015).

37. Kevin Coogan, "Lost Imperium: The European Liberation Front (1949–54)," Patterns of Prejudice 36, no. 3 (July 2002): 9–23.

38. Direction Centrale de la Police Judiciaire, "Situation des mouvements d'extrême droite en France," March 29, 1968, 2 (BDIC F8150/1); Réalités Socialistes européennes, December 1968 and February 1969.

39. Socialisme européen, September–October 1968. Pierre Vial was one of the contributors to this journal.

40. Armin Mohler, La Révolution conservatrice en Allemagne, 1918–1922 (Puiseaux : Editions Pardès, 1993 [1950]).

41. Jean-Pierre Faye, Langages totalitaires (Paris: Hermann, 1972); Dupeux, National Bolchevisme.

42. See Nicolas Lebourg, "La Fonction productrice de l'histoire dans le renouvellement du fascisme à partir des années 1960," in *Les Sciences sociales au prisme de l'extrême droite. Enjeux et usages d'une récupération idéologique*, ed. Sylvain Crépon et Sébastien Mosbah-Natanson, 213–43 (Paris: L'Harmattan, Paris, 2008).

43. Résistance, September 2003.

44. Anne-Marie Duranton-Crabol, Visages de la nouvelle droite: Le GRECE et son histoire (Paris: Fondation nationale des sciences politiques, 1988), 208–9.

45. "Alain de Benoist: L'ennemi principal," *Eléments*, no. 41 (March–April 1982), 48.

46. Le Monde, October 8, 1983 and November 17, 1984; Libération, November 12, 1984; Pierre Milza, Fascisme français. Passé et présent (Paris: Flammarion, 1987), 395; Pierre-André Taguieff, "Les Droites radicales en France: nationalisme révolutionnaire et national-libéralisme," Les Temps modernes, no. 465 (April–May 1985):1780–1842; Le Partisan européen, vendemiaire–brumaire 1986. The journal Le Partisan européen used the calendar created in 1792 by the French Revolution, not out of Republicanism, it claims, but because of anti-Christianism and the desire to create a new pagan vision of the world to ensure an "organic community of the people," the French expression for the German term *Volksgemeinschaft*.

47. MNR Bulletin de liaison, June 5, 1985 (document interne).

48. Parvulesco's writings are full of obscure references and grammatical flaws that make them quite difficult to understand. The quotes are translated from the original.

49. Jean Parvulesco, "De la libération nationale à la libération continentale," De l'Atlantique au Pacifique, February 1976.

50. Jeune Nation solidariste, March 15, 1979.

51. "Questions à Robert Steuckers: pour préciser les positions de Synergies Européennes," available at http://robertsteuckers.blogspot.fr/2012/08/pourpreciserlespositionsde.html.

52. Le Partisan européen, pluviôse 1987.

53. Manifeste du Partisan européen (Nantes: Ars, n.d.); Le Partisan européen, prairial-messidor 1986 and thermidor–fructidor 1986.

54. Alain de Benoist, foreword to Ernst Niekisch, Hitler: une fatalité allemande et autres écrits nationaux-bolcheviks (Pardès: Puiseaux, 1991), p. 55; Lutte du peuple, June 1993; Nation Europe, February–April 1996.

55. Pour la cause du peuple (manifeste de Nouvelle Résistance), n.p.

56. In the writings of Hegel, Volksgeist, or "national spirit," refers to the specific mindset of a given people and is a mediation with Weltgeist (the spirit of the world) that is, the order of the universal. Herder, German Romanticists and later on, German nationalists have given a distinctly ethnic meaning to this concept.

57. Jeune Nation solidariste, July 26, 1979.

58. Memorandum no. 10, Young Europe.

59. Interview with Ramón Bau, former secretary general of CEDADE, Madrid, January 23, 1989; ¿Qué es CEDADE? (Barcelona: Bau, 1975), 15 pages ; and ¿Qué es CEDADE? (Barcelona: BAUSP, 1978), 39 pages.

60. Lorenzo Castro Moral, Estudio de un movimiento (Madrid, 1974). Work for a course in the Faculty of Political Sciences and Sociology, Complutense University of Madrid.

61. Jorge Mota, Hacia un socialismo europeo: ¿Falange o comunismo? (Barcelona: Bau, 1974).

62. "Proyecto Bronwyn," Más allá del Sur: Revista Negra de las Artes Literarias y Políticas, no. 1, (November 1986), 12–13.

63. Fernando Márquez, "Sobre Zhirinovsky: hablando en plata," El corazón del bosque, no. 23 (spring 1994), 34.

64. "Orientándonos con Aleksandr Duguin," El corazón del bosque, no. 4 (fall 1994), 22–23.

65. El Mundo, September 30, 1993 and February 25, 1994.

66. Fernando Márquez, "Hacia el Frente Ibérico de Salvación," Punto de Vista Operativo, no. 1 (fall 1995), 3–4.

67. Tribuna de Europa, no. 4 (October 1993), 16–18; no. 6 (June 1994), 14–15.

68. "El nacional bolchevismo ruso," Tribuna de Europa, no. 4 (October 1993), 19–23.

69. Juan Antonio Llopart, "¿Nacionalbolcheviques?," Tribuna de Europa, no. 6 (June 1994), 34.

70. "La oposición social-patriótica rusa: Christian Bouchet entrevista a sus líderes," Tribuna de Europa, no. 6 segunda época (summer 1996), 22–25; "Winnig y Paetel líderes nacional bolcheviques," Tribuna de Europa, no. 7 segunda época (October–November 1996), 33; "Richard Scheringer: Del nacionalsocialismo al comunismo," Tribuna de Europa, no. 9 (March–April 1997), 30–32.

71. This journal was produced in Logroño and Madrid between 1995 and 1998, and defined itself as a "national revolutionary vehicle of critical information and opposition." Its editor and several collaborators were neo-Nazis or very sympathetic toward Nazism: Juan Colomar, Ramón Bau, and Francisco Meana. In issue no. 4, May 1996, on pages 14–15, the journal published an article in support of the "Russian nationalist communist Gennadii Ziuganov," a candidate for election, in "Desde Rusia con amor"; see also "El bolchevismo, revolución nacional rusa," Resistencia, no. 5 (September 1996), 16–17.

72. "Entrevista con Alexandre Duguin. Elecciones presidenciales en Rusia," Nosotros somos quien somos, no. 9 (April 1996), 10; other articles also appeared, including one on Russian politics: "Rusia en política exterior," Nosotros somos quien somos, no. 30 (March–April 1999), 4–5. The title of this publication is borrowed from a very famous poem published in 1955 by Gabriel Celaya, "Espana en marcha." Celaya opposed Franco and his poem became an anthem of the Left. Obviously his words, "we are who we are" were intended to be a slogan for the Left, but they were hijacked by Falange Española de las JONS, a fringe political party carrying on the extreme-right ideology of the pre-Franco phalangists, the enemies of the Left in the Spanish Civil War.

73. Robert Steuckers, email to Nicolas Lebourg, October 22, 2001.

74. "3° congrès de Nouvelle Résistance Motion présentée par le secrétariat général de l'organisation" (internal document; 1996), 4.

8. Strasserism in Germany

1. Manfred F. Boemeke, Gerald D. Feldman, and Elizabeth Glaser, eds., *The Treaty of Versailles: A Reassessment after 75 Years* (Cambridge: Cambridge University Press, 1988).

2. Bruce Kent, *Spoils of War: The Politics, Economics, and Diplomacy of Reparations, 1918–1932* (Oxford: The Clarendon Press, 1989).

3. Sebastian Haffner and Gregory Bateson, *Der Vertrag von Versailles* (Berlin: Ullstein Verlag, 1988); Wolfgang Elz, "Versailles und Weimar," *Aus Politik und Zeitgeschichte*, no. 50–51, 2008: 31–38.

4. John Kenneth Galbraith, *La crise économique de 1929: Anatomie d'une catastrophe financière* (Paris: Payot, 1989).

5. Klaus Kinner, *Der deutsche Kommunismus: Selbstverständnis und Realität* (vol. 1: *Die Weimarer Zeit*) (Berlin: Dietz, 1999); Klaus-Michael Mallmann, *Kommunisten in der Weimarer Republik: Sozialgeschichte einer revolutionären Bewegung* (Darmstadt: Wissenschaftliche Buchgesellschaft, 1996); Jean François Fayet, *Karl Radek, 1885–1939. Biographie politique* (Bern: Peter Lang, 2004).

6. Ernst von Salomon, *Der Fragebogen* (Hamburg: Rowohlt, 1951).

7. Otto-Ernst Schüddekopf, *Linke Leute von rechts: Die nationalrevolutionären Minderheiten und der Kommunismus in der Weimarer Republik* (Stuttgart: Kohlhammer, 1960).

8. Patrick Moreau, "La Communauté de combat nationale-socialiste révolutionnaire et le Front noir: Action et idéologie en Allemagne, Autriche et Tchécoslovaquie, 1930–1935," Doctorat de IIIe cycle de l'Université de Paris I, 1978, 2 vols; Patrick Moreau, *Nationalsozialismus von links: Die "Kampfgemeinschaft Revolutionärer Nationalsozialisten" und die "Schwarze Front" Otto Strassers, 1930–1935* (Stuttgart: Oldenbourg, 1985); Markus März, *Nationale Sozialisten in der NSDAP: Strukturen, Ideologie, Publizistik und Biographien des national-sozialistischen Strasser-Kreises von der AG Nordwest bis zum Kampf-Verlag 1925–1930* (Graz: Ares-Verlag, 2010); Stefan Wannenwetsch, *Unorthodoxe Sozialisten: Zu den Sozialismuskonzeptionen der Gruppe um Otto Strasser und des Internationalen Sozialistischen Kampfbundes in der Weimarer Republik* (Frankfurt am Main: Lang, 2010).

9. Richard Schapke, *Die Schwarze Front* (Leipzig, 1932); Günther Bartsch, *Zwischen drei Stühlen: Otto Strasser; Eine Biographie* (Koblenz: Verlag Siegfried Bublies, 1990).

10. Oswald Spengler, *Der Untergang des Abendlandes: Umrisse einer Morphologie der Weltgeschichte*, vol. 1 (Vienna: Verlag Braumüller, 1918); vol. 2 (Munich: C.H.Beck, 1922).

11. Arthur Moeller van den Bruck, *Das Recht der jungen Völker, 1919: Das dritte Reich* (Berlin: Ring Verlag, 1923).

12. Strasser always speaks about "Russia" in his texts in the beginning of the 1920s; he is convinced that the Soviet Union will not exist for long. Armin Mohler, *Die Konservative Revolution in Deutschland, 1918–1932: Ein Handbuch* (Graz: Ares-Verlag, 2005).

13. Udo Kissenkoetter, *Gregor Strasser und die NSDAP: Schriftenreihe der Vierteljahrshefte für Zeitgeschichte* (Stuttgart: Deutsche Verlagsanstalt, 1978). The party obtained 6.5 percent of the vote and thirty-two mandates in the May 1924 elections, and 3 percent of the vote and fourteen mandates in the December 1924 elections. Udo Kissenkoetter, *Gregor Strasser und die NSDAP: Schriftenreihe der Vierteljahrshefte für Zeitgeschichte* (Stuttgart: Deutsche Verlagsanstalt, 1978). It was a joint list of Nationalsozialistische Freiheitsbewegung (NSFB), Vereinigte Listen der Deutschvölkischen Freiheitspartei (DVFP), and Nationalsozialistische Deutsche Arbeiter-partei (NSDAP).

14. Jürgen W. Falter, *Hitlers Wähler* (Munich: C.H.Beck, 1991).

15. Louis Dupeux, *Stratégie communiste et dynamique conservatrice : Essais sur les différents sens de l'expression "national-bolchévisme" en Allemagne, sous la république de Weimar (1919–1933)* (Paris : Honoré Champion, 1976), 366–85.

16. The Wehrwolf: Bund deutscher Männer und Frontkrieger (Werewolf: Association of German Men and Front Fighters) was a nationalist and paramilitary association in the Weimar Republic. Its membership consisted mostly of Free Corps members and officers of lower ranks. During its golden age from 1924 to 1929, the Wehrwolf had about 30,000 to 40,000 members. After 1930, the Wehrwolf was largely absorbed by the NSDAP. Between 1930 and 1931, anti-Hitler attempts were made to join forces with the Freikorps Oberland, the KGNRS, and Otto Strasser's Black Front, but they failed. (Kurt Finker, "Wehrwolf. Bund deutscher Männer und Frontkrieger," in *Die bürgerlichen Parteien in Deutschland*, ed. Dieter Fricke [vol. 2, Das Europäische Buch], [Berlin: 1968], 835–40.)

17. The Landvolkbewegung (Rural People's Movement) of Schleswig-Holstein (Northern Germany) was a protest movement that emerged in the late 1920s and soon spread to large parts of the German Reich. The movement organized demonstrations against the Weimar Republic and a tax boycott. Furthermore, it launched several bomb attacks. Its symbol was a black flag with a silver plough and a red sword. In the early 1930s, the movement lost acceptance due to its terrorist activities. Most of its members became supporters of the NSDAP; a small fringe cooperated with Strasser's Black Front (Schwarze Front). See: Gerhard Stoltenberg: *Politische Strömungen im schleswig-holsteinischen Landvolk 1918–1933. Ein Beitrag zur politischen Meinungsbildung in der Weimarer Republik* (= *Beiträge zur Geschichte des Parlamentarismus und der politischen Parteien* 24, Droste Verlag, Düsseldorf 1962. The Freikorps Oberland, a free corps founded in the early Weimar Republic in April 1919, was a paramilitary militia. Its ban in November 1921 resulted in the foundation of the Bund Oberland as a club, which constituted the core of the Sturmabteilung (SA) in Bavaria. The Bund Oberland was banned throughout Germany in 1923, but was reorganized in 1925. As early as 1930, differences evolved, and the "National Revolutionaries" left the Bund. As "Oberlandkameradschaf" (Oberland comradeship), they collectively joined the National Bolshevists under Ernst Niekisch and rejected National Socialism. Josef Römer, former chief of staff of the Free Corps, joined the Communist "Scheringerkreis" and became the leader of a secret organization called "Bund Oberland" that had been founded in 1920. For a short time, Josef Römer cooperated with Strasser's Black Front. In 1939–40, together with old free corps comrades and former members of the "Aufbruch-Arbeits-Kreises" (Working Group Awakening), Römer established resistance groups in Munich and Berlin. Together with his supporters, he passed out leaflets calling the people to rise up against Adolf Hitler. He was arrested in 1942 and executed in 1944. (Christoph Hübner: *Bund Oberland, 1921–1923/1925–1930. Bund Oberland, 1921–1923/1925–1930.* See https://www.his torisches-lexikon-bayerns.de/Lexikon/Bund_Oberland, 1921-1923/1925-1930.)

18. Moreau, *Nationalsozialismus von Links*, 102ff.

19. Douglas Reed, *The Prisoner of Ottawa: Otto Strasser* (London: Cape, 1953).

20. "Programmerklärung zur nationalen und sozialen Befreiung des deutschen Volkes," *Rote Fahne*, August 25, 1930; a version is available at: http://www.kpd-sozialgeschichte. homepage.t-online.de/quellen.html#natsozbef.

21. On the entire issue, see Dupeux, *Stratégie communiste*, 549–79.

22. Dupeux, *Stratégie communiste*, 550. The text is in *Die Kommunistische Internationale in Resolutionen und Beschlüssen*, vol. 2, *1925–1943* (Offenbach: Verlag Olga Benario und Herbert Baum, 1998), 452.

23. Siegfried Bahne, "'Sozialfaschismus' in Deutschland. Zur Geschichte eines politischen Begriffs," *International Review of Social History*, 1965, no. 10: 211–45.

24. Kurt G. P. Schuster, *Der Rote Frontkämpferbund 1924–1929: Beiträge zur Geschichte und Organisationsstruktur eines politischen Kampfbundes* (Düsseldorf: Droste, 1975).

25. Lenin, Œuvres choisies (Moscow: Éditions du Progrès, 1968), vol. 3, 465–66.

26. Dupeux, *Stratégie communiste*, 557.

27. Dupeux, *Stratégie communiste*, 557.

28. Deborah Kisatsky, *The United States and the European Right, 1945–1955* (Columbus: Ohio State University Press, 2005).

29. Richard Stöss, *Parteien-Handbuch* (vol. 1, *AUD-EFP, Die Deutsch-Soziale Union*) (Bonn: Westdeutscher Verlag, 1983), 1243–78.

30. Otto Büsch and Peter Furth, *Rechtsradikalismus im Nachkriegsdeutschland: Studien über die Sozialistische Reichspartei* (Tübingen: 1952; Berlin: Franz Vahlen, 1957).

31. Patrick Moreau, "Le Parti National-Démocrate d'Allemagne dans la vie politique de la R.F.A.: Études organisationnelle, sociologique et électorale d'une formation de l'opposition nationale 1964–1976," Doctorat d'Etat de Sciences Politiques, 2 vols. plus annexes, 1984.

32. Patrick Moreau, *Les héritiers du IIIe Reich: L'extrême droite allemande de 1945 à nos jours* (Paris: Seuil, 1994), 239ff.

33. Moreau, *Les héritiers du IIIe Reich*.

34. *George Nafziger, Organizational History of the German SS Formations, 1939–1945*, http://usacac.army.mil/cac2/CGSC/CARL/nafziger/939GXWA.pdf.

35. Harald Bergsdorf, *Ungleiche Geschwister. Die deutschen Republikaner (REP) im Vergleich zum französischen Front National (FN)* (Frankfurt am Main: Lang, 2000); Britta Obszerninks, *Nachbarn am rechten Rand: Republikaner und Freiheitliche Partei Österreichs im Vergleich* (Münster: Agenda, 1999) (doctoral thesis, University of Münster).

36. Moreau, *Les héritiers du IIIe Reich*, 263ff.

37. Moreau, *Les héritiers du IIIe Reich*; Rita Schorpp-Grabiak, *Man muss so radikal sein wie die Wirklichkeit. Die PDS: Eine Bilanz* (Baden-Baden: Nomos Verlag, 2002).

38. Andreas Malycha, Peter Jochen Winters, *Die SED: Geschichte einer deutschen Partei* (Munich: C.H.Beck, 2009); Jens Gieseke and Hermann Wentker, eds., *Die Geschichte der SED: Eine Bestandsaufnahme* (Berlin: Metropol, 2011).

39. Moreau, *Les héritiers du IIIe Reich*; Schorpp-Grabiak, *Man muss so radikal sein*.

40. Uwe Backes and Henrik Steglich, eds., *Die NPD: Erfolgsbedingungen einer rechtsextremistischen Partei* (Baden-Baden: Nomos, 2007); Marc Brandstetter, "Die 'neue' NPD: Zwischen Systemfeindschaft und bürgerlicher Fassade," *Parteienmonitor Aktuell der Konrad-Adenauer-Stiftung* (Berlin, 2012), http://www.kas.de/wf/doc/kas_30034-544-1-30.pdf?140328142648.

41. Saarland (4 percent in 2004), Saxony (9.2 percent in 2004), Berlin (2.6 percent in 2006), Mecklenburg-Vorpommern (7.3 percent in 2006), Saxony (5.6 percent in 2009), Saxony-Anhalt (4.6 percent in 2011), Mecklenburg-Vorpommern (6 percent in 2011), and Saxony (4.9 percent in 2014).

42. "'Autonome Nationalisten'—Rechtsextremistische Militanz," Federal Office for Protection of the Constitution (Cologne, 2009).

43. See http://angg.info/; on the whole question, see Jan Schedler and Alexander Häusler, eds., *Autonome Nationalisten: Neonazismus in Bewegung* (Wiesbaden: Verlag für Sozialwissenschaften, 2011). A geography of the phenomenon can be found at https://www.amadeu-antonio-stiftung.de/w/files/pdfs/braune_kameraden.pdf.

44. http://www.identitaere-generation.info.

45. https://sachedesvolkes.wordpress.com/2011/06/28/der-sozialistische-flugel -der-nsdap-und-sein-wirken/.

46. http://www.der-dritte-weg.info/index.php/menue/1/thema/69/region_thema/17/ infotext/Parteigeschehen/Politik_Gesellschaft_und_Wirtschaft.html.

47. See, for example: http://www.spiegel.de/politik/ausland/russland-wladimir-putins -rechtsextreme-freunde-in-europa-a-1075461.html; http://www.bpb.de/internationales/ europa/russland/208636/analyse-russland-und-die-europaeische-extreme-rechte-eine- seltsame-verbindung; http://derstandard.at/2000038542175/Identitaere-Gruesse-aus-Moskau -Rechtsextreme-Allianz-in-den-Osten; http://greater-europe.org/archives/910; http://www.morgen post.de/berlin/article206988615/Wie-Berlins-Rechte-um-die-Gunst-der-Russland deutschen-buhlt.html; http://de.euromaidanpress.com/2015/03/31/shekhovtsov-die-russischen -massenmedien-und-die-extreme-rechte-des-westens/.

48. David Bebnowski, *Die Alternative für Deutschland: Aufstieg und gesellschaftliche Repräsentanz einer rechten populistischen Partei* (Wiesbaden: Springer VS, 2015); Alexan- der Häusler and Rainer Roeser, *Die rechten "Mut"-Bürger: Entstehung, Entwicklung, Perso- nal & Positionen der "Alternative für Deutschland"* (Hamburg: VSA Verlag, 2015); Alexander Häusler, ed., *Die Alternative für Deutschland: Programmatik, Entwicklung und politische Verortung* (Wiesbaden: Springer Fachmedien, 2016).

9. Lev Gumilev and the European New Right

This article was first published as Mark Bassin, "Lev Gumilev and the European New Right," *Nationalities Papers* 43:6 (2015), 840–65. This work was supported by the The Foundation for Baltic and East European Studies (Stockholm) as part of the project "The Vision of Eurasia."

1. Long before the collapse of the Soviet Union, Aleksandr Yanov (*The Russian New Right: Right-Wing Ideologies in the Contemporary USSR* [Berkeley, CA: University of Cali- fornia Press, 1978]) inadvertently called attention to this European–Russian juxtaposition by referring to the then-emergent Russian nationalist movement as the "Russian New Right." See also Walter Laqueur, *Black Hundred: The Rise of the Extreme Right in Russia* (New York: HarperCollins, 1993); Wayne Allensworth, *The Russian Question: Nationalism, Modernization, and Post-Communist Russia* (Lanham, MD: Rowman & Littlefield, 1998); Thomas Parland, *The Extreme Nationalist Threat in Russia: The Growing Influence of Western Rightist Ideas* (London: Routledge, 2005).

2. Mark Sedgwick, *Against the Modern World: Traditionalism and the Secret History of the Twentieth Century* (Oxford: Oxford University Press, 2004); Andreas Umland, "Kul- turhegemoniale Strategien der russischen extremen Rechten: Die Verbindung von faschis- tischer Ideologie und metapolitischer Taktik im "Neoeurasismus" des Aleksandr Dugin," Österreichische Zeitschrift für Politikwissenschaft 33, no. 4 (2004): 437–54; Vladimir Ivanov, *Aleksandr Dugin und die rechtsextremen Netzwerke* (Stuttgart: ibidemVerlag, 2007); Anton Shekhovtsov, "Aleksandr Dugin's Neo-Eurasianism; The New Right a la Russe," *Religion Compass* 3, no. 4 (2009): 697-716; Anton Shekhovtsov and Andreas Umland, "Is Aleksandr Dugin a Traditionalist? 'NeoEurasianism' and Perennial Philosophy," *Russian Review* 68 (2009): 662–78; Marlène Laruelle, "Aleksandr Dugin: A Russian Version of the European Radical Right?" *Kennan Institute Occasional Papers* 272 (n.d.).

3. A. G. Dugin, *Aleksandr Dugin: The Fourth Political Theory* (London: Arktos, 2012); A. G. Dugin, *Konflikte der Zukunft: Die Rückkehr der Geopolitik* (Kiel: Arndt-Verlag, 2014); Irenäus Eibl-Eibesfeldt, *Ethnology: The Biology of Behavior* (New York: Holt, Rinehart & Winston, 1970); Alexandre Douguine, *L'appel de L'Eurasie* (Paris: Avatar, 2013); Alexandre Dougine, *Pour une théorie du monde multipolaire* (Paris: Ars Magna, 2014). For Alain

de Benoist's appreciation of "mon ami" Dugin, see Alain de Benoist, *Mémoire vive* (Paris: Éditions de Fallois, 2012), 119, 244. See also Michael O'Meara, *New Culture, New Right: Anti-Liberalism in Postmodern Europe*, 2nd ed. (London: Arktos, 2013), 238, 243, 256n; Lucian Tudor, "The Philosophy of Identity: Ethnicity, Culture and Race in Identitarian Thought," *Occidental Quarterly* 14, no. 3 (2014): 84, 98n, 108–11.

4. Joshua Keating, "From Russia with Cash," *Slate*, November 26, 2014, accessed December 30, 2014, http://www.slate.com/blogs/the_world_/2014/11/26/from_russia_with_cash.html; Pierre Sautreuil, "With A Far-Right Band of Frenchmen Fighting In Ukraine," *Worldcrunch*, September 4, 2014, accessed December 30, 2014, http://www.worldcrunch.com/ukraine-winter/with-a-far-right-band-of-frenchmen-fighting-in-ukraine/far-right-nationalism-mercenaries-separatists-soldiers-/c20s16888/.VKMWFRF3c6V.

5. Patrick J. Buchanan, "Is Putin One of Us?" *Patrick Buchanan (blog)*, 2013, accessed December 30, 2014, http://buchanan.org/blog/putin-one-us-6071; Harold Meyerson, "Pat Buchanan, Vladimir Putin and Strange Bedfellows," *Washington Post*, December 27, 2013, accessed December 30, 2014, http://www.washingtonpost.com/opinions/harold-meyerson-pat-buchanan-vladimir-putin-and-strange-bedfellows/2013/12/24/f8159f22-68bf-11e3-a0b9-249bbb34602c_story.html; "UK Far-Right Leader Farage Calls for Alliance with Russia," *World Bulletin*, September 16, 2014, accessed December 30, 2014, http://www.worldbulletin.net/news/144501/uk-far-right-leader- farage-calls-for-alliance-with-russia. The growing political synergy between the Putin regime and radical conservatism in the West is an important subject which merits a separate examination. See Anton Shekhovtsov, "The Kremlin's Marriage of Convenience with the European Far Right," OpenDemocracy, April 28, 2014, accessed October 20, 2014, https://http://www.opendemocracy.net/od-russia/anton-shekhovtsov/kremlin%E2%80%99s-marriage-of-convenience-witheurope an-far-right; Mitchell A. Orenstein, "Putin's Western Allies: Why Europe's Far Right Is on the Kremlin's Side," *Foreign Affairs*, March 25, 2014, accessed December 30, 2014, http://www.foreignaffairs.com/articles/141067/mitchell-a-orenstein/putins-western-allies; Alina Polyakova, "Strange Bedfellows: Putin and Europe's Far Right," *World Affairs* (September–October 2014), accessed December 30, 2014, http://www.worldaffairsjournal.org/article/strange-bedfellows-putin-and-europe%E2%80%99s-far-right; Elena Servettaz, "Putin's Far-Right Friends in Europe," Institute of Modern Russia, January 16, 2014, accessed December 30, 2014, http://imrussia.org/en/russia-and-the-world/645-putins-far-right-friends-in-europe; Luke Harding, "We Should Beware Russia's Links with Europe's Right," *The Guardian*, December 8, 2014, accessed December 30, 2014, https://www.theguardian.com/commentisfree/2014/dec/08/russia-europe-right-putin-front-national-eu.

6. For earlier studies, see Hildegard Kochanek, "Die Ethnienlehre Lev N. Gumilevs: Zu den Anfängen neu-rechter Ideologie-Entwicklung im spätkommunistischen Russland," *Osteuropa* 48: 11-12 (1998): 1184–97; Hildegard Kochanek, *Die russisch-nationale Rechte von 1968 bis zum Ende der Sowjetunion* (Stuttgart: Steiner Verlag, 1999), 216–22; Marlene Lariuel' [Laruelle], "Opyt sravnitel'nogo analiza teorii etnosa L'va Gumileva i zapadnykh novykh pravykh," *Etnograficheskoe Obozrenie* 3 (2006): 226–39, http://www1.ku-eichstaett.de/ZIMOS/forum/docs/forumruss11/a10LaruellGumilev.pdf; Victor A. Shnirelman, "The Story of a Euphemism: The Khazars in Russian Nationalist Literature," in *The World of the Khazars: New Perspectives*, ed. Peter Goldern, Haggai Ben-Shammai, and Anadrs Rona-Tas (Leiden: Brill, 2007), 358; Anton Shekhovtsov, "Aleksandr Dugin's Neo-Eurasianism; The New Right à la Russe," *Religion Compass* 3, no. 4 (2009): 703–4.

7. O'Meara, *New Culture, New Right*, 31, 43.

8. Walter Laqueur, *Fascism: Past, Present and Future* (New York: Oxford University Press, 1996), 93–100.

9. Rolf Kosiek, *Völker statt One World. Das Volk im Spiegel der Wissenschaft* (Tübingen: Grabert, 1999).

10. Alain de Benoist, "Alain de Benoist Answers Tamir Bar-On," *Journal for the Study of Radicalism* 8, no. 1 (2014): 144.

11. Roger Griffin, "Interregnum or Endgame? The Radical Right in the 'Post-Fascist' Era," *Journal of Political Ideologies* 5, no. 2 (2000): 171; Tamir Bar-On, *Rethinking the French New Right: Alternatives to Modernity* (London: Routledge, 2013), 152.

12. Pierre-André Taguieff, "Le néo-racisme différentialiste. Sur l'ambiguïté d'une évidence commune et ses effets pervers," *Langage et société* 34 (1985): 69–98; Pierre-André Taguieff, *Sur la Nouvelle Droite. Jalons d'une analyse critique* (Paris: Descartes et Cia, 1994); Alberto Spektorowski, "The French New Right: Differentialism and the Idea of Ethnophilian Exclusionism," *Polity* 33, no. 2 (2000): 283–303; Alberto Spektorowski, "Ethnoregionalism, Multicultural Nationalism and the Idea of the European Third Way," *Studies in Ethnicity and Nationalism* 7, no. 3 (2007): 45–63.

13. Ferdinand Tönnies, *Gemeinschaft und Gesellschaft. Abhandlung des Communismus und des Socialismus als empirischer Culturformen* (Leipzig: Fues, 1887); Rolf Kosiek, "Die Wirklichkeit des Volken in der modernen Welt," in *Muktikultopia: Gedanken zur multikulturellen Gesellschaft*, ed. Stefan Ulbrich (Vilsbiburg: Arun, 1991), 135; Alice Brauner-Orthen, *Die neue Rechte in Deutschland: Antidemokratische und rassistische Tendenzen* (Opladen: Leske und Budrich, 2001), 49–50; Jan Herman Brinks, "Germany's New Right," in *Nationalist Myths and the Modern Media: Contested Identities in the Age of Globalisation*, ed. Jan Herman Brinks (New York: I.B. Tauris, 2005), 125, 128–29; Richard Wolin, *The Seduction of Unreason: The Intellectual Romance with Fascism from Nietzsche to Postmodernism* (Princeton, NJ: Princeton University Press, 2004), 271.

14. Tudor, "The Philosophy of Identity," 97.

15. Alain de Benoist and Tomislav Sunic, "Gemeinschaft and Gesellschaft: A Sociological View of the Decay of Modern Society," *Mankind Quarterly* 34 (1994): 261–70, https://archive.org/details/GemeinschaftAndGesellschaft.

16. O'Meara, *New Culture, New Right,* 228.

17. Charles Lindholm and José Pedro Zúquete, *The Struggle for the World: Liberation Movements in the 21st Century* (Stanford, CA: Stanford University Press, 2010), 64 (quote); A. N. Savel'ev, *Obraz vraga: Rasologiia i politicheskaia antropologiia*, 2nd ed. (Moscow: Belye Al'vy, 2010), 65–66.

18. Griffin, "Interregnum or Endgame?," 168; Bar-On, *Rethinking the French New Right*, 141, 144–56.

19. Tamir Bar-On, "Fascism to the Nouvelle Droite: The Quest for Pan-European Empire," in *Varieties of Right-Wing Extremism in Europe*, ed. Andrea Mammone, Emmanuel Godin, and Brian Jenkins (London: Routledge, 2013), 79; Raphael Schlembach, "Alain de Benoist's Anti-Political Philosophy Beyond Left and Right: Non-Emancipatory Responses to Globalisation and Crisis," Centre for the Study of Social and Global Justice, University of Nottingham, Working Paper No. 22 (2013), 11.

20. Tudor, "The Philosophy of Identity," 85.

21. Robert J. Antonio, "After Postmodernism: Reactionary Tribalism," *American Journal of Sociology* 106, no. 1 (2000): 51; Bar-On, *Rethinking the French New Right*, 145–46, 150, 170.

22. de Benoist and Sunic, "Gemeinschaft and Gesellschaft." For de Benoist's attempt to qualify his use of the ethnos concept, see de Benoist, "Alain de Benoist Answers Tamir Bar-On." Indeed, even the German term *Volk*, which would also seem to provide an alternative to "nation" unencumbered by any nation-state associations, does not always convey the full organic sense of the more exotic ethnos, as can be seen in the demand of one New Right ideologue in Germany for the "Weiterentwicklung des deutschen Volkes als *Ethnos*" rather than a nation-*Gesellschaft* (Christian Böttger, *Ethnos. Der Nebel um den Volksbegriff*

[Schnellbach: Lindenbaum Verlag, 2014], 10, emph. original); see also Pierre Krebs, *Das Thule-Seminar: Geistesgegenwart der Zukunft in der Morgenröte des Ethnos* (Horn: Burkhart Weeke Verlag, 1994).

23. For comprehensive considerations of Gumilev's thinking, see: Mark Bassin, *The Gumilev Mystique: Biopolitics, Eurasianism, and the Construction of Community in Modern Russia* (Ithaca, NY: Cornell University Press, 2016); S. S. Beliakov, *Gumilev syn Gumileva* (Moscow: Astrel', 2012); S. B. Lavrov, *Lev Gumilev: Sud'ba i idei* (Moscow: Svarog i K, 2000); S. G. Pavochka, *L. N. Gumilev: Istoki i sushchnost'* (Grodno: IGAU, 2011).

24. On the history of the *sliianie* concept, see Gerhard Simon, *Nationalism and Policy toward the Nationalities in the Soviet Union: From Totalitarian Dictatorship to Post-Stalinist Society* (Boulder, CO: Westview, 1991).

25. On the resonances between essentialist conceptions of nationality in Stalinist Russia and prewar Germany, see V. A. Tishkov, "Post-Soviet Nationalism," in *Europe's New Nationalism: States and Minorities in Conflict*, ed. Richard Caplan and John Feffer (Oxford: Oxford University Press, 1996), 27; Yuri Slezkine, "N. Ia. Marr and the National Origins of Soviet Ethnogenetics," *Slavic Review* 55, no. 4 (1996): 853; Victor A. Shnirelman, "Politics of Ethnogenesis in the USSR and After," *Bulletin of the National Museum of Ethnology* 30, no. 1 (2005): 105.

26. Terry L. Thompson, *Ideology and Policy: The Political Uses of Doctrine in the Soviet Union* (London: Routledge, 1989), 73, 76–77.

27. L. N. Gumilev, "Istoriko-filosofskie trudy kniazia N. S. Trubetskogo (zametki poslednego evraziitsa)," in *Istoriia. Kul'tura. Iazyk*, ed. V. M. Zhivov (Moscow: ProgressUnivers, 1995), 49.

28. L. N. Gumilev and V. Iu. Ermolaev. "Gore ot illiuzii," in *Ritmy Evrazii* (Moscow: Ekopros, 1993), 182.

29. Gumilev and Ermolaev, "Gore ot illiuzii."

30. L. N. Gumilev, "'Ia, russkii chelovek, vsiu zhizn' zashchishchaiu tatar ot klevety,'" in *Chernaia Legenda: Druz'ia i nedrugi Velikoi stepi* (Moscow: Ekopross, 1994), 261.

31. L. N. Gumilev, *Etnogenez i biosfera zemli*, 2nd ed. (Leningrad: Iz-vo Lenin. Gos. Un-ta, 1989), 305; Gumilev, "'Ia, russkii chelovek."

32. L. N. Gumilev and K. P. Ivanov, "Etnicheskie protsessy: Dva podkhoda k izucheniiu," *Sotsiologicheskie Issledovaniia* 1 (1992): 54; L. N. Gumilev, "Nikakoi mistiki," in *Chtoby svecha ne pogasla : Sbornik esse, interv'iu, stikhotvorenii, perevodov*, ed. E. M. Goncharova. (Moscow: Airis Press, 2003), 51–68.

33. Iu. V. Bromlei, *Ocherki teorii etnosa* (Moscow: Nauka, 1983); S. Ia. Kozlov, *Akademik Iu. V. Bromlei i otechestvennaia etnologiia, 1969–1990-e gody* (Moscow: Nauka, 2003); V. R. Filippov, *"Sovetskaia teoriia etnosa:" Istoricheskii ocherk* (Moscow: Inst. Afriki RAN, 2010); Emma Gerstein, *Moscow Memoirs*, trans. J. Crowfoot (London: Harvill Press, 2004). In fact, there were many similarities between Bromlei's and Gumilev's conceptions of ethnos; see Bassin, *The Gumilev Mystique*, and K. P. Ivanov, "Vzgliady na etnografiiu ili est' li v sovetskoi nauke dva ucheniia ob etnose," *Izvestiia Vsesoiuznogo Geograficheskogo Obshchestva* 117, no. 3 (1985): 232–38.

34. For example, S. I. Bruk and N. N. Cheboksarov, "Metaetnicheskie obshchnosti," *Rasy i Narody. Ezhegodnik* 6 (1976): 15–41.

35. L. N. Gumilev, *Konets i vnov' nachalo: Populiarnye lektsii po narodovedeniiu* (Moscow: Rol'f, 2001), 24; L. N. Gumilev, "Glavnomu redaktoru zhurnala *Kommunist* R. I. Kosolapovu [1982]," in *Vspominaia L. N. Gumileva. Vospominaniia. Publikatsii. Issledovaniia*, ed. V. N. Voronovich and M. G. Kozyreva (St. Petersburg: Iz-vo "Rostok," 2003), 233.

36. Gumilev and Ivanov, "Etnicheskie protsessy," 51.

37. L. N. Gumilev, "Korni nashego rodstva," *Izvestiia*, April 13, 1988; Gumilev, *Etnogenez i biosfera zemli*, 145 (quote), 22, 142–45; Gumilev, "'Ia, russkii chelovek," 254; Gumilev and Ermolaev, "Gore ot illiuzii," 178.

38. Helmut Wolter, *Volk im Aufstieg: Neue Ergebnisse der Volksbiologie Grossdeutsch-lands* (Leipzig: Eichblatt, 1940); Ilse Schwidetzky, *Grundzüge der Völkerbiologie* (Stuttgart: Ferdinand Enke Verlag, 1950); Ilse Schwidetzky, ed., *Die neue Rassenkunde* (Stuttgart: Gustav Fischer Verlag, 1962); Ilse Schwidetzky, *Rassen und Rassenbildung beim Menschen* (Stuttgart-New York: Fischer, 1979). In the 1930s, Ilse Schwidetzky was the assistant to Egon Freiherr von Eickstedt, one of the leading racial theorists in Nazi Germany. After the war, she worked in the Department of Anthropology at Mainz University, where she continued to publish actively on issues of *Rassenkunde*. Schwidetzky's work is widely cited in the literature of the New Right (Jonathan Benthall, "The Schwidetzky Affair," in *The Best of Anthropology Today*, ed. Jonathan Benthall, (London: Routledge, 2002), 441–4; Pierre Krebs, *Fighting for the Essence: Western Ethnosuicide or European Renaissance?* trans. Aleksandr Jacob (London: Arktos, 2012), 21, 85). For critical studies, see Michael Billig, *Die rassistische Internationale: Zur Renaissance der Rassenlehre in der modernen Psychologie* (Frankfurt: Neue Kritik, 1981); and Patrick Moreau, "Die neue Religion der Rasse: Der Biologismus und die neue kollektive Ethik der Neuen Rechten in Frankreich und Deutschland," in *Neokonservative und Neue Rechte: Der Angriff gegen Sozialstaat und liberale Demokratie in den Vereinigten Staaten, Westeuropa und der Bundesrepublik*, ed. Iring Fetscher (Munich: Beck, 1983), 122–62.

39. Schwidetzky, *Grundzüge der Völkerbiologie*, 55; Kosiek, "Die Wirklichkeit des Volken," 117–18, 121; Krebs, *Fighting for the Essence*, 22.

40. Krebs, *Fighting for the Essence*, 14, 23. Also see Tudor, "The Philosophy of Identity," 83–112.

41. Tudor, "The Philosophy of Identity," 90 (quote), 91–92.

42. O'Meara, *New Culture, New Right*, 43–44.

43. Ludwig Von Bertalanffy, *General System Theory: Foundations, Development, Applications.* (New York: George Braziller, 1968); Kosiek, "Die Wirklichkeit des Volken," 112–15.

44. Konrad Lorenz, *Das sogenannte Böse. Zur Naturgeschichte der Aggression* (Vienna: G. Borotha-Schoeler, 1963); Konrad Lorenz, *Der Abbau des Menschlichen* (Munich: Piper, 1983);

Irenäus Eibl-Eibesfeldt, *Ethnology: The Biology of Behavior* (New York: Holt, Rinehart & Winston, 1970); Irenäus Eibl-Eibesfeldt, *Der vorprogrammierte Mensch. Das Ererbte als bestimminder Faktor im menschlichen Verhalten* (Munchen: Deutscher Taschenbuchverlag, 1984); Michael Lausberg, "Irinäus Eibl-Eibesfeldt: Steigbügelhalter für die extreme Rechte?" *Tabularasa* 100 (2014), http://www.tabularasa-jena.de/artikel/artikel_5607/. A Nobel Prize-winning scientist, Konrad Lorenz was a member of the Nazi Party from 1938 to 1945. In the 1960s, he belonged to the editorial board of the French New Right journal *Nouvelle École* (Lindholm and Zúquete, *The Struggle for the World*, 61, 192n).

45. Michael Billig, *Die rassistische Internationale: Zur Renaissance der Rassenlehre in der modernen Psychologie* (Frankfurt: Neue Kritik, 1981), 145; Kosiek, "Die Wirklichkeit des Volken," 124; Kosiek, *Völker statt One World*, 218; Brauner-Orthen, *Die neue Rechte in Deutschland*, 51–52.

46. Wolin, *The Seduction of Unreason*, 265–68; Bar-On, *Rethinking the French New Right*, 148; O'Meara, *New Culture, New Right*, 28; Schlembach, "Alain de Benoist's Anti-Political Philosophy," 10–11.

47. Alain de Benoist, "Confronting Globalization, " *Telos* 108 (1996): 26; Alain de Benoist,"What is Racism?" *Telos* 114 (1999): 11–48; Arthur Verslius and Alain de Benoist, "A Conversation with Alain de Benoist," *Journal for the Study of Radicalism* 8, no. 2 (2014): 96 (quote).

48. Michael O'Meara, "Benoist's Pluriversuman Ethnonationalist Critique," New RightAusNZ, March 29, 2006, accessed October 23, 2014, http://www.newrightausnz.com/2006/03/29/benoists-pluriversuman-ethnonationalist-critique-by-michael-omeara/.

49. de Benoist and Sunic, "Gemeinschaft and Gesellschaft"; Kochanek, *Die russisch-nationale Rechte,* 219; Alain de Benoist and Charles Champetier, "Manifesto of the French New Right in the Year 2000," accessed October 18, 2014, https://archive.org/details/ManifestoOf-TheFrenchNewRightInTheYear2000; Alain de Benoist and Brian Sylvian, "European Son: An Interview with Alain de Benoist," *Occidental Quarterly* 5, no. 3 (2005): 16–17, https://http://www.toqonline.com/archives/v5n3/53-bs-debenoist.pdf; Verslius and de Benoist, "A Conversation with Alain de Benoist," 96 (quote).

50. de Benoist and Champetier, "Manifesto of the French New Right in the Year 2000"; de Benoist and Sylvian, "European Son."

51. Friedrich Ratzel, *Der Lebensraum: Eine biogeographische Studie* (Tübingen: Laupp'sche Buchhandlung, 1901); R. Walther Darré, "Blut und Boden als Lebensgrundlagen der nordischer Rasse [1930]," in *Um Blut und Boden: Reden und Aufsätze* (Munich: Zentralverlag der NSDAP, 17–29); Woodruff D. Smith, "Friedrich Ratzel and the Origin of *Lebensraum,*" *German Studies Review* 3 (1980): 51–68; Gustavo Corni and Horst Gies, *"Blut und Boden": Rassenideologie und Agrarpolitik im Staat Hitlers* (Idstein: Schultz-Kirchner Verlag, 1994).

52. Moreau, "Die neue Religion," 124; Irenäus Eibl-Eibesfeldt, *Wider die Misstrauensgesellschaft : Streitschrift für eine bessere Zukunft,* 2nd ed. (Munich: Piper, 1995), 32, 130, 157; Kochanek, *Die russisch-nationale Rechte,* 216, 219; Schlembach, "Alain de Benoist's Anti-Political Philosophy," 11.

53. Krebs, *Fighting for the Essence,* 85–86. Strikingly, this author characterizes this attachment using the expression *le Sang et le Sol*—that is, Blood and Soil (Pierre Krebs, "L'avènement de l'ethno-socialisme," EURO-SYNERGIES, 2013, accessed November 7, 2014, http://euro-synergies.hautetfort.com/archive/2013/03/22/p-krebs-l-avenement-de-l- ethno-socialisme.html.)

54. Gert Waldmann, "Verhaltensforschung und Politik," in *Europäischer Nationalismus ist Fortschritt* (Hamburg: Verlag Deutsch-Europäischer Studien, 1973), 17-47; Alberto Spektorowski, "The New Right: Ethno-Regionalism, Ethno-Pluralism and the Emergence of a Neo-Fascist 'Third Way,'" *Journal of Political Ideologies* 8, no. 1 (2003): 115.

55. Lariuel', "Opyt sravnitel'nogo analiza," 238.

56. E. P. Aksenova and M. A. Vasilev, "Problemy etnogonii slavianstva i ego vetvei v akademicheskikh diskusiiakh rubezha 1930–1940-kh godov," *Slavianovedenie* 2 (1993): 88; Slezkine, "N. Ia. Marr," 847; Francine Hirsch, *Empire of Nations: Ethnographic Knowledge and the Making of the Soviet Union* (Ithaca, NY: Cornell University Press, 2004), 216–17, 231–72.

57. Gumilev, "'Ia, russkii chelovek," 271.

58. Gumilev, *Etnogenez i biosfera zemli,* 20; L. N. Gumilev, "Zakony vremeni," *Literaturnoe Obozrenie* 3 (1990): 8; Gumilev, "'Ia, russkii chelovek," 277.

59. Gumilev, *Konets i vnov' nachalo.*; L. N. Gumilev, "Chtoby svecha ne pogasla," 45; L. N. Gumilev, "O termine etnos," in *Etnosfera: Istoriia liudei i istoriia prirody* (Moscow: Ekopros, 2004 [1967]), 40, 41.

60. L. N. Gumilev and A. M. Panchenko, *Chtoby svecha ne pogasla : Dialog* (Leningrad: Sovetskii Pisatel', 1990), 6.

61. Gumilev, *Etnogenez i biosfera zemli,* 226; Gumilev, *Konets i vnov' nachalo,* 24.

62. L. N. Gumilev, "Letter to the Editors of *Izvestiya Vsesoyuznogo Geograficheskogo Obshchestva,*" *Soviet Geography: Review and Translation* 15, no. 6 (1974): 376; Gumilev, *Etnogenez i biosfera zemli,* 227.

63. Gumilev, *Etnogenez i biosfera zemli,* 90; Gumilev, "'Ia, russkii chelovek," 258.

64. Gumilev, *Etnogenez i biosfera zemli,* 225–26.

65. Gumilev, *Etnogenez i biosfera zemli,* 90.

66. Gumilev, *Etnogenez i biosfera zemli,* 227 (quote), 85, 87–88.

67. Quoted in Andrei Rogachevskii, "Lev Gumilev i evreiskii vopros (po lichnym vospominaniiam)," *Solnechnoe spletenie* 18/19 (2001): 363. Although these comments were made in the early 1980s, Gumilev had expressed himself in a similar spirit half a century earlier, in the 1930s; see Gerstein, *Moscow Memoirs*, 230.

68. Gumilev, *Etnogenez i biosfera zemli*, 89.

69. L. Bertalanfi, *Obshchaia teoriia sistem–krticheskii obzor* (Moscow: Progress, 1969); Gumilev, *Etnogenez i biosfera zemli*, 100, 131; V. Iu. Ermolaev, "Samoorganizatsiia v prirode i etnogenez," *Izvestiia Vsesoiuznogo Geograficheskogo Obshchestva* 122, no. 1 (1990): 26; Mikhail Kuz'min, "Social Genetics and Organizational Science," in *Aleksandr Bogdanov and the Origins of Systems Thinking in Russia*, ed. John Biggart, Peter Dudley, and Francis King (Aldershot: Ashgate, 1998), 281, 284, 291–92.

70. L. N. Gumilev, "On the Anthropogenic Factor in Landscape Formation," *Soviet Geography* 9 (1968): 601; L. N. Gumilev, "Mongoly i merkity v XII veke," *Studia orientalla et Antiqua* 416 (1977), accessed April 23, 2007, http://gumilevica.kulichki.com/articles/Article78.htm; Gumilev, *Etnogenez i biosfera zemli*, 226–27, 295, 309. Lobashev maintained that while behavioral patterns themselves were not genetically inscribed or inherited in animal populations, and had to be taught afresh to each new generation, a certain predisposition to learning them—what he called *signal'naia nasledstvennost'*—did indeed form a part of an organism's genetic inheritance (M. E. Lobashev, "Signal'naia nasledstvennost'," in *Issledovaniia po genetike*, ed. M. E. Lobashev (Leningrad: Iz-vo Lenin. Gos. Un-ta, 1961); M. E. Lobashev, *Genetika* (Leningrad: Iz-vo Lenin. Gos. Un-ta, 1967). Lobashev's ideas were fundamental for Gumilev, who explained the cross-generational transfer of the ethnic "behavioral stereotype" as an example of *signal'naia nasledstvennost'*. It is extremely interesting to note that Alain de Benoist made the same argument at roughly the same time as Gumilev: "L'homme ne nait pas avec une culture (l'idée d'une culture surgissant tout armée des chromosomes est un fantasme raciste), mais *avec la faculté d'assimiler une culture*" (Alain de Benoist, *Les Idées à l'endroit* (Paris: Hallier, 1979), 93–94, emph. added, cited in Chandler Davis and Nina Godneff, "La sociobiologie et son explication de l'humanité," *Annales. Histoire, Sciences Sociales* 36, no. 4 (1981): 534). While Gumilev did not refer to Konrad Lorenz in his writings and was not necessarily aware of his work, the strong resonances between them are noted in Onoprienko (Iu. I. Onoprienko, "Analiz kontseptsii etnogeneza L. N. Gumilev s positsii sistemno-informatsionnoi metodologii," *Visnik Natsional'nogo aviatsiinogo universitetu* 2 (18) (2013): 17–25) and Dugin (A. G. Dugin, "Lev Gumilev: Nauka 'zhivoi zhizni,'" *Evrazia*, 2002, accessed February 8, 2014, http://evrazia. org/modules. php?name+News&file=article&sid=634).

71. Gumilev, "'Ia, russkii chelovek," 131, 258, 304.

72. L. N. Gumilev, "'Menia nazyvaiut evraziitsem,'" *Nash Sovremennik* 1 (1991): 133; Gumilev, *Konets i vnov' nachalo*, 182–83.

73. Mark Bassin, "Nurture *is* Nature: Lev Gumilev and the Ecology of Ethnicity," *Slavic Review* 68, no. 4 (2009): 872–97.

74. Mark Bassin, "Nationhood, Natural Region, *Mestorazvitie*: Environmentalist Discourses in Classical Eurasianism," in *Space, Place and Power in Modern Russia: Essays in the New Spatial History*, ed. Mark Bassin, Chris Ely, and Melissa Stockdale (De Kalb, IL: Northern Illinois University Press, 2010), 54–55, 58, 60, 62.

75. Gumilev, *Etnogenez i biosfera zemli*, 180.

76. Bassin, "Nurture *is* Nature," 887.

77. Gumilev and Ivanov, "Etnicheskie protsessy," 54–55.

78. Laqueur, *Fascism: Past, Present and Future*, 99; Rasma Karklins, "Ethno-Pluralism: Panacea for East Central Europe?" *Nationalities Papers* 28, no. 2 (2000): 219–41; Spektorowski, "The New Right: Ethno-Regionalism"; Spektorowski, "Ethnoregionalism, Multicultural Nationalism," 49.

79. de Benoist and Champetier, "Manifesto of the French New Right in the Year 2000."

80. Antonio, "After Postmodernism," 63 (quote); Spektorowski, "The New Right: Ethno-Regionalism," 118.

81. Quoted in Tudor, "The Philosophy of Identity," 87.

82. Tudor, "The Philosophy of Identity," 88.

83. Eibl-Eibesfeldt, *Wider die Misstrauensgesellschaft*, 157, quoted in Krebs, *Fighting for the Essence*, 87; Lausberg, "Irinäus Eibl-Eibesfeldt: Steigbügelhalter für die extreme Rechte?"

84. Krebs, *Fighting for the Essence*, 86.

85. L. N. Gumilev, "Etnogenez i etnosfera," *Priroda* 2 (1970): 47; L. N. Gumilev, "G. E. Grumm-Grzhimailo i rozhdenie nauki ob etnogeneze," *Priroda* 5 (1976): 121, 97–98; Gumilev, *Etnogenez i biosfera zemli*, 41, 48, 51, 169.

86. L. N. Gumilev, "Etnos, istoriia, kul'tura," *Dekorativnoe Iskusstvo SSSR* 5 (1989): 33.

87. L. N. Gumilev, "Pis'mo v radaktsiiu 'Voprosov filosofii,'" *Voprosy Filosofii* 5 (1989): 157.

88. Gumilev and Ivanov, "Etnicheskie protsessy," 54–56; L. N. Gumilev, "Chernaia Legenda," in *Chernaia Legenda: Druz'ia i nedrugi Velikoi stepi* (Moscow: Ekopros, 1994), 130–31 (quote).

Gumilev, "'Ia, russkii chelovek," 267; Gumilev, "Istoriko-filosofskie trudy kniazia," 36.

89. Gumilev, *Etnogenez i biosfera zemli*, 133–34. For a somewhat different geographical arrangement of the same ethnic groups, see Gumilev, *Konets i vnov' nachalo*, 292.

90. Gumilev, *Etnogenez i biosfera zemli*, 302.

91. Guillaume Faye, *Why We Fight: Manifesto of the European Resistance* (London: Arktos, 2011); Irina Filatova, "The Awkward Issue: Some Comments on the South African Debate on Nation-Building and Ethnicity," in *Democratic Nation-Building in South Africa*, ed. Nic Rhodie and Ian Liebenberg (Pretoria: Human Sciences Research Council, 1994), 134, 139, 156; Bar-On, *Rethinking the French New Right*, 196; Tudor, "The Philosophy of Identity," 86. During the Nazi period, the *Schicksalsgemeinschaft* concept was used primarily in reference to an individual ethnos. See Paul Jackson, "The New Age," in *World Fascism. A Historical Encyclopedia*, ed. Cyprian P. Blamires and Paul Jackson, vol. 2 (Santa Barbara, CA: ABC-Clio, 2006), 464; and Wolin, *The Seduction of Unreason*, 140–41.

92. Oswald Spengler, *Der Untergang des Abendlandes: Umrisse einer Morphologie der Weltgeschichte*, 2 vols. (Vienna: Braumüller, C.H. Beck, 1918–1923); Samuel P. Huntington, *The Clash of Civilizations and the Remaking of World Order* (London: Simon and Schuster, 1996).

93. Laqueur, *Fascism: Past, Present and Future*, 93.

94. Lausberg, "Irinäus Eibl-Eibesfeldt: Steigbügelhalter für die extreme Rechte?"; Tudor, "The Philosophy of Identity," 89, 92.

95. de Benoist and Champetier, "Manifesto of the French New Right in the Year 2000."

96. Spektorowski, "The New Right: Ethno-Regionalism," 112, 124; Spektorowski, "Ethnoregionalism, Multicultural Nationalism," 45–63.

97. O'Meara, *New Culture, New Right*, 231–35; Tudor, "The Philosophy of Identity," 102–3.

98. O'Meara, *New Culture, New Right*, 234.

99. Tudor, "The Philosophy of Identity," 106, 112.

100. The author of this particular project is Guillaume Faye. Bar-On, *Rethinking the French New Right*, 187–200; Michael O'Meara, *Guillaume Faye and the Battle of Europe* (London: Arktos, 2013), 61 (quote); O'Meara, *New Culture, New Right*, 235–44.

101. V. A. Michurin, "Slovar' poniatii i terminov teorii etnogeneza L. N. Gumileva," in *Etnosfera: Istoriia liudei i istoriia prirody* (Moscow: AST, 2004), 548.

102. See the charts in Gumilev, *Konets i vnov' nachalo*, 33, 35.

103. Gumilev, *Etnogenez i biosfera zemli*, 481; Michurin, "Slovar' poniatii," 564.

104. Gumilev and Ivanov, "Etnicheskie protsessy," 53.

105. Gumilev referred frequently to Spengler (his widow remarked that he had even fancied himself a sort of "Russian Spengler"), but in fact he had more in common with the Russian tradition of civilizational discourse, in particular as developed by Nikolai Danilevskii, Konstantin Leont'ev, and especially Nikolai Trubetskoi (Gumilev, *Etnogenez i biosfera zemli*, 28, 69, 121, 131, 147, 149, 244, 358n; Gumilev, "Etnos, istoriia, kul'tura," 30; L. N. Gumilev, "Iskat' to, chto verno," *Sovetskaia Literatura* 1 (1990): 72–76, accessed February 25, 2014, http://gumilevica.kulichki.net/articles/Article06.htm). See also S. S. Beliakov, *Gumilev syn Gumileva* (Moscow: Astrel', 2012), 144–46ff; P. Shitikhin, "Sravnitel'nyi analiz istoriosofskikh vzgliadov N. Ia. Danilevskogo i L. N. Gumileva" (PhD diss., Moskovskaia Dukhovnaia Akademiia, 2012). Gumilev wrote an introductory essay to a major post-Soviet collection of Trubetskoi's writings (Gumilev, "Istoriko-filosofskie trudy kniazia," 31–54).

106. Gumilev and Panchenko, *Chtoby svecha ne pogasla : Dialog*, 8.

107. Gumilev, *Etnogenez i biosfera zemli*, 109, 89, 479; Marlène Laruelle, "Lev Nikolaevic Gumilev (1912–1992): biologisme et eurasisme dans la penseé russe," *Revue des Études Slaves* 72, no. 1–2 (2000): 179.

108. Verslius and de Benoist, "A Conversation with Alain de Benoist," 83–84; Robert Steuckers, "Foundations of Russian Nationalism," Countercurrents, April 2014, accessed November 26, 2014, http:// www.counter-currents.com/2014/04/ foundations-of-russian-nationalism-2/.

109. Steuckers, "Foundations of Russian Nationalism." See also the article on Gumilev at the *Metapedia* website (the NewRight version of *Wikipedia*): "Lev Gumilev," Metapedia, accessed December 1, 2014, http://en.metapedia.org/wiki/Lev_ Gumilev.

110. de Benoist, *Mémoire vive*, 244; Bar-On, *Rethinking the French New Right*, 204–5.

111. Böttger, *Ethnos*, 216.

112. All of the quotations in this paragraph are from Joakim Andersen, "Lev Gumilev och etnogenesis," Motpol. 2010, accessed November 4, 2014, http://www.motpol.nu/ oskorei/2010/09/11/lev-gumilev-och-etnogenesis/.

113. Rafal Soborski, *Ideology in a Global Age: Continuity and Change* (New York: Palgrave, 2013), 132.

114. O'Meara, *New Culture, New Right*, 227.

115. On the revolutionary dimension of the New Right, see Lindholm and Zúquete, *The Struggle for the World*, 52.

116. Alberto Spektorowski, "Ethnoregionalism: The Intellectual New Right and the Lega Nord," *Global Review of Ethnopolitics* 2, no. 3 (2003): 55, 58–59; Spektorowski, "The New Right: Ethno-Regionalism," 121–23.

117. Alain de Benoist, "Nationalisme: phénoménologie et critique," in *Critiques— Théoriques*, 85–88 (Lausanne: L'Age d'Homme, 2002), 85-88; Spektorowski, "The New Right: Ethno-Regionalism," 121; O'Meara, *New Culture, New Right*, 48–49; Tudor, "The Philosophy of Identity," 86 (quote), 101–2.

118. Gumilev, "Korni nashego rodstva," 3; L. N. Gumilev, "Chelovechnost' prevyshe vsego," *Izvestiia*, June 24, 1989, accessed March 19, 2014, http://gumilevica.kulichki.net/articles/Article45.htm; Gumilev, "'Ia, russkii chelovek," 261; Lavrov, *Lev Gumilev*, 354.

119. L. N. Gumilev, "Kakoi ia demokrat? Ia staryi soldat!" Nevzorov, 1991, accessed April 17, 2014, http://nevzorov.tv/2012/03/lev-gumilyov-kakoj-ya-demokrat-ya-starij-soldat/.

120. Gumilev, *Etnogenez i biosfera zemli*, 18, 49, 50.

121. L. N. Gumilev, "On the Subject of the 'Unified Geography' (Landscape and Etnos, VI)," *Soviet Geography: Review and Translation* 9, no. 1 (1968): 40; Gumilev, *Etnogenez i biosfera zemli*, 18, 21, 51, 175; Gumilev, "O termine etnos," 38–39.

122. L. N. Gumilev, "Rol' klimaticheskikh kolebanii v istorii narodov stepnoi zony Evrazii," *Istoriia SSSR* 1 (1967): 55; Gumilev, "On the Subject of the 'Unified Geography,'" 36.

123. L. N. Gumilev, "Biosfera i impul'sy soznaniia," *Priroda* 12 (1978): 103 ; Gumilev, "'Ia, russkii chelovek," 271; L. N. Gumilev, "My absoliutno samobytny," *Nevskoe Vremia*, August 12, 1992, accessed March 21, 2014, http://gumilevica.kulichki.net/articles/Article52.htm, 51; L. N .Gumilev and D. M. Balashov. "V kakoe vremia my zhivem?" in *Ritmy Evrazii: Epokhi i tsvilizatsiia* (Moscow: Ekopros, 1993), 135.

124. Kosiek, "Die Wirklichkeit des Volken," 135; de Benoist and Sunic, "Gemeinschaft and Gesellschaft: A Sociological View of the Decay of Modern Society," *Mankind Quarterly* 34 (1994): 261–70, accessed October 22, 2014, https://archive.org/details/GemeinschaftAndGesellschaft; Böttger, *Ethnos*, 19.

125. Bambi Ceuppens and Peter Geschiere, "Autochthony: Local or Global? New Modes in the Struggle over Citizenship and Belonging in Africa and Europe," *Annual Review of Anthropology* 34 (2005): 397.

126. Kosiek, "Die Wirklichkeit des Volken," 120.

127. Eibl-Eibesfeldt, *Wider die Misstrauensgesellschaft,* 130, cited in Lausberg, "Irinäus Eibl-Eibesfeldt: Steigbügelhalter für die extreme Rechte?" See also Krebs, *Fighting for the Essence,* 87–88.

128. Kosiek, "Die Wirklichkeit des Volken," 111; de Benoist and Champetier, "Manifesto of the French New Right in the Year 2000"; Verslius and de Benoist, "A Conversation with Alain de Benoist," 102.

129. de Benoist and Sylvian, "European Son: An Interview with Alain de Benoist"; Spektorowski, "Ethnoregionalism, Multicultural Nationalism," 40.

130. Spektorowski, "Ethnoregionalism, Multicultural Nationalism," 49; Bar-On, *Rethinking the French New Right,* 191.

131. Gumilev, "Iskat' to, chto verno," 72–76. He was not consistent on the point, however, and elsewhere dismissed the idea of reservations in the Soviet Union (Gumilev, "Chelovechnost' prevyshe vsego"); L. N. Gumilev and A. P. Okladnikov, "Fenomen kul'tury malykh narodov Severa," *Dekorativnoe Iskusstvo* 8 (1982): 23–28, accessed May 17, 2014, http://gumilevica.kulichki.net/ articles/Article102.htm).

132. Mark Bassin, "Narrating Kulikovo: Lev Gumilev, Russian Nationalists, and the Troubled Emergence of Neo-Eurasianism," in *Between Europe and Asia: The Origins, Theories and Legacies of Russian Eurasianism*, ed. Mark Bassin, Marlene Laruelle, and Sergey Glebov (Pittsburgh, PA: University of Pittsburgh Press, 2015), 179-81.

133. Mark Bassin, "Russia between Europe and Asia: The Ideological Construction of Geographical Space," *Slavic Review* 50, no. 1 (1991): 1–17.

134. Gumilev, "Istoriko-filosofskie trudy kniazia."

135. O'Meara, *New Culture, New Right*, 210–25. Gumilev's divergent views on Europe are noted by at least some New Right ideologues. See the discussion in Robert Steuckers, "Answers to the Questions of Pavel Tulaev," *Robert Steuckers* (blog), February 2014, accessed January 7, 2014, http://robertsteuckers.blogspot.co.uk/2014/02/answers-to-questions-of-pavel-tulaev.html.

136. de Benoist, "What is Racism?," 18; Schlembach, "Alain de Benoist's Anti-Political Philosophy," 7–8.

137. de Benoist and Champetier, "Manifesto of the French New Right in the Year 2000."

138. Gumilev, "'Menia nazyvaiut evraziitsem,'" 140.

139. Gumilev, "'Menia nazyvaiut evraziitsem,'" 140; Gumilev, "My absoliutno samobytny"; L. N. Gumilev, *Drevniaia Rus' i velikaia step'* (Moscow: Airis, 2004), 22; Gumilev and Ivanov, "Etnicheskie protsessy," 56 (quotes); Lavrov, *Lev Gumilev: Sud'ba i idei*, 352.

140. L. N. Gumilev, "Gde ona, strana Khazariia?" *Nedelia* 24, June 7–13, 1964, 9.

141. L. N. Gumilev, "'Publikatsiia moikh rabot blokiruiutsia.' Kto i pochemu otvergal L. N. Gumilevu," in *Vspominaia L. N. Gumileva. Vospominaniia. Publikatsii. Issledovaniia*, ed. V. N. Voronovich and M. G. Kozyreva (St. Petersburg: Iz-vo "Rostok," 2003), 247, 234.

142. L. N. Gumilev, "Sila epokhi." *Dekorativnoe Iskusstvo SSSR* 7 (1989): 35.

143. Gumilev "Chtoby svecha ne pogasla," 13.

144. John Sharp, "The Roots and Development of Volkekunde in South Africa," *Journal of South African Studies* 8, no. 1 (1981): 16–36; Robert Gordon, "Apartheid's Anthropologists: The Genealogy of Afrikaner Anthropology," *American Ethnologist* 15, no. 3 (1988): 535–53.

145. Peter Skalnik, "Union soviétique—Afrique du Sud: Les 'théories' d l'*etnos*,'" *Cahiers d'Etudes Africaines* 28, no. 2 (1988): 157–76; Filatova, "The Awkward Issue," 52–54; John Sharp, "Anthropology in South Africa," in *The Best of Anthropology Today*, ed. Jonathan Benthall (London: Routledge, 2002), 245–53; Alan G. Morris, "Biological Anthropology at the Southern Tip of Africa: Carrying European Baggage in an African Context," *Current Anthropology* 53 (Supplement 5) (2012): S152 (quote).

10. The Yuzhinskii Circle

A previous version of the chapter was published as "The Iuzhinsky Circle: Far-Right Metaphysics in the Soviet Underground and Its Legacy Today," *Russian Review* 75, no. 4 (2015): 563–80. I am grateful to *Russian Review* for allowing me to republish a revised version of the article.

1. The Yuzhinskii circle is discussed in Andreas Umland and A. James Gregor's debate, "Dugin Not a Fascist?" *Erwägen Wissen Ethik* 16, no. 4 (2005); Andreas Umland and Anton Shekhovtsov, "Is Dugin a Traditionalist? 'Neo-Eurasianism' and Perennial Philosophy," *Russian Review* 68 (October 2009), 662–78; Stephen Shenfield, *Russian Fascism: Traditions, Tendencies, Movements* (Armonk, NY: M.E. Sharpe, 2001); and Mark Sedgwick, *Against the Modern World: Traditionalism and the Secret Intellectual History of the Twentieth Century* (New York: Oxford University Press, 2004).

2. I am grateful to the two anonymous reviewers for their comments on this subject, and to Michael Hagemeister, Birgit Menzel, and Peter Rollberg for their comments on previous versions of the article.

3. Miriam Dobson, *Khrushchev's Cold Summer: Gulag Returnees, Crime, and the Fate of Reform after Stalin* (Ithaca, NY: Cornell University Press, 2011).

4. Quoted in Stephen F. Cohen, *The Victims Return: Survivors of the Gulag After Stalin* (London: I.B. Tauris, 2012), 57.

5. Polly Jones, *The Dilemmas of De-Stalinization: Negotiating Cultural and Social Change in the Khrushchev Era* (London: Routledge, 2006).

6. Robert Horvath, *The Legacy of Soviet Dissent: Dissidents, Democratisation and Radical Nationalism in Russia* (London: Routledge, 2005).

7. Yitzhak M. Brudny, *Reinventing Russia: Russian Nationalism and the Soviet State, 1953–1991* (Cambridge, MA: Harvard University Press, 2000).

8. Nikolai Mitrokhin, *"Russkaia partiia": Dvizhenie russkikh natsionalistov v SSSR 1953–1985 gg.* (Moscow: NLO, 2003).

9. M. Bogatyrev, "Otshel'nik: Nabroski k portretu Iu. V. Titova," *Stetoskop* 22 (1999), and Valentin Vorob'ev, "Popravki k biografii khudozhnika Iuriia Titova," http://www.yuri-titov.com/titov_titologie/titologie_ru_6.htm.

10. See "Moia Maiakovka" (2002), http://www.majakovka.artmagazine.ru/.

11. Vorob'ev, "Popravki k biografii khudozhnika Iuriia Titova."

12. Eugene Gorny, "The Negative World of Yuri Mamleyev," *Zhurnal.ru*, no date, http://www.zhurnal.ru/staff/gorny/english/mamleev.htm.

13. S. Beliaeva-Konegen, "Upyr': O proze Iuriia Mamleeva," *Strelets*, no. 3 (1992): 167–69.

14. See Dzhemal's documentary film, *Krasnyi gonorar*, broadcast on the Kul'tura channel in 2011, http://etvnet.com/tv/dokumentalnyie-filmyi-online/krasnyij-gonorar/455814/ 2011.

15. Aleksei Krizhevskii, "Barkhatnoe podpol'e: Igor Dudinskii o zhizni sovetskoi bogemy," *Russkaia zhizn'*, February 1, 2008, http://www.rulife.ru/mode/article/510.

16. More in Birgit Menzel, "Occult and Esoteric Movements in Russia from the 1960s to the 1980s," and Leonid Heller, "Away from the Globe: Occultism, Esotericism and Literature in Russia during the 1960s–1980s," in *The New Age of Russia: Occult and Esoteric Dimensions*, eds. Birgit Menzel, Michael Hagemeister, and Bernice Glatzer Rosenthal (Munich: Kubon and Sagner, 2012), 151–85 and 186–210.

17. On Gurdieff see Louis Pauwels, *Monsieur Gurdjieff: Documents, témoignages, textes et commentaires sur une société initiatique contemporaine* (Paris: Albin Michel, 1996).

18. Vladimir Kozlov and Vladimir Maikov, *Transpersonal'nyi proket: psikhologiia, antropologiia, dukhovnye traditsii* (Moscow: Transpersonal'nyi institut, 2007), vol. 2, 12.

19. Kozlov and Maikov, *Transpersonal'nyi proekt*, 13–14. More in Arkadii Rovner, *Gurdzhiev i Uspenskii* (Moscow: Sofiia, 2002).

20. Sergei Shargunov, "Iurii Mamleev: 'Eta real'nost' ne nastoiashchaia, a kakaia-to poddelka.' Sergei Shargunov pobyval v gostiakh u znamenitogo pisatelia," *Colta*, November 19, 2013, http://www.colta.ru/articles/literature/1218.

21. Ulrich Schmid, "Flowers of Evil: The Poetics of Monstrosity in Contemporary Russian Literature (Erofeev, Mamleev, Sokolov, Sorokin)," *Russian Literature* (2000): 205–21.

22. The correspondence between Aseev and Helena Roerich (Elena Rerikh) is available at "Arkhiv Aseeva," http://podelise.ru/docs/index-27664529–1.html. "Aseev Aleksandr Mikhailovich," *Rerikhovskaia enksiklopediia*, http://www.roerich-encyclopedia.nm.ru/personal/Aseev.html.

23. N. A. Toots and A. L. Rychkov, "Zabytaia istoriia," *Del'fis* 66, no. 2 (2011), http://www.delphis.ru/journal/article/zabytaya-istoriya; Eleonora Poltinnikova-Shifrin, "Mistika v nashei zhizni (glava iz budushchei knigi)," *Zhurnal-Gazeta Masterskaia*, September 2, 2012, http://club.berkovich-zametki.com/?p=1266; Eleonora Shifrin, "Protsess Dem'aiankova," *Kanal 7*, December 3, 2009, http://www.7kanal.com/article.php3?id=270886.

24. Aleksandr Dugin, "Auf, o Seele!" *Nezavisimaia gazeta*, March 27, 2003, http://www.ng.ru/kafedra/2003-03-27/3_essay.html.

25. See Vladimir Pozner's interview with Geydar Dzhemal, "Geidar Dzhemal' o sebe, 'Iushinskom krushke' i Evgenii Golovine," August 10, 2013, http://www.youtube.com/watch?v=SXxQx4K4a5U#t=1035.

26. Vladimir Dzha Guzman (Videman), *Shkola magov: Fragmenty misticheskogo dvizheniia v SSSR v 70–80 gg XX veka*, no date, http://www.guzmanmedia.com/gm2/cont.php4.

27. Author's anonymous interview with a participant of the circle's activities in the 1980s.

28. Evgenii Golovin, *Sentimental'noe beshenstvo rok-n-rolla* (Moscow: Nox, 1997).

29. Konstantin Serebrov, *Misticheskii andergraund: Germeticheskaia shkola* (Moscow: Amrita, 2002).

30. Arkadii Rovner, "G. I. Gurdieff's Influence in Russia in the 1960s–1970s," Paper presented at the international conference "The Occult in 20th-century Russia: Metaphysical Roots of Soviet Civilization," Harriman Institute/European Academy, Berlin, Germany, March 11–13, 2007, available at http://gurdjieffclub.com/en/articles-essay-arkady-rovner-g-i-gurdjieffs-influence-in-russia-in-the-1960s1970.

31. Kozlov and Maikov, *Transpersonal'nyi proekt*.

32. John Bennett, *Witness: The Autobiography of John G. Bennett* (Winnipeg: Turnstone Books, 1975). On this connection see Sedgwick, *Against the Modern World*.

33. "Geidar Dzhemal' o sebe, 'Iushinskom krushke' i Evgenii Golovine."

34. Vladimir Dzha Guzman (Videman), *Tropoi sviashchennogo kozeroga ili V poiskakh absoliutnogo tsentra* (St. Petersburg: Amfora, 2005), http://www.guzmanmedia.com/gm2/cont.php4.

35. Guzman (Videman), *Shkola magov.*

36. "Umer Evgeni Vsevolodovich Golovin," *Antikompromat*, republished on *LJR*, October 29, 2010, http://lj.rossia.org/users/anticompromat/1028836.html.

37. "Geidar Dzhemal' o sebe, 'Iushinskom krushke' i Evgenii Golovine."

38. "Geidar Dzhemal' o sebe, 'Iushinskom krushke' i Evgenii Golovine."

39. Evgenii Golovin, *Mifomaniia* (Moscow: Amfora, 2010), 12–16.

40. Evgenii Golovin, "Beseda s Aleksandrom Duginym: V poiskakh vechnogo Norda," *Elementy*, available on the Golovin Fund website, http://golovinfond.ru/content/inter-vyu-elamentam. This is confirmed by Arkadii Rovner in the last chapter of his book, "Posledovateli 'sistemy,'" *Perekrestok*, http://fourthway.narod.ru/lib/rovner/gau7.htm. "Geidar Dzhemal' o sebe, 'Iushinskom krushke' i Evgenii Golovine."

41. Franco Ferraresi, *Threats to Democracy. The Radical Rights in Italy after the War* (Princeton, NJ: Princeton University Press, 1996).

42. Marina Peunova, "The Transfer of Ideas along a Cultural Gradient: The Influence of the European New Right on Aleksandr Panarin's New Eurasianism," in *Mapping the Extreme Right in Contemporary Europe: From Local to Transnational*, eds. Andrea Mammone, Emmanuel Godin, and Brian Jenkins (London: Routledge, 2012), 306.

43. On this Nazi occultism see the seminal work of Nicholas Goodrick-Clarke, *The Occult Roots of Nazism: Secret Aryan Cults and their Influence on Nazi Ideology* (New York: New York University Press, 1992).

44. The excerpts published are entitled "Kakomu bogu poklonialsia Gitler?" *Nauka i religiia*, no. 9–10 (1966): 63–69, and no. 11 (1966): 82–89.

45. "Geidar Dzhemal' o sebe, 'Iushinskom krushke' i Evgenii Golovine."

46. Anonymous interview with Geydar Dzhemal, Moscow, 2013.

47. See Ian B. Warren, "The Heritage of Europe's 'Revolutionary Conservative Movement': A Conversation with Swiss Historian Armin Mohler," *Journal of Historical Review* 14, no. 5 (1994): 3–9, http://www.ihr.org/jhr/v14n5p3_warren.html. See also Michael Minkenberg, "The New Right in France and Germany: Nouvelle Droite, Neue Rechte, and the New Right Radical Parties," in *The Revival of Right Wing Extremism in the Nineties*, eds. Peter H. Merkl, and Leonard Weinberg (London: Frank Cass, 1997).

48. Golovin, "Beseda s Aleksandrom Duginym. V poiskakh vechnogo Norda;" and "Geidar Dzhemal' o sebe, 'Iushinskom krushke' i Evgenii Golovine."

49. Giovanni Savino, "Dugin's Italian Connections: The Impact of Neo-Eurasianism on the Italian Political Landscape," forthcoming.

50. See interview of Miguel Serrano, "Esoteric Hitlerist," *Flaming Sword*, no. 3 (1994), https://web.archive.org/web/19990508174215re_/www.satanism.net/iss/wot/Miguel_Serrano.html.

51. More in Nicholas Goodrick-Clarke, *Black Sun: Aryan Cults, Esoteric Nazism and the Politics of Identity* (New York: New York University Press, 2003), chapter 9.

52. Robert Ellwood, *The Politics of Myth: A Study of C. G. Jung, Mircea Eliade, and Joseph Campbell* (Albany, NY: State University of New York Press, 1999). See also Marcel Tolcea, *Mircea Eliade et l'ésotérisme* (Paris: Entrelacs, 2013).

53. Leon Volovici, *Nationalist Ideology and Antisemitism: The Case of Romanian Intellectuals in the 1930s* (Oxford: Pergamon Press, 1991).

54. James Palmer, *The Bloody White Baron: The Extraordinary Story of the Russian Nobleman Who Became the Last Khan of Mongolia* (New York: Basic Books, 2009).

55. Arkadii Rovner, "G. I. Gurdieff's Influence in Russia in the 1960s–1970s," 153.

56. Available at "Okkul'tnye fashisty I poeziia," Pavel Gurianov's Lifejournal, July 30, 2014, http://gurianov-pavel.livejournal.com/52156.html, and "K teme degradatsii patriotizma I sataninskogo shabala khellouin," October 31, 2013, http://maks-cccc7603.livejournal.com/378005.html?thread=1005973.

57. Aleksei Chelnokov, "Tri bogatyria v forme Waffen-SS," *Sovershenno sekretno* no. 7, 278, July 2, 2012, http://www.sovsekretno.ru/articles/id/3197/.

58. This almanac is mentioned in most biographies of Golovin; however, I could not find a copy of it.

59. "Geidar Dzhemal' o sebe, 'Iushinskom krushke' i Evgenii Golovine."

60. Cosmism is a Russian ideology asserting that mankind is intimately linked to the natural forces of the cosmos, especially the sun, that the future of humanity will be to live in the cosmos and develop superhuman features, and that the conquest of space constitutes the technological and secular version of Russia's classical Christian messianism.

61. Marlene Laruelle, "Totalitarian Utopia, the Occult, and Technological Modernity in Russia: The Intellectual Experience of Cosmism," in *The New Age of Russia: Occult and Esoteric Dimensions,* eds. Birgit Menzel, Michael Hagemeister, and Bernice Glatzer Rosenthal (Munich: Kubon and Sagner, 2012), 238–58.

62. More in Viktor Shnirel'man, *Intellektual'nye labirinty: Ocherki ideologii v sovremennoi Rossii* (Moscow: Academia, 2004).

63. Guzman (Videman), *Shkola magov.*

64. In 1957, the Lenin Library acquired the German translation of 1933 by Friedrich Bauer (the original Italian dates from 1928).

65. "Dugin Aleksandr Gel'evich," *Antikompromat,* no date, http://www.anticompromat.org/dugin/duginbio.html.

66. Even though his father left the family when Dugin was only three, and there is not much information available on the father–son relationship, it is possible that the father's status at the GRU served Dugin on many occasions, first of all in his gaining access to the *spetskhran* at the Lenin Library, then in his being received and heard in Russian military circles at the start of the 1990s. However, this version is contested by Anton Shekhovtsov. More on Dugin's biography page at http://www.anticompromat.org/dugin/duginbio.html.

67. As mentioned in Vladimir Pribylovsky's biography of Dugin, http://www.anticompromat.org/dugin/duginbio.html.

68. See Dugin's biography in *Izborskii klub. Russkie strategii*, no. 9 (2014): 47.

69. Guzman (Videman), *Shkola magov.*

70. Author's anonymous interview with a participant in the circle's activities in the 1980s.

71. More in Brudny, *Reinventing Russia.*

72. Vladimir Pribylovski, "Pamiat'," in *Natsional'naia pravaia prezhde i teper'*, ed. R. Sh. Ganelin (Saint Petersburg: Institut sotsiologii RAN, 1992), vol. 2, 151–70.

73. Pribylovsky's biography of Dugin, http://www.anticompromat.org/dugin/duginbio.html.

74. Chelnokov, "Tri bogatyria v forme Waffen-SS."

75. See Dudinskii's biography at http://www.peoples.ru/art/literature/prose/publicist/igor_dudinskiy/.

76. A detailed analysis of Dugin's first trips to Western Europe has been provided by Anton Shekhovtsov, "Aleksandr Dugin and the West European New Right, 1989–1994," forthcoming.

77. On Ahnenerbe see Heather Pringle, *The Master Plan: Himmler's Scholars and the Holocaust* (New York: Hyperion, 2006).

78. Massimo Introvigne, *Le New Age des origines à nos jours : Courants, mouvements, personnalités* (Paris: Dervy, 2005).

BIBLIOGRAPHY

Agurskii, Mikhail. *Ideologiia natsional'no-bolshevizma*. Paris: YMCA-Press, 1980.

Aksakov, Nikolai. "Germaniia i Slavianstvo." *Svidetel'* 22 (1909).

Aksenova, E. P. and M. A. Vasilev. "Problemy etnogonii slavianstva i ego vetvei v akademi-cheskikh diskusiiakh rubezha 1930–1940-kh godov." *Slavianovedenie* 2 (1993).

"Alain de Benoist: L'ennemi principal." *Eléments* 41 (March–April 1982).

Alekseev, Nikolai N. "Khristianstvo i ideia monarkhii." In *Russkii narod i gosudarstvo*, 48–67. Moscow: AGRAF, 1998. Originally published in *Rossiia i Zapad: Dialog kul'tur*. Moscow: MGU, 1996.

Alekseev, Nikolai N. *Evraziistvo i kommunizm*. Prague: Evraziiskoe izdatel'stvo, 1927.

Aleshkin, Piotr F. *Krest'ianskie vosstaniia v Rossii v 1918–1922 gg. Ot makhnovshchinii do antonovshchinii*. Moscow: Veche, 2012.

Allensworth, Wayne. *The Russian Question: Nationalism, Modernization, and Post-Communist Russia*. Lanham, MD: Rowman and Littlefield, 1998.

Anan'ich, Boris. *Rossiia i mezhdunarodnyi kapital, 1897–1914: Ocherki istorii finansovykh otnoshenii*. Leningrad: Nauka, 1970.

Andersen, Joakim. "Lev Gumilev och etnogenesis." *Motpol* (2010). Accessed November 4, 2014. http://www.motpol.nu/oskorei/2010/09/11/lev-gumilev-och-etnogenesis/.

Andreeva, Ekaterina. *General Vlasov i Russkoe osvoboditel'noe dvizhenie*. London: Overseas Publications Interchange, 1990.

Andreyev, Catherine. *Vlasov and the Russian Liberation Movement*. Cambridge: Cambridge University Press, 1987.

Antikompromat. "Dugin Aleksandr Gel'evich." n.d. http://www.anticompromat.org/dugin/duginbio.html.

Antipov, Aleksandr P. "Belye i krasnye." *Evraziiskii sbornik* 6 (1929): 59–63.

Antipov, Aleksandr P. "Frankfurtskii s'ezd." *Evraziets* 20 (February 1932).

Antipov, Aleksandr P. "Novye puti Germanii." In *Novaia epokha. Ideokratiia. Politika-ekonomika. Obzory*, edited by V. A. Pei'l. Tallinn: Izdanie Evraziitsev, 1933.

Antipov, Aleksandr P. "Novye radikal'nye techeniia v Germanii." *Evraziets* 21 (November 1932).

Antonio, Robert J. "After Postmodernism: Reactionary Tribalism." *American Journal of Sociology* 106, no. 1 (2000).

Arkhiv Upravleniia Federal'noi sluzhby bezopasnosti Rossii po Brianskoi oblasti (AUFSB-BO). File 51, Sheet 1 (n.d.).

Ascher, Abraham. *The Revolution of 1905* (vol. 2, *Authority Restored*). Stanford, CA: Stanford University Press, 1992.

Avrutin, Eugene M. "Racial Categories and the Politics of (Jewish) Difference in Late Imperial Russia." *Kritika: Explorations in Russian and Eurasian History* 8, no. 1 (winter 2007): 13–40.

Backes, Uwe, and Henrik Steglich, eds. *Die NPD: Erfolgsbedingungen einer rechtsextremistischen Partei*. Baden-Baden: Nomos, 2007.

Bahar, Aleksandr. *Sozialrevolutionärer Nationalismus zwischen Konservativer Revolution und Sozialismus: Harro Schulze-Boysen und der "Gegner"-Kreis*. Koblenz: Verlag Dietmar Fölbach, 1992.

Bahne, Siegfried. "'Sozialfaschismus' in Deutschland: Zur Geschichte eines politischen Begriffs." *International Review of Social History* 10 (1965): 211–45.

Bail, René. *Les Croix de monseigneur de Mayol de Lupé.* Etrépilly: Bartillat, 1994.

Bakhmeteff Archive on Russian and East European History and Culture. *Memorandum of A. P. Antipov to the Chairman of the Eurasianist Organization's Central Committee [P. N. Savitskii] 'On the Prospects of Relations with German Groups.'* George Vernadsky Papers, Box 7. New York: Columbia University Libraries.

Balkin, Jack. *Cultural Software: A Theory of Ideology.* New Haven, CT: Yale University Press, 2002.

Barbashin, Anton and Hannah Thoburn. "Putin's Philosopher: Ivan Ilyin and the Ideology of Moscow's Rule." *Foreign Affairs,* September 30, 2015. https://www.foreignaffairs.com/articles/russian-federation/2015-09-20/putins-philosopher.

Bar-On, Tamir. "Fascism to the Nouvelle Droite: The Quest for Pan-European Empire." In *Varieties of Right-Wing Extremism in Europe,* edited by Andrea Mammone, Emmanuel Godin, and Brian Jenkins, 69–84. London: Routledge, 2013.

Bar-On, Tamir. *Rethinking the French New Right: Alternatives to Modernity.* London: Routledge, 2013.

Bartenev, Iurii. *Okazennaia Pravda.* St. Petersburg, 1907.

Bartenev, Iurii. *Pomrachennyi ideal.* Moscow, 1907.

Bartsch, Günther. *Zwischen drei Stühlen: Otto Strasser. Eine Biographie.* Koblenz: Verlag Siegfried Bublies, 1990.

Basil, John. "The Russian Theological Academies and the Old Catholics, 1870–1905." In *Religious and Secular Forces in Late Imperial Russia,* edited by Charles E. Timberlake. Seattle: University of Washington Press, 1992.

Bassin, Mark. *The Gumilev Mystique.* Ithaca, NY: Cornell University Press, 2016.

Bassin, Mark. "Narrating Kulikovo: Lev Gumilev, Russian Nationalists, and the Troubled Emergence of Neo-Eurasianism." In *Between Europe and Asia: The Origins, Theories and Legacies of Russian Eurasianism,* edited by Mark Bassin, Marlene Laruelle, and Sergey Glebov. Pittsburgh: University of Pittsburgh Press, 2015.

Bassin, Mark. "Nationhood, Natural Region, *Mestorazvitie*: Environmentalist Discourses in Classical Eurasianism." In *Space, Place and Power in Modern Russia: Essays in the New Spatial History,* edited by Mark Bassin, Chris Ely, and Melissa Stockdale. DeKalb, IL: Northern Illinois University Press, 2010.

Bassin, Mark. "Nurture *is* Nature: Lev Gumilev and the Ecology of Ethnicity." *Slavic Review* 68, no. 4 (2009): 872–97.

Bassin, Mark. "Russia between Europe and Asia: The Ideological Construction of Geographical Space." *Slavic Review* 50, no. 1 (1993): 1–17.

Bassin, Mark, Sergei Glebov, and Marlene Laruelle, eds. *Between Europe and Asia: The Origins, Theories and Legacies of Russian Eurasianism.* Pittsburgh: University of Pittsburgh Press, 2015. Baty, Régis. *Tambov, camp soviétique.* Strasbourg, n.p., 2011.

Baumgarten, Jean. *La naissance du hassidisme.* Paris: Albin Michel, 2006.

Bebnowski, David. *Die Alternative für Deutschland: Aufstieg und gesellschaftliche Repräsentanz einer rechten populistischen Partei.* Wiesbaden: Springer VS, 2015.

Beisswenger, Martin E. "'Konservativnaia revoliutsiia' v Germanii i dvizhenie 'Evraziitsev'—tochki soprikosnoveniia." In *Konservatizm v Rossii i mire,* vol. 3. Voronezh: Voronezhskii Gosudarstvennyi Universitet, 2004.

Beisswenger, Martin. "Metaphysics of the Economy: The Religious and Economic Foundations of P. N. Savitskii's Eurasianism." In *Between Europe and Asia: The Origins, Theories and Legacies of Russian Eurasianism,* edited by Mark Bassin, Marlene Laruelle, and Sergey Glebov, 97–112. Pittsburgh, PA: University of Pittsburgh Press, 2015.

Beisswenger, Martin. "N. V. Vernadskaia-Toll i stanovlenie 'nauchnogo' evraziistvo." In

Ezhegodnik Doma Russkogo zarubezh'a imeni Aleksandra Solzhenitsyna, edited by N. F. Gritsenko. Moscow: Dom Russkogo zarubezh'a imeni Aleksandra Solzhenitsyna, 2013.

Beliaeva-Konegen, S. "Upyr': O proze Iuriia Mamleeva." *Strelets* 3 (1992): 167–69.

Beliakov, S. S. *Gumilev syn Gumileva*. Moscow: Astrel', 2012.

Bene, Krisztiàn. *La collaboration militaire française dans la Seconde Guerre mondiale*. Codex, 2012.

Bennett, John. *Witness: The Autobiography of John G. Bennett*. Winnipeg: Turnstone, 1975.

Benthall, Jonathan. "The Schwidetzky Affair." In *The Best of Anthropology Today*, edited by Jonathan Benthall, 441–44. London: Routledge, 2002.

Berdiaev, Nikolai. "Evraziitsy." *Put'* 1 (1925).

Bergsdorf, Harald. *Ungleiche Geschwister: Die deutschen Republikaner (REP) im Vergleich zum französischen Front National (FN)*. Frankfurt am Main: Lang, 2000.

Berk, Stephen M. *Year of Crisis, Year of Hope: Russian Jewry and the Pogroms of 1881–1882*. Westport, CT: Greenwood Press, 1985.

Bertalanfi, L. *Obshchaia teoriia sistem–kriticheskii obzor*. Moscow: Progress, 1969.

Beyda, Oleg. "La Grande Armée in Field Gray: The Legion of French Volunteers against Bolshevism, 1941." *Journal of Slavic Military Studies* 29, no. 3 (2016): 500–518.

Billig, Michael. *Die rassistische Internationale: Zur Renaissance der Rassenlehre in der modernen Psychologie*. Frankfurt: Neue Kritik, 1981.

Binet, R. *Socialisme national contre marxisme*. Montreal: Celtiques. 1975.

Bing, Edward, ed. *Letters of Tsar Nicholas and Empress Marie: Being the Confidential Correspondence Between Nicholas II, Last of the Tsars, and his Mother, Dowager Empress Maria Feodorovna I*. London: Nicholson and Watson,1937.

Blinkhorn, Martin. "Conservatism, Traditionalism and Fascism in Spain, 1898–1937." In *Fascists and Conservatives: The Radical Right and the Establishment in Twentieth-Century Europe*, edited by Martin Blinkhorn. London: Routledge, 1990.

Boemeke, Manfred F., Gerald D. Feldman, and Elizabeth Glaser, eds. *The Treaty of Versailles: A Reassessment after 75 Years*. Cambridge: Cambridge University Press, 1988.

Bogatyrev, M. "Otshel'nik: Nabroski k portretu Iu. V. Titova." *Stetoskop* 22 (1999).

Boiarov, Aleksandr I. *Golos naroda*. December 1, 1942.

Böttger, Christian. *Ethnos: Der Nebel um den Volksbegriff*. Schnellbach: Lindenbaum Verlag, 2014.

Bouysse, Gregory. *Waffen SS français* (vol.1: *Officiers*). n.p., 2011.

Brandenberger, David. *National Bolshevism: Stalinist Mass Culture and the Formation of Modern Russian National Identity, 1931–1956*. Harvard, 2002.

Brandstetter, Marc. "Die 'neue' NPD: Zwischen Systemfeindschaft und bürgerlicher Fassade." *Parteienmonitor Aktuell der Konrad-Adenauer-Stiftung*. Berlin, 2012. http://www.kas.de/wf/doc/kas_30034-544-1-30.pdf?140328142648.

Brauner-Orthen, Alice. *Die neue Rechte in Deutschland. Antidemokratische und rassistische Tendenzen*. Opladen: Leske und Budrich, 2001.

Breuer, Stefan. *Anatomie der Konservativen Revolution*, 2nd ed. Darmstadt: Wissenschaftliche Buchgesellschaft, 1993.

Brinks, Jan Herman. "Germany's New Right." In *Nationalist Myths and the Modern Media: Contested Identities in the Age of Globalisation*, edited by Jan Herman Brinks. New York: I.B. Tauris, 2005.

Bromberg, Yakov A. "Evreiskoe vostochnichestvo v proshlom i v budushchem." *Tridtsatye gody*. Paris: Izdanie Evraziitsev, 1931.

Bromberg, Yakov A. "O neobkhodimom peresmotre evreiskogo voprosa." *Evraziiskii sbornik* 6 (1929).

Bromberg, Yakov A. *Rossiia, Zapad i evreistvo*. Prague: Izdanie Evraziitsev, 1931.

Bromlei, Iu.V. *Ocherki teorii etnosa*. Moscow: Nauka, 1983.

Bruk, S. I. and N. N. Cheboksarov. "Metaetnicheskie obshchnosti." *Rasy i Narody. Ezhegodnik* 6 (1976): 15–41.

Buchheim, Hans. "Ernst Niekischs Ideologie des Widerstandes." *Vierteljahrshefte für Zeitgeschichte* 5 (1957): 334–61.

Büsch, Otto and Peter Furth. *Rechtsradikalismus im Nachkriegsdeutschland: Studien über die Sozialistische Reichspartei.* Berlin: Franz Vahlen, 1957.

Butmi, G. V. *Rossiia na rasput'i: Kabala ili svoboda?* St. Petersburg, 1906.

Camus, Jean-Yves and Nicolas Lebourg. *Les Droites extrêmes en Europe.* Paris: Éditions du Seuil, 2015.

Camus, Jean-Yves and René Monzat. *Les Droites nationales et radicales en France.* Lyon: Presses Universitaires de Lyon, 1992.

Castro Moral, Lorenzo. *Estudio de un movimiento.* Madrid, 1974.

Ceuppens, Bambi, and Peter Geschiere. "Autochthony: Local or Global? New Modes in the Struggle over Citizenship and Belonging in Africa and Europe." *Annual Review of Anthropology* 34 (2005).

Chelnokov, Aleksei. "Tri bogatyria v forme Waffen-SS." *Sovershenno sekretno* 7 (July 2012).

Chernovskii, A., ed. *Soiuz russkogo naroda: Po materialam chrezvychainoi sledstvennoi komissii Vremennogo Pravitel'stva.* Moscow–Leningrad, 1929.

Clowes, Edith W. "Heinrich A. Stammler, 1912–2006." *Slavic Review* 66, no. 3 (2007): 600–602.

Cohen, Stephen F. *The Victims Return: Survivors of the Gulag After Stalin.* London: I.B. Tauris, 2012.

Cohn, Norman. *Warrant for Genocide: The Myth of the Jewish World-Conspiracy and the "Protocol of the Elders of Zion."* Chico, CA: Scholars Press, 1981.

Coogan, Kevin. "Lost Imperium: The European Liberation Front (1949–54)." *Patterns of Prejudice* 36, no. 3 (July 2002): 9–23.

Coppi, Hans and Geertje Andresen, eds. *Dieser Tod paßt zu mir: Harro Schulze-Boysen—Grenzgänger im Widerstand. Briefe 1915 bis 1942.* Berlin: Aufbau Verlag, 1999.

Coppi, Hans and Jürgen Danyel, eds. *Der "Gegner"-Kreis im Jahre 1932/33.* Berlin: Evangelische Akademie Berlin, 1990.

Corni, Gustavo and Horst Gies. *"Blut und Boden": Rassenideologie und Agrarpolitik im Staat Hitlers.* Idstein: Schultz-Kirchner Verlag, 1994.

Cuadrado Costa, José. "Insuffisance et dépassement du concept marxiste-léniniste de nationalité." *Conscience européenne* 9 (October 1984).

Danilova, Ol'ga. "Frantsuzskoe 'slavianofil'stvo' kontsa XIX–nachala XX veka." In *Rossiia i Frantsiia: XVIII—XX vv.* Moscow: Nauka, 2006.

Dard, Olivier. "L'Anticommunisme des nationalistes au temps de la République gaullienne." Communisme 6263 (2000).

Darré, R. Walther. "Blut und Boden als Lebensgrundlagen der nordischer Rasse [1930]." In *Um Blut und Boden: Reden und Aufsätze,* 17–29. Munich: Zentralverlag der NSDAP, 1940.

David-Fox, Michael. "A 'Prussian Bolshevik' in Stalin's Russia: Ernst Niekisch at the Crossroads between Communism and National Socialism." In *Crossing Borders: Modernity, Ideology, and Culture in Soviet Russia,* edited by Michael David-Fox, 185–220. Pittsburgh: University of Pittsburgh Press, 2015.

David-Fox, Michael, Peter Holquist, and Alexander M. Martin, eds. *Fascination and Enmity: Russia and Germany as Entangled Histories, 1914–1945.* Pittsburgh, PA: University of Pittsburgh Press, 2012.

Davis, Chandler and Nina Godneff. "La sociobiologie et son explication de l'humanité." *Annales. Histoire, Sciences Sociales* 36, no. 4 (1981).

Daye, Pierre. *L'Europe aux Européens.* Brussels: Nouvelle Société d'Editions, 1942.

de Benoist, Alain. "Alain de Benoist Answers Tamir Bar-On." *Journal for the Study of Radicalism* 8, no. 1 (2014).

de Benoist, Alain. "Confronting Globalization." *Telos* 108 (1996).

de Benoist, Alain. "Nationalisme: phénoménologie et critique." In *Critiques—Théoriques*. Lausanne: L'Age d'Homme, 2002.

de Benoist, Alain. "What is Racism." *Telos* 114 (1999).

de Benoist, Alain. *Les Idées à l'endroit*. Paris: Hallier, 1979.

de Benoist, Alain. *Mémoire vive*. Paris: Éditions de Fallois, 2012.

de Benoist, Alain. *Orientations pour des années décisives*. Paris: Labyrinthe, 1982.

de Benoist, Alain and Charles Champetier. "Manifesto of the French New Right in Year 2000." (2000). Accessed October 18, 2014. https://archive.org/details/ManifestoOfThe FrenchNewRightInTheYear2000.

de Benoist, Alain and Tomislav Sunic. "Gemeinschaft and Gesellschaft: A Sociological View of the Decay of Modern Society." *Mankind Quarterly* 34 (1994): 261–70. Accessed October 22, 2014. https://archive.org/details/GemeinschaftAndGesellschaft.

de Benoist, Alain and Brian Sylvian. "European Son: An Interview with Alain de Benoist." *Occidental Quarterly* 5, no. 3 (2005). Accessed October 23, 2014. https://http://www .toqonline. com/archives/v5n3/53-bs-debenoist.pdf.

Die Kommunistische Internationale in Resolutionen und Beschlüssen (vol. 2, *1925–1943*). Offenbach: Verlag Olga Benario und Herbert Baum, 1998.

"Die neue Religion der Rasse: der Biologismus und die neue kollektive Ethik der Neuen Rechten in Frankreich und Deutschland." In *Neokonservative und Neue Rechte: der Angriff gegen Sozialstaat und liberale Demokratie in den Vereinigten Staaten, Westeuropa und der Bundesrepublik*, edited by Iring Fetscher, 122–62. Munich: Beck, n.d.

Dobson, Miriam. *Khrushchev's Cold Summer: Gulag Returnees, Crime, and the Fate of Reform after Stalin*. Ithaca, NY: Cornell University Press, 2011.

Documents Diplomatiques Francais, 1920–1932, vol. 3. 1992.

Dom i gimnaziia Russkago sobraniia. St. Petersburg, 1910.

Dostojewski, F. M. "Deutschland, die protestierende Macht." *Widerstand* 5 (1930): 72–76.

Douguine, Alexandre. *L'appel de L'Eurasie*. Paris: Avatar, 2013.

Douguine, Alexandre. *Pour une théorie du monde multipolaire*. Paris: Ars Magna, 2014.

Driumond, Eduard. "Revoliutsiia v Rossii." *Russkoe delo* 2 (1905).

Drobiasko, Sergei I. "Lokot'skii avtonomnii okrug i Russkaia Osvoboditel'naia armiia." In *Materialy po istorii Russkogo Osvoboditelnogo Dvizheniia*, vol. 2, edited by A. V. Okorov. Moscow: Graal, 1997.

Dugin, Aleksandr G. *Aleksandr Dugin: The Fourth Political Theory*. London: Arktos, 2012.

Dugin, Aleksandr. "Auf, o Seele!" *Nezavisimaia gazeta*, March 27, 2003. http://www.ng.ru/ kafedra/2003-03-27/3_essay.html.

Dugin, Aleksandr. *Chetvertaia politicheskaia teoriia*. Moscow: Amfora, 2009.

Dugin, Aleksandr G. *Konflikte der Zukunft: Die Rückkehr der Geopolitik*. Kiel: Arndt-Verlag, 2014.

Dugin, Aleksandr. *Konservativnaia revoliutsiia. Tretii put'*. Moscow: Aktogeia, 1994. http:// my.arcto.ru/public/konsrev/3way.htm http://my.arcto.ru/public/konsrev/3way.htm.

Dugin, Aleksandr G. "Lev Gumilev: nauka 'zhivoi zhizni.'" 2002. Accessed February 8, 2014. http://evrazia. org/modules.php?name+News&file=article&sid=634

Dupeux, Louis. *"Nationalbolschewismus" in Deutschland 1919–1933: Kommunistische Strategie und konservative Dynamik*, translated by Richard Kirchhoff. Munich: C.H. Beck, 1985.

Dupeux, Louis. *National-bolchevisme. Stratégie communiste et dynamique conservatrice*. Paris: Honoré Champion, 1979.

Duranton-Crabol, Anne-Marie. *Visages de la nouvelle droite*. Le GRECE et son histoire. Paris: Fondation nationale des sciences politiques, 1988.

Durnovo, Nil, *Godina Bozh'ego popushcheniia*, vol. 1. Moscow: Vernost', 1907.

Dzhemal, Geidar. "Geidar Dzhemal o sebe, i 'Iushinskom krushke' i Evgenii Golovine." You-Tube video, 1:24:17. Posted [August 2013]. https://youtu.be/SXxQx4K4a5U.

Edelman, Robert. *Gentry Politics on the Eve of the Russian Revolution: The Nationalist Party 1907–1917.* New Brunswick, NJ: Rutgers University Press, 1980.

Eibl-Eibesfeldt, Irenäus. *Der vorprogrammierte Mensch: Das Ererbte als bestimminder Faktor im menschlichen Verhalten.* Munchen: Deutscher Taschenbuchverlag, 1984.

Eibl-Eibesfeldt, Irenäus. *Ethnology: The Biology of Behavior.* New York: Holt, Rinehart and Winston, 1970.

Eibl-Eibesfeldt, Irenäus. *Wider die Misstrauensgesellschaft: Streitschrift für eine bessere Zukunft,* 2nd ed. Munich: Piper, 1995.

Eibl-Eibesfeldt, Irenäus. *Wider die Misstrauensgesellschaft: Streitschrift für eine bessere Zukunft.* 2nd ed. Munich: Piper, 1995. Quoted in *Fighting for the Essence. Western Ethnosuicide or European Renaissance?* by Pierre Krebs. Translated by Aleksandr Jacob. London: Arktos, 2012.

"El bolchevismo, revolución nacional rusa." *Resistencia* 5 (September 1996).

"El nacional bolchevismo ruso." *Tribuna de Europa* 4 (October 1993): 19–23.

Ellwood, Robert. *The Politics of Myth: A Study of C. G. Jung, Mircea Eliade, and Joseph Campbell.* Albany, NY: State University of New York Press, 1999.

Elz, Wolfgang. "Versailles und Weimar." *Aus Politik und Zeitgeschichte* 50–51 (2008): 31–38.

"Entrevista con Alexandre Duguin: Elecciones presidenciales en Rusia." *Nosotros somos quien somos* 9 (April 1996).

Ermolaev, V. "Samoorganizatsiia v prirode i etnogenez." *Izvestiia Vsesoiuznogo Geograficheskogo Obshchestva* 122, no. 1 (1990).

Esli zavtra voina. Directed by Lazar Antsi-Polovskii, Georgii Berezko, Efim Dzigan, and Nikolai Karmazinskii. USSR: Mosfilm, 1938.

Etkind, Aleksandr. *Internal Colonization: Russia's Imperial Experience.* Cambridge: Polity Press, 2011.

"Evraziistvo: Opyt sistematicheskogo izlozheniia." In *Puti Evrazii: Russkaia intelligentsiia i sud'by Rossii.* Moscow: Russkaia kniga, 1992. Originally published in Paris: Evraziiskoe knigoizdatel'stvo, 1926.

The Extreme Nationalist Threat in Russia: The Growing Influence of Western Rightist Ideas. London: Routledge.

Fallows, Thomas S. "The Russian Fronde and the Zemstvo Movement: Economic Agitation and Gentry Politics in the Mid-1890s." *Russian Review* 44, no. 2 (April 1985): 119–38.

Falter, Jürgen W. *Hitlers Wähler.* Munich: C.H. Beck, 1991.

Faye, Guillaume. *Why We Fight. Manifesto of the European Resistance.* London: Arktos, 2011.

Faye, Jean-Pierre. *Langages totalitaires.* Paris: Hermann, 1972.

Fayet, Jean François. *Karl Radek, 1885–1939 : Biographie politique.* Bern: Peter Lang, 2004.

Federal Office for Protection of the Constitution. "'Autonome Nationalisten'—Rechtsextremistische Militanz." Cologne: Federal Office for Protection of the Constitution, 2009.

Ferraresi, Franco. *Threats to Democracy: The Radical Rights in Italy after the War.* Princeton, NJ: Princeton University Press, 1996.

Filatova, Irina. "The Awkward Issue: Some Comments on the South African Debate on Nation-Building and Ethnicity." In *Democratic Nation-Building in South Africa,* edited by Nic Rhodie and Ian Liebenberg. Pretoria: Human Sciences Research Council, 1994.

Filippov, V. R. *Sovetskaia teoriia etnosa: Istoricheskii ocherk.* Moscow: Inst. Afriki RAN, 2010.

François, Stéphane and Nicolas Lebourg. *Histoire de la haine identitaire.* Valenciennes: Presses Universitaires de Valenciennes, 2016.

Freeden, Michael. "Is Nationalism a Distinct Ideology?" *Political Studies* 46, no. 4 (1998).

Fritzsche, Klaus. *Politische Romantik und Gegenrevolution: Fluchtwege in der Krise der bürgerlichen Gesellschaft: Das Beispiel des "Tat"-Kreises.* Frankfurt/M.: Suhrkamp, 1976.

Fröhlig, Florence. *A Painful Legacy of World War II: Nazi Forced Enlistment, Alsatian/Mosellan Prisoners of War, and the Soviet Prison Camp of Tambov*. Stockholm: Acta Universitatis Stockholmiensis, 2013.

Galbraith, John Kenneth. *La crise économique de 1929: Anatomie d'une catastrophe financière*. Paris: Payot, 1989.

Galkin, Aleksandr. "O fashizme—ego sushchnosti, korniakh, priznakakh i formakh proiavleniia." *Polis* 2 (1995).

Garau, Salvatore. "If Liberalism Steps into the Fascist Synthesis: The Diverging Views of Zeev Sternhell and Ishay Landa on the Origins of Fascist Ideology." *Journal of Political Ideologies* 19, no. 1 (2014): 60–77.

Gelen, Reinhard. *Sluzhba*. Moscow: Terra, 1997.

Gentile, Emilio. "Fascism as Political Religion," *Journal of Contemporary History* 25, no. 2/3 (1990): 229–51.

Gérard, Christopher. "Honnête et fidèle." *Magazine des amis de Jean Mabire* 22.

Gerstein, Emma. *Moscow Memoirs*. Translated by J. Crowfoot. London: Harvill Press, 2004.

Gieseke, Jens and Hermann Wentker, eds. *Die Geschichte der SED: Eine Bestandsaufnahme*. Berlin: Metropol, 2011.

Gilles, Gilbert. *Un ancien Waffen SS raconte: L'ultime assaut*. Gold Mail International: 1989.

Glebov, Sergei. "N. S. Trubetskoi's 'Europe and Mankind' and Eurasianist Antievolutionism: One Unknown Source." In *Between Europe and Asia: The Origins, Theories and Legacies of Russian Eurasianism*, edited by Mark Bassin, Sergei Glebov, and Marlene Laruelle, 48–67. Pittsburgh: University of Pittsburgh Press, 2015.

Glebov, Sergei. *Evraziistvo mezhdu imperiei i modernom*. Moscow: Novoe izdatel'stvo, 2010.

Golovin, Evgenii. "Beseda s Aleksandrom Duginym: V poiskakh vechnogo Norda." *Elementy*, http://golovinfond.ru/content/intervyu-elamentam.

Golovin, Evgenii. *Mifomaniia*. Moscow: Amfora, 2010.

Golovin, Evgenii. *Sentimental'noe beshenstvo rok-n-rolla*. Moscow: Nox, 1997.

Goodrick-Clarke, Nicholas. *Black Sun: Aryan Cults, Esoteric Nazism and the Politics of Identity*. New York: New York University Press, 2003.

Goodrick-Clarke, Nicholas. *The Occult Roots of Nazism: Secret Aryan Cults and their Influence on Nazi Ideology*. New York: New York University Press, 1992.

Gordon, Robert. "Apartheid's Anthropologists: The Genealogy of Afrikaner Anthropology." *American Ethnologist* 15, no. 3 (1988): 535–53.

Gorny, Eugene. "The Negative World of Yuri Mamleyev." *Zhurnal.ru* (n.d.). http://www.zhurnal.ru/staff/gorny/english/mamleev.htm.

Gosudarstvennaia Duma. *Stenograficheskii otchet*. (February 9, 1911).

Graziani, Antoine. *Les visiteurs de l'aube, Chemise bleue*, vol. 3. Paris: Dualpha, 2009.

Griffin, Roger. "Decentering Comparative Fascist Studies." *Fascism: Journal of Comparative Fascist Studies* 4, no. 2 (2015): 103–18.

Griffin, Roger. "Interregnum or Endgame? The Radical Right in the 'Post-Fascist' Era." *Journal of Political Ideologies* 5, no. 2 (2000).

Griffin, Roger. *International Fascism: Theories, Causes, and the New Consensus*. London: Arnold, 1998.

Griffin, Roger. *The Nature of Fascism*. London: Routledge, 1993.

Griffin, Roger. "Studying Fascism in a Postfascist Age: From New Consensus to New Wave?" *Fascism: Journal of Comparative Fascist Studies* 1, no. 1 (2012): 1–17.

Grot, K. Ia. *Platon Andreevich Kulakovskii*. St. Petersburg: Senatskaia, 1913.

Guchkov, A. I. *Sbornik rechei v Tretei Gosudarstvennoi Dume (1907–1912)*. St. Petersburg, 1912.

Gumilev, Lev N. "Biosfera i impul'sy soznaniia." *Priroda* 12 (1978).

Gumilev, Lev N. "Chelovechnost' prevyshe vsego." *Izvestiia* (June 24, 1989). Accessed March 19, 2014. http://gumilevica.kulichki.net/articles/Article45.htm.

Gumilev, Lev N. "Chernaia Legenda." In *Chernaia Legenda: Druz'ia i nedrugi Velikoi stepi,* 42–147. Moscow: Ekopros, 1994.

Gumilev, Lev N. "Chtoby svecha ne pogasla." In *Chtoby svecha ne pogasla. Sbornik esse, inter-v'iu, stikhotvorenii, perevodov,* edited by E. M. Goncharova, 7–15. Moscow: Airis Press, 2003.

Gumilev, Lev N. *Drevniaia Rus' i velikaia step.'* Moscow: Airis, 2004.

Gumilev, Lev N. *Etnogenez i biosfera zemli,* 2nd ed. Leningrad: Iz-vo Lenin. Gos. Universiteta., 1989.

Gumilev, Lev N. "Etnogenez i etnosfera." *Priroda* 2 (1970).

Gumilev, Lev N. "Etnos, istoriia, kul'tura." *Dekorativnoe Iskusstvo SSSR* 5 (1989).

Gumilev, Lev N. "Etnos, istoriia, kul'tura." *Dekorativnoe Iskusstvo SSSR* 10 (1989).

Gumilev, Lev N. "G. E. Grumm-Grzhimailo i rozhdenie nauki ob etnogeneze." *Priroda* 5 (1976).

Gumilev, Lev N. "Gde ona, strana Khazariia?" *Nedelia* 24, 9 (June 7–13, 1964).

Gumilev, Lev N. "Glavnomu redaktoru zhurnala *Kommunist* R. I. Kosolapovu [1982]." In *Vspominaia L. N. Gumileva. Vospominaniia. Publikatsii. Issledovaniia,* edited by V. N. Voronovich and M. G. Kozyreva. St. Petersburg: Iz-vo "Rostok," 2003.

Gumilev, Lev N. "'Ia, russkii chelovek, vsiu zhizn' zashchishchaiu tatar ot klevety.'" In *Chernaia Legenda: Druz'ia i nedrugi Velikoi stepi.* Moscow: Ekopross, 1994.

Gumilev, Lev N. "Iskat' to, chto verno." *Sovetskaia Literatura* 1 (1990): 72–76. Accessed February 25, 2014. http://gumilevica.kulichki.net/articles/Article06.htm

Gumilev, Lev N. "Istoriko-filosofskie trudy kniazia N. S. Trubetskogo (zametki poslednego evraziitsa)." In *Istoriia. Kul'tura. Iazyk,* edited by V. M. Zhivov. Moscow: Progress-Univers, 1995.

Gumilev, Lev N. "Kakoi ia demokrat? Ia—staryi soldat!." 1991. Accessed April 17, 2014. http:// nevzorov.tv/2012/03/lev-gumilyov-kakoj-ya-demokrat-ya-starij-soldat/.

Gumilev, Lev N. *Konets i vnov' nachalo. Populiarnye lektsii po narodovedeniiu.* Moscow: Rol'f, 2001.

Gumilev, Lev N. "Korni nashego rodstva." *Izvestiia* 3 (April 13, 1988).

Gumilev, Lev N. "Letter to the Editors of *Izvestiia Vsesoiuznogo Geograficheskogo Obshchestva.*" *Soviet Geography: Review and Translation* 15, no. 6 (1974).

Gumilev, Lev N. "'Menia nazyvaiut evraziitsem.'" *Nash Sovremennik* 1 (1991).

Gumilev, Lev. n.d. *Metapedia.* Accessed December 1, 2014. http://en.metapedia.org/wiki/ Lev_Gumilev.

Gumilev, Lev N. "Mongoly i merkity v XII veke." *Studia orientalla et Antiqua* 416 (1977). Accessed April 23, 2007. http://gumilevica.kulichki.com/articles/Article78.htm.

Gumilev, Lev N. "My absoliutno samobytny." *Nevskoe vremia* (August 12, 1992). Accessed March 21, 2014. http://gumilevica.kulichki.net/articles/Article52.htm

Gumilev, Lev N. "Nikakoi mistiki." In *Chtoby svecha ne pogasla. Sbornik esse, interv'iu, stikhotvorenii, perevodov,* 51–68. Moscow: Airis Press, 2003.

Gumilev, Lev N. "O termine etnos." In *Etnosfera: Istoriia liudei i istoriia prirody.* Moscow: AST, 2004.

Gumilev, Lev N. "On the Anthropogenic Factor in Landscape Formation." *Soviet Geography* 9 (1968).

Gumilev, Lev N. "On the Subject of the 'Unified Geography' (Landscape and Etnos, VI)." *Soviet Geography: Review and Translation* 9, no. 1 (1968).

Gumilev, Lev N. "Pis'mo v redaktsiiu 'Voprosov filosofii.'" *Voprosy Filosofii* 5 (1989).

Gumilev, Lev N. "'Publikatsiia moikh rabot blokiruiutsia.' Kto i pochemu otvergal L. N. Gumilevu." In *Vspominaia L. N. Gumileva. Vospominaniia. Publikatsii. Issledovaniia,* edited by V. N. Voronovich and M. G. Kozyreva, 246–56. St. Petersburg: Iz-vo "Rostok," 2003.Gumilev, Lev N. "Rol' klimaticheskikh kolebanii v istorii narodov stepnoi zony Evrazii." *Istoriia SSSR* 1 (1967).

Gumilev, Lev N. "Sila epokhi." *Dekorativnoe Iskusstvo SSSR* 7 (1989).

Gumilev, Lev N. "Zakony vremeni." *Literaturnoe Obozrenie* 3 (1990).

Gumilev, Lev N., and D. M. Balashov. "V kakoe vremia my zhivem?" In *Ritmy Evrazii. Epokhi i tsvilizatsiia*, 133–60. Moscow: Ekopros, 1993.

Gumilev, Lev N., and V. Iu. Ermolaev. "Gore ot illiuzii." In *Ritmy Evrazii*, 174–87. Moscow: Ekopros, 1993.

Gumilev, Lev N., and K. P. Ivanov. "Etnicheskie protsessy: dva podkhoda k izucheniiu." *Sotsiologicheskie Issledovaniia* 1 (1992).

Gumilev, Lev N., and A. P. Okladnikov. "Fenomen kul'tury malykh narodov Severa." *Dekorativnoe Iskusstvo* 8 (1982): 23–28. Accessed May 17, 2014. http://gumilevica.kulichki. net/ articles/Article102.htm).

Gumilev, Lev N. and A. M. Panchenko. *Chtoby svecha ne pogasla. Dialog*. Leningrad: Sovetskii Pisatel', 1990.

Gurko, Vladimir I. *Features and Figures of the Past*, edited by J. E. Wallace Sterling, Xenia Joukoff Eudin, and H. H. Fisher; translated by Laura Matveev. Stanford, CA: Stanford University Press, 1939.

Guzman, Vladimir Dzha. *Shkola magov: Fragmenty misticheskogo dvizheniia v SSSR v 70–80 gg XX veka*. No date. http://www.guzmanmedia.com/gm2/cont.php4.

Guzman, Vladimir Dzha. *Tropoi sviashchennogo kozeroga ili V poiskakh absoliutnogo tsentra*. St. Petersburg: Amfora, 2005. http://www.guzmanmedia.com/gm2/cont.php4.

Haffner, Sebastian and Gregory Bateson. *Der Vertrag von Versailles*. Berlin: Ullstein Verlag, 1988.

Harding, Luke. "We should Beware Russia's Links with Europe's Right." *The Guardian*, December 8, 2014. Accessed December 30, 2014. http://www.theguardian.com/ commentisfree/

Häusler, Aleksandr and Rainer Roeser. *Die rechten "Mut"-Bürger. Entstehung, Entwicklung, Personal and Positionen der "Alternative für Deutschland."* Hamburg: VSA Verlag, 2015.

Häusler, Aleksandr, ed. *Die Alternative für Deutschland: Programmatik, Entwicklung und politische Verortung*. Wiesbaden: Springer Fachmedien, 2016.

Heller, Leonid. "Away from the Globe: Occultism, Esotericism and Literature in Russia during the 1960s–1980s." In *The New Age of Russia: Occult and Esoteric Dimensions*, edited by Birgit Menzel, Michael Hagemeister, and Bernice Glatzer Rosenthal, 186–210. Munich: Kubon and Sagner, 2012.

Hellman, John. *The Communitarian Third Way: Alexandre Marc's Ordre Nouveau, 1930–2000*. Montreal and Kingston: McGill–Queen's University Press, 2002.

Herf, Jeffrey. Reactionary Modernism: Technology, Culture, and Politics in Weimar and the Third Reich. Cambridge: Cambridge University Press, 2002.

Hillis, Faith. *Children of Rus': Right-Bank Ukraine and the Invention of a Russian Nation*. Ithaca, NY: Cornell University Press, 2013.

Hirsch, Francine. *Empire of Nations: Ethnographic Knowledge and the Making of the Soviet Union*. Ithaca, NY: Cornell University Press, 2004.

History of World War II 1939–1945, vol. 3. Moscow: Voenizat, 1974.

Hitler, Adolf, André François-Poncet, François Genoud, and Hugh Trevor-Roper. *Le Testament politique de Hitler: Notes recueillies par Martin Bormann*. Translated by Jacques Brécard. Paris: Fayard, 1959.

Hobsbawm, Eric. *Age of Extremes: The Short Twentieth Century, 1914–1991*. London: Abacus, 1995.

Horvath, Robert. *The Legacy of Soviet Dissent: Dissidents, Democratisation and Radical Nationalism in Russia*. London: Routledge, 2005.

Huntington, Samuel P. *The Clash of Civilizations and the Remaking of World Order*. London: Simon and Schuster, 1996.

Iashchenko, Viacheslav G. *Antibol'shevistskoe povstanchestvo v Nizhnem Povolzh'e i na Srednem Donu: 1918–1923*. Moscow: Stereotip, 2008.

Il'in, Ivan. *Nashi zadachi: Stat'i 1948–1954 gg.* Moscow: Russkaia kniga, 1993.

Iliodor, Hieromonk. *The Mad Monk of Russia, Iliodor: Life, Memoirs, and Confessions of Sergei Michailovich Trufanoff.* New York: Century, 1918.

Institut national de formation légionnaire. *Bulletin de l'Institut national légionnaire,* 7. n.p.: Vichy, September 1943.

"Interventionskrieg—Sowjetunion? Was tun wir?" *Gegner* 11/12 (June 1932).

Introvigne, Massimo. *Le New Age des origines à nos jours : Courants, mouvements, personnalités.* Paris: Dervy, 2005.

Ischboldin, Boris. "Der Bolschewismus als ideokratisches Wirtschaftssystem und seine ideokratischen Gegenspieler." *Die Tat* 23, 11 (1931/32): 907–21.

Iudenkov, Andrei F. *Politicheskaia rabota partii sredi naseleniia okkupirovannoi sovetskoi territorii.* Moscow: Mysl', 1971.

Ivanov, A. A. *Vladimir Purishkevich—opyt biografii pravogo politika, 1870–1920.* Moscow-St. Petersburg: Alians–Arkheo, 2011.

Ivanov, K. P. "Vzgliady na etnografiiu ili est' li v sovetskoi nauke dva ucheniia ob etnose." *Izvestiia Vsesoiuznogo Geograficheskogo Obshchestva* 117, no. 3 (1985): 232–38.

Ivanov, Vladimir. *Aleksandr Dugin und die rechtsextremen Netzwerke.* Stuttgart: ibidem-Verlag, 2007.

Jackson, Paul. "The New Age." In *World Fascism: A Historical Encyclopedia,* edited by Cyprian P. Blamires and Paul Jackson, vol. 2, 463–64. Santa Barbara CA: ABC-Clio, 2006.

Jakobson, Roman, ed. *N. S. Trubetzkoy's Letters and Notes.* Berlin, New York, Amsterdam: Mouton, 1975.

Jakobson, Roman. *Evraziia v svete iazykoznaniia.* Paris: Izdanie Evraziitsev, 1931.

Joly, Laurent. *Vichy dans la "solution finale": Histoire du Commissariat général aux questions juives, 1941–1944.* Paris: Grasset, 2006.

Jones, Polly. *The Dilemmas of De-Stalinization: Negotiating Cultural and Social Change in the Khrushchev Era.* London: Routledge, 2006.

Judge, Edward H. *Easter in Kishinev: Anatomy of a Pogrom.* New York and London: New York University Press, 1995.

"K otsenke sovremennosti." *Evraziia* 35 (September 7, 1929).

Kabermann, Friedrich. *Widerstand und Entscheidung eines deutschen Revolutioners. Leben und Denken von Ernst Niekisch.* Cologne: Verlag Wissenschaft und Politik, 1973.

Kaisergruber, Fernand. *Nous n'irons pas à Touapsé. Du Donetz au Caucase, de Tcherkassy à l'Oder.* n.p.,1991.

"Kakomu bogu poklonialsia Gitler?" *Nauka i religiia* 9/10 (1966): 63–69.

Kaplin, A. and A. Stepanov. "Viazigin Andrei Sergeevich." In *Chernaia sotnia: Istoricheskaia entsiklopediia,* edited by O. A. Platonov. Moscow: Institut russkoi tsiviliztsii, 2008.

Karklins, Rasma. "Ethno-pluralism: Panacea for East Central Europe?" *Nationalities Papers* 28, no. 2 (2000): 219–41.

Karsavin, Lev P. "Osnovy politiki." In *Rossiia mezhdu Evropoi i Aziei: Evraziiskii soblazn,* edited by L. I. Novikova and I. N. Sizemskaia. Moscow: Nauka, 1993.

Karsavin, Lev P. "Rossiia i evrei" *Versty* 1 (1926).

Kazantsev, Aleksander. *Tret'ia sila: Rossiia mezhdu natsizmom i kommunizmom.* Munich: Posev, 1952 (1st ed.); Moscow: Posev, 1994 (3rd ed.).

Kaznina, O. A.. "N. S. Trubetskoi i krizis evraziistva." *Slavianovedenie* 4 (1995): 89–95.

Keating, Joshua. "From Russia with Cash." *Slate,* November 26, 2014. Accessed December 30, 2014. http://www.slate.com/blogs/the_world_/2014/11/26/from_russia_with_cash.html.

Kellogg, Michael. *The Russian Roots of Nazism: White Emigres and the Making of National Socialism, 1917–1945.* New York: Cambridge University Press, 2005.

Kent, Bruce. *Spoils of War: The Politics, Economics, and Diplomacy of Reparations, 1918–1932.* Oxford: The Clarendon Press, 1989.

Kholmskii vopros: Obzor russkoi periodicheskoi pechati s 1 ianvaria 1909 do 1 oktiabria 1911 g. St. Petersburg, 1912

Khomiakov, Aleksei S. "Mnenie inostrantsev o Rossii." *Moskvitianin* 4 (1845). Republished in *Polnoe sobranie sochinenii*, vol. 1. Moscow, 1878.

Khomiakov, Aleksei S. *Zapiski o vsemirnoi istorii*, vol. 2. Moscow, 1873.

Khomiakov, D. "Revoliutsionnye raznovidnosti." *Moskovskii golos* 27 (1906)

Kinner, Klaus. *Der deutsche Kommunismus: Selbstverständnis und Realität*. Bd. 1, *Die Weimarer Zeit*. Berlin: Dietz, 1999.

Kireev. "Neskol'ko dannykh dlia resheniia evreiskogo voprosa." *Sochineniia*, vol. 2. St. Petersburg, 1912.

Kireevskii, Ivan. "Obozrenie sovremennogo sostoianiia literatury." *Polnoe sobranie sochinenii*, vol. 2. Moscow, 1862.

Kirianov, Iu. I. "Chislennost' i sostav chlenov Russkogo sobraniia." In *Rossiiskaia imperiia: Strategii stabilizatsii i opyty obnovleniia*. Voronezh, 2004.

Kirianov, Iu. I. "Russkoe sobranie." In *Politicheskie partii Rossii: Konets XI–pervaya tret' XX veka*. Moscow, 1996.

Kirianov, Iu. I. *Russkoe sobranie 1900–1917*. Moscow, 2003.

Kiriutina, Tat'iana. *Problemy razvitiia russkoi literatury i zhurnalistiki kontsa XIX–nachala XX veka: S. F. Sharapov*. Smolensk, 2001.

Kisatsky, Deborah. *The United States and the European Right, 1945–1955*. Columbus: Ohio State University Press, 2005.

Kissenkoetter, Udo. *Gregor Strasser und die NSDAP: Schriftenreihe der Vierteljahrshefte für Zeitgeschichte*. Stuttgart: Deutsche Verlagsanstalt, 1978.

Kitsenko, Nadezhda. *Sviatoi nashego vremeni: Otets Ioann Kronshtadtskii i russkii narod*. Moscow: NLO, 2006.

Kizilov, Mikhail. *The Sons of Scripture: The Karaites in Poland and Lithuania in the Twentieth Century*. Berlin: De Gruyter, 2015.

Kochanek, Hildegard. "Die Ethnienlehre Lev N. Gumilevs: Zu den Anfängen neu-rechter Ideologie-Entwicklung im spätkommunistischen Russland." *Osteuropa* 48 (1998).

Kochanek, Hildegard. *Die russisch-nationale Rechte von 1968 bis zum Ende der Sowjetunion. Eine Diskursanalyse*. Stuttgart: Franz Steiner, 1999.

Koenen, Gerd. *Der Russland-Komplex: Die Deutschen und der Osten 1900–1945*. Munich: C.H. Beck, 2005.

Kosiek, Rolf. "Die Wirklichkeit des Volken in der modernen Welt." In *Muktikultopia: Gedanken zur multikulturellen Gesellschaft*, edited by Stefan Ulbrich, 109–36. Vilsbiburg: Arun, 1991.

Kosiek, Rolf. *Völker statt One World: Das Volk im Spiegel der Wissenschaft*. Tübingen: Grabert, 1999.

Kotsiubinskii, Daniil A. *Russkii natsionalizm v nachale stoletiia: Rozhdenie i gibel' ideologii Vserossiiskogo Natsionalnogo Soiuza*. Moscow: ROSSPEN, 2001.

Kozlov, S. Ia. *Akademik Iu. V. Bromlei i otechestvennaia etnologiia, 1969–1990-e gody*. Moscow: Nauka, 2003.

Kozlov, Vladimir and Vladimir Maikov. *Transpersonal'nyi proket: Psikhologiia, antropologiia, dukhovnye traditsii*, vol. 2. Moscow: Transpersonal'nyi institut, 2007.

Krebs, Pierre. *Das Thule-Seminar: Geistesgegenwart der Zukunft in der Morgenröte des Ethnos*. Horn: Burkhart Weeke Verlag, 1994.

Krebs, Pierre. *Fighting for the Essence: Western Ethnosuicide or European Renaissance?* Translated by Aleksandr Jacob. London: Arktos, 2012.

Krebs, Pierre. "L'avènement de l'ethno-socialisme." *EURO-SYNERGIES* (2013). Accessed November 7, 2014. http://euro-synergies.hautetfort.com/archive/2013/03/22/p-krebs -l-avenement-de-l-ethno-socialisme.html.

Krest'ianskoe dvizhenie v Povolzh'e. 1919–1922 gg: Dokumenty i materialy. Moscow: Rossiskaia politicheskaia entsiklopediia, 2002.

Krizhevskii, Aleksei. "Barkhatnoe podpol'e: Igor Dudinskii o zhizni sovetskoi bogemy," *Russkaia zhizn'*. February 1, 2008, http://www.rulife.ru/mode/article/510.

Kryzhanovskii, S. E. *Vospominianiia*. St. Peterburg: Izdatel'stvo Rossiiskoi natsional'noi biblioteki, 2009.

"Kulturhegemoniale Strategien der russischen extremen Rechten: Die Verbindung von faschistischer Ideologie und metapolitischer Taktik im "Neoeurasismus" des Aleksandr Dugin." *Österreichische Zeitschrift für Politikwissenschaft* 33, no. 4: 437–54.

Kuz'min, Mikhail. "Social Genetics and Organizational Science." In *Aleksandr Bogdanov and the Origins of Systems Thinking in Russia*, edited by John Biggart, Peter Dudley and Francis King, 278–303. Aldershot: Ashgate, 1998.

Kymlicka, Will. *Contemporary Political Philosophy: An Introduction*. Oxford: Oxford University Press, 2002.

"L'action. La recontre de Frankfort." *Plans* 12 (February 1932).

"La oposición social-patriótica rusa: Christian Bouchet entrevista a sus líderes." *Tribuna de Europa* 6, no. 2 (summer 1996): 22–25.

"La Russie et l'Europe." *Nouvelle revue d'histoire* 7 (2003).

Labaume, Eugène. *Relation circonstanciée de la campagne de Russie*. Genoa, 1814.

Labonne, "Le Traité de Lausanne et la question turque." In *Revue de Paris* and *Le Tapis vert du Pacifique*, Buchet-Chastel, 1936.

Lamanskii, Vladimir. *Ob istoricheskom izuchenii greko-slavianskogo mira v Evrope*. St. Petersburg, 1871.

Lambert, Pierre-Philippe and Gérard Le Marec. In *Les français sous le casque allemande*. Grancher, 1994.

Laqueur, Walter. *Black Hundred: The Rise of the Extreme Right in Russia*. New York: HarperCollins, 1993.

Laqueur, Walter. *Chernaia sotnia: Proiskhozhdenie russkogo fashizma*. Washington, DC, 1994.

Laqueur, Walter. *Fascism: Past, Present and Future*. New York: Oxford University Press, 1996.

Laqueur, Walter. *Rossiia i Germaniia: Nastavniki Gitlera*. Moscow: Mysl', 1991.

Laqueur, Walter. *Russia and Germany: A Century of Conflict*. New Brunswick, NJ: Transaction, 1990.

Laruelle, Marlene. "Aleksandr Dugin: A Russian Version of the European Radical Right?" Kennan Institute Occasional Papers, No. 272 (n.d.).

Laruelle, Marlene, ed. *Eurasianism and the European Far Right: Reshaping the Europe-Russia Relationship*. Lanham, MD: Lexington, 2015.

Laruelle, Marlene. *L'Idéologie eurasiste russe ou Comment penser l'empire*. Paris: L'Harmattan, 1999.

Laruelle, Marlene. "Lev Nikolaevic Gumilev (1912–1992): Biologisme et eurasisme dans la penseé russe." *Revue des Études Slaves* 72, no. 1-2 (2000).

Laruelle, Marlene. *Mythe aryen et rêve impérial dans la Russie tsariste*. Paris: CNRS-Éditions, 2005.

Laruelle, Marlene. "Opyt sravnitel'nogo analiza teorii etnosa L'va Gumileva i zapadnykh novykh pravykh." *Etnograficheskoe Obozrenie* 3 (2006): 226–39. Accessed July 11, 2014. http://www1.ku-eichstaett.de/ZIMOS/forum/docs/forumruss11/a10LaruellGumilev.pdf.

Laruelle, Marlene. "La question du 'touranisme' des Russes: Contribution à une histoire des échanges intellectuels Allemagne-France-Russie au XIXe siècle." *Cahiers du monde russe* 1-2 (2004): 241–65.

Laruelle, Marlene. *Russian Eurasianism: An Ideology of Empire*. Washington, DC: Woodrow Wilson Center Press, 2008.

Laruelle, Marlene. "Totalitarian Utopia, the Occult, and Technological Modernity in Russia: The Intellectual Experience of Cosmism." In *The New Age of Russia: Occult and Es-*

oteric Dimensions, edited by Birgit Menzel, Michael Hagemeister, and Bernice Glatzer Rosenthal, 238–58. Munich: Kubon and Sagner, 2012.

Laurent, Frédéric. *L'Orchestre noir.* Paris: Stock, 1978.

Lausberg, Michael. "Irinäus Eibl-Eibesfeldt: Steigbügelhalter für die extreme Rechte?" *Tabularasa* 100 (2014). Accessed October 19, 2014. http://www.tabularasa-jena.de/artikel/artikel_5607/.

Lavrov, S. B. *Lev Gumilev: Sud'ba i idei.* Moscow: Svarog i K, 2000.

"Le calvaire de Jean-Jacques Remetter." *Dernières Nouvelles d'Alsace* (February 27, 1984).

Lebourg, Nicolas. "Arriba Eurasia? The Difficult Establishment of Eurasianism in Spain." In *Eurasianism and the European Far Right: Reshaping the Europe–Russia Relationship,* edited by Marlene Laruelle, 125–42. Lanham, MD: Lexington Books, 2015.

Lebourg, Nicolas. "La Fonction productrice de l'histoire dans le renouvellement du fascisme à partir des années 1960." In *Les Sciences sociales au prisme de l'extrême droite: Enjeux et usages d'une récupération idéologique,* edited by Sylvain Crépon et Sébastien Mosbah-Natanson, 213–43. Paris: L'Harmattan 2008.

Lebourg, Nicolas. *Le monde vu de la plus extrême-droite, du fascisme au nationalisme-révolutionnaire.* Perpignan: Presses universitaires de Perpignan, 2010.

Lebourg, Nicolas and Jonathan Preda. "Le Front de l'Est et l'extrême droite radicale française: Propagande collaborationniste, lieu de mémoire et fabrique idéologique." In *Références et thèmes des droites radicales,* edited by Olivier Dard. Peter Lang: Bern, 2015, 101–38.

Leleu, Jean-Luc. *La Waffen-SS.* Paris: Perrin, 2007.

Lenin. *Œuvres choisies,* vol. 3. Moscow: Éditions du Progrès, 1968.

Lenin. *Du Droit des nations à disposer d'elles-mêmes.* Moscow: Éditions du progrès, 1979.

"Les incorporés de force alsaciens." *Vingtième Siècle, revue d'histoire* 6 (April–June 1985): 83–102.

Levin, Sh. M. "Materialy dlia kharakteristiki kontr-revoliutsii 1905 g." *Byloe* 21 (1923).

Levitskii, V. "Pravye partii." In *Obshchestvennoe dvizhenie v Rossii v nachale XX-go veka,* edited by L. Martov et al., 4 vols. St. Petersburg, 1909–1914.

Lindholm, Charles and José Pedro Zúquete. *The Struggle for the World: Liberation Movements in the 21st Century.* Stanford, CA: Stanford University Press, 2010.

Lipiansky, A. M. "Pour un Communisme National, la revue 'Die Tat.'" *Revue d'Allemagne* 6 (1932).

Liubosh, Semen. *Russkii fashist Vladimir Purishkevich.* Leningrad, 1925.

Llopart, Juan Antonio. "¿Nacionalbolcheviques?" *Tribuna de Europa* 6 (June 1994).

Lobashev, M. E. 1961. "Signal'naia nasledstvennost.'" In *Issledovaniia po genetike,* edited by M. E. Lobashev. Leningrad: Iz-vo Lenin. Gos. Universiteta., 1961.

Lobashev, M. E. *Genetika.* Leningrad: Iz-vo Lenin. Gos. Universiteta., 1967.

Lobsiger, François. *Un suisse au service de Hitler.* Paris: Albatros, 1985.

London, Jack. *The Iron Heel.* New York: Macmillan, 1908.

Lorenz, Konrad. *Das sogenannte Böse: Zur Naturgeschichte der Aggression.* Vienna: G. Borotha-Schoeler, 1963.

Lorenz, Konrad. *Der Abbau des Menschlichen.* Munich: Piper, 1983.

Loubet del Bayle, Jean-Louis. *Les non-conformistes des années 30: Une trentative de renouvellement de la pensée politique française.* Paris: Seuil, 2001.

Löwe, Heinz-Dietrich. *The Tsars and the Jews: Reform, Reaction and Anti-Semitism in Imperial Russia, 1772–1917.* Chur: Harwood Academic Publishers, 1993.

Luk'ianov, Mikhail N. *Rossiiskii konservatizm i reforma, 1907–1914.* Stuttgart: Ibidem Verlag, 2007.

Luks, Leonid, ed. *Zwei "Sonderwege"? Russisch-deutsche Parallelen und Konstrate (1917–2014).* Stuttgart: Ibidem-Verlag, 2016.

Luks, Leonid. "'Eurasier' und 'Konservative Revolution': Zur antiwestlichen Versuchung in Rußland und in Deutschland." In *Deutschland und die Russische Revolution: 1917–1924,* edited by Gerd Koenen and Lew Kopelew, 219–39. Munich: Fink, 1998.

Luks, Leonid. "Die Ideologie der Eurasier im zeitgenössischen Zusammenhang." *Jahrbücher für Geschichte Osteuropas* 34 (1986): 374–95.

Mabire, Jean. *La division Charlemagne sur le front de l'est.* Grancher, 2005.

Mabire, Jean. *La Varende entre nous.* Tilly-sur-Seulles: Présence de La Varende, 1999.

Makarov, V. G. and A. M. Matveeva. "A. P. Antipov." In *Obshchestvennaia mysl' russkogo zarubezh'ia: Entsiklopediia,* edited by V. V. Zhuravlev. Moscow: ROSSPEN, 2009.

Malia, Martin. *Aleksandr Gertsen i proiskhozhdenie russkogo sotsializma, 1812–1855.* Moscow: Territoriia budushchego, 2010.

Mallmann, Klaus-Michael. *Kommunisten in der Weimarer Republik: Sozialgeschichte einer revolutionären Bewegung.* Darmstadt: Wissenschaftliche Buchgesellschaft, 1996.

Malycha, Andreas and Peter Jochen Winters. *Die SED: Geschichte einer deutschen Partei.* Munich: C.H. Beck, 2009.

Manifeste du Partisan européen. Nantes: Ars, n.d.

Markov, N. E. *Istoriia evreiskogo shturma v Rossii.* Harbin, 1937.

Márquez, Fernando. "Hacia el Frente Ibérico de Salvación." *Punto de Vista Operativo* 1 (fall 1995).

Márquez, Fernando. "Sobre Zhirinovsky: Hablando en plata." *El corazón del bosque* 23 (spring 1994).

Martin, Maurice. *Le Grand Suicide,* Le Puy: Crêve-Tabous, 1984.

Martin, Philippe. *A la recherche d'une éducation nouvelle: Histoire de la jeunesse allemande, 1813–1945.* Lore, 2010.

März, Markus. *Nationale Sozialisten in der NSDAP: Strukturen, Ideologie, Publizistik und Biographien des national-sozialistischen Straßer-Kreises von der AG Nordwest bis zum Kampf-Verlag 1925–1930.* Graz: Ares-Verlag, 2010.

Massip, Mireille. *Alexandre Kasem-Beg et l'émigration russe en Occident, 1902–1977.* Paris: Georg Editeur S.A., 1999.

Mech, V. *Sily reaktsii.* Moscow, 1908.

Mel'nikova, E. "Eskhatologicheskie ozhidaniia rubezha XIX–XX vekov: Kontsa sveta ne budet?" *Antropologicheskii forum* 1 (2004).

Men'shikov, Mikhail. "Rasovaia bor'ba." In Men'shikov, Mikhail, *Pis'ma k russkoi natsii* Moscow, 1999): 130–32.

Men'shikov, "Evrei o evreiakh" [1909], in Men'shikov, *Pis'ma k russkoi natsii:* 53–59.

Menzel, Birgit, "Occult and Esoteric Movements in Russia from the 1960s to the 1980s." In *The New Age of Russia: Occult and Esoteric Dimensions,* edited by Birgit Menzel, Michael Hagemeister, and Bernice Glatzer Rosenthal, 151–85. Munich: Kubon and Sagner, 2012.

Merglen, Albert. "Soldats français sous uniformes allemands 1941–1945: LVF et Waffen SS français." *Revue d'histoire de la Deuxième Guerre Mondiale* 27, 108 (1977): 71–84.

Meyer, Henry Cord. *Mitteleuropa in German Thought and Action 1815–1945.* The Hague: Martinus Nijhoff, 1955.

Meyerson, Harold. "Pat Buchanan, Vladimir Putin and Strange Bedfellows." *Washington Post,* December 27, 2013. Accessed December 30, 2014. http://www.washingtonpost.com/opinions/ harold-meyerson-pat-buchanan-vladimir-putin-and-strange-bedfellows/2013/12/24/f8159f22-68bf-11e3-a0b9-249bbb34602c_story.html.

Michel, Luc. "Aujourd'hui Moscou, demain l'Europe. Nous sommes l'Europe combattante." Nation Europe (February 1994).

Michurin, V. A. "Slovar' poniatii i terminov teorii etnogeneza L. N. Gumileva." In *Etnosfera: Istoriia liudei i istoriia prirody,* 517–72. Moscow: AST, 2004.

Miller, Alexei. *The Romanov Empire and Nationalism*. Budapest: Central European University Press, 2008.

Milukov, Pavel N. "Russkii rasizm." *Poslednie novosti* (December 16, 1926). Republished in *Istoricheskaia nauka rossiiskoi emigratsii: "Evraziiskii soblazn,"* edited by Margarita G. Vandalkovskaia, 331–35. Moscow: RAN, 1997.

Milza, Pierre. *Fascisme français: Passé et present*. Paris: Flammarion, 1987.

Minkenberg, Michael. "The New Right in France and Germany: Nouvelle Droite, Neue Rechte, and the New Right Radical Parties." In *The Revival of Right Wing Extremism in the Nineties*, edited by Peter H. Merkl and Leonard Weinberg. London: Frank Cass, 1997.

Mitrokhin, Nikolai. *"Russkaia partiia": Dvizhenie russkikh natsionalistov v SSSR 1953–1985 gg*. Moscow: NLO, 2003.

Moeller van den Bruck, Arthur. *Das Recht der jungen Völker, 1919: Das dritte Reich*. Berlin: Ring Verlag, 1923.

Mogilner, Marina. *Homo Imperii: A History of Physical Anthropology in Russia*. Lincoln, NE: University of Nebraska Press, 2013.

Mohler, Armin. *La Révolution conservatrice en Allemagne, 1918–1922*. Puiseaux: Editions Pardès, 1993 [1950].

Mohler, Armin. *Die Konservative Revolution in Deutschland 1918–1932: Grundriß ihrer Weltanschauungen*. Stuttgart: Friedrich Vorwerk Verlag, 1950. Republished Graz: Ares-Verlag, 2005.

Moreau, Patrick. "Die neue Religion der Rasse: Der Biologismus und die neue kollektive Ethik der Neuen Rechten in Frankreich und Deutschland." In *Neokonservative und Neue Rechte:Der Angriff gegen Sozialstaat und liberale Demokratie in den Vereinigten Staaten, Westeuropa und der Bundesrepublik*, edited by Iring Fetscher, 122–62. Munich: Beck, 1983.

Moreau, Patrick. "La Communauté de combat nationale-socialiste révolutionnaire et le Front noir: Action et idéologie en Allemagne, Autriche et Tchécoslovaquie, 1930–1935." Third Cycle Doctorate. University of Paris, 1978.

Moreau, Patrick. "Le Parti National-Démocrate d'Allemagne dans la vie politique de la R.F.A.: Études organisationnelle, sociologique et électorale d'une formation de l'opposition nationale 1964–1976." State Doctorate in Political Science. 1984.

Moreau, Patrick. *Les héritiers du IIIe Reich: L'extrême droite allemande de 1945 à nos jours*. Paris: Seuil, 1994.

Moreau, Patrick. *Nationalsozialismus von links: Die "Kampfgemeinschaft Revolutionärer Nationalsozialisten" und die "Schwarze Front" Otto Straßers 1930–1935*. Stuttgart: Deutsche Verlags-Anstalt, 1985.

Morozov, Viacheslav. *Russia's Postcolonial Identity: A Subaltern Empire in a Eurocentric World*. New York: Palgrave Macmillan, 2015.

Morris, Alan G. "Biological Anthropology at the Southern Tip of Africa: Carrying European Baggage in an African Context." *Current Anthropology* 53 (2012).

Moscow State Institute of International Relations. *Vypusk 1953*. Moscow: Mezhdunarodnye otnosheniia, 2001.

Mota, Jorge. *Hacia un socialismo europeo: ¿Falange o comunismo?* Barcelona: Bau, 1974.

Müller, Rolf-Dieter. *The Unknown Eastern Front: The Wehrmacht and Hitler's Foreign Soldiers*. London: I.B. Tauris, 2012.

Munoz, Antonio J. *The East Came West: Muslim, Hindu, and Buddhist Volunteers in the German Armed Forces, 1941–1945*. New York: Axis Europa Books, 2002.

Nafziger, George. "Organizational History of the German SS Formations, 1939–1945." http://usacac.army.mil/cac2/CGSC/CARL/nafziger/939GXWA.pdf.

Nazarov, Mikhail. *Missiia russkoi emigratsii*. Moscow: Rodnik, 1994.

Newstadt, E. *Components of Pessimism in Russian Conservative Thought, 1881–1905*. PhD diss., University of Oklahoma, 1991.

Niekisch, Ernst. "Abrüstung?" *Widerstand* 5 (1930): 353–61.

Niekisch, Ernst. "Die Politik des deutschen Widerstandes." *Widerstand* 5 (1930).

Niekisch, Ernst. *Hitler, une fatalité allemande et autres écrits nationaux-bolcheviks.* Pardès, Puiseaux, 1991.

Niekisch, Ernst. "Europa betet." *Widerstand* 5 (1930).

Nikol'skii, B. "Dnevnik." *Krasnyi arkhiv* 63 (1934).

Nikolaev, A. B. and R. B. Romov. "Bobrinskii Vladimir Alekseevich." In *Gosudarstvennaia duma Rossiiskoi imperii 1906–1917. Entsiklopediia.* Moscow: ROSSPEN, 2008.

Nikolaev, A. B. and R. B. Romov, "Purishkevich Vladimir Mitrofanovich," in *Gosudarstvennaia duma Rossiiskoi imperii 1906–1917. Entsiklopediia.* Moscow: ROSSPEN, 2008.

Nolte, Ernst. *Three Faces of Fascism: Action Française, Italian Fascism, National Socialism.* New York: Holt, Rinehart and Winston, 1966.

Ob"edinennoe dvorianstvo: S"ezdy upolnomochennykh gubernskikh dvorianskikh obshchestv, 1906–1916, vol. 1. Moscow, 2001.

Oberländer, Erwin. "The All-Russian Fascist Party." *Journal of Contemporary History* 1, no. 1 (1966): 158–73.

Obszerninks, Britta. *Nachbarn am rechten Rand: Republikaner und Freiheitliche Partei Österreichs im Vergleich.* Munich: Agenda, 1999.

Odarchenko, Konstantin. *Nravstvennye i pravovye osnovy russkogo narodnogo khoziaistva.* Moscow: Tipo-lit. K.F. Aleksandrova, 1897.

Odarchenko, Konstantin. "K voprosu o den'gakh i 'zolotoi valiute' kreditnogo rublia." *Russkaia beseda* 12 (1895).

Odarchenko, Konstantin. "Narodnoe khoziaistvo s tochki zreniia nravstvennosti i prava." *Russkaia beseda* 4 (1895): 28–37.

Odarchenko, Konstantin. "Otnoshenie proizvoditelei k potrebiletiam s tochki zreniia nravstvennosti i prava," *Russkaia beseda* 4 (1896): 12–20.

Omelianchuk, I. V. *Chernosotennoe dvizhenie v Rossiiskoi Imperii 1901–1914.* Kiev, 2007.

O'Meara, Michael. "Benoist's Pluriversuman Ethnonationalist Critique." 2006. Accessed October 23, 2014. http://www.newrightausnz.com/2006/03/29/benoists-pluriversuman-ethnonationalist-critique-by-michael-omeara/.

O'Meara, Michael. *Guillaume Faye and the Battle of Europe.* London: Arktos, 2013.

O'Meara, Michael. *New Culture, New Right: Anti-Liberalism in Postmodern Europe.* 2nd ed. London: Arktos, 2013.

Onoprienko, Iu. I. "Analiz kontseptsii etnogeneza L. N. Gumilev s pozitsii sistemno-informat-sionnoi metodologii." *Visnik Natsional'nogo aviatsiinogo universiteta* 2, no. 18 (2013): 17–25.

Orenstein, Mitchell A. "Putin's Western Allies: Why Europe's Far Right Is on the Kremlin's Side." *Foreign Affairs,* March 25, 2014. Accessed December 30, 2014. http://www.foreignaffairs.com/articles/141067/mitchell-a-orenstein/putins-western-allies.

"Orientándonos con Aleksandr Duguin." *El corazón del bosque* 4 (Autumn 1994).

Osorgin, Mikhail. "Politicheskie ocherki sovremennoi Italii." *Evraziia* 13 (February 16, 1929).

Ougarov, Nicolas. "Le Haut-Karabagh, lieu éruptif du conflit Islam-Chrétienté." *Militant* (May 2015).

Paetel, Karl Otto. "Otto Strasser und die 'Schwarze Front' des 'wahren Nationalsozialismus.'" *Politische Studien* 8, 92 (1957): 269–81.

Paetel, Karl Otto. *Versuchung oder Chance? Zur Geschichte des deutschen Nationalbolschewismus.* Göttingen: Musterschmidt Verlag, 1965.

Palmer, James. *The Bloody White Baron: The Extraordinary Story of the Russian Nobleman Who Became the Last Khan of Mongolia.* New York: Basic Books, 2009.

Panfil'ev. "O fashistskoi ideologii." *Evraziets* 21 (November 1932).

Parisien [Sharapov], "U Giugo," *Novoe vremia*, no. 712 (1878).

Parisien [Sharapov], "U Lui Blana," *Novoe vremia*, no. 693 (1878).

Parvulesco, Jean. "De la libération nationale à la libération continentale." *De l'Atlantique au Pacifique* (February 1976).

Pauley, Bruce. "Fascism and the *Fuehrerprinzip*: The Austrian Example." *Central European History* 12, no. 3 (1979): 272–96.

Pauwels, Louis. *Monsieur Gurdjieff: Documents, témoignages, textes et commentaires sur une société initiatique contemporaine.* Paris: Albin Michel, 1996.

Pavochka, S. G. *L. N. Gumilev: Istoki i sushchnost'.* Grodno: IGAU, 2011.

Peillen, Txomin. *Jon Mirande, poète parisien.* Euskaltzaindia, 2012.

Penka, Karl. *Origines Ariacae: Linguistisch-ethnologische Untersuchungen zur älteren Geschichte der arischen Völker und Sprachen.* Vienna, 1883.

Penkower, Monty Noam. "The Kishinev Pogrom of 1903: A Turning Point in Jewish History," *Modern Judaism* 24, no. 3 (October 2004).

"Perepiska I. S. Aksakova i S. F. Sharapova (1883–1886)." *Russkaia literatura* 1 (2005).

Perfil'ev. "'Chernyi front.' Tezisy germanskoi revoliutsii: Osnovnaia programma natsional'-sotsialisticheskoi i revoliutsionnoi organizatsii." *Evraziets* 19 (February 1932). Reprint *'Svoi put'* 2, no. 6 (April, 1932).

Pervaia vseobshchaia perepis' naseleniia Rossiiskoi imperii 1897 g. St. Petersburg, 1897–1905.

Pervyi s"ezd Evraziiskoi organizatsii. Protokol i materialy (n.p., 1932).

Peunova, Marina. "The Transfer of Ideas along a Cultural Gradient: The Influence of the European New Right on Aleksandr Panarin's New Eurasianism." In *Mapping the Extreme Right in Contemporary Europe: From Local to Transnational*, edited by Andrea Mammone, Emmanuel Godin, and Brian Jenkins. London: Routledge, 2012.

Platonov, Oleg. "Missiia vypolnima." In *Putin v zerkale "Izborskogo kluba,"* edited by Maxim Kalashnikov et al. Moscow: Knizhnyi mir, 2015.

Pokras, Daniil and Dmitrii Pokras. *If War Comes Tomorrow.* (n.d.).

Poltinnikova-Shifrin, Eleonora. "Mistika v nashei zhizni (glava iz budushchei knigi)." *Zhurnal-Gazeta Masterskaia* (2012). http://club.berkovich-zametki.com/?p=1266.

Polyakova, Alina. "Strange Bedfellows: Putin and Europe's Far Right." *World Affairs* (September–October, 2014). Accessed December 30, 2014. http://www.worldaffairsjournal.org/ article/strange-bedfellows-putin-and-europe%E2%80%99s-far-right.

Pour une critique positive. Nantes: Ars Magna, 1997; 1st ed., 1962.

Prazdnik russkago samosoznaniia: otkritie kharkovskago otdela "Russkago sobraniia." Kharkov, 1903.

Pribylovski, Vladimir. "Pamiat'." In *Natsional'naia pravaia prezhde i teper'*, vol. 2, edited by R. Sh. Ganelin, 151–70. St. Petersburg: Institut sotsiologii RAN, 1992.

Pringle, Heather. *The Master Plan: Himmler's Scholars and the Holocaust.* New York: Hyperion, 2006.

Programma Russkago sobraniia. St. Petersburg, 1906.

"Proyecto Bronwyn." *Más allá del Sur: Revista Negra de las Artes Literarias y Políticas* 1 (November 1986).

Rabow-Edling, Susanna. *Slavophile Thought and the Politics of Cultural Nationalism.* Albany, NY: SUNY Press, 2012.

Ratzel, Friedrich. *Der Lebensraum: Eine biogeographische Studie.* Tübingen: Laupp'sche Buchhandlung, 1901.

Rawson, Don C. *Russian Rightists and the Revolution of 1905.* Cambridge: Cambridge University Press, 1995.

Reed, Douglas. *The Prisoner of Ottawa: Otto Strasser.* London: Cape, 1953.

Repnikov, Aleksandr V. *Konservativnye predstasvleniia pereustroistva Rossii.* Moscow: Academia, 2007.

Repnikov, Aleksandr V. *Russkoe sobranie* in *Russkii konservatizm serediny XVIII–nachalo XX veka: Entsiklopediia.* Moscow, 2010.

Rerikhovskaia Enksiklopediia, s.v. "Aseev Aleksandr Mikhailovich." http://www.roerich -encyclopedia.facets.ru/personal/Aseev.html.

Retzius, Anders A. *Ethnologische Schriften.* Stockholm, 1864.

"Richard Scheringer: Del nacionalsocialismo al comunismo." *Tribuna de Europa* 9 (March– April 1997).

Rogachevskii, Andrei. "Lev Gumilev i evreiskii vopros (po lichnym vospominaniiam)" 2001.

Rogger, Hans. "Was There a Russian Fascism? The Union of Russian People." *Journal of Modern History* 36, no. 4 (1964): 398–415.

Rogger, Hans. *Jewish Policies and Right-Wing Politics in Imperial Russia.* Berkeley: University of California Press, 1986.

Romanov, Ivan F. *K svedeniiu budushchego ministra zemledeliia.* St. Petersburg: Tip. S. N., n.d.

Romov, R. B. "Krushevan Pavel Aleksandrovich." In *Gosudarstvennaia duma Rossiiskoi imperii 1906–1917: Entsiklopediia.* Moscow: ROSSPEN, 2008.

Ross, Alexander Reid. *Against the Fascist Creep.* Oakland, CA: AK Press, 2016.

Rovner, Arkadii. "G. I. Gurdieff's Influence in Russia in the 1960s–1970s." Paper presented at the international conference "The Occult in 20th-century Russia: Metaphysical Roots of Soviet Civilization," Harriman Institute/European Academy, Berlin, Germany, March 11–13, 2007. http://gurdjieffclub.com/en/articles-essay-arkady -rovner-g-i-gurdjieffs-influence-in-russia-in-the-1960s1970.

Rusco, Pierre. *Stoï!* Dualpha, 2006.

"Rusia en política exterior." *Nosotros somos quien somos* 30 (March–April 1999).

Rutkoff, Peter. "The *Ligue des Patriotes*: The Nature of the Radical Right and the Dreyfus Affair." *French Historical Studies* 8, no. 4 (1974): 585–603.

Rzhevskaia, Elena M. *Gebbels: Portret na fone dnevnika.* Moscow: AST-Press, 1994.

Saage, Richard. "Fascism—Revolutionary Departure to an Alternative Modernity? A Response to Roger Griffin's 'Exploding the Continuum of History.'" *European Journal of Political Theory* 11, no. 4 (2012).

Saburov, Aleksandr N. *Otvoevannaia vesna.* Ustinov [Izhevsk]: Udmurtia, 1986.

Saburov, Aleksandr N. *Silii neischislimie.* Moscow: Voenizdat, 1967.

Sadovskii, Iakov D. "Iz dnevnika 'evraziitsa.'" *Evraziiskii vremennik* 4 (1925): 400–404.

Saint-Loup. *Jean Benvoar, un héros breton,* Collection Les cahiers de la Bretagne réelle, 275b (summer 1969).

Sautreuil, Pierre. "With A Far-Right Band of Frenchmen Fighting In Ukraine." *Worldcrunch* (September 4, 2014). Accessed December 30, 2014. http://www.worldcrunch.com/ ukraine-winter/with-a-far-right-band-of-frenchmen-fighting-in-ukraine/far-right-na tionalism-mercenaries-separatists-soldiers-/c20s16888/—.VKMWFRF3c6V

Sauveur, Yannick. "L'URSS héritière du IIIe Reich." Foreword. In *Revue d'Histoire du nationalisme révolutionnaire: Jean Thiriart et le national communautarisme européen,* no. 3 (n.d.).

Savel'ev, A. N. *Obraz vraga: Rasologiia i politicheskaia antropologiia,* 2nd ed. Moscow: Belye Al'vy, 2010.

Savino, Dzhiovanni. "Okrainy Rossii i proekt natsionalizatsii Rossiiskoi Imperii." In *Puti Rossii: Sbornik statei.* Vol. 21, *Novyi poriadok—vechnoe vozvrashchenie,* edited by M. G. Pugacheva and A. F. Filippov, 231–42. Moscow: NLO, 2015.

Savino, Giovanni. "Dugin's Italian Connections: The Impact of Neo-Eurasianism on the Italian Political Landscape." Forthcoming.

Savino, Giovanni. "Il nazionalismo russo, 1900–1917: Ideologie, organizzazioni, sfera pubblica" PhD diss., University of Naples Federico II, 2012.

Savitskii, Petr N. *Rossiia—osobyi geograficheskii mir.* Prague, 1927.

Schapke, Richard. *Die Schwarze Front*. Leipzig, 1932.

Scharapoff, Serge. "L'Allemagne et l'opinion russe." *Le Radical* (January 19, 1911).

Scharapoff, Serge. "Le Nouveau plan stratégique de la Russie." *L'Opinion* (February 18, 1911).

Schedler, Jan and Aleksandr Häusler, eds. *Autonome Nationalisten: Neonazismus in Bewegung*. Wiesbaden: VS−Verlag für Sozialwissenschaften, 2011.

Schlanger, Judith. *Les métaphores de l'organisme*. Paris: L'Harmattan, 1995.

Schlembach, Raphael. "Alain de Benoist's Anti-Political Philosophy beyond Left and Right: Non-Emancipatory Responses to Globalisation and Crisis." Centre for the Study of Social and Global Justice, University of Nottingham, Working Paper No. 22, 11 (2013).

Schmid, Ulrich. "Flowers of Evil: The Poetics of Monstrosity in Contemporary Russian Literature (Erofeev, Mamleev, Sokolov, Sorokin)." *Russian Literature* (2000): 205–21.

Schorpp-Grabiak, Rita. *Man muss so radikal sein wie die Wirklichkeit. Die PDS: Eine Bilanz*. Baden-Baden: Nomos Verlag, 2002.

Schüddekopf, Otto Ernst. *Linke Leute von rechts: Die nationalrevolutionären Minderheiten und der Kommunismus in der Weimarer Republik*. Stuttgart: Kohlhammer, 1960.

Schulze-Boysen, Harro. "Der neue Gegner." *Gegner* 4/5 (1932).

Schulze-Boysen, Harro. "Die Saboteure der Revolution." *Gegner* 7 (1932).

Schulze-Boysen, Harro. *Gegner von heut−Kampfgenossen von morgen*. Berlin, 1932.

Schulze-Boysen, Harro. "Vom kommenden Wir." *Gegner* 1/2 (1932).

Schuster, Kurt G. P. *Der Rote Frontkämpferbund 1924–1929: Beiträge zur Geschichte und Organisationsstruktur eines politischen Kampfbundes*. Düsseldorf: Droste, 1975.

Schwidetzky, Ilse, ed. *Die neue Rassenkunde*. Stuttgart: Gustav Fischer Verlag, 1962.

Schwidetzky, Ilse. *Grundzüge der Völkerbiologie*. Stuttgart: Ferdinand Enke Verlag, 1950.

Schwidetzky, Ilse. *Rassen und Rassenbildung beim Menschen*. Stuttgart-New York: Fischer, 1979.

Sedgwick, Mark. *Against the Modern World: Traditionalism and the Secret History of the Twentieth Century*. Oxford: Oxford University Press, 2004.

Serebrov, Konstantin. *Misticheskii andergraund: Germeticheskaia shkola*. Moscow: Amrita, 2002.

Sériot, Patrick. *Structure and the Whole (Semiotics, Communication and Cognition)*. Berlin: De Gruyter Mouton, 2014.

Servettaz, Elena. "Putin's Far-Right Friends in Europe." Institute of Modern Russia (January 16, 2014). Accessed December 30, 2014. http://imrussia.org/en/russia-and -the-world/645-putins-far-right-friends-in-europe.

Sharapov, Sergei. *Cherez polveka*. Moscow, 1902.

Sharapov, Sergei. *Pakhar'* 4–5 (1906).

Sharapov, Sergei. "Diary DLI," *Svidetel'* 33 (1910).

Sharapov, Sergei. *Diktator: Politicheskaia fantaziia)* Moscow: Tip. A. Suvorina, 1907.

Sharapov, Sergei. "Dnevnik," *Svidetel'* 29–30 (1909): 71–81.

Sharapov, Sergei. "Iurii Mamleev: 'Eta real'nost' ne nastoiashchaia, a kakaia-to poddelka': Sergei Shargunov pobyval v gostiakh u znamenitogo pisatelia." *Colta* (November 19, 2013). http://www.colta.ru/articles/literature/1218.

Sharapov, Sergei. *Ivanov 16-i i Sokolov 18-i*. Moscow: Tip. "Russkii golos," 1907.

Sharapov, Sergei. *Izbrannoe*. Moscow: ROSSPEN, 2010.

Sharapov, Sergei. *Kabinet Diktatora*. Moscow: Svidetel', 1908.

Sharapov, Sergei. *Mirnye rechi. Po-russki. Staroe i novoe. Tri sbornika 1900 g*. Moscow: Tipo-lit. A. Vasil'eva, 1901.

Sharapov, Sergei. "Moi dnevnik CCCXXVI," *Svidetel'* 10–11 and 13 (1908).

Sharapov, Sergei. "Moi dnevnik CLXXIV." *Sochineniia*, vol 25. Moscow, 1904.

Sharapov, Sergei. "Moi dnevnik." *Sochineniia*, vol. 6 (1901).

Sharapov, Sergei. "Moi dnevnik." *Svidetel'* 35 (1910).

Sharapov, Sergei. "Moi otvet Miliukovu." *Svidetel'* 12 (1908).

Sharapov, Sergei. *Opiat' snachala. (Razmyshleniia pered tret'ei dumoi)*. Moscow, 1907.

Sharapov, Sergei. "Otkrytie Aksakovskogo obshchestva." *Russkoe delo* 11 (1907).

Sharapov, Sergei. "Pamiati I. S. Aksakova." *Sochineniia,* vol. 3. St. Petersburg: Tip. A. Porok-hovshchikova, 1899.

Sharapov, Sergei. *Russkii sel'skii khoziain: neskol'ko myslei ob ustroistve khoziaistva v Rossii na novykh nachalakh*. St. Petersburg: Tip. M. K. Remezova, 1894.

Sharapov, Sergei. *Russkoe delo,* volumes 1–52. 1887–1904.

Sharapov, Sergei. *Samoderzhavie ili konstitutsiia*. Moscow, 1908.

Sharapov, Sergei. *Sotsializm kak religiia nenavisti*. Moscow, 1907.

Sharapov, Sergei. "Zashchititel'naia rech." In *Sochineniia,* vol. 1 by Sergei Sharapov. St. Petersburg, 1892.

Sharapov, Sergei. *Vopl' golodaiushchego intelligenta* (Moscow, 1902): 32.

Sharp, John. "Anthropology in South Africa." In *The Best of Anthropology Today,* edited by Jonathan Benthall, 245–53. London: Routledge, 2002.

Sharp, John. "The Roots and Development of Volkekunde in South Africa." *Journal of South African Studies* 8, no. 1 (1981): 16–36.

Shchegolev, Pavel E., ed. *Padenie tsarskogo rezhima: Stenograficheskie otchety doprosov i pokazanii, dannykh v 1917 g. v Chrezvychanoi sledstvennoi komissii, Vremenno-go pravitel›stva,* vol. 6 (Leningrad–Moscow: 1924–1927).

Shcherbatov, Aleksandr, *Obnovlennaia Rossiia*. Moscow, 1908.

Shekhovtsov, Anton and Andreas Umland. "Aleksandr Dugin's Neo-Eurasianism: The New Right à la Russe." *Religion Compass* 3, no. 4 (2009).

Shekhovtsov, Anton. "Far-Right Election Observation Monitors in the Service of the Kremlin's Foreign Policy." In *Eurasianism and the European Far Right: Reshaping the Europe–Russia Relationship,* edited by Marlene Laruelle, 223–44. Lanham, MD: Lexington Books, 2015.

Shekhovtsov, Anton. "The Kremlin's Marriage of Convenience with the European Far Right." OpenDemocracy (April 28, 2014). Accessed October 20, 2014. https://www.open democracy.net/od-russia/antonshekhovtsov/kremlin%E2%80%99s-marriage-of-con venience-with-european-far-right.

Shemiakin, A. L. *Ideologiia Nikoly Pashicha: Formirovanie i evoliutsiia (1868–1891)*. Moscow, 1998.

Shenfield, Stephen. "The Jewish Eurasianism of Yakov Bromberg." May 1, 2012. http://stephen shenfield.net/themes/jewish-issues/jews-in-tsarist-russia/105-the-jewish-eurasian ism-of-yakov-bromberg

Shenfield, Stephen. *Russian Fascism: Traditions, Tendencies, Movements*. Armonk, NY: M.E. Sharpe, 2001.

Shevelenko, Irina. "K istorii evraziiskgo raskola 1929 goda." *Stanford Slavic Studies* 8 (1994): 376–416.

Shitikhin, P. "Sravnitel'nyi analiz istoriosofskikh vzgliadov N. Ia. Danilevskogo i Lev N. Gumileva." Avtoreferat kand. diss., Moskovskaia Dukhovnaia Akademiia, Moscow, 2012.

Shlapentokh, Dmitry. "Yakov Bromberg: The Case of a Russian Jewish Eurasianist in the USA." In *Materialy Piatnadtsatoi Ezhegodnoi Mezhdunarodnoi Mezhdistsiplinarnoi konferentsii po iudaike*. Moscow: Tsentr nauchnykh rabotnikov i prepodavatelei iudaiki v VUZakh, 2008.

Shnirel'man, Viktor. *Intellektual'nye labirinty: Ocherki ideologii v sovremennoi Rossii*. Moscow: Academia, 2004.

Shnirelman, Victor A. "Politics of Ethnogenesis in the USSR and After." *Bulletin of the National Museum of Ethnology* 30, no. 1 (2005).

Shnirelman, Victor A. "The Story of a Euphemism: The Khazars in Russian Nationalist Literature." In *The World of the Khazars: New Perspectives*, edited by Peter Goldern, Haggai Ben-Shammai, and Anadrs Rona-Tas, 358. Leiden: Brill, 2007.

Simon, Gerhard. *Nationalism and Policy toward the Nationalities in the Soviet Union. From Totalitarian Dictatorship to Post-Stalinist Society.* Boulder, CO: Westview, 1991.

Skalnik, Peter. "Union soviétique—Afrique du Sud: les 'théories' de l'etnos.'" *Cahiers d'Etudes Africaines* 28, no. 2 (1988): 157–76.

Slavianofil, Staryi. *Chto takoe Russkoe sobranie?* St. Petersburg, 1901.

Slezkine, Yuri. "N. Ia. Marr and the National Origins of Soviet Ethnogenetics." *Slavic Review* 55, no. 4 (1996).

Slutskii, M. B. *V skorbnie dni: Kishinevskii pogrom 1903 goda.* Kishinev, 1930.

Smith, Anthony D. *Chosen Peoples.* Oxford University Press Oxford, 2003.

Smith, Woodruff D. "Friedrich Ratzel and the Origin of *Lebensraum.*" *German Studies Review* 3 (1980): 51–68.

Soborski, Rafal. *Ideology in a Global Age: Continuity and Change.* New York: Palgrave, 2013.

Sontheimer, Kurt. "Der Tatkreis." In *Von Weimar zu Hitler 1930–1933*, edited by Gotthard Jasper, 197–228. Göttingen: Kiepenheuer and Witsch, 1968.

Sontheimer, Kurt. *Antidemokratisches Denken in der Weimarer Republik: Die politischen Ideen des deutschen Nationalismus zwischen 1918 und 1933*, 4th ed. Munich: dtv, 1994.

Soucy, Robert. "The Nature of Fascism in France." *Journal of Contemporary History* 1, no. 1 (1966).

Spektorowski, Alberto. "Ethnoregionalism, Multicultural Nationalism and the Idea of the European Third Way." *Studies in Ethnicity and Nationalism* 7, no. 3 (2007): 45–63.

Spektorowski, Alberto. "Ethnoregionalism: The Intellectual New Right and the Lega Nord." *Global Review of Ethnopolitics* 2, no. 3 (2003).

Spektorowski, Alberto. "The French New Right: Differentialism and the Idea of Ethnophilian Exclusionism." *Polity* 33, no. 2 (n.d.): 283–303.

Spektorowski, Alberto. "The New Right: Ethno-regionalism, Ethno-Pluralism and the Emergence of a Neo-Fascist 'Third Way.'" *Journal of Political Ideologies* 8, no. 1 (2003).

Spengler, Oswald. *Der Untergang des Abendlandes: Umrisse einer Morphologie der Weltgeschichte*, vol. 1 (Vienna: Verlag Braumüller, 1918); vol. 2 (Munich: C.H. Beck, 1922).

Steinberg, Mark. "Melancholy and Modernity: Emotions and Social Life in Russia between the Revolutions." *Journal of Social History* 41, no. 4 (2008).

Stepanov, A. "Geiden Nikolai Fedorovich." In *Chernaia sotnia: Istoricheskaia entsiklopedia*, edited by O. A. Platonov. Moscow, 2008.

Stepanov, Klavdii. *Moskovskii golos* 1 and 2 (1906).

Stepanov, S. A. *Chernaia sotnia v Rossii 1905–1914.* Moscow: Izdatelstvo Vsesoiuznogo zaochnogo politekhnicheskogo instituta, 1992.

Stephan, John J. *The Russian Fascists: Tragedy and Farce in Exile, 1925–1945.* New York: Harper and Row, 1978.

Stern, Fritz. *The Politics of Cultural Despair: A Study in the Rise of the Germanic Ideology.* Berkeley: University of California Press, 1974.

Sternhell, Zeev. "Deroulede and the Origins of Modern French Nationalism." *Journal of Contemporary History* 6, no. 4 (1971).

Sternhell, Zeev. "Fascism: Reflections on the Fate of Ideas in Twentieth Century History." *Journal of Political Ideologies* 5, no. 2 (2000): 139–62.

Sternhell, Zeev. *La droite révolutionnaire 1885–1914: Les origines françaises du fascism.* Paris: Éditions du Seuil, 1978.

Sternhell, Zeev. *Neither Right, nor Left.* Translated by David Maisel. Berkeley: University of California Press, 1986.

Sternhell, Zeev. *Ni droite, ni gauche: L'ideologie fasciste en France.* Paris: Editions du Seuil, 1983.

Steuckers, Robert. "Answers to the Questions of Pavel Tulaev." 2014. Accessed January 7, 2014. http://robertsteuckers.blogspot.co.uk/2014/02/answers-to-questions-of-pavel-tulaev.html.

Steuckers, Robert. "Foundations of Russian Nationalism." n.d. Accessed November 26, 2014. http:// www.counter-currents.com/2014/04/foundations-of-russian-nationalism-2/.

Stöss, Richard. *Parteien-Handbuch* (vol. 1, *AUD-EFP, Die Deutsch-Soziale Union*). Bonn: Westdeutscher Verlag, 1983.

Strik-Strikfeldt, Wilfried. *Gegen Stalin und Hitler*. Mainz: Verlag Hase-Koehler, 1970.

Strogov, Dmitrii I. "Salon kniazia M. M. Andronikova i sistema vlasti Rossiiskoi Imperii." *Klio: Zhurnal dlia uchenykh* 3 (2006).

Suslov, Mikhail. "Krizis messianstva i vopros o budushchem Rossii vo vzgliadakh Sergeia Sharapova (1855–1911)." *Voprosy kul'turologii* 9 (2010): 39–45.

Suslov, Mikhail. "The Lost Chance of Conservative Modernization: S. F. Sharapov in the Economic Debates of the Late Nineteenth to the Early Twentieth Century." *Acta Slavica Iaponica* 31 (2012).

Suslov, Mikhail. "Neo-Slavophilism and the Revolution of 1905–07: A Study in the Ideology of S. F. Sharapov." *Revolutionary Russia* 24, no. 1 (2011).

Suslov, Mikhail. "'Slavophilism Is True Liberalism': The Political Utopia of S. F. Sharapov (1855–1911)." *Russian History* 38, no. 2 (2011).

Suvchinskii, Petr P. "K preodoleniiu revoliutsii." *Evraziiskii vremennik* III (1923).

Suvchinskii, Petr P. "Monarkhiia ili silnaia vlast'?" *Evraziiskaia khronika* IX (1927).

Taguieff, Pierre-André. "Les Droites radicales en France: Nationalisme révolutionnaire et national-libéralisme." *Les Temps modernes* 465 (April–May 1985): 1780–1842.

Taguieff, Pierre-André. "Le néo-racisme différentialiste. Sur l'ambiguïté d'une évidence commune et ses effets pervers." *Langage et société* 34 (1985): 69–98.

Talitskii [Sharapov], *Bumazhnyi rubl'*. St. Petersburg, 1895.

Taschka, Sylvia. *Das Rußlandbild von Ernst Niekisch*. Erlangen: Palm and Enke, 1999.

Taube, Mikhail F. "Slavianofil'stvo i ego opredeleniia." *Mirnyi trud* 6 (1905).

Thaden, Edward. *Conservative Nationalism in Nineteenth-Century Russia*. Seattle: University of Washington Press, 1964.

Thälmann, Ernst. "Programmerklärung zur nationalen und sozialen Befreiung des deutschen Volkes." *Rote Fahne*, August 24, 1930.

Thiriart, Jean. *La Grande Nation: L'Europe unitaire de Brest à Bucarest*. Brussels: PCE, 1965.

Thiriart, Jean. *Quel destin pour la Bundeswehr? Mourir pour Washington ou combattre pour la naissance de l'Europe?* n.p., 1983.

Thiriart, Jean. *Un Empire de 400 millions d'hommes: l'Europe*. Brussels, 1964.

Thiriart, Jean et Luc Michel. "Le Socialisme communautaire." *Conscience européenne* (n.d.).

Thompson, Terry L. *Ideology and Policy. The Political Uses of Doctrine in the Soviet Union*. n.p., 1989.

Tikhomirov, Lev. "Aziatskii vopros." In *Khristianstvo i politika* by Lev Tikhomirov. Moscow, 1999.

Tikhomirov, L. "Dnevnik." *Krasnyi arkhiv* 61 (1933).

Tishkov, V. A. "Post-Soviet Nationalism." In *Europe's New Nationalism: States and Minorities in Conflict*, edited by Richard Caplan and John Feffer. Oxford: Oxford University Press, 1996.

Tolcea, Marcel. *Mircea Eliade et l'ésotérisme*. Paris: Entrelacs, 2013.

Tönnies, Ferdinand. *Gemeinschaft und Gesellschaft: Abhandlung des Communismus und des Socialismus als empirischer Culturformen*. Leipzig: Fues's Verlag, 1887.

Toots, N. A. and A. L. Rychkov. "Zabytaia istoriia." *Del'fis* 66, no. 2 (2011), http://www.delphis.ru/journal/article/zabytaya-istoriya.

Tsurganov Iurii S. *Beloemigranty i Vtoraia mirovaia voina: Popytka revansha, 1939–1945*. Moscow: Tsentrpoligraf, 2010.

Travers, Martin. *Critics of Modernity: The Literature of the Conservative Revolution in Germany, 1890–1933*. Pieterlen and Bern: Peter Lang, 2001.

Trubetskoi, Nikolai S. "Mysli ob indoevropeiskoi probleme." 1936. Republished in Nikolai S. Trubetskoi, *Izbrannye trudy po filologii*. Moscow: Progress, 1987. http://www.philology.ru/linguistics1/trubetskoy-87d.htm#1.

Trubetskoi, Nikolai S. "Nash otvet." Republished in Nikolai S. Trubetskoi, *Istoriia, kul'tura, iazyk*. Moscow: Progress, 1995.

Trubetskoi, Nikolai S. "O rasizme." *Evraziiskie tetrad* 5 (1935). Republished in Nikolai S. Trubetskoi, *Istoriia. Kul'tura. Iazyk*. Moscow: Progress, 1995.

Trubetskoi, Nikolai S. "O turanskoi elemente v russkoi kul'ture." Republished in *Rossiia mezhdu Evropoi i Aziei: Evraziiskii soblazn*, edited by L. I. Novikova and I. N. Sizemskaia. Moscow: Nauka, 1993.

Trubetskoi, Nikolai S. "Ob idee-pravitel'nitse ideokraticheskogo gosudarstva." In Nikolai S. Troubetzkoy, *L'Europe et l'humanité: Ecrits linguistiques et para-linguistiques*, translated by Patrick Sériot. Liège: Mardaga, 1996.

Tudor, Lucian. "The Philosophy of Identity: Ethnicity, Culture and Race in Identitarian Thought." *Occidental Quarterly* 14, no. 3 (2014).

"Umer Evgeni Vsevolodovich Golovin." *Antikompromat*. Republished on *LJR*. October 29, 2010. http://lj.rossia.org/users/anticompromat/1028836.html.

Umland, Andreas. "Konservativnaia revoliutsia: Imia sobstevennoe ili rodovoe poniatie?" *Forum noveishei vostochnoevropeiskoi istorii i kul'tury* 1 (2006): 1–15.

Umland, Andreas. "Zhirinovskii as a Fascist: Palingenetic Ultra-Nationalism and the Emergence of the Liberal-Democratic Party of Russia in 1992–93." *Forum für osteuropäische Ideen- und Zeitgeschichte* 14, no. 2 (2010): 189–215.

Umland, Andreas and Anton Shekhovtsov. "Is Dugin a Traditionalist? 'Neo-Eurasianism' and Perennial Philosophy." *Russian Review* 68 (October 2009), 662–78.

Ustav gimnazii i real'nogo uchilishcha. St. Petersburg, 1907.

Ustav "Russkago sobraniia." St. Petersburg, 1901.

Vasil'ev, Afanasii. *Miru-narodu moi otchet za prozhitoe vremia*. Petrograd: I. Kushnereva, 1908.

Vasil'ev. "Nashi okhraniteli." *Russkaia beseda* 8 (1895).

Vasil'ev, Arkadii N. *V chas dnia, vashe prevoskhoditel'stvo*. Moscow: Moskovskii rabochii, 1974.

Velichko, V. L. "Strannye pretenzii i 'Adelaida' g. Sigmy." *Russkii vestnik* 4 (1903).

Venner, Dominique. *Les Blancs et les Rouges: Histoire de la guerre civile russe*. Paris: Pygmalion, 1997.

Vergun, D. N. *Nemetskii "Drang nach Osten" v tsifrakh i faktakh*. Vienna, 1905.

Verslius, Arthur and Alain de Benoist. "A Conversation with Alain de Benoist." *Journal for the Study of Radicalism* 8, no. 2 (2014).

Voina na Balkanakh: Rechi grafa V. A. Bobrinskago. St. Petersburg, 1912.

Volovici, Leon. *Nationalist Ideology and Antisemitism: The Case of Romanian Intellectuals in the 1930s*. Oxford: Pergamon Press, 1991.

Von Bertalanffy, Ludwig. *General System Theory: Foundations, Development, Applications*. New York: George Braziller, 1968.

von dem Bussche, Raimund. *Konservatismus in der Weimarer Republik: Die Politisierung des Unpolitischen*. Heidelberg: Universitäts-Verlag Winter, 1998.

von Salomon, Ernst. *Der Fragebogen*. Hamburg: Rowohlt, 1951.

Vorob'ev, Valentin. "Popravki k biografii khudozhnika Iuriia Titova." n.d. http://www.yuri-titov.com/titov_titologie/titologie_ru_6.htm.

Waldmann, Gert. "Verhaltensforschung und Politik." In *Europäischer Nationalismus ist Fortschritt*, 17–47. Hamburg: Verlag Deutsch-Europäischer Studien, 1973.

Walicki, Andrzej. "The Troubling Legacy of Roman Dmowski." *East European Politics and Societies* 14, no. 1 (1999).

Wannenwetsch, Stefan. *Unorthodoxe Sozialisten: Zu den Sozialismuskonzeptionen der Gruppe um Otto Straßer und des Internationalen Sozialistischen Kampfbundes in der Weimarer Republik*. Frankfurt am Main: Lang, 2010.

Warren, Ian B. "The Heritage of Europe's 'Revolutionary Conservative Movement': A Conversation with Swiss Historian Armin Mohler." *Journal of Historical Review* 14, no. 5 (1994). http://www.ihr.org/jhr/v14n5p3_warren.html.

Weeks, Theodore. *Nation and State in Late Imperial Russia: Nationalism and Russification on the Western Frontier, 1863–1914*. DeKalb, IL: Northern Illinois University Press,1996.

Weinberg, Robert. "The Pogrom of 1905 in Odessa: A Case Study." In *Pogroms: Anti-Jewish Violence in Modern Russian History*, edited by John D. Klier and Shlomo Lambroza, 248–89. Cambridge: Cambridge University Press, 1992.

Weinberg, Robert. "Workers, Pogroms, and the 1905 Revolution in Odessa." *Russian Review* 46, no. 1 (1987): 53–75.

Weißmann, Karlheinz. "Konservative Revolution—Forschungsstand und Desiderata." In *Stand und Probleme der Erforschung des Konservatismus*, edited by Caspar v. Schrenck-Notzing, 119–39. Berlin: Duncker and Humblot, 2000.

Wiederkehr, Stefan. *Die eurasische Bewegung: Wissenschaft und Politik in der russischen Emigration der Zwischenkriegszeit und im postsowjetischen Russland*. Cologne: Böhlau Verlag, 2007.

"Winnig y Paetel líderes nacional bolcheviques." *Tribuna de Europa* 7, no. 2 (October–November 1996).

Witte, Sergei Iu. *The Memoirs of Count Witte*, edited and translated by Sidney Harcave. Armonk, NY: M.E. Sharpe, 1990.

Wolfe, Lucien. *The Legal Sufferings of the Jews in Russia: A Survey of Their Present Situation, and a Summary of Laws*. London: T. Fisher Unwin, 1912.

Wolin, Richard. *The Seduction of Unreason: The Intellectual Romance with Fascism from Nietzsche to Postmodernism*. Princeton, NJ: Princeton University Press, 2004.

Wolter, Helmut. *Volk im Aufstieg: Neue Ergebnisse der Volksbiologie Grossdeutschlands*. n.p., 1940.

Woods, Roger. *The Conservative Revolution in the Weimar Republic*. New York: St. Martin's, 1996.

Wyss, Marco. *Un Suisse au service de la Waffen-SS*. Neuchâtel: Alphil, Presses universitaires suisses, 2010.

Yanov, Aleksandr. *The Russian New Right. Right-Wing Ideologies in the Contemporary USSR*. Berkeley: Institute of International Studies, University of California, 1978.

Yanov, Aleksandr. *Russkaia ideia i 2000-i god*. New York: Liberty Publishing Company, 1988.

Zalesskii, Konstantin A. *Komandirii natsional'nikh formirovanii SS*. Moscow: AST-Press, 2007.

Ziegerhofer, Anita. *Botschafter Europas: Richard Nikolaus Coudenhove-Kalergi und die Paneuropa-Bewegung in den zwanziger und dreissiger Jahren*. Vienna: Böhlau Verlag, 2004.

CONTRIBUTORS

Marlene Laruelle is the associate director of the Institute for European, Russian and Eurasian Studies (IERES), and a research professor of International Affairs at the Elliott School of International Affairs, George Washington University. She was a visiting scholar at the Woodrow Wilson International Center for Scholars (2005–2006). She holds a PhD from the National Institute for Oriental Languages and Cultures in Paris. She is the author of *Russian Eurasianism: An Ideology of Empire* (Johns Hopkins University Press, 2008), *In the Name of the Nation: Nationalism and Politics in Contemporary Russia* (Palgrave, 2009), and *Russia's Strategies in the Arctic and the Future of the Far North* (M.E. Sharpe, 2013). She recently edited *Between Europe and Asia: The Origins, Theories and Legacies of Russian Eurasianism* (University of Pittsburgh Press, 2015), with Mark Bassin and Sergey Glebov; and *Eurasianism and the European Far Right: Reshaping the Russia-Europe Relationship* (Lanham, MD: Lexington, 2015).

Martin Beisswenger is an assistant professor at the School of History, National Research University—Higher School of Economics, Moscow. He received his PhD in 2009 from the University of Notre Dame with a dissertation titled *Petr Nikolaevich Savitskii (1895–1968) and the Invention of 'Eurasia.'* He is the author of a bibliography of P. N. Savitskii's published works and of several articles and book chapters on various aspects of the history of Eurasianism and the postrevolutionary Russian emigration. He has also published selected correspondence of prominent classical Eurasianists, such as N. S. Trubetskoi, P. P. Suvchinskii, P. N. Savitskii, and G. V. Florovskii. Martin Beisswenger's fields of interest include the history of Eurasianism, the history of modern Russian and European thought, and the intellectual history of European unification. He is currently revising his doctoral dissertation for publication.

Mark Bassin is a professor at the Center for Baltic and East European Studies and the Department of the History of Ideas at the Södertörns Högskola in Stockholm. He received his doctoral degree in historical geography and Russian intellectual history from the University of California, Berkeley. He has held permanent teaching positions at the University of Wisconsin–Madison, University College London, and the University of Birmingham. His research focuses on intellectual history in Eastern and Central Europe, primarily Russia and Germany. He is interested in issues of identity, politics, and ideologies in the nineteenth and twentieth centuries. He is the author of *Imperial Visions: Nationalist Imagination and Geographical Expansion in the Russian Far East, 1840–1865* (Cambridge University Press, 2006) and of *The Gumilev Mystique: Biopolitics, Eurasianism and the Construction of Community in Modern Russia* (Cornell University Press, 2016); and coeditor of *Space, Place and Power in Modern Russia: Essays in the New Spatial History* (Northern Illinois University Press, 2010) and *Soviet and Post-Soviet Identities* (Cambridge University Press, 2012).

Jean-Yves Camus is an associate researcher at the Institute of International and Strategic Relations (IRIS) in Paris, and works on political and religious extremism and minority rights. Previously he was research director at the European Center for Research on Racism and Anti-Semitism (CERA) in Paris. He was a member of the Ile de France Equality Council, an official committee advising the municipality of Paris on antidiscrimination matters. He is the author of seven books in French about the Front National and the rise of religious and political extremism. He has published scholarly articles and opinion pieces on the Front National, Islamophobia, anti-Semitism, and racism in France in French, German, and Spanish. He recently coauthored *Far-Right Politics in Europe* (Harvard University Press, 2017) with Nicolas Lebourg.

Boris N. Kovalev is a senior researcher at the Institute of History of the Russian Academy of Sciences in Saint Petersburg. He is a member of the editorial board of the Russian Library of the Holocaust and one of the foremost Russian scholars on collaboration during the Second World War in the Soviet Union. He is the author of three monographs in Russian: *Nazi Occupation and Collaborationism in Russia, 1941–1944, Collaborationism in Russia 1941–1945: Types and Forms,* and *Everyday Life of the Russian Population during Nazi Occupation.*

Patrick Moreau holds a PhD in history and political science and works at the CNRS and the Dynam Laboratory at the Strasbourg University. A specialist on political life in Germany and Austria, he has been working for decades on both the far right and communism in Europe. He is the author, among others, of *Nationalsozialismus von links* (Deutsche Verlagsanstalt, Munich 1984).

José Luis Rodríguez Jiménez is a professor of contemporary history at the University of King Juan Carlos, a leading Spanish public research university based in Madrid. He holds a degree from Défense Nationale (CESEDEN) and coordinated the investigative group on the Spanish military in Africa. He has published several articles on terrorism, but his principal research interests are the extreme right, fascism, and neo-fascism. His findings have been published in numerous articles and volumes, including *La extrema derecha en España* (1997) and *Historia de Falange Española de las JONS* (2000). He also studied Spain's participation in the Second World War in *Los esclavos españoles de Hitler* (2002), *De héroes e indeseables,* and *La División Azul* (2007).

Nicolas Lebourg is a researcher at the Observatory for Political Radicalism in Paris (ORAP, Fondation Jean Jaurès). He is a participant in the IDREA program (Internationalisation des Droites Radicales Europe Amériques) at the Maison des Sciences de l'Homme-Lorraine and earned his PhD at Perpignan University. He has published several monographs, including *Le Monde vu de la plus extrême droite* (Presses Universitaires de Perpignan, 2010), *François Duprat, l'homme qui inventa le Front National* (Denoël, 2012), and *Dans l'Ombre des Le Pen: Une histoire des No. 2 du Front National* (Nouveau Monde, 2012). He recently co-authored *Far-Right Politics in Europe* (Harvard University Press, 2017) with Jean-Yves Camus.

Giovanni Savino is currently a visiting fellow at the Russian Institute of Advanced Studies, Sholokhov Moscow State University for the Humanities. He graduated in history from the University of Naples Federico II in 2008, with a thesis on the Ukrainian question in the Russian Empire; and received his PhD from the Italian Institute of Human Sciences–SUM in 2012, with a dissertation on the origins of Russian nationalism in the late tsarist era. His research interests are Russian nationalism in the late imperial era and in contemporary Russia, the cultural and ideological roots of national identity, and the history of ideas in the European and Russian contexts. His publications include: "La Russia ostaggio del Nazionalismo," *MicroMega* 2/2014; and "Okrainy Rossii i proekt natsionalizatsii Rossiiskoi Imperii" (Okrainy Rossii and the project of nationalizing the Russian Empire), *Sotsiologicheskoe Obozrenie* 3/2014.

Mikhail Suslov is a Marie Curie assitant professor at the University of Copenhagen. He received his PhD in history from the European University Institute in Florence in 2009 and was a Marie Curie postdoctoral researcher at Uppsala University. His research interests include Russian and post-Soviet intellectual history, conservative and right-wing political ideology, critical geopolitics, and the conceptual history of the Russian Orthodox Church. His current studies deal with post-Soviet geopolitical ideas and the new media space. He is the author of *Russian Geopolitical Utopias in Comparative Perspective: Dreams of Wars and Empires, 1880–1914* (LAP LAMBERT Academic Publishing, 2010), and he recently edited *Eurasia 2.0: Russian Geopolitics in the Age of New Media* (Lexington, 2016) with Mark Bassin, and *Digital Orthodoxy in the Post-Soviet World: The Russian Orthodox Church and Web 2.0* (Ibidem Verlag, 2016).

INDEX